Textual Conspiracies

Textual Conspiracies

Walter Benjamin, Idolatry, and Political Theory

James R. Martel

THE UNIVERSITY OF MICHIGAN PRESS

Ann Arbor

First paperback edition 2013
Copyright © by the University of Michigan 2011
All rights reserved

Published in the United States of America by
The University of Michigan Press
Printed and bound by CPI Group (UK) Ltd, Croydon, CR0 4YY

2016   2015   2014   2013   5   4   3   2

A CIP catalog record for this book is available from the British Library.

Library of Congress Cataloging-in-Publication Data

Martel, James R.
    Textual conspiracies : Walter Benjamin, idolatry, and political
theory / James R. Martel.
        p.   cm.
    Includes bibliographical references and index.
    ISBN 978-0-472-11772-7 (cloth : alk. paper)
    ISBN 978-0-472-02819-1 (e-book)
    1. Benjamin, Walter, 1892–1940—Political and social views.
2. Capitalism.   3. Liberalism.   4. Conspiracies.   5. Politics and
literature.   I. Title.

PT2603.E455Z73315   2011
838'.91209—dc22   2011007220

ISBN 978-0-472-03522-9 (pbk. : alk. paper)

Acknowledgments

I want to express thanks to many people who helped me to write this book. Two people in particular merit great thanks for this book's publication. Joyce Seltzer has been an invaluable friend, advisor, and mentor in facing the publishing world and conceptualizing my projects, this one very much included. Melody Herr has been a phenomenal editor; her advice, enthusiasm, and advocacy have made getting this book to press a truly enjoyable experience. Susan Cronin, Kevin Rennells, and Mike Kehoe have also been very helpful at University of Michigan Press. I also want to thank my university, San Francisco State University, and especially my dean, Joel Kassiola, for giving me a sabbatical to help finish this project and for his support in general. Jodi Dean was instrumental in starting this project; she got me thinking about conspiracy in the first place and has been an astute and generous reader. Karen Feldman has also been a great reader and was present at the first incarnations of my work on Kafka.

In October 2010, I was fortunate to be able to present the principal arguments for this text at a conference entitled "Dangerous Crossings: Politics at the Limits of the Human," held at Johns Hopkins University. Thank you to the conference organizers: Drew Walker, Nathan Gies, Katherine Goktepe, and Tim Hanafin. Thanks also to Jennifer Culbert, Jane Bennett, Willam Connolly, and Bonnie Honig for their excellent comments and contributions to my project as well as their friendship. Other readers, colleagues, allies, and friends include, as always, Nasser Hussain and Mark Andrejevic, and many other people whose support and wisdom are invaluable to me: Marianne Constable, Ruth Sonderegger, Jackie Stevens, Martha Umphrey, Paul Passavant, Angelika von Wahl, Melissa Ptacek, Tiffany Willoughby-Herard, Sara Kendall, Wendy Lochner, Jeanne Scheper, Zhivka Valiavicharska, Jimmy Casas Klausen, Alex Dubilet, Ramona Naddaff, Lisa Disch, Stephanie Sommerfeld, Adam Thurschwell, Kennan Ferguson, David Bates, Shalini Satkunanandan, Stuart Murray,

Anatole Anton, Sandra Luft, Anatoli Ignatov, Miguel Vatter, Libby Anker, Alex Hirsch, Vicky Kahn, Keally McBride, Dean Mathiowetz, Brian Weiner, Ron Sundstrom, Kate Gordy, Wendy Brown, Kyong-Min Son, William Sokoloff, Vanessa Lemm, Tom Dumm, Peter Fitzpatrick, Colin Perrin, Austin Sarat, Linda Ross Meyer, and many others. I want to thank my many students in my two (to date) Walter Benjamin graduate seminars at SFSU including Loren Lewis, Evan Stern, Rion Roberts, Steven Swarbrick, Sharise Edwards, Tyler Nelson, Dieyana Ruzgani, Loren Stewart, Katrina Lappin, Veronica Roberts, Kenny Loui, Joshua Hurni, Cecily Gonzalez, Rebecca Stillman, Randall Cohn, Brooks Kirchgassner, and quite a few others. Finally I want to thank my wonderful family: my husband, Carlos, my children, Jacques and Rocio, and Nina, Kathryn, Elic and Mark, Ralph, Huguette, Django, and Shalini.

I give thanks to my mother, Huguette Martel, for her painting that is used on the book cover. Thanks also go to Alice Martin at Service IMEC Images (which holds the Gisèle Freund archives) and to Julie Galant at Fotofolio (the company that made the postcard that the image came from). I also thank Rich Stim, who did the research figuring out how to obtain permission, and Javier Machado Leyva, who photographed the painting and prepared the electronic file for use here.

An earlier version of chapter 2 first appeared as "The Messiah Who Comes and Who Goes: Kafka's Messianic Conspiracy in *The Castle*," in *Theory and Event* 12, no. 3 (2009). Copyright © 2009 James Martel and The Johns Hopkins University Press. Reprinted with permission by The Johns Hopkins University Press. An earlier version of chapter 3 appeared as "Machiavelli's Public Conspiracies," in *MediaTropes* 2, no. 1 (2009): 60–83.

Contents

Preface | No Hope

What does it mean to be a leftist in our time? There are those who still call for and believe in revolution—those, that is, who conform to an earlier version of the Left—but more widely, it seems safe to say, few think such an event will occur in our lifetime. In this moment in time, it seems that for most people such a revolution is impossible, nearly unthinkable. When we speak of revolution today in much of the world, we generally mean the creation or restoration of liberal democracy, not the overthrow of capitalism. The overthrow of Hosni Mubarak and other events currently sweeping across the Middle East and North Africa may deservedly be called revolutions. They have been thrilling and promise a justice that is long overdue. But there is little or no expectation that the dictators being challenged are going to be replaced by any kind of radically democratic, anticapitalist political arrangements. These revolutions are not of that kind. While there have been moments in Egypt, Tunisia and Libya where truly spontaneous, decentralized resistance movements came into being, overall such movements have been absorbed into "normalizing" discourses of sovereignty and market order. Without the immanent possibility of radical revolution—the central theme that animated the Left for much of its early history—direct and explicit opposition to capitalism becomes murkier and more diffuse. The Left, such as it is, exists today in pieces and tatters. There is an important subculture of resistance in terms of opposition, for example, to the World Trade Organization. Examples of guerrilla theater, large and disruptive demonstrations, and other forms of protest have gained widespread media attention. There are a handful of countries, such as Cuba and (to a lesser degree) Bolivia, where opposition to capitalism remains entrenched, at least ideologically. There are also (as this book will argue further) an infinite number of microresistances and oppositions to capitalism that appear in the most ordinary and unexpected places. Yet, for all of this, capitalism goes largely unchallenged; it has been knocked back on its heels, to be sure, by the recent and massive "Great Recession," but it has been down before, and capitalism, and the political forces that accompany it (traditionally liberal democracies, but now increasingly, authoritarian states such as China and Russia as well) have proven fantastically adept at changing with the times.

Against many predictions of its demise (even many from liberals) capitalism has not only survived but thrived into the twenty-first century. It could be argued that capitalism today enjoys a monopoly of unopposed, unrivaled political, economic and social primacy that it has never had before, this not so much in terms of the "end of history" predicted by figures like Fukuyama (a perusal of any newspaper today will quickly dispel that idea) but rather in terms of serious challenges to capitalism as a totalizing norm, a global way of life.

Leftists living in the early decades of this new century seem to be facing a series of unpalatable choices in terms of what we can actually do. One choice, which many have made, is to find a way to live with capitalism, to engage in what once was called "united front" tactics, alliances with left-leaning liberals in order to stave off the scary alternatives. This tactic, however, has never worked. When the Left allied with liberals in past decades, all it got was more liberalism. There is no reason to believe that such alliances will lead to any different kind of outcome now (especially when capitalism is ascendant). The election of Barack Obama may help attest to this. The election of an African American as president surely ranks as one of the United States' finest hours in many ways, but Obama is no radical (to be fair, he never pretended to be one). Many leftists who put great store in his election have been bitterly disappointed by the compromises that he has made, by his own moderateness, and by, well, his liberalism. As I see it, Obama's election is an example of capitalist homeostasis; after the fangs of capitalism were too brutally exposed (i.e., the Bush years) a return to a "kinder, gentler" form of authority helps to keep the entire system intact and operative. Surely it is true that putting any store in liberals to help us in our fight with capitalism (and, by extension, with liberalism) is a case of misplaced trust.

Another choice would be to fight for revolution anyway, to fight against our own temporality and keep alive the original goals and values of the Left. This is an admirable, brave, and often lonely track, and yet it too seems sure to lead to just more failure. Indeed, the Left has failed for virtually its entire history, and even when it has succeeded, it has failed. The short-lived revolutions of the nineteenth century were inevitably crushed by forces of reaction. The revolutions in Russia and China that actually succeeded led, not to radical democracy (although there were moments where that was achieved) but eventually to dictatorship and misery. The history of left revolution, as Arendt attests, is a history of great, wondrous episodes, separated by long decades of reaction, capitalist domination, and failure. Jodi Dean, whose work I will discuss further in this book, argues that the Left has fallen in love with its own failure.[1] As she suggests, failure may offer its own kind of solace (a kind of romance of failure), but it does not make for a viable political alternative to capitalism.

A third choice might be to just wallow in despair, to do nothing and feel terrible about the world. Certainly there is no end to left despair (the flip side of its romance of failure), but this is, by definition, a dead end and an accommodation to capitalism. Despair in and of itself is not resistance and it is not political.

Younger leftists, less laden by the baggage of past failures (or even of past "successes" like the 1960s), are understandably less gloomy about things. They tend to be more accepting of and interested in acts of micro-resistance, and many of them have grown up without the expectation of revolution. There is something to be said for this view, and at the end of this book, I will take up this question more seriously, but to take this viewpoint on its face means, once again, to generally accept that capitalism will remain the essential bedrock of our political, social, and economic order for the foreseeable future and then some. We may resist and we may endure; is that enough for the Left today?

Overall, when we think about the Left and its prospects from a historical perspective, from the perspective of all that it sought and all that once seemed possible, we seem to live in very dark times indeed. One could be forgiven for asking whether there is in fact even the slightest modicum of hope.

As I will argue in the following pages, one answer to the hopelessness of the Left, to our respective despair, indifference, complicity, resistance, joy, anger, is to give up on (one kind of) hope altogether. In a famous line that I will return to repeatedly in this book, Franz Kafka, when asked whether there was any hope, replied, "[There is] plenty of hope, an infinite amount of hope—but not for us."[2] This seemingly "Kafkaesque" joke bears, I will argue, a great deal of wisdom and is worth thinking more about. If we find that we are trapped by time, facing an endless future of capitalism without viable alternatives (or perhaps more accurately with alternatives that are viable but thoroughly unpalatable), perhaps it is hope itself that is helping us to keep ourselves so trapped. If, as I will argue further, we seem truly unable to transcend our temporality, then our hope too is a reflection of this trap—and of our time—a perpetuation of, rather than an escape from, our conundrum.

In this book I will try to think about another form of hope, specifically a form of hope for the Left, that is "not for us." What does it mean for hope to exist outside of our own subjectivity, outside of our own time? What, if anything, does this hope do for "us," such as we are? And who (i.e., what "not us") might we have to become in order to benefit from such hope?

In order to think further about this question, I turn to the writings of Walter Benjamin (as well as many other figures that I read via his work) as a way to begin to think about how to not merely be "ourselves" and in order to avoid replicating the traps that we are already suffering from. For Benjamin, as I will show further, human beings have always been susceptible to what he calls "the phantasmagoria," a miasma of false, idolatrous forms of reality based on our misreading of the world and its objects. Capitalism for Benjamin has only amplified this tendency; through commodity fetishism, capitalism has produced an elaborate, and false, sense of time and space, a "reality" that results from capitalist forms of production. So totalizing is this reality that even the most ardent leftists among us are endowed with a secret desire for capitalism to succeed; the failures of the Left are, in a sense, an effect of our participation in the same reality that feeds capitalism. Even our "hope" for revolution or the end of capitalism is similarly informed by a dark eschatology that is a product of the phantasmagoria.

In the pages of this text, I will examine Benjamin's analysis of this predicament and also consider his possible solution: to fight the phantasmagoria we must, in effect, cease to rely on our own conscious thoughts and desires, which are thoroughly complicit with it. We must conspire against our own tendency toward idolatry, engaging in what I will call a "textual conspiracy" with the very material objects and symbols of the world that we otherwise treat as fetishes.

The hope that Kafka identified, the hope that Benjamin looks to, lies in a very literal way beyond us, but it is not too far beyond. A hope that is not for us resides in the very world that we dominate and in our own, already existing radical democratic (or, as I will later suggest, anarchic) practices that we do not recognize as such. So long as our allegiance and attention is oriented toward the idolatrous understandings of politics, community, and self that are produced by the phantasmagoria, we will not be able to see that hope lies just within our reach, hence both the need and possibility for resistance and conspiracy.

Introduction | Textual Conspiracies

Conspiring against Our Time

If it is true that we live in dark times, that we are trapped by our temporality, some solace can be taken from the fact that such periods have been
faced before. By the late 1930s, Walter Benjamin was witnessing the potential victory of fascism across Europe. The only "hope" seemed to come
from the United States, itself a prime instigator of capitalist power. Benjamin did not make much of the difference between fascism and liberal
democratic variants of capitalism (although presumably his attempt to
flee from occupied France was a de facto recognition that in the latter system he would at least be permitted to remain alive). To him, it was all different faces of the same phenomena: unbridled capitalism, a system of
governance based on the worship of commodity fetishism. Such a system
produced, or as least reinforced, the "phantasmagoria" that insinuates itself into every facet of human life. In that time, as during our own, there
seemed no hope for revolution, no respite from the ravages of capitalism
in all of its guises.

For Benjamin, the purpose of making comparisons between various
historical moments was not just solace, however, but resistance. It was
during that time, toward the very end of his life, that Benjamin composed
his "Theses on the Philosophy of History," a response to this sense of being trapped by history and time. In that essay, Benjamin famously tells us:

> To articulate the past historically does not mean to recognize it "the
> way it really was" (Ranke). It means to seize hold of a memory as it
> flashes up at a moment of danger. Historical materialism wishes to
> retain that image of the past which unexpectedly appears to man
> singled out by history at a moment of danger. The danger affects
> both the content of the tradition and its receivers. The same threat

hangs over both: that of becoming a tool of the ruling classes. In every era the attempt must be made anew to wrest tradition away from a conformism that is about to overpower it. The Messiah comes not only as the redeemer, he comes as the subduer of Antichrist. Only that historian will have the gift of fanning the spark of hope in the past who is firmly convinced that *even the dead* will not be safe from the enemy if he wins. And this enemy has not ceased to be victorious.[1]

"At a moment of danger" such as Benjamin was experiencing (and such as we are experiencing in our own time, albeit in an entirely different context) he tells us that we can connect with other such moments in order to allow us to change our relationship to time. The image of the past we use is "unexpected" because for Benjamin our conscious minds are themselves largely products of our time and context. By accepting a particular view of time and history as constituting reality, we risk "becoming a tool of the ruling classes," and succumbing to "a conformism that is about to overpower [us]," whether we know it or not.

For Benjamin, time is not a continuity but a series of moments interrelated "through events that may be separated from [one another] by thousands of years."[2] He tells us further,

A historian . . . stops telling the sequence of events like the beads of a rosary. Instead, he grasps the constellation which his own era has formed with a definite earlier one.[3]

Benjamin looks for these "constellations" for the purpose of doing battle. By resorting to these kinds of transtemporal connections described above, Benjamin is attempting to circumvent our own compromise, our own participation in a sense of time and inevitability that is inherently self-defeating. In this way, he can be said to be engaging in a kind of transtemporal conspiracy, one that occurs despite and not because of our own deeply compromised desires and wishes. It is a conspiracy not only against some external enemy but even against ourselves, a conspiracy that therefore has no members even as it is undertaken on behalf of each and every one of us.

The Green Flags of Islam

The conspiracy that I will describe in the following pages is, above all, set against our own phantasms; it is a conspiracy against our participation in the idolatry of commodity fetishism and the phantasmagoria more generally. We conspire, as already suggested in the preface, with the very objects that we fetishize—the texts, images, and things that compose our understanding of reality—in order to release the grip that they have on us. Before going into more detail about the nature and source of this conspiracy and the hope that is "not for us" that it produces, a specific example may be useful to help illustrate this concept (as well as to give a sense of some of its political dimensions).

In one of her works, Assia Djebar, one of the authors that I will treat in this book as a "coconspirator" with Benjamin, offers an image of a flag that has (at least momentarily) ceased to be a fetish. In *Children of the New World*, a novel that is set in the midst of the Algerian revolution, Djebar describes a vast protest march against French colonialism led by the "green flags of Islam."[4] Participating in this rally is Youssef, one of the protagonists of the novel. Djebar writes:

> Youssef, whose only true love was for this shifting reality, this flood tide of wretchedness, would continue his tale. Then his jaws would tighten and he'd add, "Of course, they were simple rags, bits of sheets patched and sewn by the women for their luminous songs." "Filthy rags!" the police yelled, giving their first warning that they'd have to disappear. The flags kept moving forward.[5]

We will return to this image in chapter 6, but for now let us simply note that in describing the flags as "simple rags, bits of sheets," Djebar has rendered the object legible (Benjamin would say allegorized) amid its own symbolic (or fetishistic) value. Such a reading of the flag disrupts, at least potentially, the various sorts of identities—be they national, confessional, gendered, or other—promised by the fetish (identities that collectively compose the phantasmagoria). As we will see further, such a disruption also exposes and renders legible the communities that gather in the wake of such a fetish ("this shifting reality, this flood tide of wretchedness"). Such communities are not dispelled by this exposure but instead are returned to themselves, potentially freed from the idolatrous phantasms that they otherwise subscribe to. In this way the flag ceases to overwrite and obscure the community that it purportedly stands for (as a fetish) even as it remains (as an object, a set of rags) to lend a necessary sense of coherence and commonality to a disparate, multitudinous community ("Islam").

As I will argue further, this process is only possible via conspiracy. The conspiracy in this case is quite literally between the object (the rags and sheets) and the demonstrators and/or readers. Without recourse to the object qua object, the demonstrators cannot become legible to themselves as a community, cannot be anything but what their fetishistic misreading of the object determines them to be. The conspiracy described in the following pages—a conspiracy with texts and images, with the objects that we fetishize—is a prerequisite for any kind of politics that does not simply reiterate the phantasmagoria. To avoid the sense that we are trapped in time, without hope and without options, and to avoid (as Djebar feared) simply replacing one set of fetishes with another, we need to think further about this other kind of politics, this "spark of hope in the past." Such a politics is, I will argue, Benjamin's goal in fomenting conspiracy and, by extension, the purpose of this book as well.

From Plotting to Conspiracy

While, given his own view of history, it is problematical to speak of any "development" in the thought of Walter Benjamin, it does seem to be the case that as he approached the end of his life and the apparent triumph of fascism, Benjamin's work got darker and, indeed, more conspiratorial. It will be my argument that, especially toward his later years, as he worked on *The Arcades Project* and his "Theses on the Philosophy of History," as well as various related writings on Charles Baudelaire, Benjamin's basic approach to resisting the phantasmagoria produced a greater appreciation of both the necessity for and the value of conspiracy—as opposed to revolution or open rebellion—as a mode of resistance.

It is true that Benjamin was always interested in conspiracy in one form or the other. In *The Origin of German Tragic Drama* (written quite early in his career) we already see elements of a conspiratorial stance.[6] In his examination of the baroque German *Trauerspiel* (mourning play) in that work, Benjamin offers that the genre is marked by a portrayal of monarchs who are incapable of making a decision. Scholars ranging from Giorgio Agamben to Samuel Weber have argued that this portrayal is Benjamin's answer to Carl Schmitt, who in *Political Theology* (published just a few years before the *Origin*) (in)famously stated, "Sovereign is he who decides on the exception."[7] Benjamin, in response, portrays an all-too-human sovereign who is incapable of bearing the absolute power and responsibility accorded to this position, hence offering a subversive (and conspiratorial) account of the very heart of sovereign authority.

In the face of such an equivocating monarch, Benjamin notes the role in the *Trauerspiel* of the plotter (*der Integrant*), those members of the court who occupy the vacuum produced by sovereign indecision. As is very typical of Benjamin (an attitude we will see expressed in many different ways in this book), the fact that these plotters seem to be an unattractive, reactionary lot does not immediately condemn them in his eyes. Benjamin's entire strategy is recuperative; even (or especially) with such compromised subjects, he sees the promise of subversion and redemption. In their intrigues, their undermining, and their schemes, the plotters subvert the grand notions of space, time, and history (as well as the "state of exception") that the sovereign as symbol purportedly ushers into the world. As Samuel Weber notes:

> [The plotter's] function is to in-trigue, to confuse, and the condition of such confusion is precisely the particular spatialization and localization of processes that are usually considered to be temporal or historical in character.[8]

As Benjamin writes in the *Origin*:

> It is not possible to conceive of anything more inconstant than the mind of the courtier [i.e., the plotter] ... treachery is his element. It is not a sign of superficiality or clumsy characterization on the part of the authors that, at critical moments, the parasites abandon the ruler, without any pause for reflection, and go over to the other side. It is rather that their action reveals an unscrupulousness, which is in part a consciously Machiavellian gesture, but is also a dismal and melancholy submission to a supposedly unfathomable order of baleful constellations, which assumes an almost material character.[9]

We see here that the plotters depicted in the German *Trauerspiel* are animated by "consciously Machiavellian" schemes even as they also reflect factors that seem beyond their control. In speaking of "baleful constellations" (*unheilvoller Konstellationen*) and "an almost material character," Benjamin evokes his own conviction that human intentionality is not itself adequate to the task of transcending the confines of a particular historical context.[10] As we have already seen, we need to form "constellations" with other temporal moments; we require particular "material" rescues to overcome our own subjective and all-too-human tendencies to compromise.

Of these material rescues, Benjamin goes on to write:

> Crown, royal purple, scepter are indeed ultimately properties, in
> the sense of the drama of fate, and they are endowed with a fate, to
> which the courtier, as the augur of this fate, is the first to submit.
> His unfaithfulness to man is matched by a loyalty to these things to
> the point of being absorbed in a contemplative devotion to them.
> ... Clumsily, indeed unjustifiably, loyalty expresses, in its own way,
> a truth for the sake of which it does, of course, betray the world.
> Melancholy betrays the world for the sake of knowledge. But in its
> tenacious self-absorption it embraces dead objects in its contem-
> plation, in order to redeem them.[11]

We will return to this passage in the conclusion of this book. The key
point to note here is that loyalty is being expressed not to the sovereign (or
tyrant) but to the signs and symbols—one could also say the fetishes—of
that authority. Such "loyalty" produces, not more obedience, but less; it
subverts and dissembles the very structures of authority that such artifacts
symbolize. Benjamin also tells us (in another passage that we will return to
in the conclusion) that their actions lead the plotters from a compromised
human intentionality, toward "a progressive deepening of ... intention."[12]
Even as their own intentions are plainly awful, for Benjamin the plotters
are moving, even if accidentally, toward a different, potentially redemptive
sort of intentionality through their very acts of betrayal.

Rather than condemn the plotters for their treachery or sycophantic
hypocrisy (recall that he calls them "parasites"), Benjamin celebrates the
way they subvert the very sovereign they serve and fawn over. By the same
token, Benjamin celebrates the way that the German baroque dramatists,
the authors of these characters, are themselves failures and "betrayers" of
the world. Unlike their equivalents in Spain (with Calderón) and England
(with Shakespeare), the German baroque dramatists failed to produce the
transcendent truths (whether about God, the state, or the monarch) that
they sought to demonstrate in their plays. In this way, they are exactly like
the plotters they portray insofar as they too seek to serve an ideal but fail
miserably. In their stumbling and accidental way, playwright and characters alike are undermining and countering the very spectacle of state
power that these plays formally set out to depict (and praise).

The plots depicted in the *Origin* suggest a larger project of resistance
and subversion. Yet, insofar as his focus remains on the German baroque,
the culmination of this project goes unrealized in that text. Benjamin tells

us that the baroque "remained astonishingly obscure to itself."[13] Given that their conscious minds were oriented toward the very spectacle of power that they were busily subverting, these playwrights did not recognize what they had done (nor is it clear that they would have been happy with such an outcome if it could have somehow been brought to their attention).

Long after he wrote the *Origin*, as he reached the end of his life, Benjamin gained a new focus on the ideas he conceived of in his earlier work, only now he engaged with the language of conspiracy instead of plots. In his last years, he studied late-nineteenth-century France and the myriad conspiracies that flourished (and failed) in that time. He was particularly interested in the figure of Charles Baudelaire, whom he saw as a latter-day version of the *Trauerspiel* dramatists.

Benjamin was drawn to this period and to Baudelaire because he saw that mid-nineteenth-century France was the epicenter of the articulation of the phantasmagoria in its contemporary guise. Whereas in London the unreality of commodity fetishism had come down swiftly and definitively, in France it came a bit later and in pieces. Accordingly, there was enough critical distance in France to respond and reflect upon the growing influence of capitalist delusion, and Baudelaire was situated right at the epicenter of this development. For Benjamin, Baudelaire does not pretend to have some "outside" perspective on what was happening in Paris during his lifetime; he is a full and enthusiastic participant in the development of commodity fetishism, but in his art, his poetry, and his style, he also manages to subvert and conspire against that which so deeply involves him.

In his work on Baudelaire, we see Benjamin's idea of conspiracy coming more and more to the fore, developing and extending from the work he did in the *Origin*. Much is similar to his earlier work. In his study of late-nineteenth-century France, we are once again dealing with unsavory characters; Benjamin was fascinated by the corruption and failure, the drunkenness and futility of the conspiracies that swirled around Baudelaire and his times. As with the plotters in the *Origin*, there is an accidental quality to the kinds of conspiracies that he attributes to this time. The subversive effect of conspiracy in nineteenth-century France similarly works, not through conscious effort, but through inadvertent effects. Yet in his analysis of Baudelaire in particular (as we will see further in chapter 1) Benjamin develops his strategies and methodologies for conspiracy to a much greater extent. In addition to noting the inadvertent aspects of his resistance, Benjamin tells us that Baudelaire "conspires with language itself. He calculates its effects step by step" (a phrase we will return to at several points in this book).[14] We see here shades of an intentional (dare we say "Machiavellian?") conspiracy on Baudelaire's part, perhaps suggesting the kind of "progressive deepening of . . . intention" that Benjamin hints at in the *Origin*. Without becoming any less suspicious of human intentionality, Benjamin advances a strategy for conspiracy that is both "out of our hands," produced by "baleful constellations" and "material" rescues, even as it is simultaneously performed by and for "us," those of us who are complicit, compromised, and degraded by the phantasmagoria.

Benjamin's Method

The nature of such an intentionality is a key aspect of what I will be describing in this book. A conspiracy that works against one's own intentions, that engages in a hope that is "not for us," seems to make the very concept of intentionality moot. And this must be true not only for the readers of Benjamin's work but for its author as well. As he grew more conspiratorial over the years, it seems that Benjamin grew increasingly suspicious of his own intentionality; his later writings served to decenter the author from his own texts. Books like *One Way Street* and *The Arcades Project* (at least as we have received it) have a collage-like form with quotes, ideas, bits and pieces of information placed nearly without an overarching, authorial framework.[15]

The notion of a text that has (virtually) no author, of aligning oneself with texts or objects to the point of almost disappearing, suggests a dehumanizing loss of agency that seems anathema to any kind of meaning, any kind of politics. What is the point of a conspiracy that seems to exclude or deny any human agency or choice? When Benjamin writes (in the "Exposé" of 1939, in another passage that we will return to) of a strategy that "had to remain hidden from Baudelaire," he suggests that Baudelaire is excluded from his own conspiracy.[16] Here we see a depiction of conspiracies going on without the knowledge of some of their key protagonists! Are we to presume that even Benjamin is excluded from his own conspiracy? Furthermore, in keeping such secrets from his prime coconspirator(s), Benjamin is also keeping one from us, his readers. In so describing Baudelaire, Benjamin sets up an awkward situation; we the readers of this text are being told that there is a conspiracy but that we aren't invited to join. What does it mean to be informed about a conspiracy that we are excluded from? It might seem as if Benjamin is toying with a literary and philosophical nihilism in which he writes human beings out of the picture.

And yet, for all his suspicion of human intentionality—his own very much included—Benjamin does not abandon the human perspective (as if such a thing were even possible). Nor does he abandon his own role as author. What he calls for is not the denigration or elimination of human agency but, in a sense, its restoration. From Benjamin's position, as will become clearer in the ensuing chapters, the agency that we take as our own, and the intentions that we hold to so intimately are in fact a product of the phantasmagoria. The "us" that is trapped by our hopes, that is so complicit with capitalism and the phantasmagoria more generally, is not in fact us at all. This is why hope must lie outside of "ourselves"; we must recover a connection to the material world, even to ourselves, that our idolatry has denied.

Accordingly, Benjamin offers us a method—and more accurately a conspiratorial method—that can guide our intentions back to ourselves, as it were. His method is our lodestone, one that this book will attempt to reproduce; it means we do not have to abandon ourselves and our own position as human actors even as we attempt to abandon most of our insights, thoughts, and feelings about the world we live in. Benjamin's method is the part of his authorship that he does not surrender—it serves as a model for how our own agency can "survive" our turning away from what passes for our intentionality and toward a "progressive deepening . . . of intention."

Benjamin's method offers a way to read a text, any text (including the "text" of the world we live in, the signs and symbols that compose and constitute our reality). Accordingly, in this book, I will try not only to describe the method but to model and employ it myself. In this book, I will try to read a series of texts via Benjamin's method (including Benjamin's own texts) and, in so doing, expand upon and elaborate his method and his conspiracy.

Benjamin's method has multiple elements, but I'd like to highlight the principal ones, each of which has already been mentioned: it works by forming constellations across time and space, it is anti-idolatrous, and it is recuperative. Let me describe each of those features in turn, beginning with Benjamin's constellative method.

Constellations

"Constellations," as we have already seen, is the term Benjamin uses in his "Theses" for connections between historical moments. Through such constellations, influences work both "backward" and "forward" in time, altering the perception of what is real and possible for each period.[17] "Constellation" is also the term Benjamin uses in the *Origin* to describe the kind of nonlinear, nonprogressive connections that are formed between various objects and symbols in the world.[18] Ideas, which for Benjamin stand as "the objective interpretation of phenomena," form constellations between phenomena of the world in a way that is utterly different from the way that we ordinarily—that is to say, idolatrously—make associations between things.[19] Benjamin tells us that "by virtue of the elements' being seen as points in such constellations, phenomena are subdivided and at the same time redeemed."[20] While we ourselves can never know this objectivity (ideas are exclusively the province of the divine), the fact of its existence means that we are not condemned to believe only in our own phantasms. Whereas normally we make connections between objects based on our own false assumptions about space and time (so that, for example, two things that are temporally approximate are automatically seen as associated), the method of constellation allows us to attempt to make connections between things (as we have already seen) "through events that may be separated from [one another] by thousands of years."

The effect of this constellative method is to remove objects and symbols from their phantasmagoric context, to allow us to reread and reconsider them with a new perspective. Once again, we are not gaining access to the idea itself, to "truth" or the objective configuration of things (as we will see in the next chapter, we can only rejuxtapose objects and moments at random; we can never know when we have actually reproduced a truly objective relationship). Yet through this method, we are in effect decentering our own readings of objects, making other readings and relationships possible.

And this works not only for objects but for authors as well. One of the key elements of Benjamin's methodology that guides this book will be to decenter Benjamin's own central prominence as key author of this conspiracy. The way I try to do this is to form a kind of constellation of my own. While Benjamin will hold pride of place, only one chapter in this book will actually pertain to him directly. The rest of the book will look at other authors, a mixture of political and literary thinkers, in order to move away from the reliance on one discipline or one author and her or his point of view. I will read these texts in constellation with one another, adapting Benjamin's methodology as a way to illuminate the conspiracy that I see developing between them.

In order to produce a constellation between authors, the first part of the book will deal with three central thinkers of conspiracy: Benjamin himself, Kafka, from whom Benjamin drew so much, and Machiavelli, arguably the key political theorist to treat the concept of conspiracy. Putting these authors in this order does violence to their temporality, but of course, for Benjamin, that is not a problem. While Benjamin and Kafka form a natural pairing, adding Machiavelli ensures that this discussion of conspiracy will engage with an explicitly political vocabulary (even as that vocabulary will itself to some extent be challenged or altered by the conspiratorial method).

The second part of the book will deal with a set of pairings of political and literary figures covering three moments in time across three geographical contexts. The first pairing considers Alexis de Tocqueville and Edgar Allan Poe in early-nineteenth-century America. These authors are chosen because they both address a question that was crucial to that period; given that the contemporary form of the phantasmagoria was busily forming itself during this period, both Tocqueville and Poe reveal the ways that representation can lead us astray. They both also help us to think about how we can resist such forms with counternarratives of our own. In a time when narratives of authority, personhood, race, and nation were busily being developed, these authors expose the construction of these narratives and offer how narrativity—the form by which means of representation become translated into actual lived reality—can be politicized as a form of resistance.

The second pairing considers mid-twentieth-century Europe and the crisis of fascism, looking at Hannah Arendt and Federico García Lorca. Here, in the face of a totalizing domination of the world by the phantasmagoria's full expression, the question these authors address is whether there can still be a place for human beings, for agency and identity in the face of such totalization. Does the resistance to the phantasmagoria mean the elimination of our identity, such as it is? As we will see, both Arendt and Lorca suggest how the human perspective can be preserved, in each case by turning to representation. While representation seems to be the culprit for these authors (especially for Arendt), it is paradoxically, also the only possible solution to the problem of agency.

Finally, I look at a third pairing based in Algeria in the 1960s during the revolutionary war against France, by looking at Frantz Fanon and Assia Djebar. These authors are selected because both pose the question of what kind of future is possible, what kinds of communities can we forge that do not merely replicate the same phantasmagoric structures that we have been resisting in the first place. These authors suggest, each in their own way, how the "future" of Algeria is in fact already present in the forms of resistance and identities that are generally overwritten by the exigencies of colonialism, revolution, and postcolonialism.

Placing Benjamin's theories in a constellation as I do expands and applies his method in contexts that he could not have been aware of. Using a political theorist like Machiavelli helps to give strategy and teeth to a conspiracy that might otherwise appear to be purely literary in nature. Engaging with plays, novels, political tracts, and memoirs allows us to think about our textual conspiracy in a variety of contexts, many places (including non-Western ones) and many times. The purpose of making such constellations is to think more widely about resistance and conspiracy, to think more clearly about the hope that is not for us.

Anti-idolatry

In terms of the anti-idolatrous nature of his method, Benjamin doesn't always refer to idolatry by name (although he does, for example, say appreciatively of Kafka, "No other writer has obeyed the commandment 'Thou shalt not make unto thee a graven image' so faithfully"),[21] yet his struggle with idolatry and the phantasmagoria that it produces lies at the center of Benjamin's work.

The term "phantasmagoria," as Margaret Cohen tells us, comes from a kind of "magic-lantern show" that dated from the era of the French Revolution and its aftermath. This show was meant to produce ghostly images of the dead (i.e., phantoms). By analogy, Marx used the term to describe commodity fetishism as well; the link he makes illuminates the ghostly afterlife that is given to objects when they are imbued with strange and phantasmal qualities.[22] Like Marx, Benjamin uses the term "phantasmagoria" to refer specifically to the practices of commodity fetishism, to the ghostly and fantastic "reality" that is produced via such widespread idolatry. However, in this book, I will use the term "phantasmagoria" to refer to the human tendency toward idolatry more generally. As we will see further when we explore his theology in the following chapter, for Benjamin idolatry is endemic to human beings; it is a product of the fall, the pursuit of knowledge at the expense of grace. Although the present practice of commodity fetishism is the greatest and most absolute component of the phantasmagoria, the postlapsarian world has never been without some form of it.

To help illuminate the nature and extent of Benjamin's understanding of idolatry it might be useful to turn to Thomas Hobbes, who in his own writing anticipates a great deal of what Benjamin would have to say about this subject. In *Leviathan,* Hobbes speaks of the "Error of *Separated Essences,*" an idolatrous linguistic practice that for Hobbes has vast and pernicious effects in the world.[23] This error consists of turning signs, nominally merely representations of real things, into "separated essences," phantom truths that surpass and overshadow their own referent (in the same way that a religious idol, a symbol for God, supplants and overshadows God). The prime example Hobbes offers of this error is the notion of the soul. Hobbes tells us that the term "soul," originally meant merely as a linguistic figure to represent people (such as when we say, "There is not a soul in sight"), has become a rogue (and idolatrous) metaphor; it has taken on aspects of immortality and perfection that eclipse and supersede the body or person it represents.[24] The body becomes subject to the very symbol that is meant to convey its existence (hence the soul becomes a "separated essence").

For Hobbes, as for Benjamin, this practice of idolatry is all encompassing; it extends from religion to politics, to language, and even to the most basic fabric of reality and time. What Hobbes calls the "Kingdome of Darknesse" is equivalent to Benjamin's "phantasmagoria."[25] For Benjamin the phantasmagoria, as we have already begun to see, overwrites our lives, our very reality with its meanings and truths, its great, organizing narratives and promises of salvation. The phantasmagoria amounts to a mass practice of idolatry, a practice of misreading and misattributing meaning to the signs that compose the world with profound theological, political, and linguistic consequences.

In the face of such a practice of mass delusion, for Benjamin (as for Hobbes) our only recourse is not to "reality"—since that can never be actually known—but instead to a greater attention to signs themselves, to a better and nonidolatrous practice of reading and seeing (hence the need for Benjamin's methodology). For Benjamin, we can never be fully free from delusion and the misreading of signs; the best we can expect from our conspiracy is to have our delusions become legible to us as such, without being any less compelling or necessary. Over the course of this book, I will develop the idea of "recognizing our misrecognition," which is to say recognizing that we cannot help but be misled, deluded, and seduced by the signs that compose our world. This knowledge need not, however, constitute a capitulation to delusion (the stance of the phantasmagoria). Instead, we can come to recognize the way we are affected by the sign, including in ways that are both desirable and necessary. As we will see further, we would have no meaning, no identity, no politics at all without the sign. We can learn to take advantage of the *aporias* and disruptions of the symbolic order and generally navigate (or at least understand ourselves as being able to navigate) rather than simply occupy our position in that order.[26] Although the sign will always constitute the only "truth" we can ever know, we can be complicit with, rather than simply duped by, our misrecognition of it.

The key insight that comes from the idea of recognizing misrecognition is to note, as we have already seen, that our fight against idolatry can only be conducted by and through an alliance with signs. It is Kafka—who along with Baudelaire is probably Benjamin's greatest muse—who shows Benjamin how this might work. In "Some Reflections on Kafka" (a part of a letter he wrote to Gershom Scholem), Benjamin writes:

> Kafka's real genius was that he tried something entirely new: he sacrificed truth for the sake of its transmissibility, its haggadic element. Kafka's writings are by their nature parables. But it is their misery and their beauty that they had to become *more* than parables. They do not modestly lie at the feet of the doctrine, as the Haggadah lies at the feet of the Halakah. Though apparently reduced to submission, they unexpectedly raise a mighty paw against it.[27]

We will return to this passage in chapter 2 but for now let us note the concept of Haggadah (the representation of the divine)—or at least Kafka's version of it—"raising a mighty paw" against Halakah (the divine law). In this phrase, we can begin see the full, conspiratorial and, as we will see further, messianic elements of Benjamin's conspiracy. Through Kafka, Benjamin gives us a vision of the very elements that compose an image (in this case, an image of the divine) turning against the phantasms that they produce. If we stick with a purely religious terminology for a moment, we see that such a strike against our image of God is required not because God is "wrong" but because our ideas of God—and by extension our interpretations of the world—are, by definition, wrong. Left to our own devices, we engage in the "Error of *Separated Essences*"; we fetishize the concept of God, replacing divine judgments with mythical ones and creating the perverted world of the phantasmagoria in its stead. Because God's truth is mysterious to us, we must resist false prophets; we must allow language and representation to "unexpectedly raise a mighty paw" against what passes for Halakah in our world. This is why we must "conspire with language"; only the elements that produce and form the phantasmagoria can be used against it.

What we have understood through a theological terminology can be extended to semiotic and political forms of representation as well. We see Benjamin expressing the same sentiment in the *Origin* in a more secular fashion when he tells us, "The language of the baroque is constantly convulsed by rebellion on the part of the elements which make it up."[28] All representation can potentially rise up against what it purports to stand for; it can be read idolatrously, or not, depending on how we understand the process of representation and our relationship to it, depending that is, on whether we "recognize our misrecognition" or not. In this way, the various images that compose our political life, "the green flags of Islam," the images of democracy, community, and so on, do not need to be eliminated to rid us of idolatry. In fact, as I have already suggested, to eliminate the signs that organize our lives is to eliminate politics itself. We cannot, seeking to escape the sign, just be a "real," unmediated community (an ultimate phantasm); instead, the complexity and multitudinousness of the community must become legible to itself. As an idol, the sign overwrites the community and political forms that it stands for. But the sign also produces that community in the first place; we coalesce around signs, we "know" ourselves only through them. To recognize our misrecognition is to become aware of how the sign produces ties and affiliations between us, even as we resist the overarching narratives that render those ties something totalizing and alienated.

Recuperation

The final aspect of Benjamin's method that I would like to focus on is that of recuperation, the aspect that most pertains to his notion of hope. As already mentioned, Benjamin famously recalls a conversation between Franz Kafka and his friend Max Brod when contemplating the darkness of the world (a conversation we will return to in chapter 2). When Brod asked Kafka if he agreed with the Gnostics that God was "the evil demiurge," and there was thus nothing but evil in God's universe, Kafka replied "Oh no . . . our world is only a bad mood of God, a bad day of his."

"Then there is hope outside this manifestation of the world that we know," Brod answered. To which Kafka replied, "Oh, plenty of hope, an infinite amount of hope—but not for us."[29] As I have already said, such a construction of "hope . . . but not for us" epitomizes the conspiratorial aspects of Benjamin's project. There is no hope for us because we are deeply compromised creatures. In our current conditions, our intentions are not to be trusted, not even the intentions of the theorist who would save us from all of this (such "salvation," as we will see further, would inevitably be just another iteration of the phantasmagoria). What then does recuperation mean in such a context? What, exactly are we recuperating?

In chapter 2 we will engage with much of the theological basis for Benjamin's understanding of redemption and recuperation. For now, suffice it to say that even as we are fallen and complicit with the idolatry that forms our sense of reality, for Benjamin we are simultaneously subject to "God's eye view," wherein we remain part of creation. From this perspective—which is completely opaque to us—we are already redeemed, even though we don't realize it. From God's perspective our acts of idolatry are in fact attempts to reproduce the lost unity of paradise; we are lost, not because we are condemned by God, but because we misperceive what we are doing. Even as we employ signs as idols, those same signs are also in the service of God (and we are as well). In this way, our complicity with idolatry is not totalizing; our redemption (taking this term more in the Nietzschean than a Christian sense) can become legible—or at least conceivable—to us.[30] Accordingly, texts and signs can become our allies rather than purely the source of our delusion; they can become the basis of our textual conspiracy.

In this way, we can recuperate what we are already doing, what we are already seeing and responding to, even as we are dazzled by idolatry. We do not, therefore, have to give up on human agency, on intentionality or politics. Benjamin speaks quite cryptically at times about the "intention of the sign" and also the "the intention which underlies allegory," suggesting an alien form of intentionality that we must surrender to.[31] But when we look at things in a recuperative mode, we see that these alien intentions serve as storing houses for our own intentionality. Such concepts represent what we are *also* doing when we thoughtlessly engage in idolatry. It recalls that even an idolater is also, albeit inadvertently, worshipping God; the fetish we abuse also holds and retains the means for our proper worship.

What is being recuperated then, is ourselves; we are recovering ourselves from our own phantasms. Benjamin's recuperative strategy means that no one is ever so compromised or complicit that she cannot be returned to herself. Nor is any one time period so bad that it is irremediable. As dark as our own times may seem, there is hope, only it resides in another world, a world that coexists with the one we are living in (more accurately, it *is* the one we are living in, although we are not ourselves aware of that). Benjamin's method potentially serves to bring us from one world into the other; the change requires only an alteration of our attention, a "recognition of our misrecognition," in order to usher us into another form of hope.

The Politics of Benjamin's Conspiracy

Before we get on to the rest of the book, some final words may be in order about the political connotations of this project. The conclusion will be the chapter that most directly addresses the political upshot of textual conspiracies, of "hope [that is] not for us." For now I would simply like to highlight the way that this project, for all its distinction from more traditional understandings of politics, remains critically political in nature.

When thinking about a politics based on textual conspiracy, on alien forms of hope and alliances with objects, we confront a basic question of how we think about politics, what we expect something properly "political" to look like. Generally speaking, we can say that contemporary understandings of politics presuppose an active and self-conscious political subject, one who maximizes her or his will and desires through an engagement with other political actors; certainly it suggests a direct relationship between one's political aspirations and the "hope" or effect that is actually produced. Yet one of the central arguments of this book will be that when we presuppose such a political actor, we also presuppose a lot of the politics that comes with such a model. We risk perpetually reproducing the phantasmagoria that we struggle against so long as we remain tied to the formulation of politics that it suggests to us.

The terrain that Benjamin explores for his conspiracy, his political undertaking, doesn't look like ordinary politics. His key coconspirators are often literary figures like Baudelaire and Kafka. When it comes to his treatment of great, historically recognized political actors such as Auguste Blanqui (not to mention Marx), as we will see, Benjamin takes a more circuitous path toward embracing them (although in the end, I argue, he does embrace them as well). Relatedly, Benjamin's conspiracy does not take place in the usual "political" spheres, vying with the powerful, the state, the army, or the police. As we have seen, his conspiracy takes place entirely in texts and/or with objects.

Benjamin's conspiracy also involves a different form of relationality than our understanding of politics usually involves. The word "conspiracy" (in English) comes from the Latin meaning "those who breathe together," implying a closeness and interrelationality in one moment and one place. The German term *verschwörern* similarly suggests a relationality, literally: those who swear together. Yet for Benjamin, to base a conspiracy purely on temporal or physical proximity risks reinforcing and being subject to the very certainties and inevitable fates of any one time and place that create the need for conspiracy in the first place. Benjamin conspires mainly with the dead (for "*even the dead* will not be safe from the enemy if he wins") and, by extension, with the not yet born.

There are also ways that this conspiracy and method differ from more general understandings of politics in terms of the question of epistemology. We often expect politics as a norm to be based on facts and "objective truths" (so that those who disagree with us are wrong, or delusional, or, simply misunderstanding things). For Benjamin, although such truths exist, they can never be known to us (they are the exclusive province of the "God's eye view"). Accordingly, there is no privileged position from which to "know" things that are obscure to others. In Benjamin's analysis, there is thus no group that "gets it" while others are left in the dark. We are all equally deluded by the phantasmagoria; even the theorists who describe our plight (Benjamin very much included) share in this delusion. All that Benjamin can offer, as already mentioned, is his method for negotiating the shifting and perilous forms of representation that we all, of necessity, subscribe to in one form or another.

For all of his differences with our varying understandings of politics, I argue, Benjamin's conspiracy, his method, is inherently political. Benjamin may help us to expand our understanding of what the political stands for, where it occurs, and how it works. For Benjamin, a conspiracy that did not focus on texts and materiality would be bound to fail because it would exist solely in the world of human thought and action as such; it would thus be contained within the phantasmagoria. By the same token, to believe unproblematically in the reality that we perceive (i.e., in knowable, objective truths) reflects the fallacy that what we are doing and thinking is not "representative" at all but is a direct manifestation of some kind of will, agency, or truth (i.e., something "real" instead of "literary"). From Benjamin's perspective, such a view precludes any kind of redemption from the phantasmagoria because its own representational origins are invisible. There seems to be no need, no possibility for resistance when we are faced with an insurmountable "truth."

One aim I have in writing this book is to reconcile Benjamin with political theory, to establish the ways that Benjamin is explicitly political despite his appearance as being mainly involved with literary or aesthetic principles. This is not in and of itself a novel argument; Wendy Brown and Susan Buck-Morss, among others, have already done excellent work in this regard.[32] What I am looking at in particular, the mechanism by which I make a connection between Benjamin and political theory, is the idea of conspiracy. As I see it, this concept allows us to think about the question of fetishism and representation in a political fashion. Even if Benjamin doesn't always speak of conspiracy in his later work, I argue that it underlies, unifies, and explains what he is trying to do from a political perspective. Like the atmosphere of nineteenth-century France he focuses on at the end of his life, conspiracy is always afoot in his later work, even if it is not directly referenced or visible.[33] To think of Benjamin in terms of conspiracy is to think of him in clearly political terms; it is to bring an idea from an explicitly political vocabulary and apply it to this thinker for whom the connection to politics often appears tenuous or vague. And, by extending this analysis to include many other coconspirators, we can broaden and deepen our sense of what the political consists of.

In the West, political theory has long had a troubled relationship to conspiracy. Historically, much of political theory has been devoted to battling and controlling it. When it is referred to at all, conspiracy is generally regarded as a scourge for the order and stability that is a necessary prerequisite for political life. Indeed, when one thinks of the term "conspiracy" in popular culture (just as in political theory for the most part), one thinks of dark plots to destroy legitimate forms of government. Since September 11, 2001, this way of thinking has become even more pronounced (and not just in the United States). Depending on who you are and where you are standing, conspiracy is widely held to be a very bad thing, something to be avoided at all costs.

Yet there has always been a subcurrent throughout Western political theory (not to mention other, non-Western theoretical traditions) that sees conspiracy in a different light, one that sometimes even directly calls for or engages in it.[34] One could argue that if Socrates is the source of much of Western political theory, he is also one of its first conspirators, seeking to establish alternative political strategies in the face of a society that was full of its own hubris and heading into catastrophe (much as we are in our own time). Derrida speaks of an "immense rumour" coursing through the history of Western thought, a suggestion, or a dream, of a kind of political friendship that does not quite exist.[35] Benjamin himself echoes this language when he speaks of "rumor" and "folly," offering hints of another form of politics that survives, largely unnoticed, amid the swirl and madness of the phantasmagoria.[36]

As I read the Western canon, this "immense rumour" lies a great deal closer to the surface than is often considered; it pulses among some of the thinkers who lie at the very center of the canon. In a previous book, I looked at Thomas Hobbes, who is generally held to be one of the greatest proponents of order in the Western canon, the very picture of liberal (or at least "proto-liberal") orthodoxy.[37] In that book, I argued that Hobbes could be read as subverting the very principles of sovereignty that he is said to uphold and produce (in part, as already suggested, through his anti-idolatrous practices). I further argued that in Hobbes's work, it is the text that subverts and defeats even the author's own (presumed) orthodoxy and conservatism. I would definitely include Hobbes in the conspiracy that I sketch out in this current book, despite his orthodox reputation. In the third chapter of this book, I look at Machiavelli, another canonical figure who is also often seen as opposing conspiracies, to show that he too can be read as advocating a conspiracy of his own (indeed part of the reason he is included in this book is to help us think more about how to be "consciously Machiavellian" while undertaking conspiracy in a way that doesn't simply reproduce existing "realities"). Thinking of these and other authors as forming an interlocking web—or constellation—of conspiracy, and extending this reading to more contemporary thinkers, we can move this conspiratorial subcurrent toward our own time. Such a move helps us to reevaluate our own moment, a time when more conventional understandings of open resistance and rebellion seem to have either run their course or perhaps (for many at least) have even become unthinkable, impossible, the events in Egypt and Libya notwithstanding.

To be clear, I do not believe that all political and literary thinkers and actors participate in the conspiracy I am describing in this book. In fact, the vast majority do not. Yet a sufficient number of significant thinkers keep this subterranean conspiracy going. In this book, I would like to add Benjamin and—through my analysis of his conspiracy—a number of other thinkers and writers to the ranks of those who do participate, to bring this conspiracy, this "immense rumour," up and into our own time with the aim of helping us to think further about the hope that is "not for us."

This book is animated by alien hopes: hopes from other times and other lives, hope for the Left that we are not living in a temporal dead end, hope that we have options beyond recklessly attacking capitalism outright and openly or making self-defeating alliances with "left-leaning" liberals. The options that we understand ourselves as having in our times are, from Benjamin's perspective, doomed to fail insofar as each of us is marked by a desire for capitalism to succeed, whether we are aware of it or not. Yet by aligning our intentions with the "intention of the sign," we have some kind of hope after all.

What might we become when we are "not us," the recipients of this other kind of hope? Surely the concept of "the Left" is itself a product of the phantasmagoria as much as anything else. As we will see further, what we will or could become is, in most ways, no different than what we already are. The community that emerges from the conspiracy I describe in the following pages (that is to say, the community that becomes legible to itself) may, indeed must, be no more coherent, no more unified than the fractured Left that currently exists. Any sense of an ultimate Left triumph over idolatry and commodity fetishism is highly suspect (another aspect of the phantasmagoria). But what *is* or could be different is the possibility of reading and interpreting ourselves in another way, hence the value of Benjamin's method. Perhaps above all, this turn to Benjamin offers us a hope—even if, or especially because, it is a hope that is not for us—that even in the darkest of times, times when we can't imagine anything other than what is, we can still conspire.

With this idea in mind, let us turn to the first and foremost textual conspirator this book will consider, Walter Benjamin. As we move on to an engagement with the actual authors, it is worth mentioning a general semantic practice that I adopt throughout this book. While I will be distinguishing between any given author and her or his texts (beginning with Benjamin), to avoid being tiresome, and because of the ambiguity about the nature of authorship, I will sometimes use terms such as "Benjamin" and "Benjamin's text" (or whichever other author I am considering at the time) more or less interchangeably although there will be times where I will have to specify which "author" I mean.

Part I

1 | Walter Benjamin's Conspiracy with Language

Although this is a book on Benjaminian political conspiracy, it is true that in much of his work, Walter Benjamin seems to give short shrift to conspiracy as a strategy for resistance. In both his incomplete "book" on Charles Baudelaire (the one completed section, entitled "The Paris of the Second Empire in Baudelaire") and in Konvolute V in *The Arcades Project* (the section devoted to conspiracies), Benjamin focuses mainly on the incompetence, bad luck, or corruption of various conspirators during the century of failed revolutions that occurred in France between the great revolution of 1789 and the fall of the Paris commune in 1871.[1]

Yet, as we have already seen, for Benjamin, failure, decay, and futility are not in and of themselves a reason to give up on a person or a period of time. Connecting such moments, as he does, in constellation with other moments brings out conspiratorial aspects that, in turn, change the way we think about our own time as well. In this chapter, I will lay out more carefully the transtemporal conspiracy that I attributed to Benjamin in the previous introductory chapter. I will argue that although he formally seems to despair of conspiracy as a means of resistance, and even apparently castigates a hero like Auguste Blanqui for his ultimate failure as a conspirator, such a despair disguises (or, as we will see, actually permits) a retrieval of and even participation in these old conspiracies on Benjamin's part.

As we have already begun to see in the introduction, such transtemporal "constellations" serve to address one of Benjamin's chief convictions as to the source of the failure of nineteenth-century French revolutionaries (and, for that matter, all other revolutionaries as well), namely the problem of human intentionality. For Benjamin, human intentionality (very much including his own) is marked by the *mémoire voluntaire*, the conscious and therefore complicit zone of desires and thoughts that is, by definition, deeply compromised and problematical, limited and defined by the effects of commodity (and other forms of) fetishism. Our conscious minds take up and reproduce that fetishism, and our desire becomes the desire for and of the commodity, for capitalism more broadly.

In the face of his suspicions about intentionality and its limitations, in this chapter I will argue that Benjamin conspires against the intentions of the revolutionaries he is interested in. In other words, he conspires against (and therefore on behalf of) the conspirators themselves, and as we will see, he conspires even against himself. This seems like a paradoxical claim insofar as it is not clear how even conspiracy is not in and of itself marked by the very intentionality that it would rescue these figures from. As we have already begun to see, however—and as will become clearer over the course of this chapter—to conspire against intentions does not mean to engage one's own (presumably better-knowing) consciousness to rescue those with "false consciousness." Instead it means to (re)align our own intentions—and, by extension, the intentionality of others as well—with "the intention of the sign." It means to resign oneself and/or others to the materiality of texts as a way toward the possible recuperation of a human intentionality that is not overwritten by the phantasmagoria. Thus, even as the conspirator is her- or himself fully compromised, the engagement with language allows the conspirator to avoid merely replicating the very compromises that the conspiracy is "intended" to rescue the person from in the first place.

In light of the possibility of such a conspiracy and the ethos of resistance and subversion that it suggests, we will see that for Benjamin the failure and compromise of the nineteenth-century French revolutionaries he is interested in is far from fatal. Benjamin turns the failures of these revolutionaries into an asset for his (and, by extension, their) conspiracy. He employs what I call a strategy of the antidote in turning such failures and misrecognitions into the tools of combating the phantasmagoria. Like an antidote (a term Benjamin employs) our subjection to and participation in the phantasmagoria can become the basis for resistance.

In my examination of Benjamin's conspiracy, I will argue that his embrace of bohemianism, failure, and even, as we will see, the figure of Satan points to his strategy of the antidote. In a fallen world where there is nothing but idolatry, where Halakah comes to us only as mythology, we must emulate the blasphemy of Satan, the failure to obey, the confusion and indolence of the drunkard and the dandy in order to subvert the phantasmagoria and to use its own effects against itself. By such means, the absolute certainty that the phantasmagoria is real, natural, and historical can be dispelled or disturbed.[2]

As this chapter develops, I will attempt to expand the conspiracy that

Benjamin initially attributes to Baudelaire, extending it to historical persons as disparate as Blanqui and Marx and eventually coming to include Benjamin himself. By connecting these various personages via the notion of conspiracy, Benjamin is helping to form one of his "constellations," a node of connection—as well as a method of reading—that serves dialectically to lessen the hold of the phantasmagoria on each separate member.[3] However discontinuous and paradoxical it may be, this constellation and the conspiracy that it produces—which will in turn be extended in this book to include the various other conspirators that I will treat—serves as the basis for Benjamin's political theory.

Bohemian Conspiracies

A quick perusal of "The Paris of the Second Empire in Baudelaire," the second (and only completed) part of an envisioned three-part book on Baudelaire, suggests that, on the surface at least, Benjamin has little good to say or relate about the conspirators of nineteenth-century France.

He tells us, for example, in the beginning of that writing that "as emperor, Napoleon [III] continued to develop his conspiratorial habits."[4] This claim, wherein the emperor of France continues to engage in conspiracies even after he gains power, sets the tone for much of what follows, a catalog of deeply compromised conspirators who are either actually acting on behalf of the state or are betrayed, incompetent, useless, and very often injured or murdered in the course of their activities.

One key aspect of this compromise (and indeed the main subject of Benjamin's book on Baudelaire) is the peculiar nature of bourgeois/proletariat relations during this period. In Konvolute V, the section of *The Arcades Project* devoted directly to conspiracies, Benjamin (citing Charles Benoist) describes one such conspiracy, the Société des Droits de l'Homme (Society for the Rights of Man), as a means for the bourgeoisie to "woo" the proletariat "by various attentions and tokens of respect, by joining together in balls and fêtes."[5]

In Konvolute V, Benjamin also includes a citation from Paul Lafargue arguing that a particular understanding of history was a factor in bringing the workers together with the bourgeoisie in 1848 insofar as the workers held that "the great Revolution was good in itself, and human misery could be eliminated only if people were to resolve on a new 1793. Hence, they turned away distrustfully from the socialists and felt drawn to the bourgeois republicans."[6]

Such an "alliance," if that is really what we should call it, clearly contributed to the overall failure of the various revolutions in this period and speaks to the utter compromise, the death in its moment of conception, of French revolutionary spirit in the nineteenth century. As in our own time, such "popular front" tactics, an alliance with capitalist interests, proved time and time again to be disastrous for the French Left. Benjamin tells us that Marx labels this collusion between classes as "the whole, indefinite, distinguished mass, thrown hither and thither, which the French term *la bohème*" (although for Marx, perhaps more clearly than for Benjamin, the bohemians constitute only a small part of the proletariat revolutionary movement).[7]

Rather than condemn bohemianism for its political failure, however, Benjamin seems greatly drawn to it. And in fact, the lion's share of his attention to this phenomenon seems to be focused not so much on the revolutionaries themselves as on literary personages—in particular Charles Baudelaire—who lived and wrote amid them. Here, we come to the central mystery of what Benjamin is up to in his attention to this period. Why, in his interrogation of conspiracies in nineteenth-century France, does Benjamin focus on writers like Baudelaire, who he concedes was "impoten[t]"?[8] When it comes to a "pure" or true revolutionary, like Auguste Blanqui, Benjamin certainly gives him his due, but famously consigns him to a kind of historical dead end when he writes of Blanqui's "resignation without hope."[9]

Perversely, Benjamin seems to focus on the source of failure in the first place: the compromise, the useless rage, the wasted effort, the effeteness of writers, and the incompetence and naïveté of conspirators in the face of real and serious political challenges. Is Benjamin demonstrating anything other than nostalgia for this era? Does he offer any tangible, political strategies in his admiration for the bohemians (and in particular the bohemian writers)?

Professional Conspirators

One way to think about what Benjamin is up to is to note the nature of his relationship to Marx, whose own analysis of nineteenth-century French revolutions figures heavily in Benjamin's understanding. Benjamin's relationship to Marx in these works is curiously ambivalent. He cites Marx as an authority and yet somehow fails to convey that authority perfectly. As we will see repeatedly in this chapter, Benjamin appears to agree with Marx's criticisms of the conspirators of this time, but he also invokes

Baudelaire in a way that suggests that he (i.e., Benjamin) might be sympathetic to such conspirators after all (making him, like Machiavelli—as we will see further—conspiratorial in his depictions of conspiracies).

In "The Paris of the Second Empire in Baudelaire," Benjamin begins by dwelling on a series of quotes from Marx (all coming from one long citation that he keeps intact in Konvolute V) concerning the quality of the bohemians and various conspirators during the period in question.[10] Focusing specifically on the revolutions and conspiracies of 1848, Marx tells us that even the "professional conspirators" of that period leave a lot to be desired because

> they embrace inventions which are supposed to perform revolutionary miracles . . . Occupying themselves with such projects, they have no other aim but the immediate one of overthrowing the existing government, and they profoundly despise the more theoretical enlightenment of the workers regarding their class interests. Hence their anger—not proletarian but plebian—at the *habits noirs* [black coats], the more or less educated people who represent that side of the movement and of whom they can never be entirely independent, since these are the official representatives of the party.[11]

While Marx appears to be critical of this tendency (associating them with the "dissolute" nature of the *Lumpenproletariat*), Benjamin reminds us that the same atheoretical sentiment Marx applies to the professional conspirators can be ascribed to Baudelaire as well.[12] Benjamin follows this citation by writing, "Ultimately, Baudelaire's political insights do not go beyond those of these professional conspirators."[13] Accordingly, given his own strong interest in Baudelaire, it is not clear that Benjamin shares Marx's concern with the atheoretical nature of these "professional conspirators" either.

Benjamin contrasts Marx' apparently negative appraisal of the professional conspirators with Auguste Blanqui, the radical French revolutionary, who "resemble[s] one of the *habits noirs* who were the hated rivals of those professional conspirators."[14] Presumably, then, Blanqui offers a more favorable (for Marx) model for revolution than the professional conspirators themselves. Yet, Benjamin goes on to write:

> But the measured seriousness and the impenetrability which were part of Blanqui's makeup appear different in light of a statement by Marx. With reference to those professional conspirators, [Marx]

writes, "They are the alchemists of the revolution and fully share the disintegration of ideas, the narrow-mindedness, and the obsessions of the earlier alchemists."[15]

This passage is difficult to interpret (rendered yet more complex by the fact that it is Benjamin dictating how Marx felt about Blanqui). How does this statement by Marx about alchemy affect (i.e., make "appear different") the "measured seriousness and impenetrability" of Blanqui's "makeup?" Does this suggest that Blanqui is not who we initially think he is, that he is somehow less stern and aloof from the more prosaic revolutionaries of the period? The grammar, if not the content, of this passage suggests that for Benjamin, Marx's comment connects Blanqui with the professional conspirators after all, even making it unclear whether Benjamin is including Blanqui as a "professional conspirator" or distinguishing him from them. Such ambiguity calls into question our initial assumptions about who or what Marx is actually criticizing (at least in terms of the way that Benjamin is interpreting Marx).

In other writings Benjamin refers to Blanqui by the same term "professional conspirator," further effacing a distinction that Marx seems to be making.[16] Turning to the original German offers only a little bit of help on this matter. In the English translation, the terms "professional conspirator" and "professional revolutionary" are both used, possibly suggesting a difference between these terms (and hence, a possible difference between Blanqui and the others) but in German, Benjamin makes no such distinction. Whereas in the passages quoted above (and elsewhere), Marx sometimes uses the Latinate terms *Konspirateur*—as in "*Konspirateur von Profession*"—Benjamin prefers the German-derived *Berufsverschwörern* (literally, those professionals who "swear together"—as opposed to the Latin-derived German version of conspire, i.e., "those who breathe together"—but similar to the Italian *congiura*).[17] Yet he uses this term to refer both to Blanqui and to the "professional conspirators" themselves, once again undermining the distinction that Marx draws.

Benjamin's softening of Marx's criticism may also be evident in the way that, immediately following his consideration of how Marx calls the professional conspirators "alchemists," Benjamin goes on to write: "This almost automatically yields the image of Baudelaire: the enigmatic stuff of allegory in one, the mystery-mongering of the conspirator in the other."[18] Although this reference seems derogatory on Marx's part, Benjamin has a more nuanced, even appreciative view of alchemy.[19]

Thus, whereas on his own terms Marx seems pretty clear, as Benjamin "interprets" him, he becomes muddier. This says perhaps less about Marx himself than about Benjamin's own purposes with Marx. He seems to want to connect Marx, however much it may seem to go against the grain of the text, with both Baudelaire and the professional conspirators that Baudelaire was associated with (somehow dragging Blanqui into this association as well). At the very least, if he cannot connect these personages, Benjamin may be seeking to lessen the distinction that Marx seems to suggest in his own writing. In these endeavors, we can already see evidence of some kind of stealthy—we might again say conspiratorial—style on Benjamin's part, a way of nudging these historical characters into an alignment that may have had little or nothing to do with their own conscious (read intentional) positions.[20] In short, he seems to be trying to drag both Marx and Blanqui into the same quagmire of failure as the professional conspirators themselves.

Revolution and Wine

Something of this same dynamic (albeit in a slightly less complicated mode) can also be seen with Benjamin's treatment of Marx's criticism of the professional conspirators as being overly fond of wine. Insofar as the vast majority of such conspiracies were plotted and argued in one of France's many *marchands de vin* (wine shops), drinking—even lots of drinking—became part of the revolutionary apparatus. Benjamin quotes Marx here as writing that, in the wine shops, the

> conspirator, highly sanguine in character anyway like all Parisian proletarians, soon develops into an absolute *bambocheur* [boozer] in this continual tavern atmosphere. The sinister conspirator, who in secret session exhibits a Spartan self-discipline, suddenly thaws and is transformed into a tavern regular whom everybody knows and who really understands how to enjoy his wine and women.[21]

Here, Benjamin openly calls such comments "deprecatory" on Marx's part.[22] But once again Benjamin implicitly has another take on such matters. Following this quote from Marx, Benjamin concedes that "the miasma that prevailed [in the taverns] was familiar to Baudelaire."[23] Here too Benjamin seems to cite Marx's words in order to malign the conspirators as "tavern regulars" but in associating such activities with Baudelaire, Benjamin also performs something of a retrieval of that atmosphere, and with it perhaps a retrieval of the conspirators (and their conspiracy). It seems here too that Benjamin, without explicitly parting from Marx, is once again taking Baudelaire's side on this question, refusing to condemn drunkenness even though it seems to contribute to the failure of revolution. Once again Benjamin seems to read Marx against Marx's own clearly stated intentions.

As is well known, Benjamin ties the atmosphere of drinking and plotting during this period to several of Baudelaire's poems on wine, perhaps most famously in the poems "L'Âme du Vin" and "Le Vin des Chiffoniers" ("The Soul of Wine" and "The Ragpicker's Wine," respectively). In the latter poem, for example, Baudelaire associates the ragpicker's futile drunkenness with poetry and conspiracy when he writes:

> On voit un chiffonier qui vient, hochant la tête,
> Buttant, et se cognant aux murs comme un poète,
> Et, sans prendre souci des mouchards, ses sujets,
> Epanche tout son coeur en glorieux projets.
>
> [One sees a ragpicker coming—shaking his head,
> Stumbling, and colliding against walls like a poet;
> And, heedless of police informers, his humble subjects,
> He pours out his heart in glorious devisings.][24]

In this poem, we see the ferment of drunkenness, police informants, conspiracies, and poetry that characterized the period in question. If the ragpicker becomes a figure of bohemianism (without, however, actually partaking of bohemianism as a class construct), he epitomizes Benjamin's ambivalence as to whether bohemianism is useful for, or a detriment to, revolution.[25]

It is precisely this kind of poetic reading of the ragpicker (and other poetic figures as well) that seems to have infuriated or at least irritated Theodor Adorno in his famous letter written to Benjamin on November 10, 1938. In that letter, Adorno complains that Benjamin has failed to subject the objects of his analysis to proper theory, for it is

> methodologically inappropriate to give conspicuous individual features from the realm of the superstructure a "materialist" turn by relating them immediately, and perhaps even causally, to certain corresponding features of the substructure. The materialist determination of cultural traits is only possible if it is mediated through the *total social process.*[26]

Adorno focuses on Benjamin's claim that Baudelaire's wine poems were in effect "caused" by the state implementing a raise in the wine tax. Adorno argues that "the direct inference from the duty on wine to L'Ame du vin imputes to phenomena precisely the kind of spontaneity, tangibility and density which they have lost under capitalism."[27]

Hence, in claiming that he ignores the social processes that are in effect, Adorno claims that Benjamin effectively abandons Marxism altogether. He famously places Benjamin at "the crossroads of magic and positivism."[28]

If we are inclined (as I am) to defend Benjamin against this charge, we must look deeper into what Benjamin is doing here in terms of the political utility of his inquiry into bohemianism. Why distance himself from Marx (if, in fact, that is what he is doing)? Or from theory (if Adorno is correct)? Benjamin, as Adorno paints him, has been seduced by the lure of bohemianism, by the cult of futility, wine, and magic. If Benjamin is not so seduced, what explanation can we offer for his tendency to side with such figures as Baudelaire, even if he seems to be going explicitly against (or even perverting) Marx's own critique of the nineteenth-century French conspirators?

Conspiring with Language

The beginnings of an answer to this question may be found when we look at a passage right at the end of "The Paris of the Second Empire in Baudelaire" where Benjamin directly considers Baudelaire as a coconspirator (a passage we already briefly considered in the introduction):

> Behind the masks which he used to their fullest extent, the poet in Baudelaire preserved his incognito. He was as circumspect in his work as he was capable of seeming provocative in his personal associations. The incognito was the law of his poetry. His prosody is like the map of a big city in which one can move about inconspicuously, shielded by blocks of houses, gateways, courtyards. On this map, words are given clearly designated positions, just as conspirators are given designated positions before the outbreak of a revolt. *Baudelaire conspires with language itself.* He calculates its effects step by step.[29]

In claiming that "Baudelaire conspires with language itself" (in German: "Baudelaire konspiriert mit der Sprache selbst"), Benjamin may be signaling a different kind of conspiracy.[30] In both English and German there may be two senses to the word "with" (or *mit*) either meaning using language as an instrument (as in "I'm eating with a fork") or as engaging with language as an ally or agent one associates with (as in "I'm working with Ms. Jones"). In English, the term "conspire[s]" is ambiguous, as it could carry either sense of "with." However, in German, far more than in English, the second sense as an ally or agent is preferred. Thus it may be that Benjamin is telling us that for Baudelaire, his "conspiracy with language" is in fact a case of language acting as a kind of independent agent, an ally not a tool.

"With" (*mit*) language as his ally, Baudelaire conspires in ways that may differ quite radically from other conspirators, conceivably including those who merely "employ" language for the sake of their own conspiracies. Having language as an ally somehow alters the usual traps and pitfalls of conspiracy by decentering our own (tool-wielding) intentionality. This "other" style of conspiracy somehow survives even the failure of its hero, Baudelaire himself (who Benjamin tells us is "doom[ed]" by modernity).[31]

In portraying his conspiracy with language, Benjamin displays some ambivalence about Baudelaire's own role in this alliance. On the one hand we have seen that "[Baudelaire] calculates [conspiracy's] effects step by step," suggesting an active role. Yet, shortly after this passage, Benjamin writes: "For the *coup de main* which Baudelaire calls writing poetry, he takes allegories into his confidence. They alone have been let in on the secret."[32] Here, the question of Baudelaire's agency becomes a bit more problematical. He "takes allegories into his confidence," and yet "they alone have been let in on the secret." "They alone" could imply that they are in on a secret that even Baudelaire is denied. In the original German, this ambivalence may be even stronger: "Für den Handstreich, der bei Baudelaire Dichten heißt, zieht er Allegorien in sein Vertrauen. Sie sind die einzigen, die im Geheimnis sind."[33] The pronoun in the second sentence, "Sie," could refer to both Baudelaire and the allegories as being in on the secret, but it suggests a mixing of human and nonhuman elements together (exactly the ambivalence that the brings up this question in the first place) that is unusual in German. Without some additional clarification, which Benjamin does not provide, "Sie" seems to refer only to the allegories themselves, not so much eliminating Baudelaire's subjectivity as grammatically edging him out of the sentence. Such a move may further decenter the agency or intentionality of Baudelaire in favor of an alien, textual, intention. Yet as we will see further, it does not entirely leave Baudelaire out of the process.

The Intention of the Sign

If there is an "alien" intention that replaces, or at least displaces, Baudelaire's own intentionality, what form does it take? In *The Origin of German Tragic Drama*, Benjamin tells us that intention may be held in allegory rather than in the wielder of that allegory. As mentioned in the previous chapter, Benjamin speaks of "the intention of the sign"[34] and writes:

> The intention which underlies allegory is so opposed to that which is concerned with the discovery of truth that it reveals more clearly than anything else the identity of the pure curiosity which is aimed at mere knowledge with the proud isolation of man.[35]

Here, the intention of the allegory seems to be at odds with or at least unrelated to the intention of its would-be wielder.[36] While human beings seek to discover "truth" in all of its mythological forms, the allegory, it seems, seeks merely to expose those mythologies. It is worth noting that in the original German, when speaking in particular of the intention of the allegory, Benjamin often tends to use the Latinate word *Intention* (as in "Die Intention der Allegorie") rather than the usual German *absicht*, which is more conventionally translated as "intention."[37] Elsewhere, when speaking of human "intentions" he often uses other terms altogether, such as *bestimmt* (certain or destined), as when he tells us that for Baudelaire "not a word of his vocabulary is intended for allegory from the outset" ("Kein Wort seines Vokabulars ist von vornherein zur Allegorie bestimmt," literally, not a word is originally destined for allegory).[38] His use of "Intention" (more or less) specifically for allegory may signal the separate and uncorrupted intention of the semiotic "partner" that Baudelaire "conspires with (*mit*)."

To align one's own fallible, complicit intentions with the "intention of the sign" is to seek the exposure of mythology, even as we remain otherwise under its spell. As opposed to producing "mere knowledge," that is, our intentions as dictated by our times, by commodity fetishism, and so on, the "Intention" of allegory (which could also be called the desire of the sign not to carry false meanings) disrupts this fantasy. Indeed, we see in this reading that our own intentions are not really "ours" at all but products of the phantasmagoria ("the proud isolation of man"). The intention of the sign, on the other hand, affords more of a space for human agency, a harbinger of the "progressive deepening of . . . intention" that Benjamin references (as we saw in the introduction) in the *Origin*. Although we experience the intention of the sign as alien, it is in fact our own intention—at least as it is currently constituted—that is alien (or at least alienated).

Achieving Nonintentionality

If the sign has an intention of its own, this does not change the fact that human beings find the phantasmagoria irresistible, even when we see it (or at least think we do) for "what it is." Insofar as we remain seekers and builders of mythology, even while resisting it, the question of failure becomes paramount for Benjamin. It is in a sense our failure that rescues us from being totalized by the phantasmagoria, from realizing the complicit intentions that animate each and every one of us.

Thus, in the case of Baudelaire it could be argued that because he is a failure, because his own intentions are so defeated, his own words are "not intended" (or destined) for allegory. Thanks to his personal failure, Baudelaire manages to allow allegory's own "Intention" to come into play, causing Baudelaire to "conspire with language" in ways that he might not have desired or expected. Another way to think about this is to say that in his own personal failure, Baudelaire aligns himself with another failure, the failure of the sign to perfectly convey the phantasmagoria. The "Intention of the sign" can be understood in some sense as the failure of signification, the failure to definitively mean something or the failure to become true. The combination of Baudelaire's own personal failure with the failure of the sign makes for a potent combination; failure becomes refusal, resistance, subversion, and finally, the basis for conspiracy.

In this way, Benjamin may be reversing or modifying Marx's accusation against the plotters and conspirators of nineteenth-century France. Those "professional conspirators" who reject theory and the revolutionary style of the *habits noirs* (at least in the way Benjamin conceives of them) may be experiencing the failure of their own intentions as a prelude to a different kind of intentionality, a different kind of conspiracy. These conspirators de facto mask and subvert their own complicit intentions with dissolution, with wine, and with failure in general, thus becoming available for the "Intention" of the allegory (at least potentially). It is perhaps in this way alone that we can speak of redeeming these conspirators, taking their failure to be, not the end, but the beginning of their resistance (and in a way that Marx clearly does not recognize).

In his answer to Adorno's criticisms, Benjamin notes that in future research, on Baudelairian poems such as "L'Âme du Vin," he "would concentrate not on questions of taxation but on the significance of intoxication [*Rausch*] for Baudelaire."[39] While the German term *Rausch,* as Susan Buck-Morss and John McCole among others have noted, has connotations that go beyond drunkenness (evoking transcendent or ecstatic states of being) it might be that he also means something like drunkenness after all (or as well) in this context.[40] In light of Benjamin's larger appreciation for failure and its role in neutralizing intentionality, the qualities of drunkenness, rage, and irresolution and the hostility to comprehensive thought that Marx critiqued may be assets in the arsenal of the conspirators after all (even if they don't experience or understand this as such).

One might speak here of "achieving nonintentionality," that is, doing an end run around one's own consciousness in order to allow the "Intention" of allegory to step into the void. What results is not the end of human intentionality, but a kind of built-in resistance, a conspiracy against oneself that disrupts and decenters our own compromises. In this way, human subjects can once again match the sign's failure to perfectly convey the "meaning" that we seek to impart to things with a failure (and conspiracy) of their own.[41]

The Strategy of the Antidote

In extending the possibility of redeeming the failure of the drunken conspirators of nineteenth-century France, Benjamin turns abject failure and depoliticization into its opposite; he rhetorically extends his conspiracy to those who seem hopelessly excluded from it, redeeming a past moment in order to alter his understanding of his own time. At the same time, it must be said that being a drunk or being compromised and a failure doesn't in and of itself produce conspiracy. If it did, the bars and back alleys of the world would be teeming with conspiracy, and the phantasmagoria would be in real trouble. In fact drunkenness and irresolution only provide an opportunity for conspiracy to occur, and, as Machiavelli would say, opportunity must be seized in order for it to become effective. Accordingly, in addition to his appreciation of the value of failure, Benjamin provides a strategy for resistance, for rendering failure and compromise into a means for achieving nonintentionality. I call this Benjamin's strategy of the antidote.

At various points, Benjamin employs the term "antidote" to describe his strategy for resistance. He tells us, for example, that allegory is the "antidote to myth"[42] and that *correspondance* in turn is the "antidote to allegory."[43] As with the related idea (famously discussed by Derrida) of the *pharmakon* that is both poison and remedy, an antidote frequently in-

volves using a bit of a pathogen in order to save the organism from the ill-
ness that same pathogen (otherwise) produces.[44] In Benjamin's usage of
this term, we see no absolute distinction between what is "good" and "evil"
(as evinced by the fact that allegory, as we see above, is both a cure and a
poison that needs an antidote of its own). Instead, we must in effect use
the very instruments of the phantasmagoria—instruments that we are
deeply complicit with—as weapons to use against it. In this way, we turn
our dissolute failure into conspiratorial nonintentionality (at least in
terms of the compromised intentionality that we currently possess). Although Benjamin doesn't always refer to the strategy of the antidote by
name, I believe that it is central to his entire strategy; it lies at the heart of
his conspiracy and is an integral part of his recuperative method.

In considering his strategy of the antidote (and his recuperative project more generally), we must spend some time illuminating Benjamin's
theological positions insofar as they serve as the grounds for this strategy.
Given the ongoing parallelism in Benjamin's work between his theology
and his politics, we will see that the various theological figures Benjamin
considers have valence for his political strategies as well. In particular, we
must look at three figures: Satan, Jesus, and God, largely as they are described in the *Origin*, in order to better understand both the strategy of
the antidote and the theological basis that makes such a strategy possible
in the first place.

The Figure of Satan

Let us begin with a consideration of the figure of Satan, a figure Benjamin
very often connects to Baudelaire. As we will see further, for Benjamin, the
figure of Satan is the archetype for the strategy of the antidote; Satan is
both the enemy that we fight and the model for how to engage in that
fight. In "The Paris of the Second Empire in Baudelaire," in citing from
Baudelaire's "Les Litanies de Satan" Benjamin includes the line describing
Satan as the "father confessor . . . of the conspirator."[45] Even as our conspiracy is largely directed against the evils that Satan has brought into the
world, we see that Satan is also the spirit guide for that conspiracy.

For Benjamin, the figure of Satan in intrinsically tied up with human
knowledge and hence, idolatry. In the *Origin*, he tells us that "the Bible in-
troduces evil in the concept of knowledge. The serpent's promise to the
first men was to make them 'knowing both good and evil.'"[46] Benjamin
describes Adam's original relationship to objects prior to the fall:

> Adam's action of naming things . . . confirms the state of paradise as
> a state in which there is as yet no need to struggle with the commu-
> nicative significance of words. Ideas are displayed, without inten-
> tion, in the act of naming.[47]

Unlike the postlapsarian subject, Adam does not "know" anything. His act
of naming occurs "without intention," without partaking in the hubris of
idolatry. Whereas ideas ("the objective interpretation of phenomena") are
opaque to us, they are "displayed" before Adam.[48] He doesn't "know" the
truth; rather, he sees it.

In our own time, our knowledge and intentionality, our desire to master and control the world and its objects, are products of the fall. Knowledge in general is thus satanic, a direct result of the serpent's treachery. At
the same time, Benjamin tells us:

> If the lesson of Socrates, that knowledge of good makes for good
> actions, may be wrong, this is far more true of knowledge about
> evil. And it is not as an inner light, a *lumen naturale,* that this
> knowledge shines forth in the night of mournfulness, but a subter-
> ranean phosphorescence glimmers from the depths of the earth. It
> kindles the rebellious, penetrating gaze of Satan in the contempla-
> tive man.[49]

Just as Socrates is wrong that assuming knowledge of the good makes
for good actions, knowledge of evil does not always make for evil actions
either. For Benjamin, knowledge has an ambivalent quality; it isn't readily
divisible into good or evil components. Furthermore, as we'll see further,
for all its satanic aspects, knowledge is our only recourse. Accordingly, we
must turn to Satan, the figure who inaugurated knowledge in us, in order
to negotiate its ambiguities. The "rebellious, penetrating gaze of Satan" is
in fact required for our own attempts to discern or disrupt the phantasmagoria such knowledge has produced.

Other scholars have noted a beneficial if ambiguous role for the figure
of Satan in Benjamin's opus as well. In his essay "Walter Benjamin and the
Demonic: Happiness and Historical Redemption," Giorgio Agamben similarly focuses on the potentially redemptory aspects that Satan has for
Benjamin. He notes that according to Gershom Scholem, in Benjamin's
essay "Agesilaus Santander" the figure of the angel discussed there "hides
the dark, demonic traits of '[der] Angelus Satanas' [the Angel Satan]."[50]

Citing Scholem, Agamben calls this transformation "an anagram" and notes that it heralds a complication of the redemptive figure of the angel of history in Benjamin's "Theses on the Philosophy of History."[51] The angel, as we see through this association with Satan, is as much destructive as redemptive; indeed destruction in some ways *is* redemption for Benjamin. We see this sentiment directly referenced by Benjamin when, as we saw earlier, he tells us in his "Theses" that "The Messiah comes not only as the redeemer, he comes as the subduer of Antichrist."[52] We also see this sentiment expressed at the end of his "Critique of Violence" when Benjamin discusses divine violence. By analogy (or anagram), we see that Satan too can be both destructive and redemptive, a force of good or of evil (and both at once), depending on our relationship to it.

Satan and Allegory

For Benjamin, the ambivalence of the figure of Satan is tied up with the equally ambivalent trope of allegory. For Benjamin, allegory is an evil, satanic practice, a product of the fall. He writes: "Evil . . . exists only in allegory, is nothing other than allegory."[53] Such a claim might seem baffling to a reader who comes to understand that for Benjamin the practice of commodity fetishism is itself the "evil" that allegory serves to resist. Yet for Benjamin, as we have already seen, there is no such thing as untainted or innocent knowledge. Insofar as allegory is a form of knowledge, it too is "evil" and satanic, even as it also crucial in resisting Satan's effects in the world.

The chief way that allegory combats evil is by exposing its being subjective, that is to say, a product of our intentionality. As we will see further in our discussion of God, Benjamin tells us that evil does not truly exist in the world as an independent force but "arises in man himself, with the desire for knowledge."[54] In our desire to know, we emulate the hubris of Satan, the preference of our own subjectivity over the reality of the material world that surrounds us. Such subjectivity is the origin of idolatry and the phantasmagoria.

In speaking of allegory's connection to subjectivity, Benjamin tells us: "this knowledge, the triumph of subjectivity and the onset of an arbitrary rule over things, is the origin of all allegorical contemplation."[55] Yet such "allegorical contemplation" also transforms subjectivity. Benjamin tells us that "Subjectivity, like an angel falling into the depths [i.e., like Satan] is brought back by allegories, and is held fast in heaven."[56] We see here (in a passage that suggests the redemption of even Satan) that subjectivity is not so much to be overcome as restored to its rightful position ("a progressive deepening of . . . intention"). Allegory potentially exposes the fact that even when we seek evil, we are also seeking good, whether we realize it or not. Even when we are in the service of the devil, we are also in the service of God.

Insofar as allegory is itself satanic, we are in effect using a tool of Satan to fight the Satanism of the world. Benjamin describes a delicate balancing act between engaging in Satanic knowledge as a form of resistance and being drawn and seduced by the allures of that knowledge:

> Satan tempts. He initiates men in knowledge, which forms the basis of culpable behavior . . . [S]omething can take on allegorical form only for the man who has knowledge. But on the other hand, if contemplation is not so much patiently devoted to truth, as unconditionally and compulsively, in direct meditation, bent on absolute knowledge, then it is eluded by things, in the simplicity of their essence, and they lie before it as enigmatic allegorical references, they continue to be dust.[57]

In order to seek redemption, we cannot turn our back on representation. Insofar as "something can take on an allegorical form only for the man who has knowledge," we do not have the option to say no to knowledge. The correct attitude to adopt toward knowledge is not easy or clear; there is but a razor's edge between idolatry and allegory. Our attempts at knowledge usually lead to idolatry, to grasping at an "absolute knowledge" that is no longer available to us. When we approach the object in this way it is denied to us; it lies as "dust," in the "simplicity of [its] essence." Instead we must be "patiently devoted" to a truth that we will never know and can only gesture at.

If we cannot say no to knowledge, we also cannot say no to Satan or satanic temptation either. However paradoxical it may seem, such temptation is our only way "back" toward what that knowledge has taken us from. Accordingly, we must understand that our "return" to the world can only be partial; we can never fully leave the realm of knowledge and representation but must learn to inhabit it in a different way.

It is precisely because it is an ambiguous trope that allegory is of help to us in this regard. Rather than resolve the tension between the material world and our attempts to represent it (in what Benjamin calls a "spiritual" or "demonic" fashion), allegory preserves it, and necessarily so. Without such a tension, either the materiality of the world would be reduced to a purely mute state of being "dust"—innocent but completely opaque to us—or it would become a mirror of our own delusion (a state of affairs that is constantly threatened by the phantasmagoria). Benjamin summarizes this dilemma when he writes, "The purely material and this absolute spiritual are the poles of the satanic realm; and the consciousness is their illusory synthesis, in which the genuine synthesis, that of life, is imitated."[58] Our intentionality is an imitation (an "illusory synthesis") of the "genuine synthesis . . . of life," of the reconciliation between materiality and representation that we all strive for (idolaters and anti-idolaters alike). Left to our own devices, such an imitation is insufficient; we replace a genuine alignment between thing and sign ("naming") with our own delusions and idols. Hence the need for textual—and allegorical—antidotes. With such an antidote, we have at least a chance of not merely reentering into the idolatry that we seek to resist.

Satan and Baudelaire

In his later writings, Benjamin places Charles Baudelaire into the heart of the relationship between the figure of Satan and allegory that he works up in the *Origin*. We could say that Benjamin, by entering Baudelaire into this conversation (or constellation), gives his theology a conspiratorial—and political—cast. Given that for Benjamin Baudelaire is possessed of an "allegorical genius," the latter figure serves as a site in which many of the theological arguments that Benjamin makes elsewhere come to bear on matters of politics and resistance.[59] The next section of this chapter will be devoted to an explication of how such a relationship is played out in the text, but in the meantime, let us denote the intimate connection Benjamin draws between the figure of Satan and Baudelaire.

In his comments on this relationship Benjamin writes:

> [Baudelaire's] verses hold in reserve what his prose did not deny itself; this is why Satan appears in them. From Satan they derive their subtle power to avoid forswearing all loyalty to that which understanding and humaneness rebelled against—even though such loyalty may be expressed in desperate protests. Almost always the confession of piousness comes from Baudelaire like a battle cry. *He will not give up his Satan.* Satan is the real stake in the struggle which Baudelaire had to carry on with his unbelief. It is a matter not of sacraments and prayers, but of the Luciferian privilege of blaspheming the Satan to whom one has fallen prey.[60]

This passage illustrates some of the ideas that we have seen in Benjamin's considerations of Satan more generally, but here, in a writing that comes much later than his *Origin,* we see them applied to the life and work of Baudelaire directly. Here we see once again how the figure of Satan undermines or alters our "understanding and humaneness," that is to say, our human intentionality. To say of Baudelaire that "he will not give up on his Satan" (in German: "Er will sich seinen Satan nicht nehmen lassen") is to say he refuses to renounce his own compromised status in the name of some ethereal (and hence truly compromised) sense of righteousness, of intention disguised as truth or salvation.[61]

This passage also reflects how the strategy of the antidote that we saw developing in the *Origin* becomes extended to the "modern" world. In paradise, Satan's act of blasphemy against God was evil and idolatrous, a preferring of his own delusions to divine truth, but in our own fallen world, such an act becomes a model for conspiracy against the mythologies and idols that vie for the status of truth. We who read this passage can learn from Baudelaire's specific example how to emulate Satan by blaspheming against his blasphemies, turning satanic allegories into our allies. We must, like Baudelaire himself, retain "the Luciferian privilege of blaspheming the Satan to whom one has fallen prey." Even (or perhaps especially) within the context of our fallenness and failure, we, like Baudelaire, have the ability to engage in what Peter Fitzpatrick calls "productive [failures]" (albeit in ways that will not always be clear to us).[62]

The Allegorical Jesus

This discussion of allegorical redemption would be incomplete without a discussion of the other theological figures that Benjamin considers in his quest for resistance, namely Jesus Christ and God. Let us turn first to his discussion of Jesus. While it may be surprising that the Jewish Benjamin sometimes sounds so Christian, particularly toward the end of *The Origin of German Tragic Drama,* as we will see, this figure is crucial for Benjamin's conspiracy. In speaking of the figure of Jesus, we are not, strictly speaking still dealing with the strategy of the antidote per se (since Jesus is obviously not "evil"), and yet this figure remains part and parcel of his understanding of allegory in all of its "satanic" aspects.

In speaking of Jesus, Benjamin tells us: "Even the story of the life of Christ supported the movement from history to nature which is the basis of allegory."[63] He goes on to describe how in the work of German baroque dramatists, the life of Christ is depicted in an allegorical fashion with "ex-

amples of birth, marriage, and funeral poems, of eulogies and victory con-
gratulations, songs on the birth and death of Christ, on his spiritual marriage with the soul, on his glory and his victory."[64] In this process, "The
symbolic becomes distorted into the allegorical. The eternal is separated
from the events of the story of salvation, and what is left is a living image
open to all kinds of revision by the interpretive artist."[65]

In this way Jesus, the ultimate symbol of divine immanence, becomes
"distorted into the allegorical" and thus is rendered human and material.
His birth and death, his life in all of its tangibility, is rendered legible and
available for interpretation by one and all. Benjamin tells us that "it is an
unsurpassably spectacular gesture to place even Christ in the realm of the
provisional, the everyday, the unreliable."[66] It is "unsurpassable," because
Christ is the ur-symbol; to add him to the realm of unreliability, to add his
body and life to the body and life of the objects of the world, is to commit
an act of spectacular subversion of the very heart of symbolism. If Christ
can be allegorized—if he can be represented without recourse to idolatry—then everything else can be allegorized as well.

As is often the case with Benjamin, when one examines his theological
writings in detail, aspects of central theological dogmas of Judaism and
Christianity are in fact reaffirmed, only in a way that is quite different
from or even opposed to the way they are usually understood. More
specifically, in terms of Christian belief, in keeping with the idea that
"Christ died for our sins," one could argue that by being rendered allegorical, Christ makes it possible for all of us to be similarly rendered. His
"death" as a symbol commits an act of violence against all false symbols,
saving us all from the vagaries of idolatry and misreading—a corollary
and earthly version of God's own acts of "divine violence,"[67] which similarly serve to unmake idols. This "death," in some ways leads (at least potentially) to our salvation, our move away from the "sin" of knowledge.
While this reading of Christ is utterly unlike what one would find in a
standard Christian theological argument, it echoes the same language and
sentiment, albeit from a radically altered perspective. It is thus not as symbolic savior, but as an allegorized object, that Christ gets his messianic nature from a Benjaminian perspective. *This* Christ does not redeem us;
rather, in keeping with Benjamin's cosmology, by allegorizing him, or by
reading him allegorically, we are redeemed from what he symbolizes. This
(more Nietzschean) idea of a messiah that does not save us yet enables us,
as it were, to "save ourselves" will be explored again and in more detail in
the next chapter, when we consider the work of Franz Kafka.[68]

As we have seen, in Benjamin's rendition, Christ serves as a kind of spiritual anchor, a coconspirator, with a similarly allegorized figure of Satan. Collectively these figures allow us to return to materiality and move away from the vagaries of our compromised intentionality, myth, and idolatry. Between the figures of Jesus and Satan, we find our position as resistant subjects. The allegorized Jesus shows us how to destroy the symbol from its very heart—rendering the foundation of all symbolism into an allegorical ruin and thus "saving us" from our own sins. Satan in turn shows us how to be faithless, to rebel against false prophets and misreadings of Halakah (a project we will see more clearly in the next chapter in our consideration of Kafka). Even as the figure of Jesus makes it possible for us to resist the blandishments of the phantasmagoria, the figure of Satan shows us how to rebel again when, as is inevitable, the phantasmagoria reasserts itself.

The God's Eye View

The final character in this theological drama (and the final actor at the end of *The Origin of German Tragic Drama*) is God. From the God's eye view, we see the nature of evil quite differently than from our own viewpoint. In one critical passage Benjamin writes:

> It is said of God after the creation: "And God saw everything that he had made, and, behold it was very good." Knowledge of evil therefore has no object. There is no evil in the world.[69]

As we have already seen, from this viewpoint, evil exists only in the human perspective. While we have no choice but to partake in evil, all of our clutching at knowledge is in fact in service to God and to "the underlying idea" that the world possesses (an idea known only to God).[70] Benjamin famously tells us (in a passage we partially looked at in the introduction):

> Ideas are to objects as constellations are to stars. This means, in the first place, that they are neither their concepts nor their laws. They do not contribute to the knowledge of phenomena, and in no way can the latter be criteria with which to judge the existence of ideas. The significance of phenomena for ideas is confined to their conceptual elements. Whereas phenomena determine the scope and content of the concepts which encompass them, by their existence, by what they have in common, and by their differences, their relationship to ideas is the opposite of this inasmuch as the idea, the

objective interpretation of phenomena—or rather their elements—determines their relationship to each other.[71]

While the idea as itself cannot be known (as we saw, it was "displayed" in
paradise but is now hidden from us) it yet serves, as we also have already
seen, as "the objective interpretation of phenomena." The idea offers a
God's eye perspective (or rather a gesture at such a perspective) on the
phenomena of the world, on what those objects truly are and mean. When
those phenomena are aligned in particular ways (as "concepts") their
proximity or distance to truth is denoted (only not by us). Although we do
not actually know or recognize the idea in our attempts to reproduce it,
nevertheless through the use of concepts we find "the salvation of phenomena and the representation of ideas," and in this way we find what
passes for our own salvation as well.[72]

For Benjamin, in the face of this God's eye view that is denied to us, our
task as human beings is to endlessly approximate even as we fail to reproduce the idea through the juxtaposition of concepts. He tells us, "The representation of an idea can under no circumstances be considered successful unless the whole range of possible extremes it contains has been
virtually explored."[73]

Just as the Jewish mystics used to endlessly rearrange the letters of
God's name to produce the one true name, so do we endlessly seek to reproduce and reorder phenomena of the world in order to reproduce the
lost unity of paradise. The great irony of this is that we may have already
accidentally reproduced the exact image (or at least a part) of the original
unity but not known it (either at the time or afterward). Only when every
possible combination has been exhausted can we say that an idea has been
successfully "represented," covering a span of time beyond all human
comprehension and meaning.

Benjamin goes on to tell us that "the idea is a monad—the pre-stabi-
lized representation of phenomena resides within it, as in their objective
interpretation."[74] Although he cites Leibniz as a source for his concept of
the monad, in a way (and as is typical of Benjamin) he is telling us something that may be quite opposite from Leibniz.[75] While for Leibniz the
monad is a singular, basic unit of existence, for Benjamin, the basic units
of existence are the phenomena of the world. In their endless dance of
(re)juxtaposition, these objects form a monad. This process occurs over
the course of a time line that has nothing to do with human history; the
monad is only complete when all possible combinations have been exhausted. Once again, only then do we find an "objective interpretation."

Given this kind of time line, Benjamin tells us that "the purpose of the representation of the idea is nothing less than an abbreviated outline of this image of the world."[76] As human beings, we are fated to endlessly attempt to reproduce this unity in abbreviated form. We must in effect attempt to represent the monad. And, although we will fail, in a sense we are still redeemed—at least potentially—by the fact that we act in service to God (even if we don't know it). Even the most committed idolater is unknowingly participating in the monad because all forms of representation, even false ones, are in effect part of this process. This is one of the reasons that human intentionality must not be abandoned. Even the worst idolater is intending to reproduce the lost unity of paradise, albeit in a thoroughly deluded and "evil" way.

The God's eye view of course cannot be our own (thus even God is to some extent a figure in this discourse). Yet in gesturing toward it, we find the possibility of not being completely determined by the evil forms of knowledge we partake in. The God's eye view exposes the razor-thin edge of representation, how the symbolic and idolatrous forms of phantasmagoria are in fact also in the service of heaven (whether we realize or not), rendered "simply as its own reflection in God."[77] It is for this reason that the strategy of the antidote, and Benjamin's recuperative project more generally, are possible.

When considered from the God's eye view, allegory becomes the enemy of phantasmagoria:

> Allegory, of course, thereby loses everything that was most peculiar to it: the secret, privileged knowledge, the arbitrary rule in the realm of dead objects, the supposed infinity of a world without hope. All this vanishes with this *one* about-turn, in which the immersion of allegory has to clear away the final phantasmagoria of the objective and, left entirely to its own devices, re-discovers itself, not playfully in the earthly world of things, but seriously under the eyes of heaven.[78]

Ultimately, allegory, although born along with the figure of Satan, serves not Satan but heaven (or rather, both allegory and Satan serve God). Its redemptive features are simultaneous with its status as being part of the fall. Allegory, as we have already seen, redeems or exposes our subjectivity, not in order to destroy it entirely but to reveal that it has all along been seeking what God has intended it to seek.

In light of this reconciliation (or recuperation), we see that when we realign (or resign) our own intentionality with (or to) the "Intention" of allegory, we are simply gesturing at this greater, heaven-directed reconciliation, reproducing it in a far more limited and ambiguous manner. Our reconciliation with the divine cannot itself be known by us but only reflected in our relationship to allegory. Here once again, ambiguity becomes not a dodge or avoidance but a facing of our predicament. Benjamin writes: "Ultimately, the intention [of allegory] does not faithfully rest in the contemplation of bones, but faithlessly leaps forward to the idea of resurrection."[79] It is this faithless imitation of Satan's own faithlessness that ultimately reverses the arc of evil and returns us to redemption, even if we don' t know it.

Here, as with his seeming duplication of Christian dogma, we find a strong suggestion of Kant's notion of the noumenal insofar as for Benjamin it seems as if the "idea" of God's perspective is all we need to know to rescue us from delusion. The idea of the God's eye view, it would seem, is enough to ensure that we are not "merely" the phenomenal beings we appear to be. And yet here we see how radical and subversive Benjamin is by contrast to what he sometimes seems to be. For, of course, Benjamin's goal is not to turn to the metaphysical but to the phenomenal itself. He sees metaphysics as part of what prevents us from seeing what is before our eyes; it is part and parcel of the phantasmagoria. We must turn toward and not away from the phenomena of the world (this is what our gesture toward the God's eye view permits us to do). And too, very much unlike Kant, we are not meant to use the God's eye view to guide our own morality and actions (via the categorical imperative); to do so would be to presume that the God's eye view was in any way discernable to us. Indeed, as we have seen in our discussion of the figure of Satan, we need to rebel against what appears to us as "God" in order to save us from the mythological manifestations of God that Kant, among others, has helped to create (in saying this I make Kant something of a straw man, of course, for he can be read in radically different ways as well).[80]

The God's eye view does not tell us anything at all; it merely suggests to us the limitations or nonabsoluteness of our own view. By setting up God as a judge, as he does in his "Critique of Violence," Benjamin voids that position for any other contender, be it law, sovereign, or our own projections of deity. As we will see in the next chapter, our own struggles against idolatry—this voiding of our own false depictions of God, state, and reality—are matched and even made possible by the fact that the figure of God also voids itself. When he tells us in the "Theses" that "The Messiah comes not only as the redeemer, he comes as the subduer of Antichrist,"

Benjamin is suggesting (in ways we will explore further) that even a God that cannot be known (or who is "known" only as a figure) can help us in our struggle against the idolatry we ourselves foment.[81] God too, along with the figures of Satan and Jesus, can serve as an ally for our conspiracy.

The Devil and the Hair

In order to illuminate the preceding with an example, it might be helpful to turn to an author, Franz Kafka, whom we will be considering in much greater detail in the following chapter. As we will see further, Kafka shares a great deal of Benjamin's theology and hence a similar political theory as well. In his parable "The Invention of the Devil" ("Die Erfindung des Teufels") Kafka writes:

> It simply goes without saying that the falling of a human hair must matter more to the devil than to God, since the devil really loses that hair and God does not. But as long as many devils are in us that still does not help us arrive at any state of well-being.[82]

This passage helps to illuminate Benjamin's notions of a "God's eye view." We see that, for Kafka, events on earth only "happen" (i.e., are imbued with meaning) to the devil and his ilk (i.e., us). From the God's eye view, as we have seen, there is no such thing as evil, or possibly even an event as such. Yet, despite this, we who live in this world suffer from such events, given our own devilish compromises. Accordingly, we must care, devil-like, about what occurs (or fight the devil with the devil, as Benjamin suggests). This is why for Kafka there is "hope—but not for us." So long as we have "many devils . . . in us" we suffer from things that do not even (actually) occur.

In another parable, "Paradise," Kafka writes: "[It is] nevertheless possible that not only could we live continuously in Paradise, but that we are continuously there in actual fact, no matter whether we know it here or not."[83] For both Benjamin and Kafka, we are in a sense already redeemed (the falling of a hair does not happen as far as God is concerned; we do no evil; we do not even die) but without some way to gesture at this possibility, we are lost—regardless of what we do and think. It is thus once again our own "knowing" that comes into question; the way we know things is the key to our own (sense of) salvation. For that reason, we need to turn to the devil as the only way to "know" ourselves back (at least gesturally) toward God. The human perspective is not itself helped by the God's eye view Benjamin describes except to offer that the evil of the world is not to-tal (is not even real). Like two-dimensional beings who are trying to see a three-dimensional object in their midst, we can only turn to our knowl-edge and representation—the very thing that leads us to delusion in the first place—in order to "see" the material objects around us. With allegory, we dimly echo the original Adamic act of naming; we acknowledge the re-lationship between thing and sign. The very devilishness that infuses knowledge—the twisted and perverted forms of representation that it produces—becomes our only way to "know" that we know nothing at all. It is only with such a "knowledge"—whereby our subjective delusion be-comes an antidote against itself—that we can begin to act politically, that is to say, to act without being guided by the certainties and truths that are the stuff of phantasmagoria.

Allegory, Baudelaire, and Price

Having laid out the theological and representational figures that serve as antidotes for our own intentionality (and hence as conspiratorial—and textual—allies), let us return to the original conspirator we considered in constellation with Benjamin, Charles Baudelaire. Here, once again, we re-turn to the world of human beings and politics, the world that is in fact Benjamin's ultimate focus. As we have already seen, by looking at how his theological arguments are applied to the case of Baudelaire, we can begin to see how those arguments can be applied to—and have a great reso-nance for—political questions as well.

As already noted, much (although not all) of the theology discussed above comes from *The Origin of German Tragic Drama,* part of Benjamin's earlier writings. We see in the more positive tone (for Benjamin anyway) of that book a difference from his later, darker, and more explicitly con-spiratorial writings. And yet there are vivid connections between the *Ori-gin* and his later work on Baudelaire, connections that are critical for un-derstanding his later project. In connecting his later work on Baudelaire with the earlier work, Benjamin forms, in effect, a constellation with him-self (one could even say that Benjamin draws himself into his own con-spiracy).

In returning to a consideration of Baudelaire, we move from describ-ing idolatry and satanic knowledge in general to a specific form of such knowledge, namely commodity fetishism, the central element of Baude-laire's world (and ours). Despite being an entirely secular conception, commodity fetishism is, as its name implies, a form of idolatry. It comes out of the same ferment of satanic representation as religious idolatry and is subject to the same strategies.

In Benjamin's view, commodity fetishism is also deeply related to the satanic practice of allegory; in fact, Benjamin tells us that commodification itself is revealed to be a form of allegory. In *The Arcades Project*, he tells us:

> The allegorist rummages here and there for a particular piece, holds it next to some other piece, and tests to see if they fit together—that meaning with this image or this image with that meaning. The result can never be known beforehand, for there is no natural mediation between the two. But this is just how matters stand with commodity and price.... How the price of goods in each case is arrived at can never quite be foreseen, neither in the course of their production nor later when they enter the market. It is exactly the same with the object in its allegorical existence. At no point is it written in the stars that the allegorist's profundity will lead it to one meaning rather than another.... The modes of meaning fluctuate almost as rapidly as the price of commodities. In fact, the meaning of the commodity *is* its price; it has, as commodity, no other meaning. Hence the allegorist is in his element with commercial wares.[84]

Here we can see how price is a form of allegory; it too randomly associates objects with certain "meanings" (i.e., monetary values). And, as with allegory more generally, the "satanic" nature of price does not condemn it to be perfectly idolatrous. In delivering a shifting, transitory "meaning," price is in effect antisymbolic; it undercuts its own assertion of a true value by constantly altering (and hence subverting) it, making its meaning "unreliable." As with the figure of Satan, price produces the delusions of the phantasmagoria, but it also undermines them. Thus price, the central form of commodity fetishism, is also shown to undermine our symbolic readings of the objects of the world more generally (as allegories are wont to do). It hence makes it possible for us to encounter the materiality of the world after all, at least as an *aporia*—a category whose very emptiness calls into question our larger assumptions we associate with it (to offer an admittedly frivolous example: if a cup of coffee doesn't mean "two dollars," what does it mean?).

We see here again shades of the strategy of the antidote; when price is seen as allegory, we come full circle from source of fetishism to weapon against it (for "on the second part of its wide arc [allegory] returns, to re-deem").[85]

In his discussion of commodity fetishism we see how here too Benjamin pays lip service to a form of orthodoxy (in this case, Marxist) but in a way that alters or subverts that doctrine. We see, for example, Benjamin subscribing to the Marxist conviction that capitalism leads to its own demise. In his case, this argument reproduces his basic theology: commodity fetishism, although evil, works in the service of heaven; it is part of the "monad," the endless dance of representation. What distinguishes Benjamin's version of this creed from (at least one form of) orthodox Marxism is the disruption of the kind of temporal eschatologies that Marx seemingly subscribes to. *This* capitalism will not necessarily end or die in history; its self-exposure is for naught unless we bring ourselves to see it (or are brought to see it) as such. The allegorical nature of price provides an opportunity for resistance to the phantasmagoria that it is itself busily producing. As with the figure of Jesus, we must be brought to read the allegory in the symbol or risk being condemned by what we believe (or "know") to be true, hence the need for conspiracy.

Here we come closer to understanding what draws Benjamin to Baudelaire's work. For Benjamin, Baudelaire's poetry (potentially) does for the world what price (potentially) does to commodities, and in a similar manner. In a passage in the "Exposé" of 1939 (a fragment of which was cited in the Introduction), Benjamin writes:

> The key to the allegorical form in Baudelaire is bound up with the specific signification which the commodity acquires by virtue of its price. The singular debasement of things through their signification, something characteristic of seventeenth-century allegory, corresponds to the singular debasement of things through their price as commodities. This degradation, to which things are subject because they can be taxed as commodities, is counterbalanced in Baudelaire by the inestimable value of novelty. *La nouveauté* represents that absolute which is no longer accessible to any interpretation or comparison. It becomes the ultimate entrenchment of art. The final poem of *Les Fleurs du mal:* "Le Voyage." "Death, old admiral, up anchor now." The final voyage of the flâneur: death. Its destination: the new. Newness is a quality independent of the use value of the commodity. It is the source of that illusion of which fashion is the tireless purveyor. The fact that art's last line of resistance should coincide with the commodity's

most advanced line of attack—this had to remain hidden from Baudelaire.[86]

There is a great deal to unpack in this passage. Taken as a whole, we see more evidence of the double-edged nature of representation. We see the potential for the strategy of the antidote, as when Benjamin tells us: "art's last line of resistance . . . [coincides] with the commodity's most advanced line of attack." The very same gesture, the production of commodity fetishism, is also the way to resist that attack.

We also see that no one perhaps occupies that razor's edge between being a dupe of capitalism and heroic conspirator more than Baudelaire himself. The nearly perfect ambiguity of this figure who consorts with revolutionaries and reactionaries alike, who writes a new form of lyric poetry for his age even as he exemplifies a life of compromise and failure, suggests why Benjamin is drawn to write about Baudelaire in the first place. By writing that Baudelaire's allegories are "bound up with the specific signification [of the] commodity," Benjamin reminds us of how Baudelaire is fully bought into the phantasmagoria.

Relating his later and his earlier work side by side in *The Arcades Project*, Benjamin tells us that "Baroque allegory sees the corpse only from the outside; Baudelaire evokes it from within," implying his own deeper complicity.[87] Furthermore Benjamin tells us that unlike Shelley, who "rules over the allegory," Baudelaire "is ruled by it."[88] Baudelaire's compromise and participation in commodity fetishism is critical; fetishism, whether of the theological or capitalist sort, can only be resisted from within and by its own tools. A supposedly "outside" perspective like Shelley's gives a false sense of intellectual liberty from the phantasmagoria (a sense of "ruling" over rather than being ruled by allegory and the symbolic order in general). From such a position, one might be able to utter denunciations of capitalism and its vagaries, but such denunciations are compromised by the very sort of idolatrous stance Benjamin opposes; here, the subject does not even recognize being bound by and complicit with what he or she is criticizing. Having succumbed to the delusion of being "outside" of representation, such figures can offer no meaningful resistance whatsoever (an observation that will frequently occur throughout this book).

This insight helps to explain why we need our conspiracy with language in the first place. Even the most committed foe of the phantasmagoria cannot be trusted to her own devices. The exposure of fetishism by allegory is in and of itself insufficient; if we are unwilling or unable to recognize our fetishism (if, for example, we think of ourselves as being free from or above representation), its exposure will not result in our breaking from idolatry. The exposure of fetishism (which for Benjamin occurs all the time as a series of—generally unnoticed—shocks) is an opportunity, but nothing more.[89] It is only when we align our own intention with the "allegorical intention" that opportunity turns into conspiracy, into a break with current representational practices and beliefs.

Being as firmly within the maw of commodity fetishism as he is, Baudelaire demonstrates appropriate strategies that better disrupt the phantasmagoria and the forms of idolatrous reading that produce and sustain it. Yet, as we have seen, it seems that Baudelaire himself is not quite "in the know" when it comes to his conspiracy. The knowledge that the production of commodity fetishism is at the same time the last line of resistance of art had to be "hidden" from him. We see that Baudelaire is quite deluded, particularly in terms of his sincere belief in novelty.[90] The illusion of novelty, which is a hallmark of modernity, is, for Benjamin, one of the key features that render our world into a hell. But this belief in newness also masks Baudelaire's own intentionality, conspiratorially hiding the function of his poetry from even the author himself. The illusion of newness disguises what is actually occurring: the march toward death as revealed by allegory. In a sense, Baudelaire's misrecognition permits him to ally himself with a process from which he would otherwise recoil. Even while his conscious mind is preoccupied with a disguise (i.e., with novelty), Baudelaire's poetry conveys the work of allegory. His poems allow for the "allegorical intention" to subvert the very things he is writing about.

The most conspiratorial line in the passage considered earlier is the one that describes how the subversive strategy Benjamin espies "had to remain hidden from Baudelaire." This line (and indeed the entire passage that contains it) did not appear just four years earlier in his earlier (and German language) version of the "Exposé" of 1935.[91] The notion of excluding Baudelaire from his own acts of subversion suggests a further turn to conspiracy on Benjamin's part as times grew more desperate.

Baudelaire's own failure, his "achieved nonintentionality" and his participation in the delusions of the phantasmagoria, permit him to remain almost completely determined by commodity fetishism even as the "allegorical intention" unleashed in or contained by his poetry unmasks and exposes the phantasmagoria from within; this is the heart of Benjamin's conspiracy. The extent of Baudelaire's "buy-in" to commodity fetishism means that the damage that is done by his allegorical poetry strikes directly from within the heart of the phantasmagoria with maximum destructive force.

We see here the complex form of subjectivity and resistance in Benjamin's work. Baudelaire is kept out of his own conspiracy even as he is its central actor. Although Benjamin does not always seem consistent in the way he understands human intentionality (as we have seen, his work is marked by a heavy ambivalence), it may be that we are not forced to choose between our own intention and the "intention of the sign," after all. The "progressive deepening of . . . intention" Benjamin refers to in the *Origin* comes through a series of disguises and misrecognitions. If the plotters of the *Trauerspiel* took the first fumbling steps on this path, Baudelaire advances this transformation far more. Our compromise is not easily overcome, but via the mechanisms we see described above, we can achieve a de facto alignment of our intentionality with our textual allies— one that may become, over time, something more deliberate, dare we say more "chosen?" (at least from our own perspective).

Redemption Forward and Back

For all of this, it remains difficult to imagine how Baudelaire has been in any way "redeemed" or altered by this exposure, by his participation in the conspiracy Benjamin has called him to. He is left deep in his delusion. In the next chapter, we will see that the same thing pertains to many of Kafka's characters; even after they have experienced some form of "redemption," nothing much changes for them. In that chapter and elsewhere, we will try to understand better how it is possible to be redeemed and not even realize it, and what the upshot or purpose of such redemption might be.

For the time being, I will sidestep that question and instead argue that the redemption that stems from this conspiracy is not necessarily aimed (at least not directly) at Baudelaire per se but rather at Benjamin and, by extension, the readers of his texts. It could be argued that Baudelaire effectively serves as Benjamin's Satan, a limit on his own ambitions and intentions. By wrapping himself up in Baudelaire's failure and compromise, Benjamin can possibly avoid such a fate. Rendered as a "Satan" Benjamin will not give up, Baudelaire's failure becomes figural, potentially enabling Benjamin himself to "fail" in a productive sense. Here we move from a completely passive sense of conspiracy, where nonintentionality is indeed mainly accidental, to a seemingly more active form of conspiracy where past failed historical moments and events may just become the basis for a different and more productive form of failure in present or future moments. We see once again that Benjamin does not have to give up on intentionality altogether but rather may be able to align his own intentions with the "intention of the sign" (in this case, the sign as facilitated by Baudelaire). Here, we see his method operating, once again, as a kind of lodestone to guide him through these difficult representational functions.

If such a transtemporal strategy can redeem Benjamin (however limited such a redemption may be) via his engagement with the past, it may also be the case that such a move can work the other way round, that is, that present or future realignments of intentionality (through this connection to the past) can also overcome failure in the past, perhaps even returning, retroactively, to redeem or at least affect Baudelaire himself.

And not just Baudelaire; many of the revolutionaries that Benjamin seems to slight may be redeemed as well. It may be that in his "satanic" treatment of Baudelaire, Benjamin seeks not just the overcoming or displacement of his own intentionality but also that of the greatest of all conspirators, Auguste Blanqui, and possibly Marx as well. Here we have a kind of transtemporal triangulation where Benjamin uses Baudelaire to mediate the failure of Baudelaire's own contemporaries, using himself as a temporal pivot.

We can see an example of this latter possibility when Benjamin specifically relates Blanqui to Baudelaire toward the end of "The Paris of the Second Empire in Baudelaire." After citing a description of Blanqui unexpectedly appearing and "reviewing" his troops in public in a way that no one could expect (or even recognize, were they actually present), Benjamin tells us that "Baudelaire's poetry has preserved in words the strength that make such a thing [i.e., such a surreptitious display of conspiratorial power] possible."[92] Although he recognizes that Blanqui and Baudelaire shared an "impotence which was their common lot,"[93] he tells us that nonetheless "Blanqui's action was the sister of Baudelaire's dream. The two are conjoined."[94] Here we see the promise of bohemianism as a redemption out of the heart of its own failure. We also see the fulfillment of Benjamin's own subtle conflation of Blanqui and Baudelaire and his ilk, despite Marx's clear distinctions to the contrary. At the very least, we see a form of conspiracy that might not be marked purely or only by compromise and failure (taken in its usual purely negative sense). Such a conspiracy enlists the "satanic" qualities of failure and impotence as ways to transcend or resignify such outcomes.

Benjamin tells us that Baudelaire and Blanqui are "the joined hands on the stone under which Napoleon III buried the hopes of the June fighters."[95] It may be that Benjamin is here adding a third hand, namely his own (or even a fourth: that of the reader), as a way to have both their time and his own (and ours) join in a "conspiracy with language," one that enables Blanqui to have his own intentions overcome, his own failures and impotence as a revolutionary redeemed.

In her own reading of Benjamin's treatment of Blanqui, Margaret Cohen seems to echo some of these thoughts. She cites Benjamin's comment (in the "Exposé" of 1939) that Blanqui's text *L'Eternité par les astres* (Eternity via the Stars) "completes the century's constellation of phantasmagorias with one last, cosmic phantasmagoria which implicitly comprehends the severest critique of all the others."[96] For Cohen, this idea suggests that even the phantasmagoria can serve as the grounds for redemption (something we have already also suggested in our discussion of price). To a great extent, Cohen captures perfectly the redemptive and recuperative possibilities—the strategy of the antidote—that we have been discussing with Benjamin. Yet I would argue that without a conspiracy with language, such an idea doesn't get us far enough; we see in Cohen's analysis the potential for phantasmagoria to serve as the grounds for redemption, but we do not get a sense of how this can be brought about, how we can disentangle ourselves from the fetishism that perpetuates the phantasmagoria in its current, pernicious form. Cohen makes much of Benjamin's interest in utopian thinkers like Fourier as dreaming of the redemptive possibility even in contemporary forms of production and consumption (she calls Benjamin himself "utopian"), but, as Susan Buck-Morss points out, he ultimately distances himself from such thinking.[97] In my own terms, what separates Benjamin from such utopianism is his antifetishism, his suspicion even of the idea of utopia itself. Without a focus on antifetishism, we get no true antidote, we just get more of the same. Our "dreams" for redemption remain just that.

For Benjamin to appear in all of his political relevance, we need, once again, not to take at face value his weakness and passivity, his admiration for failure, or his apparent deference to automatic processes ruled by non-human agents (where we seem to have no need or ability to do anything at all). With his method in mind, we can see that he offers a way to negotiate this failure, this passivity. He shows us how to distinguish between a hopeless idolatry and a hope that is "not for us," between a phantasmagoria that smothers and overwrites us and a set of signs that can serve as our material allies. We might recall that Benjamin spoke of Blanqui's own "resignation without hope" ("resignation sans espoir").[98] Yet when we think of the possibility he finds in Kafka of "hope, but not for us," we can see how even Blanqui's hopelessness is not a dead end but is the harbinger of other, equally productive, failures as well. For Benjamin such hopelessness serves as a beginning rather than as an end. As we have seen too, "resignation" does not have to be a purely negative act; it can serve as a kind of productive failure, a "re-signation," as it were.[99] When the old hope is dead and buried, a new hope (one "not for us") may be born.

In addition to his attempt to redeem Blanqui, it may be that in his complex relationship with Marx, Benjamin seeks to return to him or redeem him from his own "failure" as well. Or perhaps, in light of this discussion, we can better see that Benjamin has never "left" Marx, by reading him in a sense against his (i.e., Marx's) own text. It may be that in textually diverging from him Benjamin may also be seeking to administer to Marx the same antidote against intention that he has administered to himself. Perhaps he offers himself as "Satan" to Marx, just as Baudelaire was "Satan" to him. The conspiracy he foments against, and therefore on behalf of, Marx is subtle and purely textual (although Adorno certainly did not miss its overt manifestations). Yet here, once again, Benjamin's failure to read Marx "correctly" may be a marker of his conspiracy with language. If this is the case, we do not necessarily need to agree with Adorno that Benjamin works at the "crossroads of magic and positivism," or even that he has abandoned Marxism and/or politics.

Conclusion

If there is a "theory" in Walter Benjamin, perhaps even a political theory, it must lie not in the theorist himself but rather in the theorist's acknowledgment of the material realities of language and the world around us, a "historical materialism" that might be more aligned with Marx than initially appears (at least when we understand more clearly how Benjamin treats Marx, however subtly, as a coconspirator).[100]

We see in Benjamin's approach to conspiracy a typical ambivalence marked by both utterly passive and even accidental forms of resistance on the one hand and deliberate (a highly loaded term, as we will see further) forms of subversion on the other. What initially appears to be an apolitical surrender to unexamined bits of so-called reality (i.e., "magic and positivism"), a merely literary or cultural foray, may in fact lead to the possibility of active conspiracy, actual political struggle, one that, as with the "troops" of Auguste Blanqui, hides in plain sight, unrecognized and therefore allowed to continue in its conspiratorial ways.

For all its stealth, we can see, as the example of Jesus suggests, the possibility of a conspiracy that produces an "unsurpassably spectacular gesture," the exposure and subversion of the phantasmagoria from within its innermost aspects and by its very own materials (as Cohen suggests). This is an exposure committed by and in the name of even some of the phantasmagoria's greatest dupes, those who (perhaps inadvertently) turn an alienated intentionality against itself and thus bring down, even if for only a moment, the entire edifice of fetishism and evil. We can see that Benjamin has—as Machiavelli did before him—retold the stories of certain historical personages to inculcate conspiracy in them and to make their conspiracy both possible and actual when it was neither of these things before (a technique we will revisit in chapter 3 on Machiavelli).

The ambivalence about the degree of human agency that we see demonstrated here reflects the peculiar alliance Benjamin is calling for, the alignment of our own intentionality with "the intention of the sign" (which is sometimes abetted, as we have seen, by turning to signs as theological or literary figures). Ultimately, for Benjamin, there may not be as much of a distinction between active and passive forms of resistance as we ourselves tend to want to insist upon, given our own understandings of politics. Such a distinction after all presumes an "active," agentful self, an intentionality that we receive from deep within the heart of the phantasmagoria. Even passivity can, for Benjamin, be overwhelmingly powerful when it is properly conceptualized. In Konvolute J in *The Arcades Project*, Baudelaire writes, "On allegory: Limp arms, like weapons dropped by one who flees."[101] There is a weakness to the weaponry of allegory, not unlike the "*weak* messian[ism]" he attributes to every generation.[102] Weak himself, like Jesus when the latter is crucified and helpless, Baudelaire is unable to resist the blandishments of novelty and fetishism, and yet these very acts, this very weakness, lead him toward resistance and, in a way, redemption. Such weakness and impotence have allowed such figures access to the heart of the phantasmagoria; they pose no threat and seem to be able to do it no harm, yet, when read as coconspirators, they reveal a strategy for subverting the phantasmagoria from within. The conspiracy, when understood as the satanic antidote to the evil of the world, does not "redeem" us once and for all in the Christian, salvational sense of the word, but it models how to strike "unsurpassably spectacular" blows against the phantasmagoria: it directs us in how ceaselessly to raise (or have our textual allies raise) "a mighty paw" against the false idols that have replaced God and our sense of political community in our world.[103]

Yet it remains true that from a leftist position, an embracing of weakness and failure seems like a recipe for just more of the same, more powerlessness, more defeat, more capitalism. With Benjamin, we see the big picture: the potential for a spectacular, even "viral" transformation of the phantasmagoria, a subversion from within and an alliance with the very material forms of representation that build up the phantasmagoria. We see that the very strength of the phantasmagoria is also its vulnerability; the act of representation, which produces the idolatry that constructs our reality, can become instead the basis for fragmenting and dissolving that reality. Yet the path to such a destination looks harrowingly like the path of powerlessness that the Left has been traveling all along. Can we or should we trust a politics based on failure and weakness, especially in the face of an opposition that is so successful and strong? What kind of politics does a Benjaminian conspiracy produce? How is it enacted and with what consequences for the kinds of human subjects we find ourselves to be?

In the next chapter, on Franz Kafka, we will add one more crucial layer to this examination of conspiracy that will help to address some of the questions: namely a focus on the messianic features of the conspiracy, on the kinds of redemptions we receive that have nothing to do with our own wishes or deeds (in Part II of this book, we will return to a focus on the human perspective and the political upshot of this conspiracy more specifically). With Kafka, perhaps even more than with Benjamin himself, we find a powerful antifetishism and in particular a depiction of a messiah that wipes away all idols (and especially the idolatry surrounding the idea of the messiah itself). As we will see, for Kafka, such messianic forms of delivery disrupt the false icons of God and state that we believe hold us together, rendering legible the kinds of communities and collective narratives that are formed in the face of such delusions, even in the heart of the phantasmagoria. While these communities are part and parcel of the phantasmagoria, Kafka makes clear that they are not wholly beholden to it. Our relations and communities have a distinct existence that, when we become aware of it, becomes the basis for a nonidolatrous form of politics. This is a politics that eschews the phantasmagoric belief that representation can be dispensed with. A nonidolatrous form of politics does not give up on signs but clings to them all the more firmly as the best, perhaps only, way to protect ourselves from our own desire for what the phantasmagoria promises (but never can deliver).

In Kafka's depiction of messianism as well as the misrecognitions that it produces, we see his own answer to the problem of human intentionality and the political possibilities that remain available to us despite our myriad failures and delusions. The form of redemption that Kafka offers us is a purely representational one (and his messiah is, as is appropriate, purely textual). In this way, Kafka exemplifies the strategy of the antidote by turning (mis)representation into a weapon to wield against idolatry, bringing along complicit human actors, however reluctantly, in its wake.

2 | Kafka: The Messiah Who Does Nothing at All

If we look at Franz Kafka's writings from the perspective of political theory, it seems, as with Benjamin, that the politics he offers us, if any, are those of passivity, failure, and doom. We have noted several times Kafka's quip to Brod that there is "plenty of hope, an infinite amount of hope—but not for us."[1] This seems like a grim joke, a typically "Kafkaesque" commentary on the futility of resistance, on the inevitability of defeat. At the end of *The Trial,* K., the central character, who seems to epitomize the hapless, anxious characters that people a Kafka novel or story, is stabbed in the heart by his tormentors and dies, in his own words, "Like a dog!" ("Wie ein hund!"),[2] suggesting the fate of all of us, in the face of obscure and irresistible powers. Many scholars of Kafka have described his supposed Zionism or the way he uses psychological or other kinds of symbolism to denote states of despair and the tyrannies of power, but it is not clear that any of this amounts to a political theory or a model for some kind of political resistance.[3]

Yet when we read Kafka the way Walter Benjamin read him, a very different thinker emerges. To his credit, Benjamin never tries to unlock the secrets of Kafka's text, as so many other commentators have. Instead, I argue, Benjamin seeks to reread Kafka as a fellow conspirator, endowing him with the same sort of conspiratorial strategies that Benjamin espouses in his own work. Conspiracy is required for Kafka because he is as suspicious—if not more so—of human intentionality as Benjamin himself.

In earlier chapters we have already encountered a paradox that arises from a politics based on distrusting our own intentions. If we are not let in on this secret, if the hope it offers is "not for us," what use is it to us? Most importantly, from the position of political theory, what kind of politics, what sort of relationality, stems from a conspiracy that seems to deny what we have come to regard as the very basis of political life? In this chapter, I will argue that Benjamin finds in Kafka a potential answer to these questions. In Kafka, he discovers a way for human beings to act politically without simply reproducing the mythologies that both writers oppose; Benjamin finds a way to do an end run around our own compromised intentionality, without giving up on the possibility of political resistance, or even the possibility of a "progressive deepening of . . . intention."

Key to Benjamin's insight is the role of misrecognition in Kafka's texts. Kafka shows that, given our compromised status, given the failures of our intentionality, we will always misread and misrecognize the signs of order, community, and authority that compose our world. Rather than try to save his characters from their delusions, Kafka gives them over to them, but in such a way as to subvert and distort their object. Kafka's characters desperately try to conform to the various powers that they see as organizing their life, but they fail, usually miserably, in their attempt. As we have already seen, such a failure can, in Benjamin's conspiratorial light, be turned into an asset; it becomes a failure to read a faux mythology "correctly," a failure to make sense of a symbolic universe that they seem to have no choice but to submit to.[4]

In addition to this failure, this stubborn and providential misrecognition, Kafka supplies Benjamin with another, crucial element: a particular, and textual, form of messianism that subverts the central powers (of both the political and divine varieties) that unite and control his characters. As we will see further, particularly in *The Castle*, Kafka offers us a parable for what Benjamin calls "divine violence": a messiah that voids or destroys its own symbols of power, its own mythologies.[5] Such a self-voiding of the messiah disrupts the central narratives of authority, leaving the communities that are organized in the name of its worship in the strange position of becoming reluctant, or perhaps even unknowing, conspirators against that which they most urgently seek to join up and collude with.

The combination of our own failure to read the mythologies of the world correctly and the self-voiding of a messiah who makes such a misreading possible in the first place amounts to a politics of "recognizing misrecognition" wherein signs are neither worshipped as true nor abandoned altogether. From Kafka' s perspective—one that Benjamin takes much from—our misrecognition need not be the basis for the ongoing practice of political idolatry. Instead, by remaining attuned to the *aporias* and lapses in our own narratives of power and authority, we can benefit from those (relatively) unscripted spaces that appear whenever those narratives are disrupted (in part by our own acts of misrecognition). The "agency" that such disruptions produce is not so much our own (at least as we are currently constituted) as it is the result of our conspiracy; it is composed of the remnants of our fetishistic sense of self and community when those sites have been destabilized and decentered, the basis for a "not us" who may have some basis for hope after all.

The value of reading Kafka and Benjamin in "constellation" with one another is to get a better sense of the role that conspiracy can play in politics. When we read Kafka through a conspiratorial (and Benjaminian) lens, we find a sense of how communities are formed, lives are lived, apart from (even as they are intimately entangled with) the great narratives of state and divine power that seem to underlie them. As already noted, when those great narratives are disrupted, these communities are not erased. Instead they emerge more clearly as having narratives of their own, narratives that are otherwise eclipsed by the notions of state and divine power they purportedly serve.

Kafka's Secrets

Given his reading of Kafka, and given his own interest in secrecy and conspiracies, as well as his own suspicion of human intentions, Benjamin does not seek to unlock Kafka's secrets. Indeed, he characterizes those secrets in such a way that unlocking them does not really seem possible; in keeping with their shared interest in Jewish mysticism, the notion of an immanent and unfathomable doctrine that can be gestured at but not described or even remotely understood is central to both writers.[6] Benjamin tells us "Kafka could understand things only in the form of a *gestus*, and this *gestus* which he did not understand constitutes the cloudy part of the parables."[7] It is telling that for Benjamin even Kafka did not understand the nature of the gestures he describes: here, the author surrenders his traditional sovereignty over his characters and their actions.[8]

In thinking about Kafka as Benjamin's coconspirator, we see a crucial development between his two best-known writings on Kafka. The first, "Franz Kafka: On the Tenth Anniversary of His Death," was written in 1934. The short fragment "Some Reflections on Kafka" was written in a letter to Gershom Scholem four years later. Under ordinary circumstances four years is not a long period of time, but between 1934 and 1938 Benjamin's life, and the world around him, was changing radically. The second writing, however short, makes an explicit break with his first reading when he says, "my main criticism of that [earlier] study today is its apologetic character" and goes on to write:

To do justice to the figure of Kafka in its purity and its peculiar beauty one must never lose sight of one thing: it is the purity and beauty of a failure. The circumstances of this failure are manifold. One is tempted to say: once he was certain of eventual failure, everything worked out for him *en route* as in a dream. There is nothing more memorable than the fervor with which Kafka emphasized his failure.[9]

To focus on Kafka as a failure is very much in keeping with Benjamin's fascination with failure more generally, as we have already seen in his study of Baudelaire and all of the failed revolutionaries who lived, drank, and died in nineteenth-century France. As already noted, for Benjamin, particularly in his later years, failure was in fact essential in order to bypass or defeat compromised human intentions. The "successes" of this world subscribe to the dominant ideology of history, time, order, and progress. To be out of time is to be a "failure" and, therefore, to fail to acquiesce to the hegemony of global capital whether in its fascist or liberal guises.

Benjamin's first essay on Kafka is hardly sunny or optimistic, and yet it is characterized by a certain version of redemptive possibility—one that he will retreat from in his later essay. This is especially evident when he writes in the earlier essay about Kafka's book *Amerika* (aka *The Man Who Disappeared*).[10] In his reading of that book, Benjamin focuses on the end of the novel, which describes the so-called Theater of Oklahoma. Benjamin tells us, "all that is expected of the applicants [to the Theater] is the ability to play themselves. It is no longer within the realm of possibility that they could, if necessary, be what they claim to be."[11] This seems to be a kind of triumph of self over intention. What "they claim to be" could mean these characters' conscious, deeply compromised intentionality. The idea of being able "play [oneself]" seems to afford us the possibility of avoiding our own egos without falling into a naturalizing positivism (where we would just "be ourselves"). This passage is reminiscent of Benjamin's writings in "The Work of Art in the Age of Mechanical Reproduction" (written two years later, in 1936), where Benjamin lauds Soviet films in which "some of the players . . . are not actors in our sense but people who portray *themselves*."[12] This idea of a redemptive possibility for identity, whether it is produced in film (as in the Soviet Union) or by the doubly removed status of characters in a play (staged by the Theater of Oklahoma) that lies within a novel (*Amerika*), offers itself as an initial answer to the problem of intentionality.

Even in that first essay, however, Benjamin anticipates the darker view of Kafka he will espouse in 1938 (thus once again performing a kind of constellation with himself). He writes:

> [Kafka's testament,] which no one interested in Kafka can disregard, says that the writings did not satisfy their author, that he regarded his efforts as failures, that he counted himself among those who were bound to failure. He did fail in his grandiose attempt to convert poetry into doctrine, to turn it into a parable and restore to it that stability and unpretentiousness which, in the face of reason, seemed to him to be the only appropriate thing for it. No other writer has obeyed the commandment "Thou shalt not make unto thee a graven image" so faithfully.[13]

It is the last sentence of this passage especially that gives us a clue to what Benjamin is trying to work out. It suggests that Kafka was able to follow the second commandment *only* because he failed at representation. In other words, for Benjamin, the only way to avoid idolatry is to blatantly and legibly fail in one's attempt to produce an idol—even the idol of one's own self (that is, of "being oneself"). Our failure or misrecognition is all that saves us from our own implication in and compromise with the phantasmagoria, and the more clearly we fail, the better.

In the comparison between the two passages from Benjamin's 1934 and 1938 essays on Kafka, we can see another stark contrast that may help to further illuminate this developing relationship between failure and representation. On the one hand, in "Franz Kafka," Benjamin tells us that Kafka's prose pieces "have ... a similar relationship to doctrine as the Haggadah [the representation of the divine law] does to the Halakah [the divine law itself]."[14] In other words, Kafka's texts serve divine truth in the same way the representation of God's law (Haggadah) reflects the law itself (Halakah). Yet in 1938 (in a passage already cited in the introduction) he writes to Scholem that Kafka's parables "do not modestly lie at the feet of the doctrine, as the Haggadah lies at the feet of the Halakah. Though apparently reduced to submission, they unexpectedly raise a mighty paw against it."[15] Here we see a much darker and more conspiratorial view on Benjamin's part (and by extension on Kafka's as well). As World War II and the Holocaust come down over his head, Benjamin comes to appreciate ever more the virtues of failure, now recast as a form of subversion, even in a sense the subversion of Halakah. As we have already noted, the purpose of this subversion is not so much directed against God per se but against our (false) anticipation of God and law. He also tells us that Kafka "sacrificed truth for the sake of clinging to its transmissibility, its haggadic element."[16] In light of this, we might say that this "mighty paw" raised against Halakah is a gesture against idolatry; it is to favor transmissibility, the materiality of Haggadah, over the kinds of truth that are promised but never delivered.

As we have already seen in the previous chapter when looking at Benjamin's treatment of the figure of Satan, we must in effect betray God to preserve God as an *aporia*, an interruption of our own mythological narratives. Here again, the "failure" of representation, the conspiratorial use of Haggadah against Law, becomes a way to preserve Law in its own "purity" and "beauty," allowing for hope ("an infinite amount of hope—but not for us").

Whereas when left to its own devices, Haggadah "modestly lie[s] at the feet of the doctrine," when it is engaged with conspiratorially, Haggadah becomes, as we will see more clearly, a weapon of misrecognition, a "mighty paw" raised against the false manifestations of Halakah. This gesture "against" God, Law, and fate is in fact the epitome of what I am calling Kafka's and Benjamin's shared conspiratorial style. In Kafka's case this conspiracy takes the explicit (but unfathomable) form of the parable.

Kafkaesque Parables

In his discussion of Kafka's use of parables, Benjamin tells us that Kafka "took all conceivable precautions against the interpretation of his writings."[17] He also tells us that ordinarily with parables "it is the reader's pleasure to smooth [the parable] out so that he has the meaning on the palm of his hand. Kafka's parables, however, unfold in . . . the way a bud turns into a blossom."[18] Thus in terms of their legibility, for Benjamin Kafka's parables are beautiful, and possibly familiar but not necessarily illuminating.

In his own treatment of parables, Kafka openly espouses his desire to be cryptic. In his short, fragmentary (or at least just short) essay "On Parables," he tells us that "all these parables really set out to say merely that the incomprehensible is incomprehensible, and we know that already. But the cares we have to struggle with every day: that is a different matter."[19] Yet Kafka does not leave it quite at that, because as we have already seen, representation and Halakah are in a relationship for him, even if it is at times a necessarily confrontational one. Thus he goes on to write:

Concerning this a man once said: Why such reluctance? If you only followed the parables you yourselves would become parables and with that rid of all your daily cares.
Another said: I bet that is also a parable.
The first said: You have won.
The second said: But unfortunately only in parable.
The first said: No, in reality: in parable you have lost.[20]

This is of course "a parable," indeed it is a "parable about parables" (reminiscent of de Man's "metafigure," which means to "[write] figuratively about figures").[21] In this case, the parable addresses the very question of how parables are related to daily life, that is to say (at least in the emphasis I am focusing on here) on the question of politics, the ordering of our lives. Kafka tends to punish those who would painfully work out his logic by deliberately withholding that logic in the first place. It is perhaps more profitable to focus, as Benjamin suggests, on the gesture that his parable makes. Taken in this spirit, we might say that this fragment suggests that, although it is futile to attempt to understand Kafka's parables, to make the attempt nonetheless is to be "rid of all your daily cares." Our struggle with a parable, it seems, is meant to be lost, but the encounter with it is still meant to allow us to "win" in our daily life; we are not left unaffected by our brush with it even though it offers us nothing at all.

Such an interpretation of parables may be even more clear in what is perhaps the most paradigmatic moment of parable reading that Kafka executes, namely the scene toward the very end of *The Trial* where K. encounters a priest who seeks to interpret (along with K.) the parable "Before the Law." This encounter with the priest comes when K. is increasingly desperate. His "case is going badly," as the priest informs him (but K. already knows this).[22]

The parable of "Before the Law" is so well known that I will only briefly paraphrase it here: a man from the country comes before a doorway to the law, and the doorkeeper there bars his entry. The man asks if he can get in later and the doorkeeper says "That's possible,"[23] and so the man waits, on a stool the doorkeeper provides him with, for his whole life, year after year, never being let in. At the end, as he is dying, the doorkeeper bends over the man to hear his last question:

"Everyone wants access to the law," says the man, "how come, over all these years, no one but me has asked to be let in?" The doorkeeper . . . shouts to him: "Nobody else could have got in this way, as this entrance was meant only for you. Now I'll go and close it."[24]

As parables are wont to do, this parable forces us to examine it closely, to try to discern the meaning. As if not content to trust in his own inscrutability, in *The Trial* Kafka has K. and the priest themselves unsuccessfully try to discern the meaning of "Before the Law." This is one of those rare and wonderful metatextual moments when two characters in a story attempt to work out what we, the readers are meant to work out (or not work out, as the case may be) for ourselves; by this device the normal lines between author and reader become blurred; we become implicated all the more in the process of interpretation even as Kafka directly interferes with that process.

In their discussions of the parable, K. and the priest agree on nothing. Suffering from arbitrary justice, K. empathizes with the man from the country. He sees how justice is wrong, arrogant, and indeed arbitrary. The priest, who works for the state (he claims to be a prison chaplain), takes the side of the doorkeeper, offering legalistic arguments for why he is right. In the hands of many an author matters might have been left there; we come to the determination that a parable is always interpreted from our own position.

Yet Kafka pushes this further; as is often the case in his work, an alternative way to read this parable comes closer to the middle than the end of this discourse. K. tries to pin the priest down by saying, "So you think the man was not cheated, do you?" and the priest answers:

Don't get me wrong . . . I'm just pointing out the different opinions about it. You shouldn't pay too much attention to people's opinions. The text cannot be altered, and the various opinions are often no more than an expression of despair over it.[25]

Here, we see that "the text cannot be altered." In other words, we are not permitted to understand the text but that doesn't mean that the text has no effect on us; it has a form, a material presence that we continually return to. The parable thus preserves the inscrutability of parables; it insists on (and therefore gives evidence of) its secret and just as sternly lets us know that we will never come to know it.[26]

Even in the face of such an absolute denial, we see that we are not left unaffected by such a gesture. We are affected not so much by the "truth" of the parable, since that is unknown to us, but by the way we organize—and live—our lives in the face of the parable. The "daily cares" and the "truth of the parable" are thus not total strangers; in the face of the parable, our acts of interpretation, however random and arbitrary they might be, serve as a kind of anchor through which we form connections with one another, determining how we see ourselves in relation to others, for better or for worse.

In this way we begin to see the relevance of Kafka for political theory (and, by extension, for Benjamin's conspiracy as well). Whether the door-keeper is above or below the man from the country (both positions are argued), whether the priest is a stern representative of the state or an ally of K., the parable serves as a point of contact, a mode of organizing that then produces relationships based on our own responses. In this way the act of interpretation becomes profoundly, and importantly, political.

We see the effects of this interpretation in the kinds of intimacies and relationships formed in the face of law and all the horrors and small mercies that are enacted in its name. In *The Trial*, we see in the strange banality of the court's rooms, mixed up with ordinary people doing their wash and cooking cabbages, the intense jealousies produced between K., his lawyer, and other, equally hapless clients, the question of the various women that alternately intercede in K.'s situation and leave him to his fate. These relationships are all produced not despite but because of the mystery that Kafka sternly guards (not unlike the doorkeeper and with a similar kind of strange intimacy).

It is at this point that it is particularly helpful to read Kafka through the lens of Benjaminian interpretation. Kafka's gesture serves here to render parables legible qua parables, even while rendering them illegible as a font of meaning or authority. He (or rather his text) thus indeed "raises a mighty paw" against Halakah by confounding it with its symbolic representations (Haggadah). Such a move reveals our understanding of Halakah to be merely text, obscure and tantalizing at the same time; Kafka subverts the notion that there is some "hidden truth" that lies within or beneath his parables. At the same time, by stripping away their content (or rather, by making it clear that the content is unavailable to us) Kafka shows how the parable serves to organize and form our responses, our lives, nonetheless. This exposure of a parable's effectiveness even without having any authoritative meaning renders visible a process that is otherwise obscured by content, by our desire to "know what the text means." This shows us that we can and do come together in ways that are not necessarily organized by clear and authoritative meanings. While we are busy seeking "the truth" and meaning, we are in fact already engaged in a kind of community, one that is produced out of our own conspiratorial and interpretive acts. It is this unrecognized (or more accurately, as we will see further, misrecognized) subterranean community that forms the heart of Kafka's politics.

Unfolding the Parable: *The Castle*

The same dynamics that we see in *The Trial* are also clearly visible in what might be considered Kafka's magnum opus, *The Castle*.[27] Here, in the last book that Kafka wrote (and which he died without finishing), we also see how parables organize our lives without recourse to definitive and authoritative meanings. At the same time we see far more clearly the subterranean rumors, the conspiratorial resistances that amass even in the face of Halakah. In *The Castle*, for all the passivity that its narrator (also named K.) seems to display, we see the processes of conspiracy on the part of the author, the characters, and the readers alike.

Just as crucially, *The Castle* also illustrates the particular and unique form of messianism that is a necessary complement to the conspiracies of its characters. As we will see further, the fact that Kafka's messiah is never recognized—or even consciously noticed as such—is essential to the form of redemption that it brings to the community it visits. Were it to be recognized, this messiah would instantly become merely another instantiation of dogma, of myth posing as divine truth. Kafka's stealth messiah preserves our misrecognition and in this way allows us to continue to fail in bold and spectacular ways in our attempt to convey and understand Halakah. This failure permits us to succeed in our conspiracy against the mythologies that pass for Halakah in our world, a conspiracy that we are not necessarily conscious or desirous of but which is in fact what redeems us (if anything does) at the end of the day.

The Castle is a sprawling, loosely connected, and incomplete narrative, but one thing that unites it quite clearly is its strong attention to questions of representation. As is fairly well known, the book begins when the narrator, K., comes to a village dominated by a castle.[28] When K. first sees the castle, we are told it belongs to "Count Westwest," but that turns out to be the only concrete reference to the castle's chief occupant for the entire novel. The very strangeness of the name "Count Westwest" (the name is the same in German, "Herrn Grafen Westwest")[29] tends to draw attention to it as only a cipher, a stand-in for the central mystery of the novel.[30]

The denizens of the village live in the shadow of the castle both literally and metaphorically. The entirety of their lives is spent in anticipation of the wishes and whims of the Castle. There is an intense hierarchy that emanates from the Castle, forming levels within levels. There are peasants, ordinary villagers, messengers such as Barnabas (who delivers K. his first so-called message from the Castle), and then the Castle officials themselves. One of these officials in particular, a man named Klamm, is the focus of much of the book's intrigue.

Kafka's treatment of Klamm and the effect of Klamm's presence (or even absence) speaks directly to the way representation is treated in *The Castle*. He is first encountered as a mere scrawl, a signature on a letter sent to K. informing him of his service (a letter that K. reverently hangs on his wall). Thus Klamm (whose name in German as in English is redolent of silence and secrecy) is introduced as a kind of failed or obscure sign.[31] K. is told that Klamm's letter "is valuable and even venerable because of Klamm's signature, which appears to be genuine."[32] But he is also told by the local village chairman that the letter's contents (which read like a fairly straightforward letter of acceptance) are unofficial, to which K. complains that "you interpret the letter so well that all that's finally left is a signature on a blank sheet of paper."[33] Such attention to legibility, signature, and its relationship to identity and meaning reinforces and makes visible the material nature of representation. Kafka here seems to be reminding us that representation, for all its mystery and power, is nothing more than lines on paper, images, sounds, and pictures.

Klamm serves as a cipher not just in name but also in his very person. As with Kafka's treatment of the parable "Before the Law" in *The Trial*, the figure of Klamm gets taken to extremes in an attempt to evade any clear "meaning" or purpose. The novel is structured as a series of revelations, usually from long conversations (and often with women who seem, in all of Kafka's novels, to be slightly more alert to whatever passes for reality than the men). As the revelations continue, what we find is that all that we have come to believe about Klamm may be wrong and in fact Klamm might not even exist. Well into the book Olga, who is the Barnabas's sister, offers a long speech that simultaneously dispels and confuses much of what we have assumed to be true up to this point. She offers that "Barnabas doubt[s] that the official identified . . . as Klamm really is Klamm."[34] She goes on to say that his appearance is of course well known in the village, some have actually seen him, everyone has heard of him, and what emerges from this mixture of sightings, rumors, and distorting ulterior motives is a picture of Klamm that is probably correct in its essential features. But only in its essential features. Otherwise it is variable and perhaps not even as variable as Klamm's real appearance. They say he looks completely different when he comes into the village and different when he leaves it, different before he has a had a beer, different afterwards. . . . and, quite understandably after all this, almost utterly different up there at the Castle. . . . Now all these discrepancies did not of course come about by magic but are quite understandable, they are the a product of the momentary mood, the degree of excitement, the countless gradations of hope or despair in which the observer . . . happens to find himself.[35]

Klamm is only sighted, or thought to be sighted, in glimpses. Barnabas "once saw Klamm through a carriage window, or thought he saw him."[36] But later, the man who was introduced to him as Klamm looked totally different. K. himself only sights Klamm—if that is really who he was— once, through a peephole.[37]

The effect of this cumulative undermining of Klamm's existence is twofold. On the one hand, Kafka seems to be playfully but purposefully unraveling our automatic deference to certain authority structures. This unraveling includes the authority of an official like Klamm, as well as the authority of the author of the text, in this case Kafka himself (whom we otherwise generally defer to). Even before Olga's speech, but certainly by that point, we can see Kafka busily undermining these assumptions on our part. Yet, on the other hand, Kafka also seems to be highlighting the way that such authority systems (of both the political and authorial sorts) produce intense responses (at least in terms of what such systems seem to promise). The letter that K. hangs on his wall was probably not written by Klamm (that was probably not his illegible signature), and yet the letter is "venerable" nonetheless. We see how power and authority function, even (or perhaps especially) as an exposed *aporia*, how they affect and organize those who live under their spell.

In his playful undermining of assumptions, his false starts and red herrings, Kafka exposes the complicity of his characters and even our own complicity as his readers in terms of our collective desire for clear, authoritative meanings. He is thus setting the grounds for a conspiracy, one that is set exactly against those authority symbols that the characters in this book (and perhaps the readers as well) are deeply implicated with.

The Erotics of Klamm

For all of his elusiveness, and even his possible nonexistence, Klamm has a powerful effect on those around him. The very suggestion of Klamm's presence excites and activates the villagers in myriad ways. K. himself gets caught up in the worship of Klamm insofar as he becomes engaged to Frieda, a woman that Klamm "summons" (assuming that the summoner really is Klamm). The minute Frieda tells K. that she is Klamm's mistress, he becomes much more interested in her, soon falling in love with her and in effect taking her away from Klamm.

As the novel progresses, the Klamm-inspired couplings and uncouplings gain speed and become almost impossible to keep track of. In every case, Klamm serves not as an actual person or agent but as a pure marker of desire.[38] The erotic charge all of these characters receive is not from the "gentlemen" of the Castle but rather from their cipher (if there is in fact any difference between these things). In all cases, whether with women or men, the desires of the officials are conveyed by letters, by messengers and intermediaries, in other words, by signs. Barnabas, for example, is filled with joy at the letter he delivers to K. It is, in fact, the first message he has been entrusted with (even if Klamm didn't write it or send it). The allure of such semiotic power is nearly irresistible to the villagers. Olga tells K., "we know that women cannot help loving officials when the officials approach them, and indeed even beforehand they're in love with the officials, no matter how strongly they attempt to deny it."[39] The letters and the states of excitement and meaningfulness they produce organize the reality of these villagers, even though this is a system without a center, an enormously complex phantasm that nonetheless compels our responses. Kafka's parable dispels the idea the humans are "naturally" social or interested in each other as a matter of course; every relationship, no matter how intimate or mundane, is produced in relationship to these signs and symbols of authority. Yet these signs are themselves very vulnerable, hollow, and unsubstantial. It may very well be that the Castle is empty, or that only its outer halls are occupied by people who themselves imagine that there are tremendously important personages lurking in the inner halls. The actual high Castle officials, so crucial for the lives of the characters of this book, are never seen except in the most hesitant and uncertain glimpses.

Missing the Messiah

With one crucial exception: In one of the most telling moments of the whole book, K. actually has an encounter with one of the high lords of the Castle but doesn't even realize it. Hoping that he'll get a sighting of Klamm, K. stands by a fancy sleigh (he assumes it must belong to Klamm) parked in the courtyard of the "Gentlemen's Inn."[40] He is invited into the sleigh to get some cognac by the coachman. While he is taking a long sip of cognac, "it became bright, the electric light came on, not only inside, on the stairs, in the passage, and in the corridor, but outside above the entrance."[41] K. jumps out of the sleigh, very nervous at being caught, and a "young gentleman, extremely good-looking, pale and reddish, but quite grave" comes over. K. ponders:

> Actually, the worst part was that the gentleman had surprised him and that there hadn't been enough time to hide from him and to wait undisturbed from Klamm, or rather, that he hadn't shown sufficient presence of mind to stay in the sleigh, close the door, and wait there on the fur blankets for Klamm.[42]

The gentleman says, "Come with me," to which K. responds, "I am waiting here for someone." The gentleman repeats "Come." And K. repeats, "But then I'll miss the person I'm waiting for." The gentleman responds, "You'll miss him whether you wait or go." And K. responds again, "Then I would rather miss him as I wait."[43] After this exchange, the gentleman leaves. The courtyard is locked and the lights switched off; K. is left alone and once again in the dark.

In a book some say is about waiting for the messiah, the messiah comes and leaves and K. doesn't even notice. He is, in fact, so fixated on Klamm, a lowly and possibly nonexistent servant of the Castle, that when a true lord appears (and not just in glimpses but fully, tangibly), he is unable to register his presence as anything but a distraction.[44] It is not until the lord begins to leave "quite slowly, as though wanting to show K. that it was still in his power to call [him] back,"[45] that K. seems to have some regrets. Even so Kafka writes: "Perhaps he had that power, but it would have done him no good; to call the sleigh back would be to drive himself away."[46]

We see in K.'s bedazzlement with Klamm shades of idolatry—an idolatry that runs rampant in *The Castle*. Here the symbol has supplanted what it stands for. Klamm, a cipher and a joke, has become more important than a high lord and gentleman. By fixating on Klamm, K. is left (literally) in the dark. At this point, we seem to have reached the dark heart of this novel, the end of hope (for us, anyway), a failure and a dead end.

Yet when read through Benjamin's lens, as coconspirators we can read K.'s actions in a different light. We can see what K. does as an example once again of what Benjamin refers to as "rais[ing] a mighty paw" against Halakah. In this example, Haggadah (if we think of Klamm as symbol or cipher) is indeed the vehicle for this conspiracy; the cipher is used to deliver us from our expectation of redemption. Kafka here reveals his conspiratorial strategy: rather than deride the "false symbol" to embrace the true God, he uses that false symbol to void any possibility of the true deity, cleansing that site of any representational aspirations. K.'s fixation on Klamm ensures that K. will never find the meaning he is searching for, never be "saved" from his own semiotic failure.

But note that K. does not act alone. He has an ally, albeit one he barely notices, namely a true lord of the castle, we might say, a messiah. Now that the messiah has come and gone, K. experiences a kind of freedom. Having missed God confers onto K. certain strange benefits:

> It seemed to K. as if they had broken off all contact with him, but as if he were freer than ever and could wait as long as he wanted here in this place where he was generally not allowed, and as if he had fought for this freedom for himself in a manner nobody else could have done and as if nobody could touch him or drive him away, or even speak to him, yet—and this conviction was at least equally strong—as if there were nothing more senseless, nothing more desperate, than this freedom, this waiting, this invulnerability.[47]

The key thing to note here is that K. is *still waiting* at the end of this passage. Nothing has really changed (in keeping with the Jewish notion Benjamin conveys us to that the messiah "would only make a slight adjustment in [the world]").[48] This is not Simone Weil's "waiting for God" wherein the waiting itself is sanctified by what it waits for. K. now knows (at least on some level) that he is waiting for nothing and there is a modicum of peace—and despair—in that knowledge.[49]

Here, we come to the center of Kafka's parable. Suitably, this messianic arrival—and subsequent abandonment—occurs not at the end of the book but tucked away in the middle. Just like the event it conveys, this section of the book comes and goes virtually unnoticed, but it also potentially transforms our reading of the text. This moment definitively undoes any hope for a final, perfect redemption, for some great resolution of meaning wherein the parable tells us a profound truth. This is thus an ur-metatextual moment, when the text announces its own impossibility of self-resolution. We, the reader, are left, like K. in the dark, but perhaps now (also like K.) relatively freed of the need to understand or discover the parable's meaning (since such a meaning has been tantalizingly dangled before us, then removed once and for all). The structures, allures, and powers of text become more legible and perhaps available to us, but minus that great centralizing organizing principle, the sovereign voice of the author/messiah who promises us something certain as a reward for our striving to interpret.

In this way, the messianic figure in *The Castle* does what Kafka does as author throughout his texts; it forcefully intervenes in his narratives in order to demonstrate that all of the narrative structures we attribute to his agency are in fact without meaning. In the face of that meaninglessness, all of our allegiance and subservience to the symbols of power become, as it were, useless, leaving us in the position of being stooges and wannabes who have no choice now but to rebel against what they would otherwise seek to worship and obey. In this process the text, the set of signs and symbols by which we would come to "know the truth," has gone from being a tool that we strive to use in our desire for interpretation, to an ally that shows us the degree to which we are influenced and shaped by texts (even as its "meaning" is withheld from us). This is the epitome of textual conspiracy.

It might seem as if Kafka is suggesting that we can dispense with the divine and political constructions of authority altogether, that we might be able to form "sideways" communities (in this case, between K. and the villagers) unorganized, undominated, and free of any taint of representation in the face of such revelations. But Kafka is too complex, too tragic a thinker to offer such a ready solution. To think this would be to presume that the messiah really *had* freed us, even from itself, whereas Kafka's messiah, it is important to stress, does virtually nothing at all. In *The Castle* we are not so much liberated from the symbols and structures of authority as those symbols are displaced, decentered. This messiah is very much akin to the one that we found in Benjamin's treatment of Jesus as well; both authors portray messiahs whose "redemptive" features come from the way they void themselves (or are voided) as sources of divine salvation, the way they refuse any meaning that is not produced from within the symbolic sphere, returning us to our own devices, our own striving for meaning and authority, in the process. In this case the messianic retains the crucial organizing function of the symbolic; it makes meaning possible without having that meaning overwrite our lives with yet more mythology (it doesn't allow any one particular meaning to trump all the others).

Revisiting the Man from the Country

To briefly extend this analysis to another of Kafka's texts already considered, in "Before the Law," we can see that the Doorkeeper, rather than being a villain, might actually be the messiah as well. Although the man's fate of lingering at the door of law seems awful, it would have been far worse if the doorkeeper relented and let him into the door of law and exposed him to all of its secrets (although we are told that there are other, nastier, doorkeepers within the door of the law). If somehow he had finally gained access to the law, the man from the country would have been confirmed in all of his delusions about Halakah. There would have been no space for resistance, no mighty paw of haggadic uprising; the very distinction between law and its representation would have been erased. So in a way, the doorkeeper and the man from the country can be read as fellow conspirators collectively denying some great resolution and thereby keeping their conspiracy going against far greater and more irresistible powers.

In the meantime, they have established a de facto society, a society of two to be exact. What they chose to do with their time is irrelevant (at some point, the man from the country gets very well acquainted with the doorkeeper's fleas). What matters is that they are situated in a site of irresolution. Their community, by virtue of its explicit exclusion from the law, is somewhat left to its own devices, a position afforded by its members' mutual conspiracy. If the doorkeeper is the messiah, he goes unnoticed and unappreciated, even apparently the villain of the parable. He, like the messiah in *The Castle,* saves the world, but nobody notices (certainly not the man from the country). The communities that are revealed in his wake (usually) go similarly unrecognized, so fixated are we on the faux symbols, the Klamms, sovereigns, authors, and potentates that leave us truly bereft.

The Silence of the Sirens

If we think further about the relationship between these moments of messianic interruption and our own acts of conspiracy, we can begin to see that for Kafka, as for Benjamin, such events are simultaneous—possibly identical in some sense, even as they are mutually implicated. In an act of "divine violence," the messianic serves to destroy its own representation "which myth bastardized with law."[50] At the same moment, our duty is to conspire against our own time and intentions, to use Haggadah (or to go along with its use) as a "mighty paw" to raise against the false appearances of Halakah. We can see that both gestures are the same: the exposure and decentering of false idols.[51]

For Benjamin (and I'd argue for Kafka as well), these gestures must be simultaneous to succeed. In keeping with the Jewish mystical tradition that the messiah is always here, Benjamin famously tells us, "Like every generation that preceded us, we have been endowed with a *weak* Messianic power."[52] But this power is nothing, or rather provides nothing but an opportunity, if we don't act ourselves. Thus, to return to Kafka's stories, neither K. nor the man from the country is "redeemed" by the messianic gesture of self-voiding, or rather if they are, their redemption seems useless unless it somehow comes to their attention, becomes legible to them.

Here we come to the trickiest part of Kafka's notion of redemption because, as we have seen, K. cannot know that he has been redeemed—he *must* miss the messiah to avoid reasserting the very mythologies that the messiah has (potentially) voided. Given the unfinished and unresolved nature of *The Castle* (is K. redeemed? Does he know? How could we tell?) a consideration of a different writing, Kafka's short parable "The Silence of the Sirens" ("Das Schweigen der Sirenen"), may offer us some illumination about how to think further about K.'s intentionality, about his role in his own conspiracy (and, by extension, the role of any fellow conspirator as well). In "The Silence of the Sirens" (wherein, in a classic act of misrecognition of his own—whether deliberate or not—Kafka completely twists the story of Ulysses around to suit his purposes), we are told that Ulysses filled his ears with wax and chained himself to the mast in order to avoid the lure of the Sirens' song. In doing so he didn't know that "the Sirens have a still more fatal weapon than their song, namely their silence."[53] While his ears are blocked up, Ulysses imagines that he is escaping their songs; little does he know that they aren't making any noise at all.[54]

Here we see a failure, an accidental conspiracy by a human agent. Yet, via his own confusion and misrecognition, Ulysses earns redemption even though he doesn't know what that redemption means or looks like (or how it came about). His conspiracy, his turn to wax and chains *does* work but to do so, it must be simultaneous with a crucial messianic function— the *aporia* of the Sirens' silence. Indeed, Kafka suggests that the Sirens are silent because of the spectacle of Ulysses' joy at his own scheme—a mutual case of misreading with happy results for Ulysses (Kafka begins this parable by stating, "Proof that inadequate, even childish measures, may serve to rescue one from peril").[55] Such misrecognition produces, in effect, the same dynamic we saw with Baudelaire's belief in novelty in the previous chapter. Baudelaire's misrecognition allows his own role in his conspiracy with language to remain "hidden from [him]," even as it also permits him to expose the centralizing myths of commodity fetishism, if not for himself, then for us, the readers of his text.[56]

And the same construction applies to *The Castle*. Due to his obsession with Klamm, K. encounters the messiah (he would never have been in that sleigh if he hadn't been waiting for Klamm). By an act of grace, the same act of idolatry on K.'s part becomes transformed into a redemptive moment because the exact same gesture of missing God coincides with God's act of becoming missed (or miss-able). This is how the two gestures are in fact one even as they are not legible in the same way.

By voiding itself, the messianic function allegorizes the signs of the divine (or perhaps more accurately in Kafka's case, renders them into parables). The failure of the sign to mean anything becomes legible, albeit in ways K. misunderstands and only dimly perceives (without, however, annihilating the sign or K.'s attachment to it). In the face of such an exposure, the quest for meaning that drives us to idolatry is disrupted, potentially turning us from being stooges into acting as "coconspirators" with the divine.

The two acts in question, one of messianic intervention and the other of our own conspiracy, haunt and inform one another. If the messiah acted without the obscurity of our own obsessions (that is to say, if we saw it for "what it is"), we would be condemned to a perfect form of idolatry, a myth without antidote insofar as the messiah would be implicated in our belief and thus no longer able to "rescue" us. If we acted without the messiah's act of self-voiding, we risk thinking, along with Ulysses and K., that our delusions are correct; that we *were* saved by wax and chains, or that Klamm really is going to save us. Such a delusion without redemption returns us to the very mythologies that both Kafka and Benjamin are trying to save us from. In either case, it is the balance and simultaneity of these gestures, the way they cast one another into doubt, that proves redemptive, a source of "hope" if anything is.

Failure and Redemption

In order to complete this discussion of the messianic function in Kafka's work (and by extension, Benjamin's as well), it may be useful to contrast my reading with that of another Kafka scholar. In her own musings on the question of Kafka's failure and what it offers, Ewa Plonowska Ziarek makes an important argument about what Kafka is up to in his parables, and I am largely in agreement with her. Yet I would here like to suggest that to leave out an explicit consideration of messianism (as I think she does to some extent) is also to leave out part of the central mechanism of Kafka's subversion and hence a key element of textual conspiracy.

In her analysis, Ziarek offers that reading Kafka's failure as a wholly negative event misses its radical nature. She too reads Kafka through the rubric of Benjamin's own work, writing:

> Although the production of exemplary sense is undercut in Kafka's parables by their ostensible rhetoric of failure, Kafka's texts, as Walter Benjamin reminds us, do not merely dramatize the inaccessibility of truth but redefine the very function of rhetoric in terms of a paradoxical task, or an impossible obligation of transmission.[57]

For Ziarek, Benjamin helps us to explain what Kafka's parables are actually doing—a kind of radical undermining of the very bases of meaning and authority. We are left, as Benjamin tells us, with a kind of pure transmissibility, a pure reduction to the sign, and in this, I am completely in agreement with her.

Ziarek helps us identify a pattern of productive failure in Kafka's work that links a great number of his works. She talks, for example, about his writings on the Tower of Babel, such as "The City Coat of Arms" ("Das Stadtwappen"). Here, a huge city is built in order to house all of the experts and builders who expect to build a "tower that will reach to heaven."[58] Of course such a thing is impossible, and so the tower never gets built. Ziarek notes that the city, which thrives despite the uselessness of its core mission, is "decentered, heterogeneous, built without any governing idea."[59] Furthermore,

> Mirroring the predicament of the builders of the city, Kafka's own interpretation of the biblical text reflects the possibilities and risks of textual transmission. . . . When completion or supplementation of the previous text is indistinguishable from its destruction, then the process of transmissibility implied in Kafka's parables subverts the stability of transcendental ideas both in their own discourse and in the texts that serve them as antecedents.[60]

This view is in keeping with what we have already encountered in *The Castle* (and *The Trial*) as well: a community that is busily forming itself in the expectation of some great organizing principle, some great delivery that never arrives. But perhaps just as important, and not noted by Ziarek, is the very end of this parable:

> All the legends and songs that came to birth in that city are filled with longing for a prophesied day when the city would be destroyed by five successive blows from a gigantic fist. It is for that reason too that the city has a closed fist on its coat of arms.[61]

The "longing" for such messianic redemption (in the form of a clear act of divine violence), for the ridding of all delusions that might be brought by such an act, does not mean that this event will actually occur. But such a longing does suggest that the residents of this city are already in some way released from the totalizing grip of their delusion. Their dream of divine violence serves messianically to destabilize their own conviction that they are already perfectly working out God's plan. Such dreams potentially make the community they *do* have legible to these subjects, even in the face of the overarching beliefs that render the community peripheral even to itself.

As I see it, therefore, the idea of pure transmissibility, a Haggadah shorn of its requirement to represent Halakah, is only half of the equation. Without some kind of messianic self-voiding, some kind of anti-idolatrous intervention that does not merely reproduce another variant of phantasmagoria, the cities and communities that we build will simply fall into another form of mythmaking. The role of the messiah in this case is to trouble the delusions of the humans that live in expectation of its arrival—to turn their idolatrous rebellion into a redemptive and ongoing conspiracy with the messiah.

Conspiring by Design

Having laid out this argument about what could be called the accidental structure of our salvation, that is to say, our own misrecognition and failure as crucial elements in freeing us from the delusions of idolatry, it must be said that Kafka occasionally indicates what appears to be another version of conspiracy that comes a bit closer to the kind of open, conscious forms of resistance that one would expect to make for a properly "political" theory of conspiracy. After all, we expect our political actors to know what they are doing, to avoid stumbling on redemption by accident or by factors utterly beyond our control.[62]

We see something of this element in Kafka's initial decision to make K. more aware of his conspiracy, a decision that he rescinded in later iterations of *The Castle*. As Mark Harman points out, in his rewriting of *The Castle*, Kafka "flattened his characters" and especially K.[63] The original hero has a "decisive deed ("entscheidenden Tat") to perform in the Castle. As Harman tells us, the original K. "is an aggressive and duplicitous character who openly admits his willingness to cheat and lie to gain what he wants."[64] Any hint of this mission is, however, eliminated in the "final" text (that is to say, the text that Max Brod actually published posthumously, and against Kafka's explicit wishes).[65] Thus, via his editing, Kafka has produced his subject's passivity. In rendering K. as a kind of confused, stumbling everyman, Kafka is de facto reducing his own agency in the text (Harmon also notes Kafka's deletion of references that made it obvious that K. was an autobiographical foil for Kafka himself).[66] In this way, Kafka makes space for the kind of messianic delivery that K. "experiences." As author, he abandons K. as an extension of himself and his own agenda; he allows K. to similarly be abandoned by the messiah in the text and left truly to his own devices.

We see indications of this more "conscious" style of conspiracy elsewhere as well, including in "The Silence of the Sirens" itself. Kafka ends that parable by mentioning a "codicil to the forgoing that has been handed down":

> Ulysses, it is said, was so full of guile, was such a fox, that not even the goddess of fate could pierce his armor. Perhaps he had really noticed, although here the human understanding is beyond its depths, that the Sirens were silent, and opposed the afore-mentioned pretense to them and the gods merely as a sort of shield.[67]

Although "beyond human understanding," this alternative view of Ulysses does more than gain redemption by accident. *This* conspiracy might just take on the question of "raising a mighty paw" against Halakah (in this case with the wax and chains, the symbols by which the sirens are "not heard") in a more open, acknowledged way.[68] In this rendition, the joke isn't on Ulysses but on the gods themselves.

Yet in this case it is not clear that we are really dealing with another form of conspiracy; rather, from our limited and compromised position, it becomes tempting to read (or depict) such a conspiracy along the lines of how we think politics and conspiracy ought to be promulgated. We see in effect the author of these texts, Kafka himself, occasionally following the path of Ulysses, insofar as he attributes (at least some of the time) to his characters a fuller power over their own salvation (or doom) than his own writings would normally suggest were possible or desirable.

The fact that even an author as esoteric as Kafka seems to display this tendency suggests that it is difficult if not impossible from within our own perspective to perfectly portray a pure messianic event or to recognize the difference between a subject who has been redeemed by the messiah and one who has redeemed her- or himself (given that these are simultaneous gestures). Any language used to describe our own role in conspiracy will inevitably employ the vocabulary of agency and deliberate action, further muddying this distinction, Whether our actions in such circumstances are "accidental" or "on purpose" becomes a very loaded question.

Indeed, it may be that when he portrays a more "deliberate" style of conspiracy, Kafka is struggling with the temptation to project his own un-reconstructed sense of agency onto the process he describes (his alterations of his own text while writing *The Castle* suggest the ways that he may have sought to combat his own interference).

Or, perhaps, in describing a deliberate form of plotting as he does, Kafka is simply gesturing toward the same kind of "progressive deepening of . . . intention" that Benjamin describes. He is trying to imagine or depict what an agency that is "not ours" might look like from our limited, compromised perspective. But his gesture must remain only that—a gesture; to suggest that we could actually emerge out of our compromised status with our intentionality scrubbed clean of idolatry, that we are capable of a "decisive deed," is potentially to fall into the very sorts of ultimate phantasmagoria that Kafka's text is set against.

Here we see that the notion of a self that is "not us" and that is fully and finally redeemed carries its own kind of danger. As we will see further in the following chapters, in the process of aligning ourselves with signs and symbols, we must resist a sense of moving toward final resolution least we become an idol unto ourselves. The very term "progressive deepening" (admittedly Benjamin's term, not Kafka's) suggests a pathway rather than a final goal. Instead of seeking final resolution, the process must remain an ongoing method, or lodestone, by which we can continue to struggle against our own idolatry. The "us" that emerges in this process is not some free, self-actualized subjectivity but an ongoing work in progress (something we will discuss further in chapters 4 and 5). Such a self may look "deliberate" from our current perspective (where we are totally overwritten by the phantasmagoria), but it remains an artifact of our conspiracy and disappears when and if we cease conspiring.

The Coming of the Messiah

When Benjamin says of Kafka: "No other writer has obeyed the commandment 'Thou shalt not make unto thee a graven image' so faithfully," he is pointing to a way in which Kafka, perhaps even more than Benjamin, generally allows his intentionality to be decentered by the "intention of the sign." In this way Kafka not only describes but also models the method that Benjamin would apply more generally. Kafka's acts of authorial self-effacement function as and, to some extent, constitute the messianic act of self-voiding in his texts. In seeking to withdraw his conscious agency somewhat from the text, he makes room for other intentions, other voices to be heard.

In speaking of Kafka's messiah we need not be too mystical; this "messiah" is, after all, simply a character in or aspect of his text. As author, Kafka can never know (nor should we, his readers) the messianic function perfectly; here too, he can only gesture at it. Even Kafka does not have access to some kind of "outside" perspective that he is privy to; he too can only relate the messianic function through symbols and representations, through events and narratives of the text. Indeed we might say that Kafka's depiction of the messianic is perhaps itself a parable by which to gesture at the idea of human beings being "rescued" by the sign, a representation of the text as an ally and coconspirator.

Both Kafka as author and the messiah in his text do very little to transcend or disturb the ordinary operations of his novels or short stories. After all, for all his self-effacing, Kafka is still the author of his works, and his messiahs are so unobtrusive as to scarcely be noticeable as such. Yet what little that they do does not leave us unaffected. As readers we are "redeemed" by these acts of self-voiding (on both the author's and the messiah's part) insofar as by eliminating the promise of telling us the true meaning of the text, they throw us back onto our own devices. We come to the text anew without any hope for resolution, and in this way we become more available to "the intention of the sign." Kafka's messiah is the avatar of this textual intention, displacing and subverting our complicit intentionality (potentially even his own) in order to foster the habit of deferring to the text for our guidance.

In his own most direct reference to the messiah in "The Coming of the Messiah" ("Das Kommen des Messias") Kafka tells us that "The messiah will only come when he is no longer necessary; he will come only on the day after his arrival; he will come, not on the last day, but the very last."[69] We will never, indeed must never, catch the messiah at its function. To do so would be to return us to the very delusion that the messiah's arrival and departure has voided in the first place. The value of our own conspiracy, even though we are hopelessly compromised, even though we are total failures, is to give us a way to understand what has become possible even while excluding and hiding the messianic function. Such a move allows us to misrecognize the messiah's actions (and, perhaps, the actions of the author as well) and hence remain redeemed; it potentially transforms our clumsy and collaborationist acts into conspiracies.

Perhaps the key point to grasp here in reading Kafka is the need to "recognize our misrecognition," that is, to remain open to the kinds of misrecognitions that we require in order to navigate the realm of representation. Rather than either seeking "the truth," or nihilistically giving up on representation altogether (in the end both gestures lead us to the same level of delusion), Kafka suggests that we can just possibly learn to recognize how valuable our failures and misrecognitions are, to recognize that our various alliances and relationships, while equally based on misrecognition, nevertheless constitute a ground for (perhaps the only ground for) a good life and a decent politics.

We can see in the gestures that Kafka makes—gestures toward our own (redeemed) agency, gestures toward a textual messiah, gestures toward justice and community—that he is in effect engaging in his own practice of recognized misrecognition. These gestures are not "true"; they come from no inside knowledge and do not produce a decisive end to idolatry. But the genius of Kafka's gestures is that they subvert rather than reinforce the phantasms that they engage with. His gestures are not meant to illuminate truth but rather his (and our) knowledge of its absence. In that absence, in the *aporias* such gestures render legible, we have a possibility of thinking and acting without the certainty of being overwritten by phantasms.

When we recognize our misrecognition, we remain bound by the signs and symbols of authority and power. Yet when the overwhelming presence of some central narrative figure is distorted or removed, we gain more access to our own politics, our own relationality that is produced in the wake of such figures. To say that such communities now become "legible" to us does not mean, once again, that we are now "in the know," but only that these alternative forms of politics and identity have entered into our conscious lexicon. To "recognize" our misrecognition means to learn to live with what passes for reality, to take advantage of what we see and encounter and to make the best home for ourselves that we can in this context. It means to learn how to see the world not for "what it is" but for how it can best be inhabited and also to recognize the ways that we have already been so inhabiting it.

Even if we are reluctant citizens of these fragile and peripheral communities (reluctant because we never cease wanting to be members of the shining, salvational community that we are promised by our own mythologies), our membership in them affords us a political space that is not inherently overdetermined by idolatry and phantasmagoria. We may be hopeless (indeed, we must be hopeless), but in that space without hope, we can yet learn how to endure and perhaps even to thrive a little in these forgotten spaces.

In the next chapter, we will leave aside this vocabulary of messiahs and redemption and look at the conspiracy from a far more prosaic viewpoint. Turning to the writing and plays of Niccolò Machiavelli, we will look at the specific strategies that Machiavelli may be suggesting for how to engage in conspiracy not only "within" a text but without as well, in our actual lived world and in our encounters with great organizing systems of power and authority. By reading an author with such an explicit and engaged political vocabulary, we are seeking to form a constellation between Benjamin's central method of reading, Kafka's understanding of agency and messianism, and, finally, Machiavelli's own explicitly political conspiratorial strategies as a way to bolster and expand our conception of how this conspiracy works.

3 | Machiavelli's Conspiracy of Open Secrets

When it comes to his own treatment of political conspiracies, Machiavelli hardly seems like the kind of figure a leftist would seek to turn to. Although famous for discussing conspiracy at length, he seems to treat the subject in a very conventional manner; far from offering a way to overcome human intentionality, Machiavelli seems to preserve and assert intention (and especially the intention of a particular individual) in order to prevail over others. Furthermore, in his treatment of conspiracy Machiavelli offers no obvious guide to which side he is on. He can appear indifferent to whether his advice serves princes or subjects or both. In the beginning of his chapter "Of Conspiracies" in the *Discourses* (its longest chapter), he writes:

> It seems to me proper now to treat of conspiracies, being a matter of so much danger both to princes and subjects; for history teaches us that many more princes have lost their lives and their states by conspiracies than by open war. But few can venture to make open war upon their sovereign, whilst every one may engage in conspiracies against him. On the other hand, subjects cannot undertake more perilous and foolhardy enterprises than conspiracies, which are in every respect more difficult and dangerous; and thence it is that, although so often attempted, yet they so rarely attain the desired object. And therefore, so that princes may learn to guard against such dangers, and that subjects may less rashly engage in them, and learn rather to live contentedly under such a government as Fate may have assigned to them, I shall treat the subject at length, and endeavor not to omit any point that may be useful to the one or the other.[1]

If anything, in this passage, Machiavelli's understanding of conspiracies seems to favor the powerful insofar as he suggests that conspiracies tend to favor princes over subjects seeking to restore their liberty. Thus he offers that subjects might be better off learning to "live contentedly under such a government as Fate may have assigned to them."

Such a view is perhaps typical of much of Western political theory, which, as we have already seen, has long tended to hold conspiracy in great suspicion. Conspiracy seems, at best, to be a double-edged sword; it may be an effective way to battle tyrants, but it could just as easily serve would-be tyrants who scheme to usurp power from legitimate governments. Conspiracy seems merely a tool and a wildcard, not possessing any particular value or political stance of its own.

Indeed, as we see in the passage above, Machiavelli may be one of the chief sources of this belief; his views on conspiracy are one of his main contributions to the Western canon. And yet, as is so often the case with Machiavelli, in the very passage in which he delivers this verdict, he may be saying more than one thing at the same time. For example, although he offers that the conspiracy of the subject against the prince is "perilous and foolhardy," he nonetheless offers (and he follows through to show this in the rest of the chapter) that conspiracies can nonetheless be "useful" (that is the given word in the English translation; in Italian it is *notabile,* or notable, i.e., worthy of study) to the subjects.[2] In other words, conspiracies by subjects may be difficult but not impossible (indeed "many more princes have lost their lives and their states by conspiracies than by open war"). If we take this view seriously, then it allows us to read the passage in a slightly different light. If in fact conspiracies by the subjects of a prince are possible, then perhaps when Machiavelli writes that subjects "may less rashly" engage in them, he doesn't simply mean this is in a negative sense. A "less rash" approach to conspiracies may in fact improve the chances of their success against unpopular princes since—as Machiavelli informs us—"everyone may engage in conspiracies against him." This reading of how the people may conspire "less rashly" is perhaps even clearer in the original Italian, where he states, "e che i privati più timidamente vi si mettino . . ." (literally: and so that the subjects can more timidly put themselves into [conspiracy]).[3] For Machiavelli to advocate "more timidity" suggests being more careful as opposed to avoiding conspiracy altogether (i.e., acting "less rashly"). A more timid conspiracy could mean one that is more prudently and secretively exercised. Thus, despite his stated desire to help princes prevent conspiracies and advising the prince's subjects to avoid conspiracies altogether, we see that perhaps Machiavelli is offering the subjects something after all. Perhaps we might even say that Machiavelli (not unlike Benjamin) appears to be conspiratorial in his description of conspiracies.[4]

Machiavellian Strategies

If such a conspiracy within conspiracy can be found in Machiavelli's texts, we might be able to conceive of conspiracy as being something other than a tool by which to overthrow governments (it can of course also be that too). Turning our enquiry to Machiavelli enables us to better understand how such a conspiracy could be (to use Benjamin's own term) "useless for the purposes of fascism," that is to say, something that works only unidirectionally, helping democratic and radical forces even as it offers nothing to the forces of centralization and the usurpation of political power for private or nefarious purposes.[5]

As I will argue in this chapter, for all of his seeming evenhandedness, Machiavelli's strategies are in fact "useless" for princes (i.e., fascism) and help only "the people" (however they might be conceived). I will argue that when Machiavelli gives advice both to princes and to subjects, he is vastly favoring the public not so much (or not only) with sympathy but also with the effects of his writings; in publishing the secret machinations of princes he is revealing their secrets, while in publishing the possibilities of a people's actions, he is giving form and strategy to a desire that is no secret at all. In this way, Machiavelli can be considered to be engaging in a language of what might be called "open secrets" or "public conspiracies," a lopsided public discourse that is explicitly nonsymmetrical in character insofar as it does not help or hurt princes and publics equally. As I will argue further, Machiavelli's use of open secrets, as well as his advocacy of using publicness (and publicity) as a weapon of popular power, allows him to pay lip service to the support of princes even as the very fact of his writing promotes a conspiracy of the people, a conspiracy that is, as it were, performed "hidden in plain sight," in a language accessible to all but which, as we will see further, benefits only the public.

This construction of secrecy is, as it were, built into the fabric of Machiavelli's texts; rather than depending on intention or guile, he offers an inherently democratic (taking that word in its most radical sense) form of representation. For Machiavelli, the act of representation, rather than being doomed to reproduce reactionary phantasms of princely power and sovereignty, can undermine those power arrangements, thus avoiding the trap of simply replacing old hierarchies with new ones. Such a view is not unlike Benjamin's understanding of Kafka's work as "raising a mighty paw" against Halakah. Here too, the forms or representation can work against the very power systems that they otherwise serve. It is principally in this sense that Machiavelli can properly be considered one of our textual conspirators.

Another aspect of Machiavelli's approach to conspiracy that is very helpful for our own purposes is the way it offers to bring others into conspiracy by virtue of certain narratives that "explain" or also produce their status as coconspirators. This is something that we saw Benjamin doing with Baudelaire, Kafka, and so on, but Machiavelli's strategies are especially helpful because they extend from engaging with one or two individuals to engaging with whole groups of people, helping to extend Benjamin's project directly into the larger political sphere. Machiavelli shows us how to include coconspirators often without their knowledge; here again, intentionality is decentered by a strategy that permits unknowing or even perhaps unwanted participation. At the same time, as we will see further, Machiavelli's strategy of extending his conspiracy via narratives permits—or even produces—our active support for being included in his conspiracies insofar as these narratives expiate (at least potentially) our guilt for being such deeply compromised subjects in the first place. Through these narratives we become potentially re-formed as being retroactively complicit with a conspiracy we never even knew about.

As already noted, in moving from Benjamin and Kafka to Machiavelli, we leave to some extent the former thinkers' esoteric concerns with images and theology and move into the more workaday vocabulary of politics. As already mentioned too, it is useful to turn to Machiavelli insofar as he is a central canonical figure for Western political theory. Linking him with Benjamin, who is at best peripheral to that canon, helps to connect the Benjaminian conspiracy to the heart of the Western tradition. Such a connection allows us to read Benjamin in an explicitly political way (where "political" is defined according to the norms that are present at the heart of Western political theory). At the same time, Machiavelli offers strategies that directly bear upon the concerns that Benjamin and Kafka both bring to their own work. While Machiavelli is far less concerned with compromised human intentionality than Benjamin, he offers ways to alter intentionality nonetheless (as we have already seen). And while far less suspicious of representation, he offers useful strategies for how to engage with representation in ways that subvert rather than perpetuate nondemocratic notions of power and authority.

It should be further noted that by connecting Machiavelli to Benjamin's conspiracy we are leaving the "modern" world as Benjamin understood it. Machiavelli's life came at the dawn of modernity and capitalism, not the future bloom that we live under today. Machiavelli's Renaissance Italy was the era of "primitive capitalism," a shadow of what was to follow. Nevertheless, Benjamin's theory of history does not make a major break between modernity and its predecessors; as we have seen, we find it possible or even necessary in his work to connect moments "through events that may be separated from [one another] by thousands of years."[6] For this reason, we should be permitted to bring Machiavelli into our conspiracy, but we do so with certain caveats. The fascism that Benjamin battles against is obviously not the same phenomenon as the power of the prince. The desires of "the people" of Italy may not be exactly the same as what Benjamin sought in communism (although Gramsci wants to suggest that they are).[7] Still, we will use these terms as analogous for the purpose of forming transtemporal constellations. As always for Benjamin, it is not the perfect analogy but the discordant juxtapositions of times and places that help to disrupt the seamless web of reality that forms the phantasmagoria. and so we engage in this analogy with this desired effect in mind.

Public Acts and Open Secrets

To begin this argument, let us examine Machiavelli's notion of secrecy as it relates to conspiracy. To claim that Machiavelli supports public conspiracies is not the same thing as claiming that he is in favor of transparency or that he calls for conspiracies that are openly proclaimed to the prince. In the same chapter on conspiracies considered above, Machiavelli tells us:

> It requires the extremest prudence, or great good fortune, that a conspiracy shall not be discovered in the process of formation. Their discovery is either by denunciation or by surmises . . . [T]reachery is so common that you cannot safely impart your project to any but such of your most trusted friends. . . . Of such reliable friends you may find one or two; but as you are necessarily obliged to extend your confidence, it becomes impossible to find many such, for their devotion to you must be greater than their sense of danger and fear of punishment.[8]

Here secrecy, that is to say, hiding one's activities from those against whom one is plotting, is both crucial and nearly impossible to maintain. Indeed, it may be because of the extreme difficulty of keeping secrets, the treachery of fellow citizens, and the various hazards posed to such conspirators, that Machiavelli resorts to a more "open" style of plotting in the first place.

Throughout his writings, Machiavelli tells his readers that if they have the power to openly overthrow an unwanted government, they ought to do it; conspiracies are, by definition, committed from a position of weakness, of uncertain outcomes. As we have already seen, popular conspiracies seem even more precarious than princely ones. And yet Machiavelli's text confers certain advantages to the people in their struggle with princes, advantages that may help such conspiracies succeed despite their inherent difficulties.

The first advantage may be obvious but is worth plainly stating nonetheless, namely the very fact that Machiavelli pontificates upon the question of conspiracies in a public, and published, venue. Even in *The Prince*, where Machiavelli seems very explicitly to be counseling princes on how to seize and maintain power at the expense of the populace, the fact that this "advice" is given in a public forum affects the impact and meaning of what Machiavelli is offering. Although *The Prince* was not literally published during his lifetime, it was widely circulated and commented upon.[9] Machiavelli supposedly sent his intended prince (first Giuliano and then Lorenzo de Medici) one version of the manuscript "beautifully lettered on vellum and richly bound," but he also circulated the manuscript among his friends and other selected audiences.[10]

Were Machiavelli to have written *The Prince* as a private letter to one prince, the same book would take on a very different connotation. In such a case, the argument that there is any kind of republican agenda in the book would be harder to make since the prince would be the sole audience for whom the book is intended (unless you could argue that somehow Machiavelli wanted to subvert the prince by giving him bad advice). By definition, Machiavelli is "advising" the prince in public, that is to say, before an audience who is witnessing, reading, and learning about his counsel. Thus, whereas princes almost by definition have private advisors who tell them how to manage power, to publicize such counsel is in a sense to let the rest of us in on the prince's secrets (in the guise of advising him). In publishing his work, Machiavelli gives his notions a material presence: a text that can, and will be interpreted and that will exert its own influence on the political questions of his day. In that way the text creates a nonsymmetrical relationship, insofar as "telling" the prince's secrets hurts the prince and helps the people. The very existence of the text of *The Prince* as a publicly circulated document thus creates an advantage on behalf of the people.

If we keep the public and material nature of this discourse in mind, it may change the way we interpret specific passages in Machiavelli's writing. For example, in the *Discourses* (a book that is of course not directed to the prince), he writes:

> If republics are slower than princes, they are also less suspicious and therefore less cautious; and if they show more respect to their great citizens, these in turn are thereby made more daring and audacious in conspiring against them.[11]

This passage can be read in two ways: either as "advising" the prince on how to take advantage of people (republics are "less suspicious and therefore less cautious") or warning republics not to be taken advantage of by would-be princes (who are "thereby made more daring and audacious in conspiring against them"). We can see that although the language seems neutral in regard to outcome, the very fact of the text's being widely circulated inherently throws Machiavelli's lot in with the reading public, since princes by definition know how to seize or maintain power, but the people may not be so well versed (or so well guarded against a prince's machinations, as we see in this very example). Here, as we have seen with Benjamin too, the text serves as a storehouse for resistance, awaiting a reading that will reverse the politics that Machiavelli formally (we might even say intentionally) espouses.

Public Knowledge(s)

An even greater popular advantage that Machiavelli confers lies in an understanding of the quality of so-called public knowledge among both princes and people, establishing the nonsymmetrical nature of these respective forms of knowledge. In the *Discourses* Machiavelli writes:

> [The people, in seeking to "bestow office" on one of their number] do ... better ... when they base their choice upon a number of good actions known to have been performed by him; for in that case they are never deceived. .... Thus the people are always less liable to the influence of erroneous opinions and corruption than princes; although it might happen that the people are deceived by public opinion and the fame and acts of a man, supposing him to be better than he really is, which would not happen to a prince, who

would be informed of it by his counsellors. Therefore so that the people might not lack similar counsel, the wise lawgivers of republics have ordered that, in the appointment of men to the highest positions, where it would be dangerous to place inefficient persons, every citizen should be allowed, and in fact it should be accounted honorable [*e gli sia imputato a gloria*—literally "to attribute glory to them"] for him, to publish in the assemblies the defects of any one named for public office; so that a people fully informed, might form a more correct judgment.[12]

Here Machiavelli directly acknowledges the different perspectives of princes and people. Princes have one single perspective, relying on their own judgments and also on the quality of their counselors. The people, when left to their own, separate, devices, are not dissimilar, but when they are allowed access to "public" information (i.e., when they have access to each other, when they form an actual and interactive public), they have a more multifaceted and hence possibly more objective understanding of things insofar as they are "less liable to the influence of erroneous opinions and corruption than princes." Although they too can be deceived, their multitudinousness is the people's best defense against misjudgment. In this case, their knowledge is not only based on personal belief that is fallible and easily deceived but also on the experiences and knowledge of all their individual members. Collectively the people can be said to "know" everything about those who live among them, while the prince only "knows" what he himself has experienced or has been told to be true (as we see in the above passage, only the very best or "wisest" of counselors have a knowledge that may be roughly equal to that of the people).

In speaking of members of the populace "publishing" their knowledge of various other persons, Machiavelli directly acknowledges the different and potentially better epistemology of the people. Making something publicly known adds it to the collective experience; it is no longer part of the private domain of princely "advice" or private opinion.

In a similar vein, Machiavelli describes the ways that the public may be not only better informed, but a better judge, than princes. This better judgment is, once again, a product of the public's unique position and perspective. For example, in *The Art of War*, Machiavelli speaks of soldiers who fight to death for their general. He tells us that one factor that motivates these soldiers is the esteem that they have for the general: "Such esteem is a result of the opinion they have of his *virtù*, rather than of any particular favor they have received from him."[13] In other words, in this case, esteem is not simply a matter of personal favors and opinions (as it might be with a prince) but is instead a recognition of the public-spiritedness of the general. As members of that public, the soldiers are acknowledging their collective self-interest as reflected in the concept of *virtù*.

For Machiavelli, public esteem (or "glory"), like public knowledge, must be actually produced by certain practices and institutions ("e gli sia imputato a gloria").[14] Once again in *The Art of War*, Machiavelli considers that one of the reasons that the Romans were so successful at maintaining their republic for so long was that they were very good at publicly recognizing merit, particularly the merit of selflessness and courage in war:

> In this manner, each man's desert was properly taken notice of, recompensed by the consuls, and honored publicly; those who obtained any reward for services of this kind, besides the reputation and glory which they acquired among their fellow soldiers, were, when they returned from the wars, received by their friends and relations with all kinds of rejoicing and congratulations. It is no wonder, then, that a people who were so exact in rewarding merit and punishing offenders should extend their empire to such a degree as they did; they are certainly highly worthy of imitation in these respects.[15]

Here, glory is actually produced through the workings of the state such that it forms and enacts the very public who respond to it. This is a virtuous cycle of continual collective affirmation.[16] This "public knowledge" forms a collective narrative, a way for the people, as it were, to talk to itself and to produce its own collectively determined meanings, values, and judgments. Because of the shifting and protean nature of these judgments, it would not be accurate to call the public knowledge "truth," but, on the other hand, it is clearly differentiated from private (read princely) opinion.

Here again, in Machiavelli's praise for the Roman republic's practice of producing public knowledge, we see a nonsymmetry, insofar as one mainly admires (loves) or dislikes (fears) a prince for his personal qualities, whereas in case of the public it is the knowledge by and relationship to the public as such that matters. Since the prince is by definition not part of the public, he is removed from such practices. He might be incidentally better or worse for various aspects of public life or for various individuals who make up part of that public; he may earn their esteem based on his own particular qualities. But he is subject to a different calculus.

In the passages considered above, Machiavelli praises the Roman republic for institutionalizing the publicization of information and of glory and hence making the Roman public a functional, enduring entity. Yet it is true that in his own time, such conditions were no longer in evidence, suggesting that the public no longer even existed in the ways that Machiavelli might desire. Certainly the public of his day no longer had access to the very advantages that for Machiavelli are crucial in overcoming princely opposition. Machiavelli, however, partially fulfills this absent role himself by publicizing the strategy of public knowledge in the pages of his texts (and, as we will see, in the performance of his plays). In this way he reproduces (albeit in a conspiratorial rather than institutionalized form) the Roman republic's use of publicness. Or perhaps more accurately, he advertises this strategy (in the guise of merely describing it) to alert would-be conspirators to the advantages and uses of the institutionalization of "popular knowledge."

Or, perhaps still more accurately yet, we might say that it is his text that performs this subversive or conspiratorial function. Whatever Machiavelli may hold to be true (a nearly impossible question to answer), his text contains and exemplifies these strategies of publicization. The notions of *gloria* and *virtù* examined here are not only described but also enacted by these texts. Here the text serves, as we have seen, to supply a "missing" function—namely that of making such alternatives to princely power both legible and viable regardless of what its author may or may not have desired.

Adianoeta

There is yet another way in which Machiavelli's texts retain and perform a conspiratorial strategy. In light of Machiavelli's acknowledgment of the differing perspectives between prince and people (a difference he famously dramatizes in his dedicatory letter to the Medicis via his contrast between the "high" perspective of the prince and his own "low," popular perspective), we might say that a given fact, statement, or opinion can be understood according to two entirely separate epistemologies: the prince's private one and (potentially at least) the people's public one.[17] Accordingly, anything that is said or done in "public" speaks, at least potentially, to people in a way that it does not speak to the prince. Here we get a better sense of the sources of nonsymmetry for Machiavelli; how apparent evenhandedness can play into the public's hands because saying one thing doesn't mean the same thing to all members of a given society, nor help all members equally.[18]

Rhetorically speaking, this understanding can be seen as Machiavelli employing the rhetorical figure of *adianoeta* (literally "not noticed"), wherein words or phrases are understood to have two separate meanings, one "obvious" and one more subtle. We have already seen examples of this figure in our various ways of reading Machiavelli's "advice," depending on which audience is intended. As a rhetorical figure, adianoeta is particularly understood to mean that various members of an audience will understand the same words differently, some let in on the ironic nature of the figure and some not. Whereas in classical rhetoric it might be the general understanding that the use of adianoeta allows those elites "in the know" to get a better sense of the esoteric meaning of phrase or word than the general audience, for Machiavelli, the figure is given a decidedly republican cast. Here, being "in the know" is a category reserved for the ordinary citizen, while the one who is excluded from knowledge is that most elite figure of all, the prince. If we consider Machiavelli to be employing this figure, we become explicitly aware of the critical role of the audience in terms of his discourse; Machiavelli's language is not aimed at some generic audience but discriminates in terms of how it will be received. With this notion of adianoeta in mind, we can see how Machiavelli actually speaks, as it were, a double language without seeming to.

We can also see here in particular that Machiavelli's text offers us something truly "useless for . . . fascism." The strategy of adianoeta subverts, but only in one direction.

To see the workings of adianoeta, and to see how the value of publicness serves Machiavelli in a conspiratorial fashion, let us consider two of Machiavelli's best-known plays, *Mandragola* ("The Mandrake Root") and *Clizia*. Both appear on their surface to be frivolous, sexually themed farces, but in the prologue to *Mandragola,* Machiavelli warns us not to take him too lightly.[19] If we take this advice to heart we can see that in some senses these plays may reveal strategies that Machiavelli practices more subtly in his "political" texts as well. The use of plays affords Machiavelli a unique format in which to work out and even practice his strategies. After all, in the case of his plays, he has a live audience, responding to and interpreting his words. Here, in other words, he is not merely dealing with a "reading" public, but an actual one, whether composed of his fellow Florentines or other audiences. With this explicit presence of the public, some of the character of Machiavelli's "public conspiracies" becomes clearer. In looking at his plays, we will see how Machiavelli advocates and employs the figure of adianoeta. We will also see how, by ensuring that the public is informed and vigilant, public conspiracies can succeed (in *Mandragola*), while would-be princely conspiracies can be foiled (in *Clizia*), both by virtue of the same textual dissymmetry that Machiavelli calls our attention to. Finally we will see the nature of Machiavelli's "deception" insofar as what he advocates is not "lying" per se but rather deceiving only the prince, while speaking the (barely) encoded public and collective narrative to everyone else. As with his understanding of public knowledge in ancient Rome, the practice of adianoeta does not produce "truth" for Machiavelli but simply offers a reflection of a multiple, democratic perspective that is not entirely overwritten by phantasms of princely power.

Mandragola

In *Mandragola,* we see a cast of characters plotting (conspiring) to seduce a young married woman. Machiavelli's foil in the play is named Ligurio, a behind-the-scenes plotter who contrives to help a younger man named Callimaco seduce Lucretia (in Italian Lucrezia), the wife of an old, rich, and foolish man named Nicia (who is often—although not always—read as a stand-in for a prince).[20] Lucretia herself can be seen as a stand-in for Florence, for the public that has to be wooed by a younger, more deserving man. In hatching his plot, Ligurio has Callimaco pose as a doctor who offers to "cure" Lucretia's infertility (in fact it is obviously Nicia who is infertile) by having her consume a mandrake root. The "doctor" tells her that the root will allow her to become pregnant but that it is also a deadly poison that will kill the next man she sleeps with. Callimaco then affects a second disguise as a pauper who is meant to sleep with Lucretia to draw off the poison (supposedly dying in the process). Nicia, eager to become a father, actually undresses Callimaco and puts him in bed with his own wife. After Callimaco succeeds in his scheme (which can only really be called a rape), he reveals himself to Lucretia and she agrees, however improbably, to become his lover behind Nicia's back. At the very end of the play we get this bit of dialogue when Nicia (now a cuckold) and Lucretia see Callimaco approaching them. Recall that Nicia still thinks Callimaco is a doctor:

> NICIA: Doctor, let me present you to my wife.
> CALLIMACO: With pleasure.
> NICIA: Lucretia, this is the man who'll cause us to have a staff to
>   support our old age.

LUCRETIA: I'm delighted to meet him and want him to be our
  closest friend [in Italian: "nostro compare," literally our dear
  friend or, perhaps also, accomplice].
NICIA: Now bless you. And I want him and Ligurio to come and
  have dinner with us this noon.
LUCRETIA: Yes, indeed.
NICIA: And I'm going to give them the key of the room on the
  ground floor in the loggia, so they can come there when it's con-
  venient, because they don't have women at home and live like
  animals.
CALLIMACO: I accept it, to use it when I like.[21]

This bit of dialogue perfectly demonstrates the strategies of adianoeta. The audience is of course laughing at all of these lines because they have access to knowledge the Nicia is denied (very much including the bawdy sexual double entendres about "staffs" [in Italian: *bastone*] etc.).[22] They know, as Nicia does not, that the whole story of the mandrake root is fake, a conspiracy meant to trick him. Although Machiavelli is notorious for gleefully advocating lying, neither Callimaco nor Lucretia is actually telling lies; the only person being deceived is Nicia, and that is because of his limited (and private) knowledge. This is in fact not so much deception as it is adianoeta. Thus when Nicia says, "Let me present you to my wife" and Callimaco responds, "With pleasure," he is clearly alluding to the sexual pleasure he has enjoyed with her, and when Lucretia says that she wants Callimaco to be her "closest friend," here too she is telling what she perceives to be the truth. It is only Nicia who does not understand what she means by this. The audience laughs because it is in on the conspiracy and delights in the openness with which Callimaco and Lucretia can fool Nicia.

In addition to the cast of characters described above, as already noted we also have a real audience (and hence a "public") viewing and respond- ing to this play. Just as for Machiavelli princes have limited perspective, Nicia has access to only one viewpoint, his own. He is furthermore subject to myriad bad advisors (the "doctor," a self-serving priest, and Ligurio himself). The audience, on the other hand, fully understands both Nicia's viewpoint and its own enlarged, public viewpoint. This helps elucidate Machiavelli's point about the lack of symmetry between the relative per- spectives of prince and population. The population can be let in on things via the very act of the play's being performed—a revival, however altered (and conspiratorial), of the ancient Roman practice of publicization.

Callimaco and Brutus

In a way then, the play *Mandragola* might be considered to serve as a dress rehearsal for an actual, political conspiracy. This point becomes more credible when one considers the parallels between Callimaco as a character and Junius Brutus, the founder of the Roman republic and a prominent figure in *The Discourses*. In the story of Brutus, the nephew of the Tarquin king rapes a noble Roman woman named Lucretia. She subsequently kills herself. Brutus vows vengeance and claims that Rome will never have a king again, establishing the Roman republic. In both cases, the hero (Callimaco or Brutus) overcomes a compromised past to rise to the occasion. In both cases, the rape of Lucretia (or Lucrezia) is the pivotal event. Finally, in both cases a conspiracy is undertaken at the expense of some undeserving prince or rich man (and it succeeds).

There are of course, major (and telling) differences between these characters. Callimaco is in effect the rapist and not the avenger, of Lucretia/Lucrezia; he seems to play the role of assaulter, not liberator. Machiavelli reminds us that Brutus "played the fool" in the years before his establishment of the Roman republic, whereas Callimaco is not shown to be "playing a fool" so much as being one.

Yet different as they may be, we see a similar role for Machiavelli in telling their respective stories and in leading them, as it were, to a new appreciation and support for publicness. In both cases, Machiavelli demonstrates how a story can be spun to reconfigure a private person into a public citizen, a member of a mutually informed collective. According to Machiavelli, Livy offered that Junius Brutus played a fool mainly to protect his life and his property, but Machiavelli reinterprets this argument: "If we well consider his conduct we are led to believe that he had another reason, which was that by thus avoiding observation he would have a better chance of destroying the kings, and of liberating his country."[23] Here, Machiavelli plays a similar role to that of Ligurio in *Mandragola*, reinterpreting his character in order to make a conspiracy possible or effective—at least in theory—where one had not necessarily existed before.

Given that in his own lifetime, Machiavelli is faced with a more or less indifferent, depoliticized public that acts largely as a collection of private and self-interested citizens (and hence, easily subject to princely manipulations), his task, when read via the lens of Benjaminian conspiracy, is to tell a story that will convert such specimens into active fellow conspirators. In the case of Junius Brutus, Machiavelli shows how a previously indifferent citizen can be reconfigured as having been a conspirator "all along." In this way his fellow Florentines can similarly come to see themselves as "coconspirators" after the fact. This suggests a nonviolent version of Machiavelli's call to "kill the sons of Brutus" (i.e., those compromised collaborationists he lives amid), by turning them—at least rhetorically—into retroactive conspirators.[24] In the case of Ligurio's treatment of Callimaco, we can see an analogous strategy to get an indifferent son of the city to "fall in love with the public [i.e., Lucretia]" when he was initially motivated purely by private considerations (in this case, sexual conquest). Such strategies that both dramatize the point and instruct the public are made possible only via the use of "open secrets," of adianoeta. With his powers of publicity firmly in hand, Machiavelli can employ a double language, instructing and reimagining his audience members as coconspirators even as he fools and excludes the prince.

Such a strategy is, of course, not reserved for his plays. We see Machiavelli employing more or less the same technique in *The Discourses* when he describes how to plot against a prince:

> If their [i.e., the conspirators'] condition be such that their forces do not suffice for open war against the prince, then they should seek by every art to win his friendship, and for this purpose employ all possible means such as adopting his tastes, and taking delight in all things that give him pleasure. Such intimacy will insure tranquility without any danger, and enable you to share the enjoyment of the prince's good fortune with him, and at the same time afford you every convenience for satisfying your resentment ["e ti arreca ogni commodità di sodisfare allo animo tuo"].[25]

While he is careful to avoid any mention of himself, this passage can be read as a perfect explanation for what Machiavelli is up to in *The Prince*, beginning with the dedication, as well as an explanation for his seeming evenhandedness throughout his writings. If we take this passage as being addressed specifically to a public audience (being, as it is, in the *Discourses*), we can read it as instructions for how to deploy and recognize the figure of adianoeta. It is like saying, "When I appear to be cozying up to the prince, know that I do so in order to better foment my conspiracy against him." It turns Machiavelli's own seeming indifference (not unlike the indifference of Callimaco) into a conspiratorial stance and hence models for his readers a similar transformation.

This strategy, as I have suggested in the beginning of this chapter, can be considered a potent weapon in the arsenal of a Benjaminian strategy as well. Such retellings offer refuge from our own compromise. We discover that rather than being agents of delusion and phantasmagoria, we have been "conspiring all along" for its downfall. Such a move seems like a typical "Machiavellian" manipulation until we recall Benjamin's notion of a God's eye view. From this perspective, although we are fallen, we are also always in God's service, whether we realize it or not; the signs that we engage with are both the stuff of deception and the means for our redemption. Thus we are therefore indeed all "fellow conspirators" regardless of how implicated we are in the workings of the phantasmagoria. Such a perspective allows this strategy to be something other than a mere trick, another contribution to the phantasmagoria. Even though it seems to be based on a lie or deception, this strategy in effect makes it possible for us not to be merely and perfectly determined by what we currently take to be the field of truth and possibility.

Clizia

In *Clizia*, we see something of a similar dynamic as in *Mandragola* although in this case, it is not adianoeta that is dramatized and employed so much as an assertion of the power of publicness. In this case, as I interpret the play, the focus changes from how a public conspiracy can be employed to how princely counterconspiracies can be thwarted. In this way, reading *Mandragola* and *Clizia* in tandem, we can read these plays as the complement to Machiavelli's long chapter on conspiracies in *The Discourses,* which similarly handles both kinds of conspiracy.

In the case of *Clizia,* there is not one conspiracy but two. Here too the "prize" is a woman, in this case Clizia herself, who never actually appears on stage. Cleander (Cleandro in Italian), a young man, is in a competition against his own father, Nicomaco, to seduce Clizia, who is a ward of the family. In order to get access to Clizia, both son and father try to get their personal servants to marry her, reasoning that with such a husband, they can then make Clizia their own mistress. This play, however, has a tellingly different outcome than *Mandragola*. Rather than have the younger Cleander triumph as Callimaco does in *Mandragola,* in *Clizia* Machiavelli has both conspiracies essentially fail. Sofronia, the mother of Cleander and wife of Nicomaco, initially conspires with her son to keep her husband away from Clizia. She plays a trick on her husband by having her male servant dress up as Clizia and beat up Nicomaco when he makes advances on "her" after a phony (and same-sex) wedding. Yet after the short-term triumph of Cleander's conspiracy, Sofronia decides that Cleander's proxy can't marry Clizia either, effectively denying Cleander's quest. It is only at the end of the play that Sofronia changes her mind. Clizia's rich father from Naples arrives and a proper marriage between Cleander and Clizia is arranged.

In this play, we see again the power of publicness. For either Nicomaco's or Cleander's conspiracy to succeed, it must rely on secrecy and guile. Sofronia's own conspiracy, on the other hand, relies upon the public in order to succeed. Sofronia counts on the shame that her husband or son would incur if his plot were exposed; she uses their secrecy as a weapon against them. When Sofronia triumphs over her husband she tells him:

> I never wanted to make a joke of you; but you're the one who's wanted to do it to all the rest of us, and finally to yourself. Aren't you ashamed to have brought up a girl in your house with such care, and in every way as daughters of the best families are brought up, and then to try to marry her to a rascally and shiftless servant, because he's willing you should lie with her? Did you think you were dealing with blind people, or with those who couldn't upset these shameful plans of yours? I confess that I've managed all those tricks that have been played on you because, if I was to make you come to your senses, there was no other way than to get so many witnesses to your actions that you'd be ashamed, and then shame'd make you do what nothing else could.[26]

To which a defeated Nicomaco replies: "My Sofronia, do what you like; I'm prepared not to go beyond the limits you set, if only the thing doesn't get known [*non si risappia*]."[27]

In this case, Sofronia is not employing the figure of adianoeta directly, but she nonetheless is taking advantage of various forms of knowledge, both public and private, and using that difference to her advantage. Here, as with *Mandragola,* the nature of Sofronia's deception is different from either Cleander's or Nicomaco's. Sofronia deceives these two men, but she does not deceive the audience. Unlike these two figures, who are moved only by their private lusts, Sofronia's goal is to inform, and earn the esteem of, the public.[28]

Although it is true that Cleander ends up with Clizia, he gains her only through the ministrations of his mother, who has the true power in the family. While father and son operate from fear of exposure, Sofronia enlists the audience, which is omnipresent, as her ally; in her case exposure (i.e., "publicness") is not to be feared but is rather her prime weapon, the key to her strategy. The audience here is both figural and literal. It is figured in the play as a kind of viewing public whose scrutiny both Nicomaco and Cleander fear, but it is also a literal audience composed of the members of the Florentine (or other Italian) public who have come to watch the play. In this way, the audience is, as it were, let into the conspiracy, brought in on the joke at Nicomaco's (and Cleander's) expense. In this way, both *Clizia* and *Mandragola* can be shown to represent attempts to dramatize and reveal the strategies of conspiracy (and counterconspiracy). Both plays draw upon, even as they produce, a sense of "publicness" that then serves as a weapon against princes (or at least princely figures).

As I have already begun to suggest, the power of such conspiracies may be such that they overcome the compromises even of their author. Several scholars have noted the similarity between the names "Nicomaco" and "Niccolò Machiavelli," arguing that Nicomaco is a foil for Machiavelli himself.[29] *Clizia* was written relatively late in Machiavelli's life and may suggest his own ambivalence about the compromises he was forced to make to regain some of his lost status in a postrepublican Florence. Clearly he had more or less successfully "cozied up" to the Medicis by that point, sitting out, or at least not being implicated in, the 1522 plot by many of his friends, including Zanobi Buondelmonti, to whom *The Discourses* is dedicated.[30] But even if Machiavelli has become too compromised by his own comportment (i.e., even if his conspiracy remains on a purely rhetorical level), through his plays Machiavelli shows how his compromised status can be defeated by publicness. He shows that some kind of *virtù* can be brought even to the tired, the old, and the compromised, at least symbolically, thanks to the strategy of publicity, a strategy that neither favors nor protects any one individual person, not even Machiavelli himself, but works solely on behalf of the public as a whole.

Machiavelli and Benjamin

Examining the strategy of adianoeta and the employment of publicness from the perspective of Benjaminian conspiracy, we should note that in the interplay between prince and people we do not seem to have left intentionality behind us. The foils for popular opinion seem no less opinionated than those who stand in for more official positions. From a Benjaminian perspective, why should we care whether Callimaco or Nicia ends up with Lucretia when both of them seem so venal, so intention driven?

This question suggests why the distinction between lying and adianoeta is so crucial from the perspective of a Benjaminian conspiracy. We need to be careful not to romanticize the people's perspective and, in doing so, confine them to their own intentionality (which is, as we see even without reference to Benjamin, deeply compromised). In thinking further about the distinctions between public and private forms of intention, we see that both the prince and the people are engaged in a form of representation but that the latter form is more conducive to the "recognized misrecognitions" that I argue constitute the best kind of resistance to phantasms of control and unity. The people are not "right" or seeing "truth" in their own form of knowledge, but, via the device of adianoeta and the strictures and powers of publicization, theirs is a more overtly and clearly *representational* activity. Given that the prince has no checks on his own belief in truth, no other persons he needs to clear his ideas through, he has no need for a clear recourse to representation. What his advisors tell him, what he himself thinks, will seem to him to be "wrong" or "right," that is, not representations per se but truths (or falsities). While the prince may believe what he thinks to be true, the people on the other hand have no choice but to knowingly "represent" their ideas to one another, whether by speech, writing, or other medium. The delusions of the public are thus explicitly and necessarily rendered legible as acts of representation—with all of the flaws and distortions that such recognition entails. The public's use of the strategy of adianoeta thus allows the prince's unlimited delusion, his ability to consider himself as having stepped outside of representation altogether, to become a weapon against him. The people thus retain the power of "recognizing misrecognition"; the asymmetry between prince and people is produced by the fact that the prince may believe he knows the truth while the people, by virtue of their very plurality, know that they do not.[31] In this way, as mentioned earlier, representation need not be ceded to princes and other sovereign figures as a game that always favors the elites and the powerful.

In an idea that will be echoed when we get to our consideration of Tocqueville—and later with Fanon and Djebar as well—we will see that the knowledge of the people serves not as an accurate depiction of "what is really true" so much as a record of a collective process of producing narratives; it can be seen as accurate only in the way it conveys and reproduces that process. As individuals, members of Machiavelli's public hold onto their intentions as much as ever, but in their plurality we see those intentions held in check, at least to some extent, by the resort to collective representation, by a collectivity rendered as text (this offers perhaps a good working definition of what Machiavelli means, textually speaking, by the term *virtù*).

When they exist in their individual, separate lives, the people are exactly like the prince but without all of his accouterments of power; in this position, they are weaker than he is, susceptible to his manipulations and obfuscations. But when the people are connected to material representations of their own plurality through the recourse to publicization (a practice institutionalized in ancient Rome and potentially revived by reading Machiavelli as a fellow conspirator), they gain, at least potentially, a "crisis-proof" (to cite another term of Benjamin's) position.[32] From this position, various strategies, including adianoeta, become potentially quite devastating to the illusions and hierarchies of princely power, to the earliest manifestations of the phantasmagoria (at least in its modern guise). And Machiavelli's books and plays offer a primer on how these alternative forms of community can be formed and sustained.

The ambiguity that Benjamin displays toward the question of human intentionality is far from perfectly resolved in Machiavelli's work. Yet Machiavelli suggests an intriguing possibility wherein there can actually be a coincidence of interests between human intentionality and "the intention of the sign" (something that we also saw in the *Origin,* where "consciously Machiavellian" plots coincide with "baleful constellations"). Callimaco, to take one example, when left to his own devices, is self-interested, deluded, and deeply compromised. Yet with the intervention of Ligurio/Machiavelli (who certainly has intentions of his own), his intentions become something else. What that "something else" amounts to depends on our reading of the text, but it becomes at least conceivable to read a public mindedness—we might even say *virtù*—in a figure who otherwise is hopelessly lost in his own fantasies. This publicness is not so much found in "real life" as it is produced in and by texts, by a set of speech acts, beliefs, and practices that collectively compose and constitute "the people." In this way, Callimaco's intentions can be said to have become aligned with the "intention of the sign"; his goals become the goals of the public he has been brought into (or, the public he already belonged to, as we saw with Kafka, but which was previously overwritten by idols of self, sensuality, etc.). In this process, Callimaco has been transformed from cad to citizen; he has become a conspirator without ever consciously wanting to or even realizing it.

As for Ligurio, we can see that the role of the "theorist," the conspiratorial mastermind, need not be defeated by his or her own intentionality. Ligurio, like Machiavelli, certainly has his share of nefarious intentions. He seems to be motivated by greed for reward, by resentment against Nicia's ability to have such a wife, and also by the sheer joy of meddling. Yet such motivations do not condemn Ligurio to be unable to actually help or conspire with Callimaco.[33] Ligurio (and perhaps, by extension, Machiavelli as well) is in effect rescued from his own intentionality by the same device that he uses to rescue Callimaco; in both cases a turn to textuality, to fables, disguises, and conspiracies affords these figures an outcome that surpasses whatever they may have originally intended. Similarly, their engagement with the public, via the device of adianoeta, renders the outcomes of their deeds not merely something of their own devising and wishes but something that reflects a larger and more public context.

The one character who seems to get the least from this arrangement is Lucrezia. She bears the indignity of Callimaco's (and Machiavelli's) treatment of her with little, if any, recognition for what she has done and borne (not unlike the historical Lucretia herself). We could conclude from this that Machiavelli's sexism and misogyny ruin (and not in a positive, Benjaminian sense) any promise that his model of conspiracy holds out. At the very least, the fate of Lucrezia alerts us to an aspect of conspiracy that we might otherwise overlook, namely the fact that old injustices and hierarchies do not disappear when conspiracies succeed but remain to trouble us and to be contended with. Whereas some theorists who speak of moving from our current political practices to an "agonic" form of politics imply that all old divisions and hierarchies are somehow erased by our transformation so that we are essentially starting with a clean slate, we see here that the past, the lure of the fetish that compromised us in the first place, is not so easily displaced. The troubling example of Lucrezia reminds us (as we will see further in chapter 6) that the "future" that we seek may not be so different from the past. What might be different however is that through the device of conspiracy a community might become more legible to itself, might have a chance to act in ways that do not simply replicate the perverse ways we are arranged as fully docile subjects of the phantasmagoria. This is not to say that if our conspiracy succeeds, Lucrezia (or Lucretia) will finally get justice, but it means that a different outcome (that is to say, an outcome where the future is not predestined by what has come before it) is possible.

Machiavelli's key insight overall is perhaps that a community is formed by the way it represents itself both to itself as a whole and to its individual members. When that form of representation is controlled by "princes," representation goes underground; it becomes hardened into fantastic "truths" and becomes subject to the prince's whim (or the whim of his advisors), leaving the people destitute and depoliticized. When, on the other hand, representation is rendered a public good and a public activity, the narratives that constitute a community can be allowed to function more openly, more readily identifiable as "representative." We can see how in the face of this visible representation, lives are altered, intentions are displaced (something we will see further in chapter 5). Even from a position of defeat and failure, we see from Machiavelli that the power to take charge of and display representation never leaves a people; whenever they choose, they can, through the conspiracies that Machiavelli depicts in his books and plays, retrieve the power of representation and, in the process, radically alter the landscape of their political existence.

While Machiavelli helps us to conceive what such a politics would look like, how it might actually work, a caveat is perhaps in order. Insofar as Machiavelli *is* emblematic of the Western canon and of the ways that politics is generally conceived, we need to be careful not to read too much "hope" into his strategies. That is to say, we need to watch out (as Kafka does) for the possibility that our conspiracy might fall back into our phantasmagorical sense of agency after all. The vision of a freestanding and self-sustaining republic—Machiavelli's rendition of an updated Roman republic—is surely alluring for the Left in our own time. But as we began to see with Kafka already, such a vision might serve as an idol that interferes with the actual promulgation of left politics. I will return to these questions in the conclusion of this book, where I ask more directly what a politics of conspiracy would look like. For now, let me adopt a certain wary agnosticism in which, for all of his critical strategic help, Machiavelli's vision of a widespread and sustainable form of public discourse may be too good to be true. Or perhaps, more accurately, it remains useful but does not necessarily function on some grand national or international scale (where the dreams of the Left have traditionally resided). It seems that the lessons from Kafka and Benjamin that we draw show us a tougher, more problematic, and more fragmented and ordinary form of politics than what Machiavelli potentially promises (something we began to see in our consideration of Lucrezia as well). To say this does not lessen Machiavelli's importance for this conspiracy, however. In forming a constellation among Machiavelli, Benjamin, and Kafka, I seek to have Machiavelli inform the latter thinkers with tangible, practical strategies that they may themselves be lacking. But at the same time, I seek to have these later thinkers temper Machiavelli's own vision (or visions) of politics with the doubts and limitations that come out of their own, more esoteric form of political theory.

At this point of the book, we have completed our survey of the three chief conspirators we will engage with: Benjamin, Kafka, and Machiavelli, thus finishing Part I. In the following three chapters, which constitute Part II, we will, as already explained, be turning to three pairs of thinkers and writers. In each case I look at a political theorist and a literary figure who share a particular context, both in terms of time and geography. The purpose of this juxtaposition is to bring out the literary qualities of the theorist in question and the political qualities of the literary figure, somewhat effacing the lines between these approaches in a way that is typical of Benjamin himself. Each of these pairs is also intended to further illuminate some of the central questions and concerns about the politics that emerge from our considerations of conspiracy so far. In chapter 4, I will address the question, "How can the phantasmagoria be rendered legible and thereby resisted?" In chapter 5, I return to the question, "What is the place for the human being in the face of a conspiracy that excludes our own intentions?" In chapter 6 I ask, "What positive steps can we take, what ideas of the future may we produce, in the face of the implacable and deeply entrenched nature of the phantasmagoria?"

The following chapter, which tries to answer the first question, examines the work of Tocqueville and Poe in the United States during the early nineteenth century. By looking at these two authors, I seek to show how a rapidly developing phantasmagoria can be rendered legible, how it can be allegorized. Once again, this does not mean that we see "the truth" about the phantasmagoria, but merely that we learn to read it through its component parts. If the phantasmagoria is made of signs, to see those signs qua signs is to resist seeing the world they construct as natural, real or without alternatives (it is to "recognize our misrecognition").

In turning to these thinkers, we are seeking to apply some of Benjamin's own analysis of Baudelaire (who similarly witnessed a growing phantasmagoria in mid-nineteenth-century France) to another time and place. At the same time, we will see, in the intense attention each of these authors pays to the question of representation as a source of political structure, a further elaboration of the powers—and vulnerabilities—of the sign in constituting a society. In Poe in particular, we will see (as Benjamin appreciated) a writer whose works almost forced readers to encounter the physical materiality of the text they were reading. By extension, he also potentially enables his readers to see the world around them as also being material, as composed of signs and hence ripe for conspiratorial resistances.

In our treatment of these authors, we will see further evidence how our individual and collective acts of resistance must remain acts of misrecognition. Even as we seek to "expose" and render legible the phantasmagoria, we must not take recourse to a fantasy of being free of representation. The space that is opened up by our conspiracy remains determined and organized by the sign, but, as we will see further, it also affords us the helpful delusion (not unlike Ulysses himself) that we are navigating ourselves in the course of our resistance. The ability to simultaneously "resign" ourselves to the intention of the sign (and to believe in our own self-determination in so doing) becomes the required stance for the human agent. Our conspiracy with language produces this complicated dance of messianic redemption and "self-delivery," a prerequisite for the nonidolatrous form of politics that we seek.

Part II

4 | Rendering the World into Signs: Alexis de Toqueville and Edgar Allan Poe

Born just a few years apart during the first decade of the nineteenth century, Alexis de Tocqueville and Edgar Allan Poe lived and wrote during much the same period. Tocqueville's *Democracy in America* and Poe's *Narrative of Arthur Gordon Pym* were published within a few years of each other and stand as each author's commentary on the development and nature of the United States in the 1830s. As individuals, Tocqueville and Poe have nearly nothing in common. Tocqueville was a French aristocrat with liberal leanings. He served in French politics in various capacities, including helping to draft the constitution of France's Second Republic. He came to America ostensibly to study the U.S. penal system and ended up writing the hugely influential two-volume *Democracy in America* (of which the second volume seems far more troubled and doubtful than the first). Poe was a troubled, alcoholic, and brilliant American writer. He is mainly known for his short stories, especially in the genres of mystery and horror. He experienced fame in his life ("The Raven," published in 1845, was an instant success), but his life was marred by a hard beginning, his drinking, his wife Virginia's struggle with tuberculosis, and his own premature death at the age of forty.

Despite these differences, when we focus less on these authors as individuals, with their political views and foibles, and more on the texts that they have produced (and in particular, the two texts already mentioned), we find the points of commonality that suggest their respective roles in the conspiracy I am sketching out here.

On the surface of it, Edgar Allan Poe is an easy candidate for this conspiracy—in terms of constellations, he is directly linked, as we will see further, with Baudelaire, who translated *The Narrative of Arthur Gordon Pym* into French, among other writings (and of course Benjamin pays serious attention to Poe as well). Tocqueville, on the other hand, seems completely unrelated and "out of constellation" with the figures I am treating in this book. Of all the writers I am dealing with, he is the most enamored with liberalism and hence the elaboration of the phantasmagoria that it spawned. In his political career, Tocqueville often opposed the Left, and some of his writings on Algeria, as well as the United States, seem to anticipate later formulations of apartheid.[1] Yet as we have seen in chapter 1, even the most compromised of figures (such as Baudelaire) can possibly be candidates for conspiracy when we treat their texts qua texts and not as missives from these individuals' own intentionality. Tocqueville's conscious fascination with liberalism was mixed with a strong distress about where America (in his view, the ultimate liberal society) was heading. He can be (and often is) read as a prophet for all that has gone wrong with America, I would say a prophet of the coming iteration of the phantasmagoria.[2]

Rather than excluding Tocqueville from our conspiracy, I see him, not unlike Baudelaire, as someone who is fully in the maw of what he describes. Both Tocqueville and Poe experienced a phantasmagoria in the making, but if anything, Tocqueville was deeper inside what he describes, precisely because he is not, on the surface, radical in any way.

In terms of choosing the time and place of early to mid-nineteenth-century America more generally, we can recall that Benjamin saw the value of looking at a society as it began to fall under the grip of commodity fetishism, when the phantasmagoria such a fetishism produced had not yet achieved the status of a full-blown "reality." This is why, as already mentioned, he chose to look at Paris during the time of Baudelaire. Through Baudelaire's responses to his time, Benjamin gained a perspective on a phenomenon that in his own time had simply become "how things are," an irrefutable and nearly invisible (because so naturalized) part of the fabric of ordinary life. To turn a similar lens onto the phantasmagoria as it was emerging in America is to truly encounter "the belly of the beast," a witnessing of what was to become (and what remains to this day) the core of global capitalism and liberalism.

Accordingly, in this chapter, I will focus on the advent of industrialization and commodity fetishism in America during the early part of the nineteenth century. In the 1830s, the phantasmagoria (at least the modern version of it) was busily spinning itself into a new and vastly complex form of existence in the United States. The drama of industrialization, the rise of a robust and unfettered capitalism, was transforming a largely agricultural society into a new and powerful nation.

Both authors capture the excitement, the allure, and the dark side of this phenomenon, but they also capture its vulnerability. We see in both

Tocqueville's and Poe's accounts of the growing phantasmagoria (a term that neither of them actually uses, of course, but which has a corollary in their writings) a focus on the question of representation. As we will see further, both authors simultaneously expose the phantasmagoria as "nothing" but representation. At the same time, both of them warn us that representation per se is not the problem for the United States (and, by extension, the rest of the world). On the contrary, the phantasmagoria is produced, as we have already begun to see, by obliterating or forgetting the representational nature of the world, of the communities we have made. For these authors, idolatry comes not from the sign as such, but from our (satanic) hubris, from our considering our own delusions to be "true," "natural," and/or "divine."

Reading Tocqueville and Poe in constellation mutually illuminates the conspiratorial side of both writers. Reading Poe through the lens of Tocqueville serves to politicize Poe's writings; it shows that some of his concerns that appear primarily literary in character have a political valence, one connected to some of the same themes that Tocqueville was dealing with himself. Reading Tocqueville through Poe's lens helps to render subversive and conspiratorial what might otherwise be read as a text that on the whole contributes to (as much as it "describes") the growth of capitalist culture and narratives in the United States. The value of reading Tocqueville in this way is several-fold. On the one hand, portraying an author who plays such a central role in America's own self-understanding as a subversive and a conspirator troubles and complicates that narrative. Perhaps more importantly, if we see Tocqueville as being, in part, an architect of the American narrative, we gain access to ur-narrative codes that a great text like *Democracy in America* offers, thus having greater access to the American narrative more generally (with all the subversive possibilities that implies).

To simplify the comparison that I am making, I will stick largely to the two aforementioned texts, Tocqueville's *Democracy in America* and Poe's *The Narrative of Arthur Gordon Pym* (I will focus on *Democracy in America* exclusively in the case of Tocqueville, while in Poe's case, I will treat other texts as well). Looking at these texts side by side helps to establish some of the parallels between these authors in the way they render the semiotics of American nation-building legible. In the case of both authors, I will pay especially close attention to the question of race as it is pertains to depictions and understandings of the American nation and polity. For each of these authors, race becomes a way to get at the issue of representation and a sense of national identity. For both Tocqueville and

Poe, race is largely a matter of semiotics (unlike for Jefferson, for example, who—at least when it came to African Americans—sought to some extent to impart race with an absolute essentialism).[3] For Tocqueville, as we will see further, race is largely a matter of narratives. Tocqueville offers that the African and Native American races were in danger of having their narratives forgotten, distorted, or stolen even as Anglo Americans were in the process of developing a narrative of their own (one that Tocqueville played a big part in fomenting). For Poe, race relations reflect the logic and treacheries of the issue of representation more generally. The insistence on the meaning of texts, the question of legibility, becomes, as we will see in our analysis of *The Narrative of Arthur Gordon Pym,* a template for a racialized violence, a reflection of the insistence that black letters serve meanings dreamed up and projected onto white pages. In this analysis, semiotic urges both reflect and spill over into the kinds of politics that are actually practiced in the new burgeoning American society. With both writers, race emerges as a symptom of a larger semiotic struggle, one between the insistence on having a given, naturalized narrative or meaning on the one hand, and an acknowledgment of how vulnerable and fungible such narratives actually can be on the other. Both authors suggest that the tension between the ideals and limitations of narrative endeavors leads to the actual practice of politics in the United States, to slavery and genocide.

Reading these texts from our own time allows us to render the fabric of our own contemporary narratives more legible and accessible; we can see the role that semiotics and representation continue to play in the formation of our sense of community, reality, and time. We can also see that, however formidable it may be, the phantasmagoria in both its past and present incarnations is neither inevitable nor impregnable as a model for how we constitute ourselves and our relationships with others.

Alexis de Tocqueville

The Idol and Image of Power

In his introduction to *Democracy in America,* Tocqueville famously tells us that in America he seeks an "image of democracy."[4] Throughout the text—and in a way that accords with other conspirators we treat in this book—Tocqueville makes a running parallel between questions of representation in a semiotic sense and representation as a political process.

"Representation" for Tocqueville thus has a double sense, both a basic building block in producing a polity and also the conduct of that polity's political process. We come to see right away that Tocqueville's approach to the United States and its political system (i.e., democracy), taken as an "image," focuses on the semiotic basis of political life.

This interest in the intersection of semiotics and politics is reinforced by Tocqueville's concern with the "mores" and "passions" of the American people. For Tocqueville (as for other related French writers of his own time and the preceding century such as Montesquieu) the way the citizens of a given nation understand and interpret their own condition—in other words, the way they represent themselves to themselves—has vast importance for the way they actually practice politics.

Yet while he saw it as basic to politics in all of its senses, the question of representation is fraught for Tocqueville. For Tocqueville, as for Benjamin, the more representation as a process is legible as such, the less it poses as true (i.e., "fails"), the better. In his view, there is no question of representation serving to actually produce "truth"; what is being represented, somewhat as we saw with Machiavelli in the previous chapter, is a permanently shifting and unstable set of beliefs and values. At best, representation can offer a snapshot of an endless and myriad work in progress. Yet in the United States Tocqueville sees representation as often veering toward claims of truth nonetheless (and, as we'll see, he participates in such language himself). In his view, this fallacy is particularly marked in the case of Anglo Americans; in their self-regard, Anglo Americans (according to Tocqueville) see themselves not really requiring representation at all insofar as they are just "being who they are" (something that is not true for other communities both in the United States and elsewhere). From a Benjaminian perspective, this kind of hubris can be understood as a kind of idolatry, a chief part of what leads the United States toward the current form of the phantasmagoria.

Tocqueville raises the issue of problematical representation, specifically including the language of idolatry, for example when he describes the relationship between religion and democracy in America. After writing that "The homage due to saints and angels became an almost idolatrous worship [un culte presque idolâtre] amongst the majority of the Christian world,"[5] Tocqueville goes on to state that in "democratic ages . . . it is more particularly important not to allow the homage paid to secondary agents [agents secondaires] to be confounded with the worship due to the Creator alone."[6] Insofar as idolatry falsely promotes such "secondary agents," it threatens the "idea of an only and all-powerful Being, dispensing equal laws in the same manner to every man," the basis, in his view, for democracy itself.[7]

In thinking about this threat, Tocqueville displays an ambivalence that, as we will see, marks much of his work when it comes to the question of representation and its uses. On the one hand, he tells us that the tendency of people living in a democracy (and in particular those living in the United States) is to be contemptuous of figures and their possible idolatrous uses:

> In speaking of philosophical method among the Americans, I have shown that nothing is more repugnant to the human mind in an age of equality than the idea of subjection to forms. Men living at such times are impatient of figures; to their eyes symbols appear to be the puerile artifice which is used to conceal or to set off truths, which should more naturally be bared to the light of open day.[8]

Yet for all the "impatien[ce] of figures" the Americans demonstrate, Tocqueville suggests that we must not abandon representation altogether (an attitude we will see Arendt duplicating in the next chapter). This, despite the ongoing danger of idolatry:

> I firmly believe in the necessity of forms, which fix the human mind in the contemplation of abstract truths, and stimulate its ardor in the pursuit of them, whilst they invigorate its powers of retaining them steadfastly.[9]

Tocqueville goes on to tell us that for all their impatience and contempt for figures and forms, Americans are vulnerable to the temptations of idolatry, perhaps because of that very impatience. As we will see further (and in ways that Tocqueville is not always consistent about) the very attitude of being "nonidolatrous" can itself be the source of a kind of ultimate idolatry. The idea that Americans (and in particular Anglo Americans) see themselves as experiencing "truths . . . bared to the light of open day" suggests as much. Insofar as forms are required to "fix the human mind" when it considers abstractions like equality and democracy, to pretend that one can do away with these representational forms altogether—that is to say, to take one's anti-idolatrous sentiments to the extreme point of dispensing with representation altogether—can in fact lead to an even deeper idolatry, one that is completely disguised as "truth" and hence irremediable.

We see some of this concern for an idolatry that is not recognizable as such when Tocqueville describes the phenomena of centralization in America, another (and possibly related) threat to democracy:

> Centralization succeeds more easily, indeed, in subjecting the external actions of men to a certain uniformity, which at least commands our regard, independently of the objects to which it is applied, like those devotees who worship the statue and forget the deity it represents [*comme ces dévots qui adorent la statue, oubliant la divinité qu'elle représente*].[10]

While in the text it appears that Tocqueville is only talking about centralization in Europe (as opposed to the Americans, who offer "the appearance of disorder"),[11] he tells us that "far from supposing that the American governments are not sufficiently centralized, I shall prove hereafter that they are too much so."[12] Here we see other evidence of the parallels between Tocqueville's semiotic understanding and his analysis of the practice of politics in the United States, for he goes on to write:

> The legislative bodies [in the United States] daily encroach upon the authority of the Government, and their tendency, like that of the French Convention, is to appropriate it entirely to themselves. Under these circumstances the social power is constantly changing hands, because it is subordinate to the power of the people, which is too apt to forget the maxims of wisdom and of foresight in the consciousness of its strength: hence arises its danger; and thus its vigor, and not its impotence, will probably be the cause of its ultimate destruction.[13]

Here, we see once again, a danger of pushing a pure view of representation too far; the people, so sure that they are "representing themselves," allow a faux and idolatrous sense of themselves as a body to replace their own effective self-expression. Here the people's hard-won "maxims of wisdom and of foresight" are eclipsed by their own hubris (the "consciousness of its strength"). He makes a similar point when he writes:

> I am convinced that democratic nations are most exposed to fall beneath the yoke of a central administration, for several reasons, amongst which is the following. The constant tendency of these nations is to concentrate all the strength of the Government in the hands of the only power that directly represents the people, because

beyond the people nothing is to be perceived but a mass of equal individuals confounded together. But when the same power is already in possession of all the attributes of the Government, it can scarcely refrain from penetrating into the details of the administration.[14]

One could chalk up viewpoints such as these to Tocqueville's own aristocratic distaste for populism and egalitarianism (and there is no denying that he had these tendencies, however moderated they were in his case). Yet by focusing on his understanding of such behavior as being potentially "idolatrous," we can also read such a sentiment as betraying a belief that so-called populism—and for that matter democracy—in America masks a collective delusion (as opposed to the specific imposition of the delusions of a ruler or oligarchy that one finds in most, if not all, other countries).

Tocqueville's point here is that both Europe and the United States are centralized despite the latter's appearance as a very decentralized and even "anarch[ic]" space.[15] In both cases, centralization involves subjecting a political community to a particular, and idolatrous, style of reading. In the case of the United States, it seems as if centralization is even more pernicious than in Europe, especially in the long run, both because it disguises itself (as semianarchic) and because it is collectively held and practiced by Anglo Americans as a whole (and thus not resolvable by a simple case of "regime change"). For Tocqueville this collective idolatry represents a kind of mass hubris wherein the rough-and-tumble of decision making is replaced by some great and imaginary "image," we might say an image of democracy itself. As we see, this image or idol actually substitutes for and displaces actual democratic practices, leaving a faux semblance in its stead.

Read in this way, Tocqueville can be seen as a prophet of the phantasmagoria to come; the lack of some clearly legible "central" power (which permits centralization to continue while disguised as its opposite), the spread of delusion to one and all, the idolatrous nature of reading and perception, and, above all, the use of images of democracy in a way that denudes the political process it supposedly represents, amount to a practice of political idolatry in America. Such a view aligns Tocqueville's analysis of the United States with Benjamin's own comments that fascism (and presumably by extension, capitalism as well) "render[s politics] aesthetic."[16] That is to say, he too seems to see that the forms of representation (as opposed to its content) can hijack the political process, replacing substantive and collection action with empty promises. The aesthetics of such a politics can be seen most clearly in Tocqueville's dire warnings about the future: the phantasmagoria that we know today was new in his time, but it was weaving a narrative that was in short time to become for all intents and purposes the "reality" that we continue to inhabit.

Sovereignty and Opinion

Reading Tocqueville in this darker and more subversive way might illuminate and destabilize his claim that Anglo Americans are the first "to establish and maintain the sovereignty of the people."[17] While such a claim is usually read in a positive light, reading Tocqueville through the lens of conspiracy suggests a much more problematic meaning for such a term. As mentioned earlier, it is generally held that Tocqueville begins his study by being ambiguous about the United States and that his opinions only grow darker, especially by the time he sits down to write volume 2.[18] In his treatment of the idea of sovereignty, we see some of this developing ambiguity. For Tocqueville, sovereignty is a stealth principle, one that operates behind the scenes even as it serves as a prerequisite for the functions of political life that are contained within its grand narrative structure. He writes:

> The principle of the sovereignty of the people, which is to be found, more or less, at the bottom of all almost all human institutions, generally remains concealed from view. It is obeyed without being recognized, or if for a moment it be brought to light, it is hastily cast back into the gloom of the sanctuary.[19]

For Tocqueville the idea of the sovereignty of the people is one that is frequently (or maybe always) misrepresented either by "the wily and despotic of every age" or by "the votes of a timid or an interested minority" or even by "the silence of a people."[20]

Yet in America, Tocqueville seems, at least initially, to see an exception to this inevitability. In chapter 4 of volume 1, he writes:

> At the present day the principle of the sovereignty of the people has acquired, in the United States, all the practical development that the imagination can conceive. It is unencumbered by those fictions which have been thrown over it in other countries [*Il s'est dégagé de toutes les fictions dont on a pris soin de l'environner ailleurs*], and it appears in every possible form, according to the exigency of the occasion.[21]

Despite the contrary warnings he gives elsewhere in *Democracy in America,* we see Tocqueville here subscribing to the idea that "unencumbered by . . . fictions" as it is, American popular sovereignty seems to be "true," not so much a representation of the people's "will," but that will itself, directly expressed.

Yet such a sentiment goes against the vast bulk of his writing in *Democracy in America*. As we have already begun to see, in much of Tocqueville's account, the citizens of the United States are no more immune to fictions than anyone else. Such fictions can be seen in particular in the case of popular opinion, which for Tocqueville has an unusual prominence in the United States. While opinion may seem to offer an inherently "democratic" (that is to say, decentralized, plural, and unscripted) basis of representation, for Tocqueville, the power and even tyranny of opinion actually collude with and produce the unprecedented centralization of power he espies in America more generally. Thus, for example, in chapter 3 of volume 2, Tocqueville writes:

> [The] never-dying, ever-kindling hatred, which sets a democratic people against the smallest privileges, is peculiarly favorable to the gradual concentration of all political rights in the hands of the representative of the State alone. The sovereign, being necessarily and incontestably above all the citizens, excites not their envy, and each of them thinks he strips his equals of the prerogatives which he concedes to the crown. The man of a democratic age is extremely reluctant to obey his neighbor who is his equal . . . he loves continually to remind him of the common dependence in which both of them stand to the same master.[22]

Thus can a multitude "freely" will itself into subservience. We saw something of this same sentiment in Machiavelli's conviction that a people who did not have the institutional capacity to mutually inform one another, that is to say, a people who were "represented" *in toto* rather than in their myriad diversity, became, for all intents and purposes, subject to the manipulation of princes, who learned to speak on behalf of this mass. For Tocqueville, even without "princes," such a process leads to a kind of mass tyranny; in American democracy the opinions of the people are shared by the state in the form of a mutuality that in fact reinforces the centralizing power of the state:

> [The] common sentiments [such as love of equality and uniformity] which, in democratic nations, constantly unite the sovereign

and every member of the community in one and the same conviction, establish a secret and lasting sympathy between them.[23]

Here, a system of government wherein each individual seems to be left to
do pretty much as she or he pleases eventually devolves into a depoliticized space, a place where one's own passions (read intentions) collude
with the very sorts of oppressions that democracy is supposed to release
them from:

> Thus [the sovereign government] every day renders the exercise of
> the free agency of man less useful and less frequent; it circumscribes
> the will within a narrower range, and gradually robs a man of all
> the uses of himself.[24]

What we see here is a description of the new phantasmagoria that is coming, wherein the appearance of democracy, of "free will" and agency as a
basic principle of government disguises a usurpation of power, a state that
"provides for [the people's] security, foresees and supplies their necessities, facilitates their pleasures, manages their principal concerns" and generally "spare[s] them all the care of thinking and all the trouble of living."[25] These passages describe the rise of the very sort of compromised
intentionality, disguised as one's own "opinion," that we see Benjamin doing battle against one century later.[26]

Once again, all of this could be read (as many have) as the grousing of
an aristocrat who, while in awe of democracy, fears the loss of a power and
privilege that came as his birthright. Yet, if one pays attention to Tocqueville's treatment of representation, we see something more potentially
subversive afoot. Rather than committing to a wholesale condemnation of
democracy, Tocqueville's criticism may simply be oriented toward the
form of "representative" democracy practiced in the United States. It is
well worth noting that in the original French version of *Democracy in
America*, Tocqueville does not say that in America he sought "the image of
democracy" as we find in most English translations, but rather "an image"
[*une image de la démocratie*].[27] However inconsequential this difference
may seem, it suggests that there may be more than one form, or image, of
democracy, and that the one that he finds actively being practiced in the
United States may not be the best or only alternative. In reading Tocqueville conspiratorially, and by focusing on his analysis of representation
qua representation, we can see a radical and subversive possibility in this

author, one that does not turn its back on democracy but rather understands that democracy is not possible without a corresponding theory of
(semiotic) representation that affords it the radical decentralization that it
seeks (and pretends to already have).

Race and Narrative

We can perhaps see most clearly the dangers and costs of the Anglo American version of representation when we consider Tocqueville's treatment
of the question of race in America. Like Jefferson before him, and many
other authors who wrote about America, Tocqueville responded to the
atrocities of slavery and genocide that marked racial relations in the
United States. In his approach to race, Tocqueville shares racist beliefs
with many of his contemporaries (as evidenced, as we have already seen,
by his writings on Algeria).[28] At the same time, by rendering race itself a
question of representation, he—or rather his text—offers a means by
which to potentially subvert or resist more widespread contemporary
racial constructions.

Consistent with his analysis of politics in general, the question of race
is for Tocqueville at least in part a matter of semiotics and narrative. Of
the three main races he considers, African, Native, and European (and in
particular Anglo) Americans, we see three different styles of narrative and
three different outcomes.

To begin with African Americans, for Tocqueville, this community was
unable to assert itself and rebel against slavery (at least in any kind of
widespread and effective way) because its own narrative was effectively
erased. Tocqueville writes:

> [The African American slave] has lost all remembrance of his coun-
> try; the language which his forefathers spoke is never heard around
> him; he abjured their religion and forgot their customs when he
> ceased to belong to Africa, without acquiring any claim to Euro-
> pean privileges. But he remains half way between the two commu-
> nities; sold by the one, repulsed by the other; finding not a spot in
> the universe to call by the name of country, except the faint image
> of a home which the shelter of his master's roof affords.[29]

Here again, we see a basic problem of representation: in Tocqueville's rendition: the African American has no tale to tell, cannot even remember her or
his own language. Tocqueville is either unaware of or not interested in the

various forms of religion, dance, music, song, and, indeed, language evoking Africa that did and do persist among African Americans. According to Tocqueville, without any ability to determine their own narrative, to represent themselves, as it were, African Americans are utterly disempowered.

For Tocqueville, Native Americans are also displaced, albeit in different ways:

> When the North American Indians had lost their sentiment of attachment to their country; when their families were dispersed, their traditions obscured, and the chain of their recollection broken; when all their habits were changed, and their wants increased beyond measure, European tyranny rendered them more disorderly and less civilized than they were before.[30]

For all of Native Americans' similarity with African Americans in terms of narrative disruption, the key difference for Tocqueville comes in the way each community views itself. Critically, for Tocqueville, African Americans have no choice but to emulate the European, to take their narrative as their own, even though this narrative explicitly excludes them. Thus the African American "makes a thousand fruitless efforts to insinuate himself amongst men who repulse him; he conforms to the tastes of his oppressors, adopts their opinions, and hopes by imitating them to form a part of their community."[31] In this telling (which once again ignores or is ignorant of the myriad forms of African American resistance), Africans Americans are forced to occupy someone else's narrative framework, a deep and possibly permanent disadvantage. The Native American, on the other hand, "has his imagination inflated with the pretended nobility of his origin, and lives and dies in the midst of these dreams of pride. Far from desiring to conform his habits to ours, he loves his savage life as the distinguishing mark of his race."[32] Thus Native Americans still have a narrative, but it is one that is distorted by their encounter with Europeans (they are "more disorderly and less civilized than they were before"). In part, Native Americans are forced to perceive themselves via the projected fantasies of the Europeans (including their "pretended nobility"). Their new narrative portrays them to themselves (according to Tocqueville anyway) as the Europeans see them: doomed, noble, fading. Such a narrative does not stem from their own experience or traditions and hence ensures their demise, at least in terms of being a people that is able to represent itself.

In his discussion of race, Tocqueville does not ignore the question of color, especially as it relates to slavery. Yet once again, for him, color is largely a semiotic rather than an immutable, biological marker of race. He tells us that whereas among the ancients (Europeans), slaves and their masters were of the same race, "amongst the moderns, the abstract and transient fact of slavery is fatally united to the physical and permanent fact of color."[33] Color does not necessarily reveal something "natural" about slavery (Tocqueville calls the arrangement unnatural at several points); rather it designates a targeted community; in the American context, having a darker shade of skin is meant to be read as signifying slavery itself.

The loss or distortion of narrative is not unique to people of color either. Tocqueville gives an example of French Canadians who have in effect swapped a European narrative for something more "indigenous." He writes, "These French settlers were worthy people, but idle and uninstructed: they had contracted many of the habits of savages."[34] He also says that due to their greater propensity to intermarry with Native Americans, French Americans came to resemble them and to share their fate and— even more critically—their narrative (itself a product and reflection of colonialism and genocide):

> [The French in North America] were not slow in connecting themselves with the daughters of the natives, but there was an unfortunate affinity between the Indian character and their own: instead of giving the tastes and habits of civilized life to the savages, the French too often grew passionately fond of the state of wild freedom they found them in. They become the most dangerous of the inhabitants of the desert, and won the friendship of the Indian by exaggerating his vices and virtues.[35]

In this way, the French become, perhaps even more than Native Americans themselves, subscribers to a narrative that is a product of fantasy, in this case a fantasy that is of their own creation. Such fantasies are projected onto a people who have the misfortune to be in the way of Anglo American ambitions. The "wildness" the French succumb to is not "natural," not really "native" at all, but a product of the clash of narratives that occurs across the North American continent. For Tocqueville, their change of narrative condemns French Americans to a marked inferiority to Anglo Americans themselves: "The [Anglo] Americans, who were perhaps [the French Canadians'] inferiors, in a moral point of view, were immeasurably superior to them in intelligence: they were industrious, well informed, rich, and accustomed to govern their own community."[36]

In considering the relations between the three races in America (or at least the three races he treats) Tocqueville offers an illuminating vignette: As he was traveling through a wood by a fountain (or spring) in Alabama by a pioneer's house,

> An Indian woman appeared, followed by a negress, and holding by the hand a little white girl of five or six years old, whom I took to be the daughter of the pioneer. A sort of barbarous luxury set off the costume of the Indian; rings of metal were hanging from her nostrils and ears, her hair, which was adorned with glass beads, fell loosely upon her shoulders. . . . The negress was clad in squalid European garments. They all three came and seated themselves upon the banks of the fountain; and the young Indian, taking the child into her arms, lavished upon her such fond caresses as mothers give; while the negress endeavored by various little artifices to attract the attention of the young Creole.[37]

For Tocqueville, this tableau was "peculiarly touching," speaking to the intimacies as well as the vast distances between the "three races of men which people North America."[38] The scene also serves as a kind of allegory for race in America; while the Native American woman is clad in "barbarous luxury," the African American woman is clad in "squalid European garments." The first has a semblance of her own past to draw upon (or rather a "past" as projected by Tocqueville's own fantasies) while the latter is depicted as being bereft and abandoned. While the Native American seems to feel a real affection for the European girl, the African American must resort to artifice to keep her position. In either case, the result is the same: a subservience to the European narrative that is so totalizing in its representational authority that Tocqueville does not even feel the need to tell us how the European girl herself is dressed.

Given this depiction of the respective peoples of North America, it is tempting to say that Anglo Americans have a fully robust narrative while African and Native Americans do not. Yet this is not the case for Tocqueville. In his view, it is not true that Anglo Americans are "authentic" or "genuine" in a way that African Americans and Native Americans are not. Indeed for Tocqueville, as we have already seen, the Anglo American narrative is perhaps the most distorted of them all. Insofar as we have already seen that Anglo Americans often do seem to consider themselves as not requiring representation (whether of the political or semiotic varieties), their narrative, for Tocqueville, is perhaps particularly subject to the idolatrous errors he sees being practiced in the United States more generally (and which, as we have seen, he practices himself on occasion).

It seems that the very power that Anglo Americans enjoy vis-à-vis other races and nations, be they Native, African, French, or Spanish, has left them a sense of privilege with vast (and negative) semiotic consequences. The sense of manifest destiny, of race privilege and similar forms of hubris are part of why Anglo Americans, in Tocqueville's view, engage in political and social idolatry, why they feel free to inflict on other peoples the dehumanizing practices they engage in.

We see in this juxtaposition of three races the true costs of a narrative that does not even regard itself as such. On the one hand, for Tocqueville, Anglo Americans are slowly sinking (they will sink a great deal further in the coming decades) into a collective delusion from which there is no easy escape. Far from Anglo Americans having a valid narrative of their own,

> Not only does democracy make every man [presumably he means every Anglo American man—and woman] forget his ancestors, but it hides his descendents, and separates his contemporaries from him; it throws him back forever upon himself alone, and threatens in the end to confine him entirely within the solitude of his own heart.[39]

At the same time, the sense of entitlement, of being "without fiction," also engenders a lopsided racial politics whereby other communities, and other ways of seeing and organizing the world, are cast aside as inferior. Other communities, in this rendition, are savage and somehow less real exactly because they must suffer from representation while the Anglo American apparently doesn't need to.

Tocqueville's work stands both as an appreciation of the energy and power of Anglo Americans and as a warning about the hubris of thinking one is more authentic than anyone else. In the end, I do not read *Democracy in America* as a call for a "true" narrative of a people, but rather as a call to recognize all narratives as being flawed, imperfect, and vulnerable, even while remaining absolutely necessary for any community. As we have seen with Kafka as well, communities are always organized by the collective delusions we all subscribe to, but that does not mean that they are totalized by those delusions. When the representational functions of community building are denied, they become idols, unseen and depoliticized sources of mythology. When, on the other hand, they become legible as such, when our acts of self-representation become tangible and politicized, a "conspiracy" with language becomes possible as a way to decenter and dislodge the primacy of such myths.

For Tocqueville, without the ability to tell one's own, collective story, however arbitrary or delusional such a telling might be, a community loses itself. In the case of America we see such a loss occurring, both for those communities that have been targeted by Anglo Americans and for Anglo Americans themselves (albeit in dramatically different ways). A community is anchored not by the "truth" of its narrative but by the narrative's mere existence as a record of its actions and viewpoints. To be represented is in some sense to exist as a community, to have a political space in which one's own practices can emerge, however partially and imperfectly.

Even as Tocqueville vigorously promotes various sets of delusions as regards the three races that he treats in America, his text offers a way to step aside from the "truth" of his narrative, the authority of his own voice, and see instead the representational function at work. The text offers the means by which such constructions can be resisted and conspired against, even as it apparently promotes the very racist views that a particular notion of representation produces (and the views that Tocqueville himself held). In this way, when we read Tocqueville through a subversive lens, we can appreciate certain potentials in his texts even while the author was complicit in many of the phenomena he worries about. He himself subscribes to many of the racist fantasies and projections that he ascribes to Americans (as we have seen), and yet he—or rather his text—also renders those fantasies legible and therefore potentially vulnerable.

Tocqueville and the Future

For all of his overt allegiance to the conventions and politics of his own time, there are moments when Tocqueville evinces, despite himself, a view of time and narrative that seems outright Benjaminian. There are moments in his text, in other words, when he moves more readily into constellation with the other thinkers we are reading alongside him. In his introduction to *Democracy in America* Tocqueville describes the need for a new "science of politics," one that threatens to produce the precise phantasm of "truth" that so much of the rest of the two volumes sets out to expose.

> This, however, is what we think of least; launched in the middle of a rapid stream, we obstinately fix our eyes on the ruins which may still be described upon the shore we have left, whilst the current sweeps us along, and drives us backwards towards the gulf.[40]

Such an image suggests the subversive side of Tocqueville; even if he wants to join the Anglo American experiment in certainty and "nonrepresentation" (i.e., "science"), he reverts, even by negative example, to a view of the world that is perfectly allegorical (a view offered to us, as is appropriate, by an actual allegory). He says we "obstinately fix our eyes on the ruins" that are behind us rather than in front us, thus reproducing, however accidentally, the same stance and gaze as Benjamin's angel of history (which the latter discusses in his "Theses on Philosophy of History"). In the original French, this passage of Tocqueville's is perhaps even more redolent of Benjamin: "placés au milieu d'un fleuve rapide, nous fixons obstinément les yeux vers quelques débris qu'on aperçoit encore sur le rivage, tandis que le courant nous entraîne et nous pousse à reculons vers des abîmes."[41] Here, we go back, not toward the gulf [of Mexico], but toward the "ruins" (*les abîmes*) we have spotted on the shore. To look at the ruin instead of the shining truthful future is, for Benjamin, the correct posture to take; it offers the appropriate and conspiratorial stance vis-à-vis the concept of history and the idea of "progress," focusing not on truth but on the debris and failure of representation.

Although Tocqueville tells us that the "science of politics" that rescues us from such delusions is what we "think of least," in fact, and in part thanks to his own interventions, it has become part and parcel of our reality, what we "think of most." Yet in a book that attempts a systematic and perhaps even scientific view of a society, we also see, particularly in his poetic or allegorical modes, exactly the sort of subversive, explicitly representational forms of reading and perceiving that such a science serves to oppose and overwrite. Such moments speak of an undercurrent in *Democracy in America,* one that is indeed moving "backwards towards the ruins" and that suggests another way, another form of democracy and relationality altogether, "an[other] image of democracy."[42]

Edgar Allan Poe

Moving from Tocqueville to Poe, we come to a figure that occupies a much clearer and more unambiguous position in Benjamin's conspiracy. When it comes to our treatment of Poe in particular, a connection to Benjamin is easy to make. Poe was a major source of inspiration for Baudelaire, who in turn inspired Benjamin himself.[43] As R. E. Foust tells us: "Poe's mystic writing is the core of Baudelaire's symbolist theory of 'correspondences'" (an idea that Benjamin makes much of in his "On Some Motifs in Baudelaire").[44]

For both Baudelaire and Benjamin, their connection to a prior source (Poe and Baudelaire respectively) came as a kind of rescue when times were particularly dark. In his comments on Poe, offered in the beginning of his translation of some of Poe's best-known writings into French, Baudelaire sees the same strange mixture of damnation and salvation that Benjamin spotted in Baudelaire himself. In his appraisal of Poe, Baudelaire also demonstrates the same appreciation for the benefits of failure that Benjamin discovers in him. Evoking a similar sort of "Satanism," Baudelaire writes that for Poe "the devil will enter through a keyhole. Any perfection will be the flaw in [his] armor and a superlative quality the germ of [his] damnation."[45]

Despite his own allegiance to "modernity," Baudelaire appreciates Poe's rejection of the idea of progress and, with it, a certain pattern of understanding time and history (again, very much like Benjamin). He even includes Machiavelli (or at least "Machiavellianism"), useful for our own purposes, in this rejection of temporal linearity, hence widening the interconnections of our conspiracy a bit further:

> Poe thought progress, that grand modern idea, was an ecstasy of flycatchers, and he called the *perfecting* of the human habitation scars and rectangular abominations [*des cicatrices et des abominations rectangulaires*]. Poe was over there [i.e., in America] a singularly solitary mind. He only believed in the unchanging, in the eternal, the *self-same* [in English in original], and he enjoyed—cruel privilege in a society in love with itself!—the great good sense, in a Machiavellian way, which went before the wise men, like a shining column, across the desert of history.[46]

By including Poe (and, at least gesturally, Machiavelli) in the conspiracy Benjamin advocates we are merely bringing things full circle. And there are circles within circles; Kafka was influenced by Poe as well, and, of course, Kafka influenced Benjamin too, as we have already seen. Being aware of these shared connections allows us, once again, to decenter Benjamin's own role as "author" or origin (taken in its more ordinary sense) of this conspiracy, to see the influences that run both backward and forward (and sideways) through time.

In many ways, Poe can be read as conspiratorial even without the benefit of Benjamin's analysis. Paranoia and a sense of menace animate nearly every one of his stories, and often his work is downright baroque in its rendition of violence and danger; truly a conspiratorial atmosphere pervades his fiction.

As with Kafka's work, many authors have spent enormous amounts of time and energy seeking to determine Poe's underlying motivations.[47] These studies are helpful and important but from a conspiratorial angle—at least of the Benjaminian sort—it almost doesn't matter what Poe thought or intended. Even as Tocqueville's own quasi-liberal leanings do not mean he cannot be read as a coconspirator, so too with Poe, we can't assume that his dark and subversive style automatically makes him a radical. Even without delving into his conscious and deliberate forms of subversion, a reading of Poe's texts uncovers many of the same conspiratorial devices that we note in the other authors in this study. What distinguishes Poe in this regard, his main contribution to our conspiracy, is the fact that he is a master at exposing the materiality in and of texts. Few authors match Poe's intense attention to the physicality of material objects: in his hands, bodies become corpses, letters become signs.[48] Perhaps even more to the point, in Poe's hands the physical materiality of the text we are actually reading is brought to our attention. While ordinarily the whiteness of the page and the blackness of the text disappear into the background, so that we become completely unaware of the process of representation, Poe brings this materiality into focus, thus making the process of reading more legible, part of what the text conveys or does.

When we read Poe in constellation with an explicitly political writer like Tocqueville, we are better able to grasp the political valence of his work. Poe makes his texts so legible qua texts that they become in a sense undeniably allegorical; the connections he makes between the materiality of the text and the world that text conveys suggest how such an allegorical process can be extended to matters of politics. At the same time, Poe's treatment of texts does not offer some kind of "behind the scenes" clarity that is otherwise unavailable to us as readers; as with other conspirators we have looked at, what Poe makes visible is not the "truth" that the narrative points to but merely the facticity of the narrative process itself. We see Poe's work as a testament to both the power and the limits of textual materialism; he shows the text's power to expose and disrupt the hold of the phantasmagoria that was busily being reproduced during Poe's lifetime, as well as the limits of a textual materiality that gives no insight, produces no truth, and ultimately, does not free us from the burdens and promise of representation and misrecognition. These basic aspects of Poe's work, and the political implications they convey, come out perhaps most clearly in Poe's great (and only) novel *The Narrative of Arthur Gordon Pym.*

The Narrative of Arthur Gordon Pym

The *Narrative of Arthur Gordon Pym* explicitly sets up a parallel between a geographical journey depicted in the pages of the text and a semiotic journey to the end of meaning, language, and text. In the story we sail from the safe harbors of the symbolic universe that we inhabit (in this case New Bedford, Massachusetts) to the far reaches, or limits, of representation (the southernmost oceans). At the end of the book, we encounter the raw, terrifying void at the bottom or limit of the world and also, by extension, at the bottom or limit of the page. *The Narrative of Arthur Gordon Pym* is extremely self-reflective insofar as it constantly reminds us that we are in fact reading a book, one composed of white pages and marked with black symbols; in performing its own plot of sailing to the limits of representation, it reminds us too that the text has definite and limited physical dimensions.[49] In so firmly anchoring a metaphor in our actual experience of reading, as well as making ongoing analogies between the symbols of this text and the world that the text represents, Poe's *Narrative* once again shows both the power and limits of representation. The power of representation is manifest in the way it organizes and animates our lives, even, as we will see further, when we have seen it "for what it is" (i.e., "only" representation). The exposure of its limits (i.e., the fact that it is merely and only text, black marks on white paper) prevents us from slipping into the ultimate delusion that what the text conveys is actually "true," something that breaks free from representation (and hence the text) altogether.

The ongoing parallel that the book makes between textual representation and the "real world" can be demonstrated from the outset by the book's title. As with many books of that period, *The Narrative of Arthur Gordon Pym* has a long, descriptive title. In this particular case, in addition to serving as a summary of the book's plot, the title also establishes the connection between the geographical journey it describes and the physical materiality of the book in which that description is to be found. More specifically, it establishes the connection between the direction "south" and the lowest boundaries of the pages of the text. The title, as it was printed in the original 1838 edition, reads:

THE NARRATIVE
OF
ARTHUR GORDON PYM
OF NANTUCKET

COMPRISING THE DETAILS OF A MUTINY AND
ATROCIOUS BUTCHERY
ON BOARD THE AMERICAN BRIG GRAMPUS,
ON HER WAY TO
THE SOUTHERN SEAS, IN THE MONTH OF JUNE, 1827

WITH AN ACCOUNT OF THE RECAPTURE OF
THE VESSEL BY THE
SURVIVERS; THEIR SHIPWRECK AND
SUBSEQUENT HORRIBLE
SUFFERINGS FROM FAMINE; THEIR DELIVERANCE BY
MEANS OF THE BRITISH SCHOONER JANE GUY; THE
BRIEF CRUISE OF THIS LATTER VESSEL IN THE
ANTARCTIC OCEAN; HER CAPTURE, AND THE
MASSASCRE OF HER CREW AMONG THE
GROUP OF ISLANDS IN THE

EIGHTY-FOURTH PARALLEL OF SOUTHERN LATITUDE;
TOGETHER WITH THE INCREDIBLE ADVENTURES AND
DISCOVERIES

STILL FURTHER SOUTH

TO WHICH THAT DISTRESSING CALAMITY GAVE RISE.[50]

Here, the physical form of the words, including the way the lines are spaced, forms a kind of arrow (or prow of a ship) pointing downward to the bottom of the page. As the adventures described in the text become more dramatic and amazing, the text becomes more cryptic and evocative, capped off by the claim to go "still further south" in bold, large letters which are indeed written in the "south" of the page. In this way, the title serves as a map for the narrative, both figuratively and literally. Poe, a master of semiotics, suggests here that the mysteries of the plot may be accompanied by mysteries that affect our act of reading this book as well.

This connection between the physicality of the text and the plot is re-inforced relatively early in the actual narrative. The hero of the book, a young man—Arthur Gordon Pym himself—is a stowaway in a boat where his friend Augustus is working as a sailor. While hiding from the crew, he is enclosed in total blackness and falls into a deep sleep. Pym wakes up starving and wracked with thirst with a sense that a great deal of time has passed, yet Augustus, who is supposed to feed him and give him water, mysteriously fails to appear. After Pym has sat a long, awful time in the pitch black, his dog—also a passenger on the ship—appears with a piece of paper tied around its neck. At first, Pym is forced to simply feel the paper and wonder at what is written upon it. Then he manages to create a dim and brief light by rubbing some phosphorous that he happens to have with him onto one side of the page. With this light, Pym is crushed to see that the paper contains nothing but a "dreary and unsatisfactory blank."[51] It then occurs to him that he might have been looking at the wrong side of the page. He writes: "It was very probable, I considered, that some words were written upon that side of the paper which had not been examined—but which side was that?"[52] He tries to feel the thickness of the pen marks but cannot; both sides of the page are equally flat and featureless in a tactile sense. Eventually, he manages to ascertain which side of the paper still has phosphorous, conjecturing that the message must be on the other side. Finally, rubbing on the remaining few bits of phosphorus in his possession, he sees the text but the light being so brief, he can only read the last few words, which are "*blood—your life depends upon lying close.*"[53] Responding to this note, Pym tells us:

> Had I been able to ascertain the entire contents of the note . . . even although it should have revealed a story of disaster the most unspeakable, could not, I am firmly convinced, have imbued my mind with one tithe of the harrowing and yet indefinable horror with which I was inspired by the fragmentary warning thus received.[54]

The single word "blood," taken out of its context and grammar, particularly horrifies the narrator:

> And "*blood*" too, that word of all words—so rife at all times with mystery, and suffering, and terror . . . how chillily and heavily (disjointed, as it thus was, from any foregoing words to qualify or render it distinct) did its vague syllables fall, amid the deep gloom of my prison, into the innermost recesses of my soul![55]

Here Poe is anticipating something that Benjamin will write some one hundred years later in *The Origin of German Tragic Drama*. After noting (as we have already seen) that "the language of the baroque is constantly convulsed by rebellion on the part of the elements which make it up," Benjamin goes on to give an example of what he means.[56] He describes a passage from the "Herod-drama" of Calderón:

> By chance, Mariamne, the wife of Herod, catches sight of the fragments of a letter in which her husband orders that, in the event of his own death, she should be killed in order to preserve his supposedly threatened honour. She picks up these fragments from the ground and gives an account of their content in extremely evocative lines. 'What do they contain? / Death is the very first word / which I encounter; here is the word honour, /And there I see Mariamne. /What does this mean? Heaven help me! / For much is said in the three words / Mariamne, death, and honour. / Here it says: secretly; here: / dignity; here: commands; and here: ambition; / And here, it continues: if I die / But what doubt can there be? I am already informed / By the folds of the paper, / Which are related / to the crime they enfold. / O field, on your green carpet / Let me piece them together![57]

Benjamin goes on to write of this:

> Even in their isolation the words reveal themselves as fateful. Indeed, one is tempted to say that the very fact that they still have a meaning in their isolation lends a threatening quality to this remnant of the meaning they have kept.[58]

In the case of both authors, when language is fragmented, its materiality emerges more clearly, and, as a result, the basic gesture of the language works more immediately and legibly upon us to produce intense states of fright and curiosity.[59]

What we have in this series of events Poe describes is an encapsulation of the literal experience of reading a novel, a journey through representation that moves from the physicality of the page that tells nothing, to the text that can't be felt, to the particle of meaning that hints at great profundities, perhaps exactly because it is merely a fragment. When we finally find out the full text of the passage, "*I have scrawled this with blood—your life depends upon lying close*"—we find out that his friend's absence is due to a mutiny on the ship. It is indeed a bit anticlimactic.[60] We see here how representation works within and in response to the physical limits of the page. The more this system of representation fails to achieve meaning, the more fraught it becomes; we come to experience the text as a "fragmentary warning."

What this short segment allegorizes is the frantic need for meaning that we bring to the act of reading and interpretation. Pym is driven to desperation to discern the meaning of this text, but the author, in a style very reminiscent of Kafka, playfully withholds that meaning and even shows that the actual meaning is far less powerful than Pym (the author's foil in the text) imagines it to be. As we already saw in the earlier chapter on Kafka, texts and representations demand and produce a response in us qua texts. We remain determined by them even or especially when we recognize them for "what they are."

A Voyage to Tsalal

Another, richer, example of this understanding of the power (and limits) of representation comes late in the book when, after many adventures and after changing vessels, Pym crosses the "eighty forth parallel of southern latitude" (the point where the "ship" of the narrative sails across the line of the title proclaiming: "STILL FURTHER SOUTH") and enters a world of fantastic imagery with strange lights and weird plants and creatures floating in the water. Here, Pym and his crewmates come across a black island. Everything on this island is black, even the water. The island's inhabitants are a black-skinned people called the Tsalalians who have an abject horror of whiteness. The island is set with huge mysterious black gorges. When they enter into and explore these gorges, Pym and his crewmates discover that they are actually giant carved letters. The self-referentiality of the book begins to close in on itself when we see these characters examining and exploring (reading?) the very letters that convey their existence to the readers of the book.

Here, at the extreme ends of symbolization, we see an almost absurd literalization of the question of representation; in the far south, the literal becomes embodied. The text virtually forces the reader to see representation for what it is, black marks on a white page.

The Tsalalians' fear of whiteness becomes literally enacted when they try to kill all of the white sailors, including Pym. Violence and hatred are endemic throughout this novel but become most clearly actualized as the novel nears its conclusion. As we get closer to the heart of the mystery long promised by the novel's extended title, the root of that violence seems to be linked to the question of representation itself. The Tsalalians seem meant to stand in as living representatives of the blackness of letters and in this case, as embodied symbols, they have their own agenda. Here, at the limits of representation, it might be said that the symbols see themselves as no longer needing to represent anything at all, to be freed from the tiresome restraints of "meaning" whatever the white sailor/authors want them to mean.[61] In another version of Kafka's notion of raising a mighty paw against Halakah, the symbols themselves have rebelled against what they symbolize, in this case instigating a full-fledged race war.

We can see too that in this parable Poe helps to explain how actual race relations in America are affected by our approach to representation. As in Tocqueville, in Poe the burden of representation is shunted onto one community ("the black letters") while the other appears not to be representative at all (the "white page"). In rebelling against the idolatrous nature of representation in America, the Tsalalians are demonstrating how to resist the faux orderings of the symbolic order that have led, Poe may be suggesting, to slavery and genocide.

The semiotic and political implications of this narrative become even more legible as the story moves inexorably to its conclusions. Escaping from Tsalal, the surviving white sailors (with Pym in their company) head toward the absolute edge of the world, the bottom of the page, the end of the novel. Here, the very oceans become milky white and the sky is filled with bright white lights. Nu-Nu, a Tsalalian whom they take with them as a prisoner, is increasingly terrified as they make this journey, and it is no wonder; the world itself is becoming white. The reality of the page that contains this narrative becomes literalized as a giant white sheet that lies before them. White "ashy material" falls from the sky, and they find themselves sailing into a wall of whiteness—a "gigantic curtain [that] ranged along the whole extent of the southern horizon."[62] Here we come to the noumenal curtain; the abyssal limit turns out to be the page itself, the radical limit of meaning. The novel proper ends with the following passage:

> The darkness had materially increased, relieved only by the glare of the water thrown back from the white curtain before us. Many gigantic and pallidly white birds flew continuously now from beyond the veil, and their scream was the eternal *Tekeli-li!* [a Tsalalian term previously associated with whiteness] as they retreated from our vision. Hereupon Nu-Nu stirred in the bottom of the boat; but, upon touching him, we found his spirit departed. And now we rushed

into the embraces of the cataract, where a chasm threw itself open
to receive us. But there arose in our pathway a shrouded human
figure, very far larger in its proportions than any dweller among
men. And the hue of the skin of the figure was of the perfect whiteness of the snow.[63]

Here, at the end of the novel an abyss of meaninglessness—a complete absence of symbols—looms up and defeats the very text that represents it.
Nu-Nu, the living embodiment of representation, dies upon seeing this
absolute limit.

What do the sailors see in that figure, in the blankness of the page, the
literal limit of representation itself? They might be seeing God. They
might be seeing a sheer image of authorship or personhood—no one in
particular. They might be seeing the ghostly image of the author himself—Edgar Allan Poe hiding behind his syllabically similar namesake,
Arthur Gordon Pym. Like Kafka, Poe will not reveal his secrets; he refuses
to rescue us with a meaning that would merely return us to the delusions
that his *Narrative* might decenter.

In the very undecidability of this image, we see another iteration of the
messianism that we found in Kafka (and Benjamin) as well. In this figure
we potentially see a ghostly outline of the true narrator of this text (whoever that may be), the source of "meaning." Rendering the figure of the author as part of the text reminds us both of the godlike power of the author
(within the context of his or her novel) and also of the fact that such
power comes only from within the confines of symbolism and representation. Here, as with Kafka's strange messiah (or also Benjamin's depiction
of the allegorized Jesus), we find a godlike figure whose uncanniness, both
familiar and infinitely elusive, demonstrates the way that the text elicits
our desire for resolution and meaning even as this figure (once again) delivers nothing at all. After our own expectation for textual redemption is
made quite literally legible to us (via this figure and our responses to it)
and after this expectation is thoroughly frustrated, we are returned instead
to the fact that we are merely gazing upon a white page. In this way a "conspiracy with language" may be inculcated in the reader, so that our attempts at idolatry are undermined by the idols themselves. In its uprising,
the text ceases to be our slave, a tool for our own phantasms (the very attitude toward representation that elicited the attack of the Tsalalians on
the sailors); it becomes instead an independent force, potentially an ally
(or also, an enemy), which undermines our own complicity with the fantasy of "knowing the truth."

Back to New Bedford

In the aftermath of such an event, we must ask what happens to representation. What kind of representational acts can we commit in the face of the exposure of its physicality, its limitations (as well as its seductions)? Poe's answer is, of course, that in fact we can and will continue to engage in representation, exposed or not, because, after all, we have no choice. In the afterword of the book, Poe brings the narrative back to more ordinary forms of symbolism. Here Pym is dead and "Edgar Allan Poe" becomes a character in his own story, a ruse that begins in the introduction written by "Pym" in which Poe agrees to publish some parts of the narrative in a magazine "*under the garb of fiction.*"[64]

Once back in the "normalcy" of New Bedford we seem to be where we started, with nothing much different than before. But having encountered or described the limits and materiality of representation as he has, Poe does leave us with one final sentiment. In his notes that follow the novel, Poe explains the true meaning of the mysterious giant letters that the characters explored on the black island of Tsalal; they mean "to be shady," "to be white," "the region of the south."[65] This so-called explanation is once again anticlimatic because we have already gotten a much stronger response to the story by virtue of its very undecipherability, its exposure as text qua text. Back in the firm embrace of the symbolic (that is to say, a symbolic order that does not present itself to us as such), we are returned to clear "meanings" and values as well as the "normalcy" of America (very much including American race relations). What was once rendered clearly legible has reverted to its unread, phantasmagoric condition.

After this "explanation" however, strangely and without warning, Poe leaves us with one final line that has nothing to do with his explanations and visions of normalcy, a line that comes seemingly out of nowhere. He writes, or rather in the text it is written: "*I have graven it within the hills, and my vengeance upon the dust within the rock.*"[66] In this sentence's strange grammar and eerie tone, we see again the power of representation when it is pushed to the limits of decipherability. What is the meaning of this last strange line? Is it the voice of the author? Does it issue from that ghostly white figure we glimpsed at the end of the world? Once again in its very unintelligibility Poe's text demonstrates that even back in New Bedford, where the basic fact of representation is not constantly exposed (as it is on Tsalal to the point where it becomes unbearable) and where we can believe ourselves (as Tocqueville suggests too, at least for Anglo Americans) not to be engaging in representation at all, we still have not escaped from it. Even in New Bedford, representation remains both present and potentially subversive, even when we are not always aware of it as such. The text—which is not gone but has gone back into the background of our reading experience—bears this violent dangerous and sundering possibility, in this case quite literally. The text is "graven . . . within the hills" of the novel. Its "vengeance" (not unlike the vengeance of the Tsalalians it depicts) is upon us, the readers who hold so dearly to the sensibility of an order and truth that does not actually exist. Even when we cling to our idolatry, to a "normal" state of phantasmagoria, the text continually threatens to render us coconspirators whether we like it or not, to turn our misrecognition into a weapon (a "mighty paw") against the idols themselves, revealing them to be "nothing" but black words on white paper.

The Maelstrom

When we begin to think of Poe's conspiracy in explicitly political terms, we come up against a seeming problem; the *Narrative* suggests that even when representation is fully exposed for "what it is," utter complicity and passivity can still ensue (both for the characters and, presumably, for the readers of the novel as well). The white sailors (including Pym) do not in fact conspire with the Tsalalians. Indeed, they capture and enslave Nu-Nu, perpetuating the cycle of slavery and exploitation. When they return to New Bedford, the sailors seem much the same as before; the warning that the book ends with is not addressed to anyone in particular but just stands as a mute and seemingly unread (by the characters) or unreadable (by the readers) testament to the fact of representation. In the face of such passivity and even active participation in the regime of idolatry, is there a viable resistant stance that a subject of the phantasmagoria can take? Can we join rather than just benefit from this "conspiracy" with (or, in this case, by) language so that the text is our ally rather than our slave? For a potential answer to such questions, we can turn to another Poe story entitled "A Descent into the Maelström."

"A Descent into the Maelström" takes place in Norway. In the story, a man is telling someone else about his encounter with a giant whirlpool that almost took his life. The man describes how he and his brothers were on a boat that got sucked into the orbit of the whirlpool. While his brothers get sucked into the maw, the narrator himself survives by circumnavigating the whirlpool.

In looking at this story, I want to pay particular attention to Slavoj Žižek's interpretation of it. Žižek, one of Lacan's best-known contemporary readers, is very much at home in a discussion of the role of the symbolic and how best to navigate it (as we will see further as we delve deeper into the connections between Benjaminian conspiracy and Lacanian psychoanalytical theory more generally). Through a most useful misrecognition of his own, Žižek reads "A Descent into the Maelström" in a way that richly illuminates the strategies that we ourselves can bring to our conspiracy with language, and the role that misrecognition in particular can play in that process.

In his retelling, Žižek subtly misreads Poe's story; he writes that the narrator survives the whirlpool by "deftly steering the wreck on which he is stuck, which circulates around the maelstrom, miraculously avoid[ing] being swallowed up."[67] But in fact there is no question of steering in the actual story. In the midst of his despair about being sucked into the vortex he is helplessly circling in a boat, Poe's narrator gets a flash of hope: he recalls that in a whirlpool not all materials are treated equally and that "a cylinder, swimming in a vortex, offered more resistance to its suction."[68]

Accordingly, the narrator tells us, "I resolved to lash myself securely to the water-cask upon which I now held . . . and to throw myself with it into the water."[69] Watching his hapless brothers get sucked into the maelstrom, the narrator tells us that "the barrel to which I was attached sunk very little farther than half the distance between the bottom of the gulf and the spot at which I leaped overboard."[70] He is thus carried by the whirlpool's momentum in a circular rather than downward fashion, thus surviving until the whirlpool subsides. In Žižek's interpretation simply holding on and floating becomes "steering." The two activities may seem similar but Poe's character is staying where he is, or rather he is only being moved by the force of the storm. Žižek interprets this as a kind of self-moving across the face of the storm as if the human actor were in fact the central agent in recognizing and then resisting the power of the abyss.

This misreading on Žižek's part is similar to what we saw with Kafka's Ulysses (a story that Kafka also usefully misread) insofar as here too a great deal of agency is attributed to an act that is only peripherally related to human decision-making. It is true that Poe's character did save himself; had the narrator not lashed himself to a cylindrical object and jumped into the water, he would have shared his brothers' fate. But this is not so much a matter of "steering" or bending the symbolic to his will, as accommodating himself to the vagaries of that order, to discovering and following its patterns (however chaotic), that is to say, to "conspiring with language."

The (false) agency that Žižek attributes to his character is, however, both useful and necessary. As we already saw in the case of both Ulysses and K., our misrecognition permits us to attribute our redemption to our own agency, keeping the messianic function hidden from us. We are rendered into beings who believe themselves to be capable of resistance and conspiracy when, formerly, we were not so capable. In this way, while we do not escape from the symbolic order and its delusions (just as Poe's narrator doesn't escape from the maelstrom so much as he rides it out), we are able to live more or less safely on its periphery.

For Žižek, the "Descent into the Maelström" illuminates the correct strategy for engaging with a world of delusion and fantasy, in the process demonstrating a basic principle of Lacanian ethics. He writes that, like the narrator in Poe's story, "the postmodern subject must learn the artifice of surviving the experience of a radical Limit, of circulating around the lethal abyss without being swallowed up by it."[71] Žižek's analysis of the Lacanian model has many resonances with the notions of representation we have been working with in this book. For Žižek, too, delusion is inescapable. The symbolic order that we all live under represents and at the same time protects us from what Žižek, citing Lacan, calls "the real." For Žižek the real is a rent in the fabric of the symbolic; it is the failure of the symbolic to perfectly convey what it represents. In our own, Benjaminian terms, we could call this a version of the "intention of the sign," the resistance that signs give toward the act of representation. In Lacanian terms, the real is what gives a sense of meaning and "reality" to the entire edifice of representation. It is almost as if a fantasy that is too perfect, too totalizing, would not pass for "reality" at all. We need the flaw in order to believe in the delusions that we subscribe to (again, in Benjaminian terms, we could say that we need the reminder, however slight, of the "God's eye view," the fact that our reality is not what it appears to be, in order to make both our idolatry and our anti-idolatrous gestures seem worthwhile, seem connected to something that is bigger than us).

For Žižek, as for Lacan, the real lies at the center of our system of fantasies and beliefs; it compels us and serves (like Kafka's Castle) as our ultimate desire, the object of everything that we do and strive for. As we approach it, its horrible emptiness becomes apparent without being any less compelling. For Žižek, at least in this reading, Lacanian ethics consists of taking refuge in the symbolic order as a way to circumnavigate the abyss of the real without fully succumbing to it.[72] In my own view, this is tantamount to calling for a textual conspiracy, an alliance with, rather than submission to, the signs that compose our world as well as a call to occupy the periphery of our world despite (or perhaps because of) the exposure of the central mythologies which organize our reality.

Žižek is not the only Lacanian who makes this point. Joan Copjec, another important Lacanian thinker (whom we will consider again in later chapters), argues that the symbolic must be our home (despite the fact that the "truth" it represents is both awful and empty). But, she tells us, it doesn't have to be merely a poor substitute for what we really want (our goal, to use the Lacanian parlance). Although it is, by definition, not as ideal and perfect as what our delusions promise us, the symbolic need not be a source of permanent loss and dissatisfaction.[73] Indeed, she suggests that it may be exactly because the symbolic is not what we really want that it offers any hope for human satisfaction. Representation is not "the real thing" for us, but it may in fact offer us something that we will never otherwise find in our grasping after "truth" and "reality": an anchor and a safe haven (much as Poe's narrator finds safety in the barrel that he clings to).

This all seems well and good, but we could yet again (as we saw in the previous chapter on Machiavelli) be facing yet another solution to the problem of representation that is too good to be true. As Jodi Dean points out, the "satisfaction" that we take from the drive, that is to say, the satisfaction that can be derived from giving up the false object and embracing the "journey" (in this case our circumnavigation of the object), can itself be empty and apolitical, a neurotic repetition in which we take satisfaction in our own failure and loss.[74] This is, as already mentioned in the preface, Dean's explanation for the position of the Left today. We have given up on our goal—revolution and a just and equitable society—and now we take a strange, guilty pleasure in its loss.

There is thus a real danger, Dean tells us, in treating objectlessness itself as a destination. In my own terms I would argue that the risk that Dean describes (contra Copjec) is akin to the risk of reasserting idolatry after our fetishism has been exposed. The circumnavigating subject could adopt (and this is, I think, what Dean's criticism implies) the stance of a fetishist who understands that the real has been "exposed" (i.e., the decentering of mythology has been made legible) but doesn't care.[75] In *Politics Out of History* Wendy Brown, citing Freud, describes the position of such a fetishist who, despite the fact that her fetish has been revealed, says, "I know, [it is just a fetish] but still . . ."[76] One could, it is to be presumed, still cling to the symbolic without giving up on the fetish. The person might even be worse off than the ordinary fetishist because she would think, in her own mind, that she was "in the know," thus once again thinking herself free from representation, whereas she is, in fact, all the more deeply held in its embrace.

Such a view may well be the fate of the sailors in Poe's *Narrative;* the fact of representation was revealed to them in all its raw materiality, but they remained (it seems) fetishists at the end of the day. They "knew," but such knowledge imparted no resistance, no conspiracy. We are reminded here once again why for Benjamin (especially toward the end of his life) the mere exposure of idolatry is not sufficient; we also need a change in intention, a move away from our own subjectivity and the traps of time, space, and reality that form it.

All of this leads to a question: is it possible to find satisfaction with the symbolic order, with our lives and communities that are formed in the face of the phantasmagoria, in a way that doesn't simply reiterate the romance of failure that animates so much of the Left? Poe's tale of the maelstrom is extremely useful in this regard because it suggests a relationship to the symbolic (the "conspiracy with language" itself) that may help avert such a repetition. While the action of clinging to the object may be common to both the fetishist and the conspirator, Poe's tale illustrates the key difference.

To see how this is so, we must return to the moment in the story when the narrator begins his "rescue." As the boat is circling the maelstrom, the narrator initially clings to a ringbolt attached to the boat while one of his brothers clings to the water cask (the other brother gets swept overboard after the mainmast he is lashed to breaks off and pulls him into the sea). Then, as the terror builds, the narrator's brother lurches across the boat to reach for the ringbolt as well, even though there is not room for both of them. The narrator is saddened by his brother's attempt to save himself even at the expense of the narrator's own life ("I never felt deeper grief than when I saw him attempt this act"), yet he claims that "I knew it could make no difference whether either of us held on at all; so I let him have the bolt, and went astern to the cask."[77] The narrator at this point has already begun to make his peace with his inevitable death; he begins "to reflect how magnificent a thing it was to die in such a manner" and begins to feel "a *wish* to explore [the maelstrom's] depths."[78] This desire for what in Žižekian (or Lacanian) terms could be called the drive allows the narrator to let go of the assurances of stability, order, and normality that the brother refuses to surrender.

The brother, still a fetishist, clings desperately to the "solidity" of the ringbolt, even though it is attached to a paltry boat circling the storm. The narrator clings to the water cask "instinctively," but in this clinging, he stumbles on his own redemption (with a bit of help from some hastily recalled physics about the rotation of bodies).

This aspect of Poe's tale beautifully illustrates the distinction between a conspiracy with language and a continued fetishism. Having given up on any kind of grand rescues or salvation, the narrator becomes available for a nonfetishistic relationship to the sign, to the barrels and objects that are caught up in the swirl of the maelstrom. Fetishists cling to the symbolic not for itself but for the fantasy they continue to subscribe to, even when they "know better." The narrator's brother in this case was in a state of total panic; he, like the narrator, knew he was doomed, but he could not give up on the hope that actually condemned him to his death. Rather than ally with the objects in his midst, he abandoned the thing that would have saved him, futilely clinging to the appearance of normality and safety (the ringbolt) in a situation where such promises had already been utterly eradicated and exposed. Here we see how false hope, the hope that we currently possess, leads to our own undoing (literally in this case; the boat, the ringbolt, and the brother all got sucked into the empty center of the maelstrom).

It is crucial to understand that Poe's narrator is not "seeing the truth" or escaping delusion; he is instead "recognizing his misrecognition." Even in the face of the perfect meaninglessness that the narrator faces at the center of the maelstrom, the narrator still contends with the symbolic and its "rules" (such as how whirlpool's work, etc.). By still following these rules (even, one could say, when he "knows better"), the narrator is able to survive. In Žižek's terms, the narrator remains a captive of the symbolic order but is lucky to navigate (or to be navigated) within it without fully succumbing to the horror its delusions both lead us to and protect us from. He "recognizes his misrecognition" by avoiding the two extremes, either fetishism or a nihilistic rejection of all meaning (as we have already seen, in the end these two gestures become the same).

Thus the narrator finds his own agency—however delusional it may be—in giving himself over to his "conspiracy with language." In so doing, the narrator finds that the symbolic is not as "empty" as it seems; even when denuded by the exposure of the real, rules still apply, water casks still float. As we already saw with Kafka, the individuals and communities that are formed in the face of some central referent (God, the state, the green flags of Islam, etc.) have an existence that is distinct from that referent; they can survive and even flourish when such a referent is decentered. But they can do so only if they give up on "hope," on the assurances of delivery by the referent itself.

Thus even when truth and meaning are decentered, the world still makes sense to us, and, accordingly, our own sense of agency (and life) is also preserved even though it too is a misrecognition. Žižek's helpful misreading of the agency of Poe's narrator demonstrates that we tend to assume our own self-motivation in all contexts, projecting agency onto our actions even when they have completely heteronymous sources. Indeed, in the next chapter on Arendt and Lorca I will argue that our agency (as opposed to the false agency of the phantasmagoria) is effectively produced by such misreadings. From this perspective, clinging becomes steering, and putting in wax earplugs become silencing the Sirens. Such misreadings are necessary and in fact are the way that we can overcome our own sense of doom and defeat, our sense of being trapped in time. By conspiring with language, by clinging to the barrels for dear life, we are moved in a different direction, we escape a certain fate.

After the Maelstrom

As Poe shows in "A Descent into the Maelström" the encounter with the abyss of meaning has a profound impact on us. His narrator, who started out with a head of black hair, finds that it has turned absolutely white on encountering the maelstrom (with all the semiotic connotations that changes of color implies for Poe).[79] As in the *Narrative* we see here that even when he returns to the full embrace of phantasmagoria, to "normalcy," the fact (and threat) of representation does not go away. But in "A Descent into the Maelström" it seems fair to say that the narrator (and perhaps the reader?) is even more affected by the encounter with the materiality of representation than the characters in the *Narrative*. The fact of having experienced the radical decentering of his reality and the concomitant (and nonidolatrous) relationship with signs that saves him means that the narrator will never be quite the same again. In the beginning of the story, we see that rather than seek to forget what happened to him, the narrator is compelled, not only to tell his story over and over again, but to tell it while gazing at the monstrous whirlpool that repeatedly forms and unforms itself just beyond the shore he inhabits. While the "threat" uttered at the end of the *Narrative* is uttered to no one in particular, the narrator in "A Descent into the Maelström" is specifically drawn to see that threat over and over again. In full view of this embodied undoing of the very normalcy that he has miraculously returned to, we are reminded of the narrator's "*wish* to explore [the maelstrom's] depths," which he expresses at the height of his crisis. Whether he acts on such wishes or not, he now knows that there is something that lies beyond hope itself, beyond our desire for "normalcy" and safety. He sees other opportunities, other understandings of the possible (or even of the desirable), whereas the existence of such alternatives would not even have been conceivable to him before his encounter with the maelstrom. Whether he continues with his "conspiracy with language" or not, the narrator is clearly a different man now; he no longer sees the world in the way that "normalcy" and phantasmagoria insist on organizing it.

Conclusion

In this chapter we have seen the potentially subversive power of revealing the materiality of representation and—by extension—the immateriality, the idolatry of what representation supposedly makes "present" to us. This exposure is twofold; first, these authors reveal (particularly Poe) the basic material quality of the signs that compose our reality—the building blocks of the phantasmagoria. Second, they show how these signs are actually present even when we no longer see them, even when they have successfully constituted our "reality." Allegorizing the building blocks of this reality, we see how fragile it is, how quickly the maelstrom beneath the surface of the symbolic becomes palpable.

As we have seen, Poe is the more openly subversive of this pair. He plays with our desperate belief in our own agency, in our requirement for "reality" and the fact that in the "New Bedfords" of our world, we appear not to be representational at all. The voyage that Poe describes in the *Narrative of Arthur Gordon Pym* does not actually go anywhere—it remains located exactly wherever it is being read—but it dramatizes a move to the limits of representation to show that representation cannot and should not be escaped. As with Benjamin too, for Poe representation is all that we have by which to organize our lives and our world.

Poe's *Narrative* also shows the dangers of continuing to believe in nonrepresentation (the delusion of the idolater); especially when read in conjunction with Tocqueville's own writings, we see slavery, racism, and genocide as part of the price that is paid (usually by nonwhite people) for refusing to recognize the phantasmal quality of a particular approach to representation. The fantasy that human subjects are in control of their own meaning leads, as Poe and Tocqueville both show, to dominance, hierarchy, rages, and bitter resentments on all sides (and as we will see in chapter 6, this genocidal tendency gets extended via colonialism and imperialism to the rest of the world as well).

Whereas Tocqueville is formally more of a liberal (or protoliberal) and hence more complicit in the phantasmagoria he describes, as we have seen, none of us avoid some form of deep complicity. This complicity is not, however, the end of the story. Tocqueville offers a viewpoint from well within the confines of the construction of the American narrative (indeed, he is one of its prime architects) without being any less helpful for the purposes of conspiracy. By reading these two disparate authors in constellation, we find that they can be mutually illuminating; although Tocqueville is redolent, and even generally in favor (especially in volume 1 of *Democracy in America*), of the very forms of thinking about politics that reproduce the phantasmagoria, his political focus and its links to semiotic representation help to reveal the political dimensions of Poe's work more clearly. Similarly, Poe's relentless exposure of the materiality of signs helps us to read Tocqueville more clearly in terms of the semiotic implications of the latter's own work. Read together, they show some of the subversive possibilities, the messianic gestures, and the conspiracies that can be fomented from within the confines of the symbolic order (a good thing, too, since there is nowhere else for human beings to go).

Just as crucially as understanding the subversive power of the kinds of exposure we see in Tocqueville's writings and in Poe's *Narrative,* we also see, through an analysis of Poe's "A Descent into the Maelström," how a subject can go from being a deeply complicit colluder with the phantasmagoria to a conspirator with language. As our analysis of "A Descent into the Maëlstrom" shows, when we treat the object or sign—much less another person—as a tool (or slave), we share its/their (reified) fate, we bring vengeance onto ourselves for our hubris and assumptions about reality. When, on the other hand, we treat the sign or other as an ally, we are in effect altering our own fate (or having it altered for us); we gain access to a different (purely representational) reality. The troubling stances of passivity, privilege (including race privilege), and obfuscation are called into question or altered (without, I would argue, being completely erased or forgotten). What in the *Narrative* (and for that matter in *Democracy in America* as well) serves as an *opportunity* for conspiracy becomes in "A Descent into the Maelström" a *strategy,* a way to involve ourselves directly in the conspiracy that otherwise excludes us. This strategy affects not just the characters in the text but us readers as well. As readers of these texts, we are almost automatically placed in a privileged and complicit position; we engage with meaning, we seek "truth" in the process of reading. Without a sense of how we can engage in conspiracy, the idea of conspiracy remains alluring but empty; with a strategy for *how* we conspire (granting that this "how" does not so much eliminate as coordinate our passive and accidental stance with the actions of the text) it may just become possible to actually do so. What "A Descent into the Maelström" teaches us, finally, is that in order to enter into a conspiracy with language (as well as with materiality in general), we must dramatically break with the (false) hopes that keep us trapped in the phantasmagoria. Only then do we become available for the hope which is "not for us."

In the next chapter, we will continue to look at a question that we began to consider when we engaged with Žižek's reading of "A Descent into the Maelström," namely the role of human agency in a conspiracy that seeks to decenter human subjects. By looking at Hannah Arendt and Federico García Lorca and their respective approaches to what I call "a place for the human" in this conspiracy with language, we will see further some of the strategies (as always, guided and produced by our own misrecognition) that enable us to benefit from a conspiracy that formally excludes us. These authors, in their confrontation with the rise of European fascism (and for Arendt, its aftermath as well), can be seen as facing the very maelstrom that Poe only guessed at. In their own circumnavigation of the symbolic realm, both Arendt and Lorca demonstrate a set of strategies for holding fast to a sense of agency, even (or perhaps especially) at a moment in time when human choice seemed minimal and when all hope was truly lost. It may well be that only at such moments, only when we are forced to give up hope, do we also have a chance, however slight, of earning the kind of redemption that a conspiracy with language may afford us.

5 | Hannah Arendt, Federico García Lorca, and the Place for the Human

In a conspiracy dedicated to the overcoming of human intentionality, one that is marked by a profound distrust of human actions, thoughts and deeds, and even the possibility of hope, the question of a place and a role for human beings is central. What, we have already asked several times, does it mean to enter into a conspiracy that offers no hope for "us," the human subjects of the phantasmagoria? We have seen that the conspiracy we have been examining seems to exclude our own agency, our own ability to engage in politics in the ways we usually understand the term. And yet, as we have also begun to see in the last chapter, such an exclusion is not absolute; when we align our intentions with the intention of the sign, instead of seeking to use the sign for our own phantasmic purposes, we gain a sense of agency. Indeed, the agency we receive from our alliance with texts, however much it remains a misrecognition, offers us far more than the "agency" we receive in the phantasmagoria, wherein much is promised but little (or nothing) is delivered.

In this chapter, we will further our examination of what a conspiracy with language offers our own agency; that is, what it offers us in terms of our own lives, powers, decisions, and actions, even on the most intimate and personal level. More specifically, we will look at strategies that can enhance, or produce, our own agency in the face of our conspiracy. To look at such strategies, we will engage with two writers, Hannah Arendt and Federico García Lorca. As with the previous chapter (and the one that is to follow), these thinkers are paired because they mutually illuminate a particular question. Here again, these writers roughly share a geographical and temporal context, in this case Europe around the time of World War II, a period shaped and marked above all by the crisis of European fascism. Having survived the war, Arendt lived much longer than Lorca did; she was thus able to witness the full panoply of European fascism and its aftermath. Her writings are a direct response to fascism, and especially National Socialism, as a dark echo of the Enlightenment ideas of progress and democracy. As with Benjamin, such events led Arendt to question the platitudes of liberalism, to detect the maelstrom at the center of the various grand narratives of her day. On the other hand, in no small part because Lorca was an early victim of fascism, much of his work anticipates what was to come; the two Lorca plays that I am looking at in this chapter, dating from 1928 and 1931 respectively, come a bit before the full expression of Spanish fascism, which, in any event is quite different from the phenomenon of Nazism. Yet, whether by prescient insight or by virtue of his own conspiracy with language, Lorca's work poses a challenge to what fascism (and by extension the phantasmagoria more generally) stood for in a way that complements much of what Arendt was to discover as a historical eyewitness.

As with the authors in the previous chapter, Arendt and Lorca have very little in common. Arendt, who has enjoyed a central canonical status as a political theorist for many decades, grew up as a Jew in Germany. She studied philosophy with Martin Heidegger, among other mentors, and when racial laws prevented her from pursuing a career in her own country, moved from Germany to France (where she befriended Benjamin). She finally left Europe altogether for the United States just ahead of the Nazi killing machine. Most of her most famous writings such as *The Origins of Totalitarianism, The Human Condition,* and *On Revolution* were written in exile. Lorca, on the other hand, had very little to do with politics per se. He grew up in Granada, Spain, eventually moving to Madrid, where he became an influential member of the Spanish avant-garde art movement (befriending figures like Luis Buñuel and Salvador Dalí in the process). He achieved a great deal of success as a poet, playwright, and theater director. His best-known plays are the *Rural Trilogy* of *Bodas de Sangre* (Blood Wedding), *Yerma,* and *La Casa de Bernarda Alba* (The House of Bernarda Alba). Right around the time that the Spanish civil war broke out, Lorca moved back to Granada, where he was one of the early victims of the war. He was targeted mostly for his association with the cultural Left, for his strange plays, and for the fact that he was a (more or less openly) gay man.[1] He was widely considered to be a leftist but in a rather amorphous way, mostly by association and temperament.[2] He was shot and killed by local fascists in August 1936.

Once again, despite their having virtually nothing in common except for their contention with fascism in its various guises, it remains fruitful to read these authors in constellation with one another. In their respective opposition to the way that fascism aestheticizes politics—as Benjamin puts it—these writers oppose the grand narratives of truth, order, and subjectivity (which for Lorca can be taken in both a political and a literary sense) that reach their apotheosis in fascist ideology.[3] As a response to such constructions of ideology, both authors turn to and struggle with materialism, with the heteronymous sources of our resistance and agency and what they mean for the human subject. As with the other coconspirators I treat in this book, these writers see a form of materialism, and in particular textual or representational materialism, as a way to save the subject from being utterly determined by her or his own intentionality (Arendt would say by her or his will) as well as from a sense of being totally determined by context (Arendt would say by "what" we are). This in and of itself makes these writers stand apart from much of Western thought, wherein materialism itself is the source of determinism, not a source of resistance to it, and it links them to one another. In Arendt's case, our actions, our appearance to ourselves and to others, are what saves us from a fate of being totalized either by our own wills (i.e., intentions) or by the "will" of some great, sovereign power (whether of the fascist or liberal capitalist variety). In the case of Lorca, a kind of textual deus ex machina delivers his characters from a certain and apparent fate (although as we will see, what it delivers them to is not necessarily what they would have chosen).

Yet for all of their textual materialism, both of these authors complicate this picture by struggling to maintain a human position in the face of these textual rescues. If their responses to the totalizations threatened by fascism, capitalism, and other social, economic, and political forces are a turn toward self-determination, that "self" threatens to be overwritten, at least potentially, by the very materiality that saves (or produces) it. We see this struggle with Arendt insofar as she evinces a conflict between her wish for a pure exteriority, a perfect spontaneity on the one hand and the enduring edifices of political life, a *res publica* on the other. In other words, Arendt has a basic conflict between the rescue that is provided by materiality on the one hand and the world that human beings themselves create (including the all-important possibility of a political life) on the other. With Lorca, we find a literary version of this conflict between the power of the text to liberate his characters, to lift them out of their contexts entirely, and the ongoing question of the role and power of the characters (including Lorca the author), of their (his) own acts of self-narration and imagination.

In the case of both authors, I argue that this conflict, rather than being disabling, reveals better how a place for human perspectives can and must be maintained in the face of these textual conspiracies. As we will see, for both authors, the human perspective they seek is in some sense generated by and from their engagement with materialism. Yet, particularly in Arendt's case, there is a (valuable) reluctance to acknowledge this source. As we have already seen, to maintain a "human" perspective in some sense means to misrecognize the way materiality delivers us from our own internal phantasms. Indeed, as I have also already suggested, such misrecognition constitutes the human perspective itself. In their respective struggles with this question, Arendt and Lorca jointly illuminate strategies that perpetuate a human position and perspective even as they demonstrate its limitations and travails, its ongoing and necessarily delusional nature.

Hannah Arendt: Appearance versus Representation

In looking at Arendt's work on the relationship between politics and materiality, we immediately come across a series of ambivalences on her part. As already indicated, Arendt is highly suspicious (as is Benjamin) of human intentionality, and more specifically in her case, of the human will. For Arendt, the will—at least in the form that we currently experience it—is a modern and generally pernicious phenomenon; as we will see further, for Arendt, the will denies the reality of human plurality (and hence politics) in favor of its own internal phantasms.

In order to bypass the will, Arendt seeks a kind of perfect and political exteriority, what could be called a "politics of appearance." Here each of us exists as "an appearance among appearances," a cipher that evokes our condition as existing amid other people.[4] When Arendt speaks of appearance in this way, she does not mean our actual physical presence before others so much as the Greek idea of *dokei moi* ("it appears to me"), that is to say, the way that human beings intrude onto other people's interiority (and will), bringing in a perspective or appearance that is not within the other person's control. This is not so much representation for Arendt as "presentation." While the "materiality" of the other's appearance to us is based more on how we see them than what they actually (ontologically) are (hence she speaks of "appearance" vs. something like "being"), such a seeing does not come under the control of the interior mind or will and hence is not *re*-presented so much as just seen or noted by the self.

Arendt's conception of action is deeply tied to the understanding of politics that comes out of her interest in appearance. In her view action causes us to "appear" to ourselves and to others in ways that are unexpected; action thus rescues us from our inner phantasms, delivering us to political life. It seems here as if Arendt has indeed sought out an external, material source of personhood as a counterweight to our own subjectivity.

Yet, as we will see further, even as Arendt makes these arguments, we also find her often holding back from a full embrace of this vision, compromising with many of the internal and subjective aspects of the social that in her view threaten the vision of politics that is so dear to her. At the heart of her ambivalence lies the troubling question of representation. On the one hand, representation determines how we relate to one another, both ethically and politically—we see this for example in Arendt's notion of "representative thinking."[5] Yet at the same time representation also is tainted by our subjective phantasms; the will is a representative faculty. It is tempting to say that Arendt seeks to dispense with representation altogether, that she prefers, as already suggested, "appearance" as a pure marker of presence, a kind of non- or antirepresentative understanding of human interactivity.[6] And yet, as we will see, Arendt is more complicated than this. Arendt does not abandon representation; even as she holds it in deep suspicion, she sees representation as a necessary and, I would further add, even desirable part of modernity. In this way she is aligned with the other textual conspirators that I consider in this book. Insofar as she sabotages (as we will see) her own antirepresentational ideals, we can see Arendt as practicing a kind of "recognized misrecognition," or at least its functional equivalent, an embrace, however reluctant, of the symbolic order, even given its dangers and distortions.

I argue that in her promotion and then undermining of fables, in her hesitations, in her compromises, Arendt is seeking to maintain a place for human action and responsibility in the face of two dangers. The first danger, which she depicts quite clearly throughout her work, is that of internal phantasm, the perils, I would say (she would not put it quite this way), of idolatry, of failing to take the plurality of human beings as "real." We could call this a failure of insufficient materialism, of turning too far inward and therefore abandoning the proper sphere of politics. The second danger is less noted in Arendt, but equally crucial. This is the danger of becoming lost in the very sorts of spontaneity and freedoms that Arendt seems to call for (an idea she perhaps evokes when she speaks of "the abyss of freedom").[7] This could be called a failure of excessive materialism— where the subject becomes purely an externality and has lost any sense or possibility of herself, making a complete surrender to the text or fable that is meant to rescue her. While the first danger is far keener for Arendt, the second one tempers her political theory.

This is far from asserting that Arendt is somehow an "antimaterialist."

In the end, I am not sure that Arendt is all that different from a thinker like Foucault or even Hobbes, despite their more evident and full embrace of materialism. Arendt's hesitations may even render a service to materialist thought insofar as they stave off a kind of faux, perfect materialist delivery that is just another phantasm. As we have already seen, the idea that we can in fact be rid of our misrecognitions, that we could be "free" or find "truth" via a surrender to materialism, can be just as pernicious, just as subject to manipulation and phantasmagoria as a complete surrender to mythology. As we have already seen too, such a notion can produce an even worse fantasy because in this case materialism itself is implicated and thus cannot be turned to for redemption (no messiah can lead to our rescue if we think we've already been saved).

In my view, Arendt's continued interest in representation despite all the perils she attributes to it suggests an acknowledgment that a politics that is free of representation altogether (a pure "politics of appearance") is both impossible and not even necessarily desirable. By holding onto the misrecognitions that are inherent in representation, we avoid replacing one set of phantasms with another. Arendt can be viewed as a fellow conspirator because her hesitations protect her from embracing any one set of mythologies too deeply. While such a move does affect the overall coherence of her argument, it demonstrates how the human perspective can and must always be a moving target, determined by nothing but its own self-positing, its own continuous act of self-misrecognition.

The Problem of the Will

To flesh out this argument, let us explore the ways that Arendt denotes the relationship between representation and human interiority. Throughout her work but perhaps most particularly in *Willing,* written toward the end of her life, we see Arendt demonstrating a keen distrust of and ambivalence toward human interiority, as we have already suggested, particularly in terms of the human will. In *Willing* Arendt associates the will with the idea of the *liberum arbitrium* (a connection she makes in earlier works as well), a term often translated as "free" will but which for Arendt deals only with the predetermined, the already true (as far as it is concerned), negating or precluding the very sorts of spontaneity that Arendt seeks as a basis for political action and freedom:

> The *liberum arbitrium* decides between things equally possible and given to us, as it were, in *statu nascendi* as mere potentialities, whereas a power to begin something really new could not very well

be preceded by any potentiality, which then would figure as one of the causes of the accomplished act.[8]

For Arendt, the will is a quintessentially modern faculty, with roots in Christian doctrine. She tells us that whereas in modern times, the idea of freedom is connected to the notion "I will," for the Greeks and Romans, the idea of freedom was better summarized by "I can."[9] Arendt writes that "when we deal with experiences relevant to the Will, we are dealing with experiences that men have not only with themselves, but also *inside* themselves."[10] The will seeks to deal with the world around it by taking recourse in its own interiority, projecting itself into the wider world and seeking to remake it in its own image. It is for this reason apolitical or even antipolitical because, as we have already seen, it denies or at least struggles with the basic fact of human plurality (in more Benjaminian terms, we can see the will as the avenue by which the phantasmagoria extends itself into our innermost reaches, posing as—and constituting—our own interiority).[11]

By contrast, Arendt tells us that the ancient world had a completely different approach to the self in relation to others. She writes that Socrates spoke of the "two-in-one," our conscience or internal dialogue between me and myself that is "not thematically concerned with the Self but, on the contrary, with the experiences and questions that this Self, an appearance among appearances, feels are in need of examination."[12] Herein lies the difference: the (modern) will privileges itself and therefore renders itself in its own self-regard as *not* being an appearance, whereas the rest of the world, the other, and so on, are "merely" appearances *to it*. This dissymmetry could be said to be the basis of the problem of representation for Arendt; with representation something is always presented to a particular, and privileged, subject that understands itself as not being "representative" at all (echoing a problem that we saw with Tocqueville and Poe as well).

The Socratic/classical notion of conscience, on the other hand, sees both itself and the worldly matters it concerns itself with as appearances, thus reading itself as having a kind of material existence (an "appearance") that denies or undermines such a privileged and purportedly nonrepresentational perspective.

This distinction between classical and modern forms of self-conception has great relevance for questions of politics. Arendt writes that for the Socratic conception of self,

This mediating examination of everything given can be disturbed by the necessities of life, by the presence of others, by all kinds of urgent business. But none of the factors interfering with the mind's activity rises out of the mind itself, for the two-in-one are friends and partners, and to keep intact this "harmony" is the thinking ego's foremost concern.[13]

This harmony is absent from later, Christian notions of willing. She tells us that for Paul the "two-in-one" are "not friends or partners; they are in constant struggle with each other."[14] The other is experienced through law and prohibition; she or he represents the one who must not be killed, coveted, or otherwise serve as a cause for sin. Such a relationship "arouses the passions," as well as resistances.[15]

From a Benjaminian perspective, at this point we have already introduced idolatry, failed representations of the divine "bastardized with law."[16] The privileged perspective of will sees itself as an agent that must either obey or rebel against a divinely mandated law, hence setting up an adversarial relationship with the world. Arendt shows that the most accurate motto for freedom in Christian-influenced modernity might be "I-will-but-*cannot*" due to the impossible obligations of a perfect divine law (echoing here, however faintly, the impotence of the baroque sovereign that Benjamin examines in the *Origin*). She summarizes this by writing:

> Hence, when we come to Paul, the accent shifts entirely from doing to believing, from the outward man living in a world of appearances (*himself an appearance among appearances and therefore subject to semblance and illusion*) to an inwardness which by definition never unequivocally manifests itself and can be scrutinized only by a God who also never appears unequivocally. The ways of this God are inscrutable.[17]

Perhaps the most critical line to grasp here is the one she commits to parentheses. For Arendt, the Greek self is "an appearance among appearances and therefore subject to semblance and illusion." Such a self is not "true," not objective at all but a delusion, we could say a misrecognition, by definition. The inward Christian self on the other hand, accessible only to God, is equally mysterious yet it is rendered in some sense *not* a delusion by virtue of its manifestation to God. In our earlier chapter on Benjamin, we saw that the "God's eye view" was the basis for a materiality of subjecthood, a font of resistance to our delusions. But Arendt, drawing on an alternative and problematical version of this theology, implies here as elsewhere that the injection of God into the question of subjectivity naturalizes or depoliticizes the appearance of the other as a representation; knowing that God can read us, we tend to think we too can read one another and hence "know" the other as an inner projection. From this hubristic assumption, we begin to take on God's viewpoint as our own, asserting "meaning" and "truth" onto the other (and when the other does not conform to this view, we seek to impose that "truth" on the other, as we have already seen in the previous chapter). This offers a very different version of the "God's eye view" than Benjamin. In this case, such a "perspective," as we see, leads to more, not less, idolatry.

The consequences of the shift to willing for Arendt are thus grave, ushering in a new era of delusional antipolitical activity culminating in totalitarianism (and to some extent, capitalism as well). Of course the Greeks and Romans were capable of doing, and thinking, awful things (we only need to read a few Greek dramas to know that), but by having a foundation for subjectivity in will, modernity is faced with an especially pernicious and intractable problem. What Socrates would have considered a "weakness of reason when confronted with the passionate drive of the desires" is in our own times considered a "free choice of the Will."[18] Hence through the concept of the will, our compromise becomes truly "part of us." One could even say it defines "what" (as opposed to "who") we are.[19]

Although with Arendt we have an entirely different history than we do with Benjamin—especially in terms of the theological ramifications—we see a similar notion of the utter compromise of the self. The will for Arendt is the equivalent of Benjamin's notion of intentionality; it occupies a position that does not even see itself as having a position. The will produces a depoliticized space of representation and, I would add—although here again I'm fairly sure Arendt would not put it this way herself—a space of idolatry, whereby a false reading of the sign as not even being a sign allows for a great deal of what Arendt and Benjamin would both call "evil."[20]

Given the way the will perceives and orders the world, there is no room for appearance, and without appearance, we also lose touch with reality, with materiality itself. As Arendt famously tells us:

> To men the reality of the world is guaranteed by the presence of others, by its appearing to all ... and whatever lacks this appearance comes and passes away like a dream, intimately and exclusively our own but without reality.[21]

We can also see this sentiment expressed in Arendt's treatment of forgiveness, as when she writes:

The fact that the same *who*, revealed in action and speech, remains also the subject of forgiving is the deepest reason why nobody can forgive himself; here, as in action and speech generally, we are dependent upon others, to whom we appear in a distinctness which we ourselves are unable to perceive. Closed within ourselves, we would never be able to forgive ourselves any failing or transgression because we would lack the experience of the person for the sake of whom one can forgive.[22]

When we are "closed within ourselves" as we are with the will, we take in the other as a representation we make to ourselves. The other is hence not real to us. Nor are we real to ourselves. It is only when "we appear in a distinctness," expressed via our speech and action, as a material presence that we become a "*who*." Our "who," as opposed to our "what," is revealed via action and speech. It is not summoned in our mind's eye but appears before us, a surprise to both ourselves and to others. Our "who" is hence spontaneous, that is to say, not preordained by our "free wills."

A Politics of Will

Stemming from this philosophical basis of opposition or at least resistance to the will, we see a corresponding, and derivative, political stance as well in Arendt. In *On Revolution*, written quite a bit earlier than *Willing*, Arendt often seems to be distinctly against the concept of representation as a basis for political life. When speaking of the revolutionary struggle between councils and parties, the former being the spheres of action and appearance, the latter being the imposition of ideologies, of willing itself, she writes:

> The conflict between the two systems, the parties and the councils, came to the fore in all twentieth-century revolutions. The issue at stake was representation versus action and participation. The councils were organs of action ... [the parties] knew well enough that no party, no matter how revolutionary it was, would be able to survive the transformation of the government into a true Soviet Republic.[23]

Here we see that the party, an organ of representation, "represents" nothing but its own phantasms. The parties' only recourse is to destroy and coopt the councils that serve as a rival to, and in fact a completely alternative form of politics from, the parties themselves. Unlike the parties, the councils are not representative of anything but rather simply serve as sites for appearance, as zones of mutuality and action.

For Arendt, the ultimate consequence of the pernicious form of representation embodied by parties is the concept of sovereignty.[24] For Arendt, sovereignty is merely the projection of the will outward into the world. Through sovereignty, the will seeks to extend its illusions of control and indeed "representation" onto an entire community, displacing any genuine political life in the process (a process that is once again perhaps best epitomized by Nazism and the *Führerprinzip*). As Arendt tells us:

> Because of the philosophical shift from action to will-power, from freedom as a state of being manifest in action to the *liberum arbitrium,* the ideal of freedom ceased to be virtuosity in the [classical] sense. . . . and became sovereignty, the ideal of a free will, independent from others and eventually prevailing against them.[25]

Sovereignty is, for Arendt, the (pseudo) political form par excellence in modernity exactly because of the predominance of the will. Just as the will gives itself a privileged position in terms of representation (due to the delusion that it doesn't need to be represented to others, but others need to be represented to it) so too does sovereignty partake of an idolatrous form of representation in which a single, privileged perspective is packaged as a collective will (one that is said to "represent" the other wills that it in fact has overshadowed). In Benjaminian terms we could call this delusion the political basis for the contemporary form of the phantasmagoria (something that Machiavelli and Tocqueville both warn us against as well).

Can (Should) Representation Be Redeemed?

Thus we seem to have a very clear preference in Arendt for appearance over representation, a "politics of appearance" that dispenses with representation altogether. Yet, for all of her opposition to representation, at least in the forms we have encountered it, Arendt remains nuanced on this issue. Lisa Disch, a well-noted Arendt scholar, notes that contra thinkers like Iris Marion Young, who believe that "'authentic democracy' is unmediated, and representation 'derivative, secondary, distanced, ambiguous, and suspect,'" Arendt is in some cases is actually supportive of representation.[26] In the case of *On Revolution,* for example,

Arendt presents Council governance not as direct democracy but as an "alternative for representative government" that, unlike the party system, fosters and depends upon political participation. . . . To clarify, because Arendt's own polemics sometimes confuse the matter, she recommends Councils as an alternative *to* party systems *for* representative government, not an alternative to representative government *per se.*[27]

In Disch's view it is not representation itself that is at issue but a *style* of representation that Arendt opposes (reminiscent of what we saw with Tocqueville as well). But what that style consists in is not immediately clear. In *On Revolution,* Arendt makes a distinction between two kinds of representation, the Federalist/Madisonian model whereby the people are represented "virtually" by their elected leaders (through the party) and the Anti-Federalist/Jeffersonian model whereby the people are represented more "literally" (through councils which then instruct delegates on how to vote).

One might surmise that Arendt simply favors the Anti-Federalist position (and hence that style of representation as well), but Disch shows that this is not quite the case. Arendt muddies her own distinction by depicting it as a choice between two problematic options, a choice between "representation as a mere substitute for direct action of the people and representation as a popularly controlled rule of the people's representatives over the people."[28] She tells us that such a choice produces "one of those dilemmas which permit of no solution."[29] In this reading, neither form of representation is portrayed as being particularly desirable.

In fact, as Disch notes, when push comes to shove, Arendt seemingly (and surprisingly) comes down on the side of the centralizers, that is, the Federalists. In the very same book in which she bemoans how parties have supplanted councils, thus suppressing genuinely democratic movements, Arendt notes that with the Anti-Federalist view of representation "government has degenerated into mere administration, the public realm has vanished."[30]

The idea that only a centralized government could provide a public realm flies in the face of much of what Arendt argues in *On Revolution.* It ignores her own point that the councils themselves—those local political bodies—could constitute a public realm that would only need to be coordinated at the "representational" level of government. Yet, for all of this, Arendt worries that with a government that is so reduced in terms of its own function, there is no space either for seeing and being seen in action, John Adams' *spectemur agendo,* or for discussion and decision, Jefferson's pride of being "a participator in government" [or] Madison's "medium of a chosen body of citizens" through which opinions must pass and be purified into public views.[31]

Such a concern emphasizes once again the idea that seeing and being seen (politically speaking) must be orchestrated on a grand, national level to exist at all.

In Disch's view, such a preference for Federalist models of representation is a deformation of Arendt's political theory suggesting Arendt's own misreadings of the histories involved. She writes:

> Arendt's confident assertions that the Founders had acted "out of the uninterrupted strength" of the tradition of federalism suggest that she fell for what Brutus, Gerry and other Anti-Federalist dissidents rightly viewed as a clever political ruse: marketing a proposal for "national" or "consolidated" government under the "federal" brand.[32]

And further that:

> Arendt takes the Federalists at their word. She lauds their fidelity to the "basic federal principle," faulting them only "for being inadequately conscious of themselves as innovators" (Honig 1991, 98). She defends as an accidental casualty of their timidity the vision of small-scale republicanism that the Federalists deliberately and skillfully dismantled. In short, Arendt puts forward Anti-Federalist *arguments* while contributing to Federalist *ideology.*[33]

Whereas for Bonnie Honig, Arendt's turn to fables allows her to alter and adjust the context and possibility for freedom, for Disch, Arendt's turn to fables actually made it more difficult for her to recognize and preserve what was best about the American practice of politics.[34]

Arendt and Misrecognition

For my own part, I don't see Arendt as being quite as bewitched by Federalist rhetoric as Disch suggests. Nor do I see her work as being quite as disabled by such inconsistencies. Instead, I see Arendt demonstrating, as already suggested, a true—and necessary—ambivalence toward representation, one that reflects some of the deepest paradoxes of her work.

In her own analysis, Agnes Heller helps us to understand how this ambivalence on Arendt's part may play itself out. Heller speaks of a "paradox of freedom" in Arendt wherein the possibility of the kind of perfect and spontaneous politics she lauds threatens the very political community it is meant to save. As Heller tells us:

> Beginning anew as the interruption of continuity is the essence of human action. But only continuity can be interrupted, for interruption cannot be interrupted. Political action cuts the thread that binds actors to tradition. Yet it is also true that a loss of tradition means a loss of what Arendt calls "treasure," or rather of *the* treasure, the past: If there is no treasure to inherit, there is no continuity at all, no past, no future, just the eternal recurrence of the same. ... How can one begin something absolutely new at any time and also preserve and cherish the treasures of the past?[35]

Here we see a potential conflict between the nonrepresentational, spontaneous, and interrupting action aspects of political community on the one hand (the politics she ascribes to Athens, perhaps to the Anti-Federalists as well) and the need for continuity, for "a place for the human," for tradition, and an ongoing narrative (or indeed self-representation) of a community on the other.[36]

In her own response to this question, Heller suggests that Arendt's promotion of a "pure" action is not quite what it seems:

> The Arendtian *pure* action (a very Kantian expression) is entirely free, free from everything, not just from constraints, but also from the situation in which it occurs. But actions, political actions included, are never "pure." Arendt knows this very well. She does not put the emphasis on pure action, on action as pure initiation and pure freedom, just to make a pleasing typology or to exclude from action everything that is impure ... Arendt speaks of pure action for the sake of the future. Nothing but the concept of pure action can offer hope for the almost impossible, for the omnipresence of the eruption of freedom everywhere, in every situation and at any time.[37]

In Heller's analysis, Arendt's love for a "politics of appearance," a purely material, purely antirepresentative understanding of politics, functions less as a desired alternative form of politics than as a way to disrupt the sense that we must live within the bonds set by our current conceptions of politics (and representation). For the "sake of the future," Arendt engages with these visions as a way to resist our conviction (one that she shares herself) that we are trapped in our context, in our own temporality.

Here Heller helps us to think of Arendt's ambivalence as a rhetorical strategy rather than an assertion of a clear and unambiguous truth (wherein we would have to determine which mode of representation best conveyed that truth). Such a claim accords very well with reading Arendt through a Benjaminian, and conspiratorial, lens. As we have seen, for Arendt, materiality is indeed what rescues us from our own phantasms. Her vision of a politics of pure exteriority, the politics she ascribes to the Greeks (and to a lesser extent to the Anti-Federalists), subverts and resists the present, giving us a sense of alternatives even when we don't actually have any. But to assert this pure exteriority as an actual, practicable form of politics would be to risk succumbing once again to the idea that we can or should do without representation.[38] To turn completely to a politics of appearance that is entirely outside of representation would be to create an ultimate and depoliticized fetish. Such a move threatens to repeat the hubris of the will that it is not representative at all. In the end the dangers of too much and too little materialism bring us to the same position.

The act of representation, while deeply faulty for Arendt, is the only way to make us aware of the degree to which our perspectives are just that, "an appearance among appearances and therefore subject to semblance and illusion." To be "free" of representation is to lose this sense of semblance, and thus lose a sense of how for Arendt those perspectives are "real," that is to say, subject to politics, external and available for mutual (mis)recognition.

For all the reasons above, I would argue that the style of representation that Arendt effectively favors is that of "recognized misrecognition." Her ambivalence toward representation allows Arendt a healthy skepticism without giving up on the necessity and centrality of representation as a whole. Her ambivalence is not meant to be resolved but sustained; she avoids the fetish of internal phantasms via a turn to the material, and she avoids the fetish of the pure material via a reassertion of the value and place of human agency and perspective.

We see that in jettisoning her own dreams of a perfect and pure appearance and clinging instead to the highly suspect fact of representation, Arendt is not unlike the narrator of "A Descent into the Maelström," who abandons the allure of his boat's ringbolt in favor of the uncertainties of the water cask. Like that narrator, Arendt too is perhaps guided as much by instinct as by conviction, but in either case, it is her attention to language and sign, to the benefits and necessity of representation that allows her to, as it were, overcome her own will or intentionality (at least to the extent that it is overcome). With respect to "recognizing her misrecognition," it is far from clear that Arendt is consciously choosing a messier and interactive notion of representation over a "politics of appearance." Yet, this "choice" is nonetheless produced in her texts by the paradoxes that her work presents to us. The incongruities and contradictions of her fables are therefore perhaps less distortions of her theory than they are indications that misrecognition—and hence, representation—is endemic to and necessary for the human perspective.

Rather than try to "solve" the problem of representation, as we have seen, Arendt engages with misrecognition as the only way to preserve some modicum of a freedom that she sees as being under assault from all sides (a Lacanian might call this move "traversing the fantasy"). By holding onto representation, despite all the idolatrous threats that it poses, and by refusing to turn textual rescues into perfect moments of salvation, Arendt can be seen as preserving (or serving to preserve) the very human perspective that her political theory has always foremost been in service of.

The Castle *Revisited*

Both the necessity for and powers of misrecognition in Arendt's work come out even more clearly when we consider her comments (as is quite appropriate) on Kafka and, in particular, her own reading of *The Castle*. Here we form yet another constellation in our conspiracy. In Arendt's view, which she sets out in "The Jew as Pariah," Kafka's *Castle* is a book about Jewish identity, about how a Jew can find her or his place in a world that is determined by other (in this case Christian) and often hostile narratives. She also sees *The Castle* as a book that suggests misrecognition (and hence representation) offers a limited redemption.[39] In her reading, it is the Jew's mistaken belief in things like "rights" and "justice" that makes such things conceivable (if not possible) in a world where they do not and cannot exist. Arendt picks up on the value of misrecognition for Kafka and in the process helps us to better understand how the misreading and misinterpretation of signs can lead (or not lead, depending on how we think about *The Castle* as a whole) to something like redemption in her own work as well.

In her analysis, Arendt does not focus on the messianic aspects of the text (although reading it as a Jewish text may inevitably brings with it some messianic associations). Instead she reads it as a metaphor for the problem of assimilation. For Arendt, in order to assimilate, or at least attempt to, K. must shed all of his Jewish characteristics and become a person of near perfect generality. He wants to be "normal," to have "'a home, a position, real work to do,' to marry and to 'become a member of the community.'"[40] But K. cannot escape his "Jewishness" because of his association with the Castle. The villagers come to suspect him for his desire to be one of them even when he has opportunities for a higher status. While K. is trying to achieve basic human rights and dignities, the villagers understand (as he does not) that such rights do not exist:

> The plain villagers, controlled to the last detail by the ruling class, and slaves even in their thoughts to the whims of their all-powerful officials, have long since come to realize that to be in the right or to be in the wrong is for them a matter of pure "fate" which they cannot alter.[41]

The villagers, who have no formal barrier to their full humanity (as K. "the Jew" does), know that the "privileges" of normality are hardly what an outsider thinks they might be. In their world, the space for humanity and freedom is denied by a totalizing power structure. The villagers experience power and agency as "fate," a random occurrence over which they have no control. They don't even quite object to this circumstance (since they are "slaves even in their thoughts"). K. alone finds this situation "unjust and monstrous."[42]

Thus, what for K. was a "commonplace and obvious" goal is in fact "exceptional and magnificent."[43]

> The simplest inquiry into right and wrong is regarded as querulous disputation; the character of the regime, the power of the castle, are things which may not be questioned. So when K., thoroughly indignant and outraged, bursts out with the words "So that's what the officials are like," the whole village trembles as if some vital secret, if not indeed the whole pattern of its life, had been suddenly betrayed.[44]

In his attempt to be an "everyman," then, K. inadvertently exposes the fantasies of universality that he aspires to. K. himself does not quite understand this. Arendt tell us that the villager's tales of woe "fail to rouse in him that sense of haunting fear with which they take pains to invest them" and that "since he cannot share this feeling he can never really be one of them."[45]

In Arendt's view, K.'s particular position, his discoveries, does little to help K. himself (since "what he strove to achieve was beyond the strength of any one man").[46] Eventually (although this doesn't happen in the novel itself, which remained unfinished), Kafka intended to have K. die of exhaustion, no more or less part of the village than the day he arrived. Yet for Arendt he does not leave the village unaffected; his failure is not in vain:

> The very fight he has put up to obtain the few basic things which society owes to men has opened the eyes of the villagers, or at least of some of them. His story, his behavior, has taught [the villagers] both that human rights are worth fighting for and that the rule of the castle is not divine law and, consequently, can be attacked.[47]

From the perspective of a Benjaminian conspiracy, we can read this as a testament to the possibility of carving out "a place for the human" even in the midst of overwhelming obstacles (and only because of ongoing acts of misrecognition) and a sense of complete totalization.

Yet crucially it is not the case that in misrecognizing rights, K. has actually produced them out of thin air. His delusion does not bring some shining and true rights into the world. It is rather that in his pursuit of such a belief, K. has rendered the false (and supposedly divine) appearance of rights into a weapon to wield against the Castle. Given his outsider perspective and his resultant false belief in rights, K. has rendered his misrecognition legible to the other villagers so that they can see that "the castle is not divine law," potentially allowing them to share in his misrecognition. Although K.'s own will is as subservient as anyone else's (he desperately wants to join the Castle, the village, someone or something), he inadvertently exposes the "Halakah" of the Castle as being empty. He radically undermines the phantasms and projections of the will, engaging in a spectacular act of anti-idolatry even though he is a true believer, indeed the truest (perhaps only) believer that there is.

For her own part, Arendt certainly does not share K.'s naïveté. Still, she recognizes (as Kafka does as well) the value of not letting go of your fantasies—or perhaps she recognizes that one cannot actually let go of them, that representation and fantasy are the building blocks of our reality, for better or worse. Arendt sees that K. (and maybe Kafka as well) is wrongheaded in his belief in the possibility of "simple, decent life," yet she also sees the benefits of this misrecognition. If she imputes K.'s position to something "Jewish," she may well be drawing upon her own feelings of Jewishness, her belief in things that do not exist, exactly because of her personal feelings of exclusion from the universal. Similar to K., Arendt believes in—or at least textually commits herself to—things that seem impossible (although as we have seen she tempers her beliefs in a way that K. does not).

For all of their similarities, Arendt's version of Jewishness is not Kafka's. While he focuses on the mystical and messianic aspects of misrecognition, Arendt emphasizes the political. She reminds us that even the "modest" goals of Kafka are not enough. Arendt concludes that the strategy that K. outlines is not viable for a particular individual since one individual "is no longer strong enough to fulfill the basic demands of human life."[48] She goes on to say that "only when a people lives and functions in consort with other peoples can it contribute to the establishment upon earth of a commonly conditioned and commonly controlled humanity."[49] A simple, decent life for one figure is not enough and is in fact not even possible apart from a commitment to a political process (arguably Kafka's texts show precisely the same thing, even if she doesn't see things that way).[50]

Yet for all this, Arendt sees a political benefit in K.'s (and Kafka's) text: the effect of his (and her) storytelling interferes with the structure of collective fantasy and meaning, allowing a different (and political) kind of community to emerge. We see this possibility in Arendt's own work as well; Arendt too may spread her own misrecognitions to her readership. Her engagement with mythology and representation may too "open . . . the eyes of the villagers [in this case, her readers], or at least some of them."

K.'s conspiracy against the Castle may have amounted to nothing at all, but, as Arendt takes pains to demonstrate, it shows that such a conspiracy is possible, that it may lead to a properly political and collective response. After all, Arendt tells us that the villagers learn from K. "that human rights are worth fighting for." This does not mean that rights now exist (in fact we see that they do not), but it suggests the possibility of politicizing a question that the phantasmagoria has rendered moot with its own delusions. This is not so much a happy ending (after all K. dies a miserable and lonely death, albeit outside of the confines of the novel) but a contingent one, an ending that is neither predetermined (by the will) nor rescued (by some great materialist salvation). It represents a future of struggle and uncertainty, and this contingent, partial, and halting future may be all that Arendt means in the end by her use of the term "freedom."

Federico García Lorca

In moving from Arendt to Federico García Lorca, we seem to have abandoned the most basic political struggle that Arendt dedicates her life and work to. On the surface, as already noted, Lorca seems to be fairly apolitical, a purely literary figure. To some extent, however, this may be an artificial distinction. Benjamin himself shows that politics is always concerned with the aesthetic and with representation, even as he shows the political aspects of art and literature. Even if we leave such considerations to one side, I hope to show in the rest of this chapter that Lorca's writing engages with strategies and possibilities similar to those of Arendt (as well as other writers that we are treating in this textual conspiracy) and furthermore that these strategies have important political connotations for the kinds of resistances we are describing in this book.

In terms of his contributions as an artist and writer, Lorca demonstrates throughout his work a strong attention to the transformative power of texts, offering a level of textual materialism that approaches what we have seen in Poe. In his writing, Lorca reveals a set of strategies that may be familiar to us by now. His strategies deliver textual redemption to characters who are impossibly trapped by their contexts. Even if this redemption is not always recognizable as such from the perspective of the characters themselves, it is delivered to them nonetheless. His characters are offered a "self-determination" even if the self in question is one that is produced largely or entirely via textual strategies. In this way, Lorca is very much in keeping with Kafka's form of misrecognized redemption, and, by extension, he writes in constellation with Arendt as well.

Yet, given his own focus on language and the craft of writing, Lorca adds a dimension that is even clearer than what we see in Arendt's own work, namely the way in which the text can be the source of and storehouse for our misrecognition. This is true for Lorca in terms of both the way that the text resists and subverts the characters' own desire for redemption (that is to say, the way that the text "redeems" the characters in unintended ways) and the way the text enables the characters to misrecognize even the manner in which the text determines (and rescues) them. As Lorca helps to make clear, the "place for the human" we seek to find in conspiracy is produced not so much in defiance of or struggle with the text (as it sometimes seems for Arendt) as through the texts; even our sense of stepping away from the text toward a form of self-determinism is itself an artifact of our conspiracy with language (something we already began to see with Žižek's [mis]reading of "A Descent into the Maelström").

Such "self-determination" remains highly paradoxical insofar as the self is precisely what is in question in Lorca's work. Even the "selfhood" of the author comes into question; while Lorca is undeniably the sole "author" of his plays, we will see that he, like Arendt, acts to overwrite or engage with his own desires by acknowledging and rendering legible the "intention of the sign." Even his foils in the text—the narrators and prologuists—are shown, upon close examination, to be, not omniscient and all seeing, but rather the ones who are in a sense most excluded from the play's revelations. In Lorca's plays, those who are portrayed as the most deluded, the most lost in the mimicry and pantomime of their roles, are in the end the most redeemed. The characters who fare best are those who engage (even if not willingly) in textual "rewritings" of themselves, surrendering what they took to be their own agency in the process. Such characters engage in conspiracy by disguising themselves, taking on new roles and new identities. Their initial motivations are sometimes venal (as with Machiavelli) and always come out of their own conscious intentions, but in the process of their conspiracy, they discover that they are not in fact "in charge" of the persona they have created but are rather swept along by the new "self" that their disguise produces.

This slippage between the author's desire for the text to "represent" his own position on the one hand and the resistance of the text to that authority on the other is particularly highlighted in Lorca's work. And yet, despite this paradox, we will see that the characters that Lorca portrays do in a sense "find themselves," exactly by surrendering (or resigning) themselves to their textual alliances. Such an insight helps us to think further about the "progressive deepening of . . . intention" Benjamin hints at in the *Origin*.

In order to demonstrate the workings of textual redemption in Lorca, let us look at a few of those texts. For the sake of brevity, I will focus on two plays, *La Zapatera Prodigiosa* (The Shoemaker's Wonderful Wife) and *The Love of Don Perlimplín*, which illustrate these strategies particularly well. As with the two plays by Machiavelli examined earlier, both of these plays involve conspiracies about questions of love, sexuality, and marriage. Both sets of plays are sexual farces (although Lorca is always more tragic than Machiavelli). And both authors can be said to have an "ironic" style insofar as—at least in *La Zapatera Prodigiosa*—we have a narrator (not unlike the one who opens *Mandragola*) who seems somehow "in the know," aware of the manipulations of theater and willing to expose these schemes because he knows the audience will be manipulated nonetheless. Lorca takes this even further than Machiavelli does; frequently characters will suddenly talk to the audience or to each other in ways that break out of the traditional illusion of theatricality. Still, for all of their similarities, Lorca's irony collapses in a way that Machiavelli's never quite does. Let us recall that in *Mandragola,* Machiavelli's foil is Ligurio; he is the one character who is always in command of the story (although Callimaco certainly fits the bill for the subject who is redeemed without knowing why or how). With Lorca on the other hand, such a position is never sustained; it is almost as if the author gives up trying to control the direction of the play, as if the characters themselves are conspiring, not only against one another, but against the author himself. If Machiavelli's plays show us how to commit conspiracy while hiding in plain sight, Lorca's plays show us how a purely textual conspiracy can nevertheless produce a place for human beings and a politics of misrecognition.

La Zapatera Prodigiosa

In *La Zapatera Prodigiosa* we see a husband (the Shoemaker) and wife (the Wife) who are unhappily married. The wife is a stunning beauty and seems vain; she is obsessed with other men's opinion of her, and a tyrant to her hapless husband. We find, then, a situation that is vaguely akin to what we find in *Mandragola:* a loveless marriage, disparities in age and beauty, schemers who wish to seduce the wife, and other such fare. The play begins with a fairly typical ironic stance by a narrator called "The dramatist" who comes in holding a letter and begins by telling the audience:

> Distinguished ladies and gentlemen . . . (*Pause*) Or rather, ladies and gentlemen, which is not to say the writer doesn't think you are distinguished. In fact, the opposite. But the word contains the tiniest hint of fear, a kind of plea for the audience to be kind to the actors' performance and the writer's brilliance. The writer doesn't ask for kindness; just for attention once he's leapt that barbed and dreadful barrier of fear that writers have of writing for the theatre.[51]

Here, we see the dramatist "confessing" his anxiety, personalizing the opening of the play in ways that make the audience hyperconscious of the fact that they are, in fact, watching a play. In short, the dramatist is engaging in that kind of ironic stance that is quite common even in the Renaissance but which by the early and middle twentieth century had become a ritual of theatrical "self-exposure," something meant to startle the audience out of complacency or to seduce viewers into the "realism" of the drama (by showing them "a behind-the-scenes look"). Indeed, at the end of his monologue (or rather would-be monologue, since he gets interrupted, as we'll see in a moment), as the dramatist departs, the stage directions say "*His manner is ironic.*"[52]

Such an ironic stance seems problematical from the perspective of a Benjaminian conspiracy because it appears to preserve an authorial stance, a kind of all-knowingness that also contaminates the audience by bringing it also into "the knowledge" that the playwright has to impart (suggesting once again the possibility of being "true" or nonrepresentational). But Lorca is a writer of sublime complexity, and so his prologuist's monologue is, as already mentioned, interrupted by one of his characters. The dramatist tells us, "But don't be surprised if [the wife] enters furiously or bitterly complains. You see, she always struggles, either with reality around her, or with her fantasies when they become reality." Immediately after, the wife can be heard shouting offstage: "I want to make my entrance."[53] To which the dramatist replies, "All right, all right! Don't be so impatient. It's not a gown with a train or fantastic feathers you're about to appear in. It's just a rag, do you hear? The dress of a shoemaker's wife!" To which she replies, still offstage: "Let me make my entrance."[54]

The plot of the play contains the broad strokes of conspiracy: after endless bitter feuding and after the wife seems poised for all sorts of extramarital affairs (although crucially, she never moves beyond flirting; she requires praise from other men but seemingly nothing more), the husband finally leaves, at the time we think for good. After the husband leaves, the wife becomes even more morose and bitter. She now claims that she always loved her husband and heaps her scorn on the succession of men that proclaim their love for her. In fact, the husband returns, disguised as a puppeteer who puts on a play within a play in the wife's home in front of an audience of neighbors and would-be suitors. Even before the "play" begins, one character tells the wife, "When the puppet-master speaks, he sounds exactly like your husband. Don't you think so?" to which the wife replies "His [i.e., her husband's] voice was much more gentle."[55] A strange brew of reality and fiction is being concocted here where it becomes difficult to tell whether the storytelling is responding to reality or if it is the other way around ("either with reality around her, or with her fantasies when they become reality"). In denying that the puppeteer is her own husband (even after having the conspiracy essentially exposed from the outset) the wife seems to cling to a radically different "truth" about who her husband really is.

In his play within a play, the shoemaker tells the truth as he sees it: he depicts a meek but virtuous husband with a scornful, ungrateful wife. As he describes the wife's perfidy, the actual wife keeps interrupting with statements like "What a horrible woman!"[56] As if attesting to the intertwining of "reality" and "fiction," the shoemaker, interrupted once too many times by his wife and his audience, says "Please don't interrupt! You can't imagine how hard it is to remember the piece by heart."[57] As the shoemaker describes a plot by the wife's suitors to kill the husband, the play is interrupted by the shouts of men outside. These are the voices of thwarted suitors who are "in real life" plotting to kill the wife at that very moment.

At that point, everyone rushes out into the street except for husband and wife. Continuing his disguise, he talks to her and she tells him how she has remained devoted to her husband. Now it is her turn to tell her version of reality (albeit minus the textual disguise). She describes their marriage as loving, speaking of how he'd recite stories to her in bed and how those stories used to frighten her, to which he replied (in her story within a story), "But my dearest darling, it's only a story!"[58] Afterward, we find this exchange:

SHOEMAKER (*indignant*). A pack of lies!
WIFE (*startled*). What? Are you mad?
SHOEMAKER. All lies!
WIFE (*angrily*). What on earth do you mean, puppet-master?
SHOEMAKER (*standing angrily*). Your husband was quite right.
   Those stories are nothing but lies! Pure fantasy!
WIFE (*sharply*). Of course they are. Do you think I'm a fool? . . .
   But you can't deny they do make a strong impression.[59]

Here we see an acknowledgment that stories, even stories that we know are false, can have a great effect ("a strong impression").[60] This is something we have seen in many other writers in our constellation, especially perhaps Kafka and Poe.

The above passage marks a turning point in the narrative as the various constructions of truth converge. After debating whether people really are so impressionable, the husband allows that he knows a woman who has no such feelings. He describes his wife, this time without the falsifying details (in his "play" she is a tanner's wife, but here he mentions that she is a shoemaker's wife). The wife cries, "You are talking about me, aren't you?"[61] In his denial, and in her moment of "self-recognition," the two become much more sympathetic to one another, approximating the relationship that the wife imagines they have had (in retrospect) all along. He tells her that his wife abandoned him. Both of them begin to praise their lost spouse. She says, "My heart belongs to the man who's out there, wherever he is, the man I must be faithful to. My husband!" He says, "I love my wife, my lawful wedded wife, and no one else!"[62] These declarations seem to finally produce the actual love that eluded this couple during their real marriage. Here, it seems, via the devices of a textual conspiracy (i.e., the play within a play) a real love is (miraculously) produced.

Up to this point, we see the workings of the text as a delivery from the despair of its characters. It is through the textuality of their subterfuge (a play within a play, lines that the Shoemaker fears he will forget in the face of the reality he is busy respinning) that these characters are able to change their lives and produce a love that never existed before. This is similar to Arendt's strategy of misrecognition, of telling fables to produce new concepts of what is possible. By misrecognizing one another (in this case quite literally) these characters are somehow redeemed. This is in part why the author's own stance of all-knowing "irony" collapses upon itself. "Being in the know" is not what redeems these characters. They are redeemed precisely by *not knowing*, by being wrong and false. What the text does is render their misrecognition legible. It allows us to see that misrecognition (which in the end, is all recognition, all representation) can change (even as it constitutes) the world.

Even so, Lorca has one more trick up his sleeve, and it is a necessary one for the purposes of a Benjaminian conspiracy. In fact, when they finally declare their true identities to one another, we get this unexpected exchange:

> WIFE (*responding*). Rogue, scoundrel, blackguard, liar! Do you hear that [the taunting songs from the villagers about the wife's alleged (but actually untrue) infidelities]? It's all your fault!
> *She throws chairs.*
> SHOEMAKER (*emotionally, going to his bench*). My dear wife!
> WIFE. You vagabond! Oh, I'm glad you decided to come back! I'm going to lead you such a dance! [In Spanish: "¡Qué vida te voy a dar!" literally: what a life I'm going to give you!] You'd be better off with the Inquisition or the Templars of Rome!
> SHOEMAKER (*at his bench*). My true happiness is here![63]

From this exchange you might surmise that nobody has changed after all. The wife has reverted to her sharp ways and the husband seems to have reverted to being a weak-willed dupe. Surely this is not the fate either character intended when this masquerade began. Were their conspiracies truly being guided by their own conscious wishes, this is most likely not the outcome they would have chosen (what they would have chosen in fact is made evident by each spouse's fantastic [re]appraisal of the other). Yet, although they do not become one another's ideal, fantasy lovers, they are in fact not quite what they were when the play began either. As the threatening neighbors approach with their vicious singing, the wife has this to say (the final lines of the play):

> WIFE. Such rotten luck! To have to put up with a man like this! (*Going to the door.*) Shut up, loud mouths! Obscene creatures! Come on, come on! There are two of us now to defend the house! Two of us! Myself and my husband! (*Turning to the* SHOEMAKER.) This wretch, this good-for-nothing![64]

We are left with a new situation. After the conspiracy is revealed, the wife reverts to type, ceasing to romanticize her husband even as we gain a new sense of their solidarity. This is not some miraculous production of a new, perfect form of love. The manipulations and the deceptions of conspiracy do not produce a brand-new reality. Instead, and very much in keeping with the Benjaminian style, they simply rescramble, rejuxtapose the existing materials of the character's lives.[65] The love that is produced here is a failed representation of their fantastic desires, the love they wanted and pretended to have. This failure is crucial and functions in two ways. First, there is a failure to perfectly represent the shoemaker and his wife "as they are" (i.e., as we find them when the play begins). Second, there is a failure to deliver the couple to some pure, perfect phantasm of love. Thanks to the failure(s) engendered by the textual conspiracies in this play, this couple is given a chance, a redemption that comes in a form they neither expected nor would necessarily have chosen or desired. Yet it is redemption all the same, even if they don't appreciate it or realize it (witness the wife's complex mix of love and negativity at the very end of the play).

The textual conspiracy both sides engage in (he via the device of his disguise, she by the device of a new set of memories) allows this couple to encounter the symbolic forms that constitute their relationship and the world around them. As with Arendt, they navigate (or are navigated through) a course between the phantasms of a "reality" that appears unchangeable and the phantasms of "salvation" that promises but offers no change.[66] Their engagement in conspiracy renders their lives a legible—

and alterable—narrative (only not alterable by them but by the texts they turn to). As such, it produces the very sense of agency that they believe themselves to be already in possession of.

We can see that when left to their own devices, these characters have no agency at all, only pure phantasm. Before her husband's (disguised) re-entry into her life, the wife was trapped in a fantasy world; she was a prisoner of her own intentions. If her husband's intention in his own disguise was to prove that his wife was faithless, this too was a trap insofar as it sought to reaffirm a "reality" that was entirely tenuous and fantastical.

Although he is continually in his wife's presence for the vast majority of the play, the husband only becomes legible to her as someone not within the control of her own phantasms by first disappearing from her and then reappearing through the distortions of a conspiracy. Now the wife knows that her husband, for all his (ongoing) failures, is made present and real to her ("There are two of us now"). The love that we find at the end of this play is not a romanticized perfect bond but a simple—and happy—act of (mis)recognition. The independent agency each member of the couple experiences in the other comes, not from that person per se but from their mutual conspiracy; the selfhood this conspiracy produces offers this couple a haven, perhaps even a source, for their own deluded but crucial sense of agency.

It is vital not to confuse the "reality" of this textually produced agency with ontological reality (or what passes for it). As a result of their conspiracy, the husband and wife do not suddenly "get each other" or "realize what they have had all along"; to argue thus would be to return to the fantasy that they have so recently, and just barely, emerged from. Nor is this quite an example of Arendt's pure "politics of appearance" (which, in any case, her own text subverts, as we have seen). This is not recognition but misrecognition as facilitated by and through texts. Although the way the husband and wife become "real" for each other looks a great deal like Arendt's notion of appearance, I'd argue that Lorca does a somewhat better job than Arendt of resisting this move. Although, as we will see in our analysis of the next play, Lorca, like Arendt, flirts with the notion of a nonrepresentational, immediate response to the material presence of the other, he allows his text to subvert such a move far more definitively than Arendt does. Instead of any kind of true, nonrepresentative acts of mutual recognition, what we see here is another case of "recognizing misrecognition"; each spouse becomes an other who defies and alters his or her partner's expectations without becoming "authentically" that person.[67] The reality of the selves that comes out of this conspiracy is explicitly and only representational; it is representation itself and not what it points to that is "recognized" and made legible in this context.

When the illusions of recognition and mutuality are subverted and exposed by the textual conspiracy both wife and husband participate in, then and only then do we acknowledge the (productive) failures of representation. The idol of the other has been exposed as such, and in the wake of that exposure (as with Kafka, Arendt, and Benjamin himself), something truly common can, just possibly, also come into being—without being any more "true." We find that the barest hint of such a possibility is evident at the end of *La Zapatera Prodigiosa*.

The Love of Don Perlimplín

In *The Love of Don Perlimplín* (*Amor de don Perlimplín con Belisa en su jardín*), another play by Lorca, we get a very different kind of conspiracy and a correspondingly different sort of outcome, even as the basic conspiratorial strategy it demonstrates remains the same. In this play, at the outset, Don Perlimplín is depicted as a very old, virginal, and rich man. His servant Marcolfa talks Don Perlimplín into seeking to marry a neighboring beauty, Belisa.[68]

In this play, Belisa is depicted as a vain seductress; she agrees to marry Don Perlimplín only because her mother insists on it (due to his great wealth). On their wedding night, Don Perlimplín appears to be impotent and terrified of his bride. Their marriage appears to instigate a serious identity crisis in him; at one point he calls out, "Oh, Perlimplín! Where are you, Perlimplín?"[69] Yet, somehow, and quite suddenly, he finds himself in love with Belisa. He says:

> I married . . . who knows why? . . . but not for love. I could never imagine your body until I looked through the keyhole and saw them dressing you in your bride's dress. It was then I experienced love. At that very moment. Like a sharp needle plunged into my throat.[70]

He falls asleep, seemingly without laying a finger on his bride. When he wakes up he sees the window open and five discarded ladders below, obviously left by five other men that she has slept with that night. Belisa says of the ladders that it is "the custom in my mother's country" to leave such ladders lying around on a bride's wedding night.[71] She tells Don Perlimplín that the corresponding five hats left on the balcony are "only the passing drunkards."[72] Rather than get angry at what he knows to be her deception, Don Perlimplín tells her, "Your explanation's perfect. I believe you. Why shouldn't I?"[73]

At this point Don Perlimplín begins his conspiracy to win over his bride.[74] His plan is to produce for Belisa a perfect, fantasy lover. In getting her to love that false lover, he will in effect be getting her to fall in love with Don Perlimplín himself. Picking up a letter from one of her actual lovers, Don Perlimplín pretends it's from the fantasy one. He asks Belisa, "Has he been here?" Belisa, playing along (perhaps because she is relieved he only thinks she has one suitor), says, "Twice."[75] She claims that he is hateful and awful (and by implication that she has spurned him) but Don Perlimplín says:

> I saw the young man for the first time two weeks ago. I can honestly say his good looks dazzled me. I've never seen a man who so perfectly combined masculinity and delicacy. For some reason I thought of you.[76]

Taken up by this fantasy, Belisa tells her husband that she does receive other letters but whereas those letters speak of "wonderful countries, of dreams and broken hearts," this dream lover's letters speak only of "[her] body."[77]

In participating in what amounts to a dual conspiracy, Belisa is allowing herself to admit what she most craves in a lover: a total adoration of her physical self. For his part, Don Perlimplín also succumbs to this fantasy (and in fact he does love her only in this way, as we have seen). When he proceeds to set up a "meeting" between Belisa and this lover, Marcalfo chides him, saying, "How can you encourage your wife to commit the worst of sins?" To which he gleefully replies, "Because Don Perlimplín has no honour and wants to amuse himself. Imagine! Tonight Belisa's new and unknown lover will come."[78] Here Don Perlimplín is participating in his own humiliation and destruction. Belisa's love for the man Don Perlimplín invented has them both captivated. The climax of the play comes when Belisa and Don Perlimplín meet as she is searching for the fake lover in the garden. Don Perlimplín tells Belisa that this lover will be wearing a red cloak and endeavors to walk around in one to give "sightings" of him. When he realizes how madly in love Belisa now is with this fake lover, Don Perlimplín says:

PERLIMPLÍN. This is my triumph!
BELISA. What triumph?
PERLIMPLÍN. The triumph of my imagination.
BELISA. It's true you helped me to love him. [Es verdad que me
ayudaste a quererlo.][79]

In her reply, Belisa acknowledges, however indirectly, the role Don Perlimplín plays in producing her love, albeit for another (nonexistent) man.
Don Perlimplín tells Belisa he will kill the lover, so that "When he's dead,
you can caress him forever in your bed, so handsome, so elegant, and not
be afraid to lose his love."[80] Belisa, in desperation, seeks to kill Don Perlimplín, but she finds him already dying, stabbed by his own dagger (for
he has indeed "killed" the phantom lover). Keeping up the illusion, but
also attesting to what he's done, he responds to Belisa's question "Who has
killed you?" by saying, "Your husband with this emerald knife." But then he
goes on to say that the lover "killed me because he knew I love you most of
all"[81] and also that "Perlimplín has killed me . . . I was the one who loved
your flesh . . . only your flesh! [Yo en cambio amaba tu cuerpo nada más]
. . . and he's killed me."[82] In other words, only Don Perlimplín loved his
wife as she desired to be loved, for her body, her flesh alone. He asks her to
let him "die holding your body."[83]

As he is dying, in a way that is similar to what we saw in *La Zapatera
Prodigiosa,* narrative and reality begin to converge for Don Perlimplín.
Belisa says: "But the young man! Why did you trick me?" To which Don
Perlimplín replies "What young man?" After he dies she has this final ex-
change with Marcolfa:

MARCOLFA. Madam!
BELISA (*weeping*). Don Perlimplín is dead!
MARCOLFA. I know. Now he shall have for his shroud the bright
red cloak [the one he ascribed to the young lover] he wore to
walk beneath his own window.
BELISA (*weeping*). I never thought he was such a complex person.
MARCOLFA. And now you know, it's too late. I shall make him a
wreath as bright as the mid-day sun.
BELISA. Perlimplín! What have you done, Perlimplín?
MARCOLFA. Belisa, you are a different person now, clothed in my
master's glorious blood.
BELISA. But who was this man? Who?

MARCOLFA. The lovely young man whose face you shall never
   see.
BELISA. I love him, Marcolfa, truly. With all the passion of my
   flesh and my spirit. But where is the young man in the red cloak?
   ...Where is he?
MARCOLFA. Don Perlimplín, sleep peacefully ... Listen, Don
   Perlimplín, listen to her![84]

Belisa never quite realizes that her lover is not real even though she has in
a sense knowingly participated in this conspiracy and even though both
Don Perlimplín and Marcolfa more or less reveal it to her. Her love for the
young man seems unchanged, but in the meantime she has fallen in love,
however impossibly, with Don Perlimplín himself. The grammar (in English as well as in Spanish) suggests as much: when Marcolfa says she will
never see the young man's face, Belisa replies "I love him" ("le quiero"),
seemingly alluding to the young man, but then she asks, "But where is the
young man in the red cloak?" ("Pero ¿dónde está el joven de la capa roja?")
as if she was not talking about him at all but rather about Don Perlimplín.[85] By misrecognizing what he has done, Belisa responds to her
husband's conspiracy, allowing her love for a phantasm to become the basis for a love for her husband.

The Temptations of Nonrepresentation

But what, exactly, is the nature of this love? How "real" can it be when it is
based on conspiracy and masquerade? As previously suggested, in *The
Love of Don Perlimplín,* far more than in *La Zapatera Prodigiosa,* Lorca
verges on the same appreciation for a pure, nonrepresentational notion of
appearance that we sometimes see in Arendt. After all, Don Perlimplín
falls in love with Belisa when she "appears" to him through a keyhole. The
pure image of Belisa alters him fundamentally ("Like a sharp needle
plunged into my throat"). Don Perlimplín's objectification of Belisa's
body seems redolent of (and is certainly consistent with) old-school sexism, yet it does not appear that Don Perlimplín is interested in Belisa sexually. He does not even try to sleep with her on his wedding night and is
content to die merely holding her body. His love for her is almost perfectly
materialist in nature. He truly loves her as a physical object in a way that is
seemingly not "representative" at all.

   And yet, not unlike with Arendt, Lorca's character retreats from this idealization. This love for her appearance does not give Don Perlimplín access to some level of truth about Belisa that is denied to other characters in the play. Don Perlimplín does not necessarily believe Belisa's stories or think her to be chaste; his creation of a phantom lover suggests he is trying to outfox her, to beat her at her own (representational) games.

Indeed, rather than have access to some perfect truth about Belisa (via her "appearance"), Don Perlimplín is clearly deceived (or perhaps allows himself to be deceived) about the virtues he sees in her. When Belisa tells him her fabrications about why she has five ladders and five hats leading to her bedroom, recall that Don Perlimplín tells her, "Your explanation's perfect. I believe you. Why shouldn't I?" In the original Spanish, Lorca writes: "¿Y por qué no? Todo lo explicas bien. Estoy conforme. ¿Por qué no ha de ser así?" Literally this means: "And why not? You explain everything well. I am satisfied. Why can't it be this way?"[86] Even as her falseness is made readily apparent, Don Perlimplín still finds a way to believe his wife ("Why can't it be this way?"). He clings to his misrecognition despite all evidence to the contrary and in fact it is his misrecognition that allows him to love her, to make Belisa worthy of his love.

Thus, not unlike as in Arendt, Don Perlimplín negotiates between various forms of his delusion. His love for Belisa's pure materiality causes him to pursue a love that he knows is impossible and wrong. At the same time, he still engages (again like Arendt) with the world of symbols and representation. Don Perlimplín beats Belisa at her own game because he has an ally that she does not: the sign itself. Whereas Belisa is merely a liar, turning to manipulation and obfuscation to get her way, Don Perlimplín is guided by a vision that is not of his own devising. He is as much a dupe as he is "in command" of his own conspiracy. The conspiracy takes on a life of its own, producing new phantasms even as it disassembles old ones. Were these delusions fully under the control of his own conscious will, Don Perlimplín would be returned to the full embrace of these delusions (and hence worse off than Belisa, who tends to deal with delusion on a purely instrumental basis). With the sign as his ally, on the other hand, Don Perlimplín avoids being so narrowly determined even as he remains entrapped by the structures and allures of the symbolic order. He thus avoids the ideal of a pure, nonrepresentative love that initially seems to overtake him (the love of Belisa's appearance) in favor of a more nuanced, representational (and conspiratorial) form of love (which is indeed the "love of Don Perlimplín").

As I suggested earlier, Lorca seems to have an easier time resisting the temptations of appearance and nonrepresentation than Arendt does her-self. What for Arendt comes from a very complex process and a set of deep ambivalences is for Lorca a function of his deep trust of his own text, of his relative ease in surrendering his status as author to the various subversions that the text may perform. Paradoxically, however, to resist the temptation toward a nonrepresentational form of connection too much would be just as pernicious as not resisting it at all. In Arendt's case, as we have already seen, the pull toward materialism gets her away from the other extreme, too much interiority, too much determinism by the will. In Lorca's case, at least in the context of *The Love of Don Perlimplín*, we see that the hero's belief in or obsession with Belisa's appearance is what preserves his delusion, what gets him into conspiracy in the first place.

The Love of the Sign

We see in the love that emerges between Don Perlimplín and Belisa (as in *La Zapatera Prodigiosa*) the central role of misrecognition. Like Kafka's rendition of Ulysses, or Poe's narrator in "A Descent into the Maelström," Don Perlimplín must not quite understand what he is doing. If he did, his whole scheme, his conspiracy, would not work; it would just produce greater delusion. In the end, Don Perlimplín is redeemed by his conspiracy with language; the signs and objects that he would fetishistically worship (the red cloak, Belisa's body) become instead the means of his own rescue. And Belisa is in her own way redeemed as well. She is transformed, becoming something she did not expect (and certainly did not want to be).

Of course this play hardly has a "happy ending"; Don Perlimplín dies in the end (and by his "own" hand). But he has achieved his dearest goal; he has won Belisa's love, transforming her and in some sense "releasing" Belisa from one set of delusions (and into another). And it is here, especially when read in conjunction with Arendt, that we see the more political side of Lorca emerging. One could argue that if he loves Belisa purely as an appearance, as a mere sign, he could be content living out his life as a cuckold, "having" Belisa as an image that cannot be taken away from him regardless of what she does or says. I would argue that Don Perlimplín conspires against Belisa not so much for his sake as for hers, or maybe for theirs, a small, but nonetheless political community of two. By offering her this phantom lover, a walking sign produced only by words and by a red cloak, Don Perlimplín shows Belisa the same form of love he experiences himself. Ready for a pure love, a perfect and transcendent, nonrepresentational love, the couple receives instead a love they never sought. This is a love made and composed by signs, one that is only and merely representational.

The relationality that emerges here is the same that we saw in Kafka, a relationship that becomes legible (or possible?) only in light of the deflation of grand narratives and great expectations. Yet in Lorca's hands, this kind of relationality becomes something quite intimate. Without being any less political, the relationships that Lorca leaves us with are often very basic, very human: love, family, kinship are all made possible not despite but because of the conspiracy with material objects that subvert our own conscious intentions. What *The Love of Don Perlimplín* suggests, most of all, is how powerful, how seductive the sign can be. When we love with the love of the sign, when our desire is its desire ("the intention of the sign"), we see that we have a powerful way to resist and reshape the world we live in (even if that reshaping is not done by us). Thanks to his conspiracy with the sign, with language itself, both Don Perlimplín and Belisa are brought to love. Crucially (and just as we saw with *The Castle*) the sign's power over us works even (or again especially) when exposed as such. As we see, love does not end when we see and embrace our misrepresentation. In fact, it could be argued that love only really begins at this point.

Conclusion: Finding a Place for the Human

In their mutual quests for exteriority, Arendt and Lorca demonstrate many of the pitfalls and opportunities that an alliance with materiality affords these authors. For Arendt, exteriority is both a goal and a threat. In her almost stubborn insistence on subverting her own ideals of a politics of appearance that eschews representation altogether, Arendt avoids turning the very materiality that she engages with into just another idol, an ur-materiality. What Arendt achieves by instinct (if that is what it is) Lorca achieves by literary device—he too pulls back from a fantasy of pure materiality. We saw in both *La Zapatera Prodigiosa* and *The Love of Don Perlimplín* that material rescues do not produce perfect, happy endings, but complicated and partial resolutions.[87]

We see here in the end another piece of evidence that the mere exposure of the allegory is not in and of itself sufficient. We want very much to be deluded; we want the phantasmagoria to save us. That is why it is possible to have the fetishist that Wendy Brown alludes to, who says, "I know, [it is a fetish] but still . . ."[88] Thus we need the conspiracy with language to render us the kinds of subjects who can and will resist (and not merely see) the symbolic order that we occupy. We not only need to relearn how to see and read but need to perceive with a new sense of self, one that can only be produced via the conspiracy with language. We can perhaps see how Benjamin himself, later in his life, sought to further and deepen his conspiracy, to save even himself from a hope that resistance came from exposure and legibility alone (i.e., from the mere fact of allegory).

In terms of the question of a place for the human and the politics that are produced via misrecognition, we see that for both Arendt and Lorca delusion (and for that matter representation itself), rather than being a necessary evil, can and must constitute and create the "place for the human." It is our delusions that preserve a sense of our own agency even when that agency is delivered to us via our textual conspiracies. It is our delusions that permit us to allegorize the process of representation, even as we are utterly contained within and formed by that process. Finally, it is our delusions that give us a sense of an "outside" perspective from which we can derive impossible and unimaginable outcomes when in fact, to roughly paraphrase Derrida, "There is no outside" (at least not one that we can perceive), only our misrecognition of such.

We ask about "the place of the human" in this context because we fear that without some sense of agency, politics would be impossible. The values of freedom, of action, all the things most dear to Arendt, seem to be tied up with a human subject who regards her- or himself as capable of autonomous decision-making. This is the subjectivity that both Arendt and Lorca sought to discover and/or preserve in the face of the growing mythology of authenticity and order that fascism represented. Such autonomy has to be housed—and even created—somewhere, and we surrender such terrain with great reluctance and trepidation. But as our engagement with Arendt and Lorca suggests, we need not be so fearful. Our choice is not whether to have agency or not, but rather what kind of agency we should have. Our agency, it seems clear, always comes from outside of us, so the only question is whether we get it from the phantasmagoria or from a "conspiracy with language."[89]

The writers we engage with in this chapter have different approaches to this question. We see, for example, in Arendt's notion of a "who" an attempt to think about a self that is externally derived but is still somehow more "authentic" than "what" we otherwise are. But we need to remind ourselves that for Arendt both authenticity and reality are relative concepts. For Arendt, the authenticity of the "who" ultimately comes not from its achievement of a kind of pure perfection (as Agnes Heller explains) but rather from the messy and partial reflections of our own personal and collective narratives that compose the world of representation.

Where Arendt is driven by an often fearful defense of a human perspective (one that preserves, as we have seen, her misrecognition), Lorca embraces a more overt form of textual materialism. He reveals, quite poignantly, that the "self" that is produced by such material alliances is a fully human one, capable of love and the most basic of intimacies. Lorca shows us perhaps more clearly than any of the thinkers that we engage with that a conspiracy with language does not force us to choose between our humanity and our redemption; in fact, both are produced by and in response to the same (textual) source.

In seeking to reconcile a hope that is "not for us" and our own limited and complicit perspective, we see the possibility of a reconciliation, the "progressive deepening of . . . intention" that is anticipated in Benjamin's analysis of the *Trauerspiel.* If selves are, by definition, representational creatures, then we see in this reconciliation not a final, "authentic" self that emerges but instead a reflection of what the self has been all along, a textual—even while it is intimately human—production. What has changed through conspiracy is that this textual self has now (finally) not only become legible to us (at least potentially) but has, in a sense, become "us."

In the next chapter, we will engage in our final pairing of a theorist, Frantz Fanon, and a writer, Assia Djebar. These authors too share a context, in this case the Algerian revolution and its aftermath. In turning to these writers, we are also turning away from Europe and the United States, and toward the question of politics as it is practiced on a global scale. We will see how this conspiracy can and must be extended to consider questions of colonialism and postcolonialism, racism and gender relations, in other, non-Western contexts. In addition to moving beyond the narrow canon of Western political theory and literature, in looking at these two writers in constellation we are attempting to think, finally, about the future, about what happens "next." From our trap in our own temporal contexts, it seems clear that there is no future at all (this is what Benjamin explains to us in his "Theses on the Philosophy of History"). Does a conspiracy with language produce something like a future, some kind of direction that we can move to that is not totally determined by what has already been? In the case of Fanon and Djebar, their challenge is to imagine an Algeria that is not overdetermined by the pitfalls of either colonialism or postcolonialism, despite acknowledging that it is impossible to escape this temporal and spatial context. In their attempts to think about an Algerian future nonetheless, these authors display textual acts of recognized misrecognition that are crucial for any thought of resistance to a phantasmagoria that is global. Despite the fact that it cannot be done, they engage with an idea of the future, offering us one final way in which we can think about a textual conspiracy in a wider, global, and explicitly political context.

6 | Reconstructing the World:
Frantz Fanon and Assia Djebar

In turning to Fanon and Djebar, we come finally to one of the most crucial aspects of our inquiry: the problematization of politics from the perspective of colonialism, globalized racism, and imperialism. Here, in addition to the woes of alienation and commodity fetishism, we see some of
deepest evils of the phantasmagoria at work, the effects of mythology and
commodity fetishism as a worldwide practice. In looking at these writers'
respective responses to that global practice, we also expand, as already
noted, from an exclusive look at texts from the Western canon, to other
texts, other perspectives.

In the writings of Frantz Fanon and Assia Djebar, especially when we
read these authors through the lens of Benjaminian conspiracy, we see a
renewed attention to the question of action, of reconstruction and moving on from a past and a present that feel like an irresistible destiny. Reading Fanon and Djebar in constellation helps to focus our inquiry on one
place, one revolution and its aftermath: Algeria in the late fifties and early
sixties and what has happened since. Our reading of the events of the Algerian revolution cannot help but be informed by subsequent events.
Through its revolution, the country now has, in Djebar's terms, "an Algerian night that is no longer colonial."[1] Yet Algeria is hardly "free," the Algerian people are hardly "self-determining." The very revolutionary apparatus of the state has become harshly antidemocratic, and the nation has
been roiled by the often extraordinarily violent struggle between the state
and Islamic radicals. In the face of such events, the hopes for a "free Algeria" seem quixotic, never possible in the first place; the revolution seems to
have been doomed from the start.

Here we are returned to a familiar gloom—the very one Benjamin
faced toward the end of his life. In a sense the "failures" of the Algerian
revolution are no different than the myriad other failed revolutions witnessed by Benjamin, as well as Arendt, Baudelaire, and many others. There

is perhaps therefore nothing unique about this revolution or those writers and activists who were involved in it. Yet by examining the work of Fanon and Djebar in particular, we can see an ethos of salvaging resistance and a sense of a future even given their respective certainties (Fanon mainly by intuition and insight and Djebar by the subsequent developments of post-colonialism) that this revolution could not and would not succeed—at least not in the way that it was intended to.

The challenge facing Fanon and Djebar is to form, out of the chaos of events, people, and experiences that forms Algeria's "history," some notion or gesture toward what Algeria means or could mean, some notion of what Algeria is when it is not simply determined by France, by its own leaders, by Islamic radicals, and by the failure of its revolution. What is Algeria besides the various competing mythologies that are vying to remake it in their image (with many of these mythologies bearing their own acronym: the OAS, the FNL, the FIS)? To tie this back to Tocqueville, these authors face the question of how to produce or recognize a narrative for a community that is neither "authentic" (because to say so would be once again to succumb to utter delusion) nor handed to them by the colonial and postcolonial experience.

At bottom, this question of what Algeria is or means is once again a question of representation and the difficulties and paradoxes that it produces. How does one "represent" Algeria in all of its complexity? What, if anything, remains when the various mythologies that currently constitute it are disrupted or exposed? As with many of the writers we have examined in this book, both Fanon and Djebar seek to engage with the power of texts, with signs and writing as a way to come to grips with the power of representation. They both recognize that wars and revolutions are not just conducted in the streets and with guns, but also occur on the level of the psyche, in culture, in gender relations, in language and thought. In Fanon's quest to overcome the psychic degradations of racism, in Djebar's engagement with questions of gender and the persistence of colonial relationships of power long after the revolution has ended, we see an acknowledgment of this requirement to confront colonialism and the phantasmagoria on all levels, and perhaps especially at the level of semiotics.

In terms of their respective biographies, Frantz Fanon was born in Martinique and studied psychiatry in France. He eventually moved to Algeria to practice psychiatry there, but he got increasingly radicalized over the course of his life; both personally and professionally, he experienced the ravages of racism and colonialism on people of color all over the world. Exiled from Algeria, he got very involved in the revolutionary movement but fell ill with leukemia and died in 1961. His most famous book, *The Wretched of the Earth* (which I will consider in significant detail in this chapter), helped make a name for him as a fiery revolutionary. Assia Djebar (the pen name of Fatimah-Zorah Imalayen) was born in Algeria and eventually became a student in Paris, where she has lived much of her life, along with time spent in Switzerland, Tunisia, and Algeria. Her novel *Children of the New World* (which I will also treat at length in this chapter) helped make her reputation as a writer. Some of her other well-known books include *So Vast the Prison, Women of Algiers in their Apartment,* and *Algerian White* (which I will also consider in this chapter).

Forming a constellation between Fanon and Djebar is easy in the sense that they actually knew each other. At one point, Djebar worked as a reporter for a revolutionary paper *El-Moudjahid* in Tunis for which Fanon served as editor. She also remained friends with his wife Josie long after Fanon's death (she writes about both of their deaths in *Algerian White*).[2]

Despite their connection, there are important differences between Fanon and Djebar. Fanon's rhetoric is far more fiery and confident, Djebar's more reflective, less polemical. At the same time, a close (and conspiratorial) reading of Fanon reveals that his texts often undermine or call into question his own assertions. Not unlike Arendt and Lorca, Fanon's texts allegorize and problematize his own ideals, in this case in terms of his contributions to the mythologies of Algeria, thereby aligning him more closely with Djebar than might first seem evident.

Both of these authors are deeply ambivalent. As we have seen in previous chapters, while ambivalence can be a source of prevarication and incoherence, when read through a conspiratorial lens, such ambivalence serves to deepen and further resistance. The ambivalence these authors display helps keep them focused, not so much on "what can be done" (since that is a work in progress and not determined by what we imagine to be the case) but rather on how and in what manner we "do things" in the first place, how and if our very thoughts and actions can avoid merely replicating the same failures over and over again.

In this regard, Fanon and Djebar offer us yet another view of the power (and limits) of recognizing misrecognition. Both authors engage in repeated acts of misrecognition: Fanon by continuing to believe in and advocate for revolution even when he "knows better," Djebar by believing in the possibility of an Algerian future that is not determined purely by colonialism and the postcolonial experience when she too sees the impossibility of what she seeks. Yet these are not naive acts of delusion and false hope for these authors. As we will see further, both Fanon and Djebar allow their fantasies of deliverance and salvation (i.e., the fantasy of total revolution, of full and self-determining national identity and democracy) to be undermined and altered by the very texts that deliver them. So decentered, these phantasms do not disappear; their authors do not stop believing in them. Yet, in their altered form, such fantasies change and undermine a particular sense of historical defeat and certainty. The communities and resistances that already exist in Algeria become legible and "possible" even in a context where they are manifestly inconceivable.

In this chapter, we are looking particularly at the act of reconstructing the world, reordering and reshuffling the symbolic order in ways that defy and resist the strong sense of doom and predetermination that permeates our (and their) time and condition. As we have already seen in chapter 4, we must give up on hope for our salvation, in order to be available for some kind of salvation after all. Fanon and Djebar follow the strategy of clinging (like Poe's narrator) to the sign as a way to save themselves from being condemned by their own hopes and beliefs.

As we will see further, looking at Fanon and Djebar through a conspiratorial, Benjaminian lens allows us to see that the "future" that we seek, the "next" step that we must take, is in fact already "here." That is to say, while striving to find out what Algeria "means" or "is" when it is not defined by its past and present context, to find out what Algeria could yet be, we need only to understand what Algeria is and has always been when not read through the idolatrous lens of the phantasmagoria (more specifically in this case the phantasmagoria of colonialism and postcolonialism).

Throughout this book we have been seeing that even in the heart of the phantasmagoria, in the veritable "belly of the beast," there are always communities and identities that are being formed, lives that are being lived that are not recognized insofar as they are overwritten by (even as they are formed in response to) the phantasmagoria. In Algeria too, we will see that when such an overwriting is disrupted by a conspiracy with language, what emerges is an Algerian "future" that is already here, already possible. This "future" is humbler, more inchoate, and less definitive than the promise of future that the phantasmagoria seduces us with. *This* Algeria will always be more scattered, fragmentary, and problematic than the shining and perfect "Algeria" that these authors look to and hope for. The Algeria that is already here, as we will see further, is rather (and merely) a rejuxtaposition of all of the complicit and problematical forms of Algeria that are held in contestation (an idea that Fanon evokes when he speaks of "struggle" as the basis for a different ontology). To find an Algeria that can be their home amid the ruins of their dreams of a different, truer Algeria stands as the key challenge posed to these writers. Let us examine each of them in turn.

Frantz Fanon

For all this talk of failure, in some ways, Fanon has already succeeded, and wildly, as a textual conspirator (and as a conspirator taken in the more ordinary sense as well). As Homi K. Bhabha writes in his foreword to *The Wretched of the Earth*:

> In 1966, Bobby Seale and Huey Newton read *The Wretched of the Earth* in a house in Oakland, and—so the story goes—when they were arrested some months later for "blocking the sidewalk," the text provided foundational perspectives on neocolonialism and nationalism that inspired the founding of the Black Nationalist Party. . . . In the early seventies, Steve Biko's room in the student residence of the University of Natal became . . . the intellectual center of the black consciousness movement. That dorm room in Durban was the place where Biko, "the person who brought ideas," first circulated *The Wretched of the Earth* to his friends and comrades—writers, activists, community workers, actors, students—who were also conversant with the poetry and the politics of the Black Panther movement.[3]

Bhabha goes on to show how this text inspired other radicals ranging from Bobby Sands in prison in Belfast to Ali Shariati, a leading intellect in the Shiite revival who in turn helped inspire the Iranian revolution. We see here a clear example of a transtemporal constellation, an idea, communicated purely in a text that is deeply implicated with other generations of revolutionaries. Fanon's text is unique in our own examination insofar as it is already powerfully connected in a chain of revolutionary moments, thoughts, and actions.

At the same time, to be sure, none of these revolutions have quite turned out the way Fanon might have intended. Except for a few, partial cases, such as Cuba, the visions of third world radicalism, shorn from colonialism and engaged with an entirely new set of realities, cannot really be said to have taken place in our world to date—at least not in a sustained and ongoing manner.

Is it too much to ask of one text, or one author, to do more than Fanon has already done? Perhaps it is. Yet that is exactly why we must engage in intertextual conspiracies in the first place. One text informs another and is, in turn, informed. In this mutual interaction, a change is effected and produced in our own response to the phantasmagorias of power. The value of such conspiracy comes in the unexpected and unintended consequences of such juxtapositions of readings.

Thus, when we look at Fanon, not by himself, but in constellation with other writers, we can possibly further benefit from our inclusion of his texts in a textual conspiracy, adding a new dimension to his already impressive effects as a conspirator. As with each author that we have studied so far (Benjamin very much included) there is space for considering Fanon's work in ways that Fanon himself may not have intended or imagined (to some extent, that is the point of this exercise).

And yet it should be said that this author—and in particular this author's most revolutionary and inspirational of texts, *The Wretched of the Earth*—may have as much or even more to offer than he receives from such an act of juxtaposition. For example, we see that unlike Benjamin, Fanon is caught up in an actual revolutionary movement: that of Algeria against its former colonial power, France. While Fanon gave himself over body and soul to this struggle, Benjamin tended to keep himself far away from the actual practice of politics except insofar as his interventions in radio, collage, and writing can (and should) be deemed political—hence his move toward conspiracy in the first place. Even as we implicate Fanon in Benjamin's conspiracy, it is helpful to engage Benjamin with an author like Fanon (Machiavelli is another example) who does not shy away from such overt engagements. Such an association may help to better connect this conspiracy to that very thing which it tries to redeem—revolution.

Yet, for all of his radicalism, in his exhortations for third world radicalism and revolution, Fanon often strikes many (although certainly not all) contemporaries as being out of our time; his talk of revolution speaks of an age that seems no longer to exist. It becomes difficult to think of Fanon as seriously offering some model of political resistance when his vision seems manifestly impossible and anachronistic. One benefit of reading Fanon's texts through the lens of a Benjaminian conspiracy is to help bring his work back into an engagement with our time and other times as well. In this context, Fanon's work becomes (relatively) immune to the phantasms of time by which capitalism puts boundaries upon certain historical moments and the various concepts (such as revolution) associated with them.

In this way, Fanon's concept of revolution becomes something other than a temporally determined narrative of liberation. While his personal and professional commitment to the revolution he was part of required a certain stance on the part of the author, his text often fails to convey this stance properly (as already suggested). As we will see further, Fanon's text in a sense redeems Fanon's revolution, making it not simply an artifact of his intentionality (which then truly would be bound by his time and context) but a series of strategies and textual misrecognitions that we can engage with to this day. In examining the nature of Fanon's "recognized misrecognition" we begin to get a sense of what revolution still means when it is not simply bound by our desire for a perfect and pure redemption, how by aligning ourselves with the "intention of the sign," we come to find a form of redemption, a "future" after all, even if not what we hoped for or expected.

The Phantasms of Colonialism

For both Fanon and Benjamin the question of the production of reality (or what passes for it) is paramount. Both writers seek to resist a stream of phantasms that not only issues from but also constitutes the framework of a hateful political structure, the phantasmagoria.

In Fanon's case in particular, the prevalence of phantasm can be directly attributed to the colonial experience. For Fanon, the colonial subject (and perhaps the postcolonial subject as well) is in many ways a fantastic creature. In *The Wretched of the Earth* he writes: "It is the colonist who *fabricated* and *continues to fabricate* the colonized subject."[4] As with Benjamin, this spectral reality extends not only through space (via the vicissitudes of colonialism) but time as well. Fanon sees that under conditions of colonialism, the "traditions" of a people, their very notion of their own past and its meaning, become in effect a tool of colonization:

> In scaring me, the atmosphere of myths and magic operates like an undeniable reality. In terrifying me, it incorporates me into the traditions and history of my land and ethnic group, but at the same time I am reassured and granted a civil status, an identification. The secret sphere in underdeveloped countries is a collective sphere that falls exclusively within the realm of magic. By entangling me in this inextricable web where gestures are repeated with a secular limpidity, my very own world, our very own world, thus perpetuates itself. Zombies, believe me, are more terrifying than colonists. . . . The magical, supernatural powers prove to be surprisingly ego boost-

ing. The colonist's powers are infinitely shrunk, stamped by for-
eignness. There is no real reason to fight them because what really
matters is that the mythical structures contain far more terrifying
adversaries. It is evident that everything is reduced to a permanent
confrontation at the level of phantasy.[5]

We see in this passage once again how "reality" can be a production of
images, often working at cross-purposes with the struggle against colonialism. Any sense of "authenticity" and a people's "true nature" is revealed in Fanon's astute observation as just another facet of power. In the
time of colonialization, there is no past, no present that is not itself an
artifact of rule. Even objectivity seems to be a product of colonialization,
as when Fanon writes: "For the colonized subject, objectivity is always directed against him."[6] Thus Fanon, like Benjamin, finds himself facing a
dead end of time, a position from which there seems to be no way out. But
Fanon, perhaps more than anyone else in this book (possibly including
Benjamin), refuses to accept these terms; his struggle is absolute; he offers
a total resistance to being determined by temporal and conceptual norms.

At first blush, the form of Fanon's resistance seems to lie in a recourse
to "reality" as a counterweight to the phantasms of colonialism. He tells
us, "To politicize the masses is to make the nation in its totality a reality
for every citizen."[7] Fanon turns to violence (a loaded and complex concept, as we will see), to nationalism (as a stepping stone to "a social and
political consciousness"), and to struggle as a way to redeploy the bases
of reality in a way that resists, rather than supports, colonialism.[8] He
further writes:

> After years of unreality, after wallowing in the most extraordinary
> phantasms, the colonized subject, machine gun at the ready, finally
> confronts the only force which challenges his very being: colonial-
> ism. And the young colonized subject who grows up in an atmo-
> sphere of fire and brimstone has no scruples mocking zombie an-
> cestors, two-headed horses, corpses woken from the dead, and
> djinns who, taking advantage of a yawn, slip inside the body. The
> colonized subject discovers reality and transforms it through his
> praxis, his deployment of violence and his agenda for liberation.[9]

Here we see an "agenda for liberation"; the pseudo past gives way to a new
kind of "real" future.

And yet, for all of his seeking of reality, Fanon seems at times in real despair about where to find it, about how to know what it actually consists of. Fanon is always clear that although the "reality" of colonialism may be bogus, as a lived experience, it is all too tangible (all too "real," one might say). The experience of colonialism has a stranglehold on the very psyche of the colonized subject (as we will come to see more clearly) that survives the "regime change" that Fanon officially advocates.

In speaking of the struggle against or even demise of colonialism, Fanon speaks of a "vertigo" (*vertige*) during such moments.[10] This is a confusion that arises from the loss of the very revolutionary clarity that Fanon often asserts; it is a reflection of the complexities and entanglements of the colonial legacy that defy easy and decisive solutions. He describes, for example, one of his psychiatric patients, a former member of the resistance who suffered from anxiety and insomnia. He had bombed a crowded café and, after having met people from the colonizing nation who sympathized with his revolution, he worried that some at that café (although it was "known to be the haunt of notorious racists") might also have been sympathetic to his cause.[11] This realization produces in the patient a "kind of vertigo."

> In other words, our actions never cease to haunt us. The way they are ordered, organized, and reasoned can be a posteriori radically transformed. It is by no means the least of the traps history and its many determinations set for us. But can we escape vertigo? Who dares claim that vertigo does not prey on every life?[12]

The anxiety he describes here derives from a psychological confusion that even the militant cannot quite escape. When certain oppositions become less certain, a deep psychic crisis follows for the would-be revolutionary. If the "Other" is not who we thought, then who are we? The bonds between subject and colonizer do not readily give way even in the face of revolutionary violence. And Fanon indicates that this crisis is not limited to psychiatric patients ("Who dares claim that vertigo does not prey on every life?").

In this way, we can see Fanon as describing an anxiety that troubles his own revolutionary fervor. Insofar as Fanon sees even reality itself as being a shifting arena of effects, it becomes difficult to locate the very kinds of revolutionary certainty that he calls for. "Reality" does not therefore serve as the alternative to colonialism that Fanon sometimes suggests. This reality is, after all, also of necessity representative and as such is neither firm nor sure but always an open question.

The Shifting Grounds of Race

We can see many of these same questions and ambivalences on Fanon's part when he considers the all-important question of race. It would seem that race is the main anchor for Fanon's ontology, the basis for his resistance and the source of his materiality (or "reality"). In *Black Skin, White Masks,* he writes: "I am the slave not of the 'idea' that others have of me but of my own appearance."[13] It would seem as though his own blackness becomes a fact, an unshakeable identity that Fanon fiercely embraces. Yet David Macey cautions us not to confuse facticity for experience in Fanon's work. This confusion may be worse among his English-speaking readers than his French-speaking ones. Macey tells us, for example, that the English translation of the title for the fifth chapter of *The Wretched of the Earth* is "The Fact of Blackness," whereas the French title means something more like "The lived experience of the black man" ("L'expérience vécue du Noir").[14] According to Macey, for Fanon, there is no "fact" of blackness; rather skin color becomes a site of semiotic contestation:

> the point of Fanon's exercise in socio-diagnostics is to demonstrate that there is no "fact" of blackness (or, by the same criterion, whiteness); both are a form of lived experience (expérience vécue; Erlebnis). To mistake a lived experience for a fact is to betray Fanon's text to such an extent as to make it almost incomprehensible.[15]

Echoing this idea, Lewis R. Gordon reminds us of Fanon's roots in existentialism. Gordon tells us that "as a radical humanist [Fanon] stands in a critical relation to ontology. He rejects all ontology that puts existence to the wayside. His sentiment is fundamentally existential."[16] Race, as it emerges in Fanon's text, is a disturbed and shifting phenomenon without being any less crucial or definitive. It remains definitive for Fanon because race and racial identity can often be an instrument of power and manipulation (even as it is also a fulcrum for resistance to that power):

> The people who in the early days of the struggle had adopted the primitive Manicheanism of the colonizer—Black versus White, Arab versus Infidel—realize en route that some blacks can be whiter than whites, and that the prospect of a national flag or independence does not automatically result in certain segments of the population giving up their privileges and their interests.[17]

In *A Dying Colonialism,* Fanon tells us that "it is the white man who creates the Negro."[18] The production of a distinction between "white" northern Africa and "black" southern Africa is for Fanon typical of the kind of false dichotomies that allow colonialism to succeed (and even after colonialism ends, to linger on in the form of racism).

The shifting grounds of race as measured against Fanon's own lived experience and self-expression as a man of color can be seen, for example, in the differing perspectives of *Black Skin, White Masks* and *The Wretched of the Earth.* In the former text, he writes fully from an Antillean perspective. In his introduction to *Black Skin, White Masks,* Fanon writes, "Since I was born in the Antilles, my observations and my conclusions are valid only for the Antilles—at least concerning the black man *at home* [*chez lui*]."[19] Yet, by the time he writes *The Wretched of the Earth,* we find that he has transformed himself, at least textually, into an Algerian. He uses the term "we Algerians [Nous, Algériens]"[20] and also notes that "We have taken the Algerian example . . . not to glorify our own people."[21] On the next page he also writes, "We African politicians."[22] This new "we" attests, at least in terms of his own person, to the fluidity of the very categories that are so integral to him. It also marks a change from his self-perception in *Black Skin, White Masks* when he writes: "Some ten years ago, I was astonished to learn that the North Africans despised men of color. It was absolutely impossible for me to make any contact with the local population."[23] In his experiences between the writings of these two books, Fanon seems to have left one set of ontologies and possibilities for another.[24]

Yet, even in *Black Skin, White Masks* we see the shifting grounds of race identity at play. As someone from Martinique, he is (or his fellow Martinicans are), in his own words, "closer to the white man" than Africans are.[25] Even among his fellow Antilleans, there are fine and meaningful gradations. He writes that those from Guadeloupe are "farther away from the white man" than the Martinicans themselves.[26]

It is almost as if, in "becoming" an Algerian by the time he writes *The Wretched of the Earth,* Fanon has purged himself of a particular pathology (one that he described in depth in *Black Skin, White Masks*), and yet the markers and pathologies of race are not so easily gotten rid of. The text permits him to put on and take off these identities and in a sense undermines his absolute identification(s) at any one time. This does not mean that the text "proves" that race is somehow consciously (or even unconsciously) enacted; the fervor of identity that the author expresses in each case is evidence that it is not. Rather it shows how the text complicates and renders more ambiguous the strictures of race, even as it permits what seems impossible—the alterations of racial identity in the span of a few years. In this way we can see how the text allegorizes race, rendering race legible both in its power to produce absolute identifications and in its transmissibility and its vulnerability as a category. It reveals that the intentions and self-identification of the author are, in this case, not so much to be discarded as read as part of the functioning and iterability of race as a semiotic practice.

A Psychology of Signs

We can see a similar dynamic of textual subversion or complication in Fanon's treatment of one of the central components of the "reality" that is built by colonialism, namely psychology. Here, once again, Fanon's authorial position as an advocate of a revolution in the psyche of colonized people is complicated and rendered more ambiguous by the very texts that deliver his judgments.

Trained as a psychiatrist, Fanon sees the traumas of racism and colonialism as having their primary effect in the psychological makeup of the subject.[27] His approach to psychology is a highly semiotic one; in Fanon's view, the fabrication of a self is both produced in and contested by a series of readings and structurings. Accordingly, Fanon seeks to strategically conceptualize the psyche as a zone of combat and resistance. As he tells us in *Black Skin, White Masks:* "I believe that the fact of the juxtaposition of the white and black race has created a massive psychoexistential complex. I hope by analyzing it to destroy it."[28] In making such a claim, Fanon suggests the possibility of a new form of psychic formation that is not simply another iteration of this "psychoexistential complex."[29]

Yet this hope for destruction and cure is complicated by the way Fanon conceptualizes the psyche in the first place. In his embrace of psychology, Fanon both works with and refutes Lacan. In *Black Skin, White Masks*, Fanon tells us that Lacan's mirror stage is the key to understanding black self consciousness as well as white, but with one key difference; racializing Lacan's conception, Fanon argues that the "Other" that is produced for the white subject is the black subject and the black subject is the converse to the white.[30] Yet this relationship is not symmetrical by any means: "Only for the white man The Other is perceived on the level of the body image, absolutely as the not-self—that is, the unidentifiable, the unassimilable. For the black man, as we have shown, historical and economic realities come into the picture."[31] When whites dream, he tells us, their nightmares are invaded by a black other. When blacks dream, they "ha[ve] no color," or if they do, it is white or pink.[32]

Thus for Fanon, the black subject (at least the Antillean one he focuses on in that book) has a kind of second subjectification experience. "Historical and economic realities" that impinge on subjectivity mean that the black Antillean subject's own self-recognition is finalized by an act of interpellation. David Macey references this when he describes Fanon's experience (described in *Black Face, White Masks*) of being spotted by a young white child in Lyons who turned toward him and said, "tiens, un nègre" ("look, a negro").[33] Such interpellation (à la Althusser) inserts itself into or interacts with the "psychoexistential complex" of lived black experience. Such interpellation comes as a surprise to the black subject, who up till then had not understood the nature of his subjecthood (at least as Fanon understands and experiences it). Thus Fanon writes:

> As long as the black man is among his own, he will have no occasion, except in minor internal conflicts, to experience his being through others. There is of course the moment of "being for others," of which Hegel speaks, but every ontology is made unattainable in a colonized and civilized society.[34]

Given this form of psychic formation, it is not clear that the racialization of the Other can be so easily "destroyed" or "cured." The very premise of Fanon's psychology is that the formation of black subjectivity reflects the "historical and economic realities" of the colonial—and postcolonial—world. Thus, a psyche based on struggle against colonization will not destroy so much as resist the ravages of colonialism. To put this in the language of a Benjaminian conspiracy, to allow the allegorical nature of the psyche to become legible to the subject is not to free the subject from it or to offer redemption in the normal meaning of that term. Instead it serves as an opportunity for resistance, for struggle, and, ultimately, for a rejuxtaposition of the materials that make up identity in the hopes of avoiding some of its traps as it is currently constituted.

This may seem a disappointing message from the perspective of Fanon's own stated authorial intention to "destroy" the psychoexistential complex of colonialism. But the text resists that perfect destruction, that dream of a pure (and nonsemiotic, nonrepresentational) "reality." Accordingly, as it is rendered by Fanon's text, the psyche becomes less a place to clear of colonial influences than what it has always been: a semiotic battle-ground, a potential site for conspiracy.[35]

The "Reality" of Resistance

In terms of what is produced by this battle, what that new version of "reality" might consist of, we see unsettlement rather than resolution. If the grounds of race shift as much as they anchor, if the psyche cannot be destroyed so much as held in tension, then Fanon is not offering solutions so much as strategies. This is why reading him in constellation with Benjamin is especially helpful. If we look for Fanon to "answer" the problem of race and psyche, he will disappoint us; he will be returned to his temporal prison, too removed from us to be of any help. But if we read him as a conspirator, as someone who shows us how to struggle, how to resist in the midst of an ongoing form of resistance or process, then we do have something to learn from him: namely, how the rearrangement of existing reality can, even if in limited or partial doses, alter or subvert a particular mode of being, an "ontology." In this spirit we can read many of Fanon's hesitations and enthusiasms as attempts, however varied, to enact this rearrangement or realignment; even if the particular rearrangements he (or his text) offers do not always satisfy, they suggest a style of being that can adapt and even find its solace in the shifting forms of reality and resistance, disappointment and tenacity that characterize this conspiratorial style.

The upshot of the cumulative textual undermining we have been examining is that it prevents Fanon from realizing his own wish for "reality," for an escape from the onus of representation, very much as we saw in the case of Arendt, Lorca, and other coconspirators. In the absence of such certainty or ontological salvation, we are left instead with the need for struggle, for an ongoing grappling (and conspiracy) with the signs and symbols that form (in this case) the postcolonial world. In continuing to believe in revolution, a total cleansing and new beginning that his own text has rendered impossible, Fanon is not naively and fetishistically clinging to a kind of false hope. Insofar as his texts repeatedly defeat or complicate his hopes (again, not unlike what we already saw with Arendt), Fanon engages in his own form of recognized misrecognition. Here, revolution itself becomes an ongoing realignment and rejuxtaposition that remains fully engaged with (and seduced by) the symbolic order even as it thoroughly resists the particular manifestation of colonial and postcolonial authority that such an order has, up till now, entailed. We can see the functioning of this understanding of revolution most clearly when we consider Fanon's famous (and infamous) writings on violence.

"On Violence"

Many authors have tried to argue that Fanon's claims about violence are misunderstood. Even Hannah Arendt, who is famous for denouncing Fanon in her own essay entitled "On Violence," writes in a footnote to that essay that

> Fanon himself . . . is much more doubtful about violence than his admirers. It seems that only the book's first chapter, "Concerning Violence," has been widely read. Fanon knows of the "unmixed and total brutality which, if not immediately combatted, invariably leads to the defeat of the movement within a few weeks.[36]

I don't want to really take sides on this issue per se, but rather to note that the ongoing centrality of violence to Fanon's argument (whether it is meant metaphorically or literally or some combination of the two, as I suspect) suggests the need for the demarcation or dramatization to the self of a break with colonial ontologies. Insofar as in Fanon's case we are dealing with a rejuxtaposition of existing forms of representation rather than an absolute new (and therefore inherently mythical) beginning, such a break must be clearly noted and rendered legible to the subject whom it affects. Indeed the dramatization of a break with the past (and present) serves as the very basis for the new "self" that emerges out of existing semiotic constructions.

Fanon's notion of violence can thus be seen as integral to his practice of recognized misrecognition. His belief in the ability of violence (however it is considered) to achieve a break with past practices is critical because it gets at (or produces) a renewed sense of agency and its possibility. To believe in violence is to believe in one's own ability to change a world that manifestly cannot be changed (and in that wrong belief, as we have already seen with Arendt and others, such change becomes conceivable after all, albeit not in the form we expect and desire).

Here again, for Fanon, the practice of violence rejuxtaposes rather than radically alters that which it breaks with. Despite using language of "cleansing," of "ridding" and "achieving," I would suggest that violence for Fanon is less a cure (my word, not his) than it is an antidote (taken in the Benjaminian sense).[37] Violence entails having the tools—and in particular the semiotic tools—of the colonial masters used against them. The people learn "tangibility" when they take on the violence of colonialism as their own project; they earn a place at the ontological table by employing the same brute forms of mastery that have rendered them colonial subjects in the first place. In other words, Fanon's call to violence may be less a desire for revenge and giving the French a taste of their own medicine (although it surely is that as well) than a way to teach a community how to wield its own semiotic force, to deploy the theatricality and spectacle of politics of its own accord and in so doing, multiply the ways that reality is read, produced, and fomented. By advocating physical violence as he does, Fanon is also suggesting a kind of semiotic violence, a kind of collective misrecognition (implemented, however, on an individual basis) wherein we somehow align ourselves with the signs that constitute the grounds of our own subjection (a set of actions that he models in his own text). Here, narrativity, the formation of a group's collective identity, becomes politicized, becomes available for alterations and/or reflections of that community's own practices.

Arendt and Fanon

In order to clarify these points, and also in order to align Fanon with one of his more vociferous critics (who I nevertheless treat as his coconspirator), I seek to reconcile or at least approximate Fanon's understanding of violence with that of Hannah Arendt. In her own essay "On Violence," Arendt famously opposes Fanon, lumping him together with Pareto and Sorel (and Sartre as well, to some extent). Arendt, it should be said, is not absolutely opposed to violence per se. What she opposes is the systematic or "rationalized" use of violence as a substitute for (and ultimately destroyer of) political space:

> To use reason when reason is used as a trap is not "rational"; just as to use a gun in self-defense is not "irrational." This violent reaction against hypocrisy, however justifiable in its own terms, loses its *raison d'être* when it tries to develop a strategy of its own with specific goals: it becomes "irrational" the moment it is "rationalized," that is, the moment the re-action in the course of a contest turns into an action.[38]

As we already saw above, there is a sense in which Arendt separates Fanon himself from Pareto and Sorel in that she claims he does not romanticize violence to the degree that the others do. She implies that Sartre, in his own reading and response to Fanon, is swayed by the latter's "worst rhetorical excesses" and that in fact Fanon is "closer to reality than most."[39] Yet this is hardly a compliment on her part; Arendt's complaint is that *any* call to violence is inherently antipolitical. While in private instances such a response may well be justified, it is never justified when violence comes to replace the collective actions of people that underlie political life (such a power, she tells us, "needs no justification, being inherent in the very existence of political communities").[40] Violence, for Arendt, is instrumental; it denies human plurality, and, worst of all, it simply replicates itself, rather than building something new (i.e., power). What Fanon is calling for, she is telling us, is not a political revolution at all, but instead an uprising based on rage and vengeance.

Arendt depicts Fanon as a writer who is less bloodthirsty than he initially appears to be but who has somehow gotten swept up—whether as himself or at least as a figure that influenced other radicals—in the mythologies of revolution. Among those mythologies, Arendt writes (quite controversially at the time) that "The Third World is not a reality, but an ideology."[41] She tells us that the very idea of Third World solidarity is based on an erroneous connection to the Marxist slogan "Workers of the World Unite!" which she says has been "thoroughly discredited."[42] Here we come back to a point that can often be raised against Benjamin as well; the notion that some kind of romantic and ineffectual view of revolution can derail a theorist's effectiveness. But I would argue here that Arendt is missing something crucial in her rush to condemn Fanon's approach to violence.

What she misses is precisely the kinds of semiotic strategies that Fanon—and Arendt herself for that matter—is involved with. To miss this aspect of Fanon is to literalize the violence he calls for (although, to be fair, she doesn't always say this, and furthermore, it is not clear that he doesn't sometimes mean it literally). This is not to argue, as many others have, that Fanon means violence "metaphorically" instead of literally (although he may do that too). Rather, it is to insist that his advocacy for violence should be understood at least partly in terms of a semiotic strategy; in my view, it is the rhetorical effect of the call for violence, rather than the practice of violence itself, that anchors Fanon's strategies of resistance.

Arendt's critique of Fanon misses out on the textual dimension that I have been describing, wherein the text resists even as it promulgates some of Fanon's "rhetorical excesses." In his expressions of violence and third world solidarity, Fanon may in part be getting swept up in some kind of dream, as Arendt suggests, but he, or at least his text, is certainly also dramatizing and suggesting new juxtapositions, new possibilities and readings in his constant semiotic struggle with the legacy of colonialism. Fanon may or may not believe in third world solidarity (his biographies suggest that he has a complicated attitude on this question), but he advances this notion in the same way he advances the idea of violence, in the service of his attempt to reconfigure the signs and images of his time.[43] Rather than seeking to begin again or turn to some kind of "authentic" third world identity (which he—and/or his text—renders impossible), Fanon shows how one can radicalize a given set of signs and employ them in a way that subverts and threatens the very status quo from which it is derived, here again evoking a strategy of the antidote, as we saw earlier with Benjamin.

Where I would part company most firmly with Arendt's interpretation is that, where she sees him as being, to some extent, a victim of his own phantasms, I see Fanon as being quite deft and agile, quite strategic in his engagement with such devices. Indeed, as we have already noted, in embracing a third world that may or may not have existed in his lifetime, in embracing a violence that threatens to undermine many of his own most cherished goals, Fanon is evincing a strategy that Arendt herself practices—namely the strategy of misrecognition (as I have begun to suggest). Just as Kafka's "K." misrecognizes the idea of human rights—mistakenly believing in an idea that the supposed beneficiaries of such "rights" know to be false—so too does Fanon misrecognize the "third world" and even the value of violence and revolution. But whereas Kafka's character's misrecognition comes from a kind of naive optimism, Fanon is practicing a (textually derived) strategy. In so doing, Fanon refuses to allow himself to be dictated to by his time or his circumstances.

In seeking to reconcile Arendt with Fanon, I would not argue that they are actually in agreement on violence after all. While one could argue that the mass movement against the French in Algeria could be called an instance of power, instead of violence (using Arendt's terms), Fanon's explicit calls for cutting throats and so on probably makes such a link too unpalatable for Arendt (although surely some throats were cut in the American Revolution as well). Furthermore, Arendt's view of Algeria and Fanon's role in it may very well be colored by the question of color itself.[44] Yet through their collective acts of misrecognition, we can see some commonalities, some constellations, after all.

Misrecognition and the "Future"

Fanon's approach to politics and to the legacies of colonialism may look like mere stubbornness or a refusal to "understand reality," but when we think about his consistent focus on semiotic forms of resistance, we can see this misrecognition in a new light. As we have seen, what saves Fanon from a merely stubborn advocacy of what is in fact impossible is the way that his texts void or complicate the very center of his ideals—thus echoing the kind of messianic "rescues" that we saw with Kafka as well. So voided, Fanon's key notions, of race, of postcolonial reality, of the "third world," even of revolution, do not disappear. They remain as categories but categories marked by an *aporia* that protects them from degenerating into just another (false) truth.

In this way, Fanon's texts answer his own most pressing anxiety: that the revolution he calls for will simply replace one set of false ontologies with another, one myth with another. Read as a coconspirator with Benjamin—even with Arendt—Fanon shows how this danger can be avoided precisely by having his own texts save his misrecognitions from becoming just more renditions of the phantasmagoria. Instead, the self-inflicted ambivalences his text displays keep these categories shifting: as we have seen, they become sites of struggle rather than of determination.

Thus for Fanon, struggle is not merely a weary, endless way of saying no. Instead it suggests a way of engaging with the signs that compose the world, to seek out, rather than merely be subject to, the dance of representation that continually forms and reforms "reality." The ethos of resistance that comes out of Fanon's "conspiracy with language" does not need to reinvent the world out of thin air (it could never and should never do such a thing). Instead, it allows Fanon access to a "future," a "self" and a political community that are, as we have seen, already "here" and "now."[45] In that way, and perhaps in that way alone, can we speak of these categories as determining and producing a new (and better) sense of a "reality" that already exists but of which we are barely aware.

As we have seen, the (re)occupation of such a reality does not involve surrendering a hard-fought sense of identity or truth. The "reality" that Fanon seeks—or at least the reality that his texts produce—is neither authentic nor merely a reiteration of colonialism. It is rather a reflection of its component parts, of the lives, struggles, and experiences of colonial and postcolonial subjects. But it is a reflection that is distorted by textual conspiracy; like our image in a funhouse mirror, what we see is altered or failed replicas of ourselves, but in such alterations we find a way to avoid both a total determination of ourselves as well as a dehumanized and perfectly exteriorized world in which there is no "self" (no delusion or sign) at all.

Although Fanon may have failed to deliver an Algeria free of its colonial past, or a revolution that managed to avoid replacing one set of mythologies with another, Fanon's misrecognition of revolution leaves revolution as an ongoing possibility. Fanon offers us a vision of resistance as a way of life as allowed for by the resistance of the text. He offers a space we can occupy and a strategy for altering and reworking reality, even if those alterations and reworkings don't always—or ever—produce some perfect and genuine other (third?) world. In this way, he avoids treating the text instrumentally, as a device to deliver his desires, thus merely re-iterating the phantasms he would resist. Instead, by throwing himself into the maw of textual resistance, Fanon models a way to ally with textuality—and hence materiality more generally—transforming his life and times into a conspiratorial, ever shifting potentiality.

Assia Djebar

In her contention with the multiple overlying realities that compose Algeria, Djebar, no less than Fanon, practices a recognized misrecognition. In her case, what she misrecognizes is not so much the Algerian revolution per se (she tends to see it from a critical perspective even as she portrays it with grace and sympathy) as the question of Algeria itself.[46] In her writing, Djebar paints a full picture of the multiple strands that constitute Algeria and the Algerians; her characters are women and men, speaking Arabic (both classical and local dialects), Berber, and French. Old histories of fallen heroes and powerful emirs are mixed with contemporary citizens in all of their complexity. Resisters and prevaricators are depicted as well as collaborators and colonizers. The many voices and attitudes that characterize her novels complicate the idea that there is one reality, one people or one future for Algeria. Even the question of time is complicated in Djebar's text; it is often "chopped up," such that one moment in time is juxtaposed with another, and ghosts and dreams are allowed to haunt her texts in a way that suggests that reality is, once again, more fluid than we usually imagine.[47]

While the diversity of her textual depictions makes it seem as if it would be literally impossible to speak meaningfully of Algeria or "being Algerian," Djebar still engages in such language. She also considers the possibility of an Algerian future that is not completely determined by the past even when her text attests to the deep entanglements, the near total-izing hold of the colonial experience, on the present. In her evocation of these "impossible" visions, as with other figures in our conspiracy, Djebar avoids the fetish of a "true" Algeria without giving up on Algeria itself. In-deed, as already suggested, like Fanon, her texts refuse such a vision, even if it may (or may not) be the author's own goal (or intention). In looking at Djebar's work, we begin to understand more clearly (as we did with Tocqueville as well) that a community's narrative is not an "authentic" record of a people (no matter how much the author might desire such au-thenticity) but rather a textual enactment of struggle over questions of representation and identity. More specifically, Djebar is able to convey the existence and experience of the myriad "side communities" that are formed in and around the grand narratives (be they historical, Berber, French, Islamic, issuing from the contemporary Algerian state or from other, myriad sources) that are in turn promulgated, destabilized, and contested in the Algerian context.

Djebar's texts thus serve as a resource for our quest for the future, for the notion of what comes "next" after conspiracy. As we have already seen, when viewed through a conspiratorial lens the "future" is, in many ways, already here. In her conspiracy and alliance with texts, Djebar's texts allow "Algeria" in all of its complexity, diversity, and struggle to be misrecog-nized in a way that does not merely reproduce the phantasmagoria. Al-though impossible, an Algerian community, an Algerian future is nonetheless present in and amid the very representational struggles that seem to mire this community in a temporal trap. Djebar's careful atten-tion to the daily lives and responses of Algerian people in all of their vari-ety helps us to recuperate a sense of what an Algerian future might already look like, what it might already be, even if we aren't (yet) aware of it.

As already noted, despite their personal connection, in many ways, Djebar and Fanon differ quite markedly. Djebar never quite shared Fanon's form of enthusiasm for the revolution. For his part, while far more radical than she was, Fanon treated Djebar with a great deal of kind-ness and tolerance. David Macey writes that when Fanon and Djebar both lived in Tunis, he was one of the only persons associated with the revolu-tionary movement who "was willing to discuss her books and her plans for future novels on her own terms."[48] Others in the leadership found her work insufficiently revolutionary in character. The two writers also had different views on the role of women in the revolution.

On the other hand, there are ways in which these two authors are sim-

ilar. Like Fanon, Djebar is a transplant. Where Fanon goes from being Antillean to Algerian, Djebar, born and raised in Algeria, finds herself today
living in France and writing in French. It may be that in both cases their
cosmopolitan experience helps them to articulate the fungibility of seemingly fixed realities.

Similarly, Djebar's texts, like Fanon's, complicate what would otherwise be a fairly straightforward appraisal of the "success" or "failure" of the
Algerian revolution. Over the course of her career as a writer, Djebar has
witnessed both the revolution and its aftermath. In this way, she has a perspective denied to Fanon, who died before the full repercussions of the
revolution became fully apparent. At the same time, Djebar asserts that
Fanon himself saw the flaws in the revolution he espoused. In *Algerian
White,* she asks of Fanon: "Did he already suspect the coming of the time
of the jackals?"[49] Even more pointedly, she asserts that "if Fanon had come
back to life ten years later, he would have turned his back on these new
[Algerian] masters, he would have gone back and shut himself up in his
hospital in Blida."[50]

In looking at Djebar's understanding of the revolution and its aftermath, I will focus on a comparison between two of her books. *Children of
the New World,* as already mentioned, was written during the revolutionary era and demonstrates a guarded optimism for what it might lead to.
Algerian White was written decades later in the face of the clear and abject
failure of the revolution. The contrast between these two books sets out
some of the parameters of Djebar's response to revolution and its failure
as well as the question of an Algerian future. As we will see, even in her
darkest moments, Djebar does not turn her back either on what the revolution was or what it might yet be. As with Fanon, Djebar's struggle takes
place on a largely semiotic level and, on that ground, the revolution can
never said to be "done," "doomed," or "complete"; its significance, its representation, remains an ongoing, endlessly renegotiable process.

By reading Djebar's books in constellation with Fanon's, and by focusing on the limits and possibilities of recognized misrecognition as a strategy for facing what is manifestly impossible, we can avoid both an absolute historical determinism wherein the failure of the future condemns
the past as well as a myopia or romance of the present wherein the hope
for revolution is itself a guarantor of success. In Djebar's case in particular
we see the major role that the revolution has played in the production of
an Algerian identity, which, for all of its paradoxes, complexities, and even
impossibility, yet serves as a site by which to politicize the community
whose name it purports to serve. Djebar shows that no narrative of the Al-

gerian people can be valid without reference to the revolution and the ongoing struggles that the revolution set into motion. As with Fanon, once the revolution's mythologies have been destabilized and made legible, what remains for Djebar is the sense of struggle, resistance, and rejuxtaposition that is the hallmark of the conspiracy with language these authors are engaged with.

The New World

We can see Djebar's particular mixture of hopefulness and despair even in her most "revolutionary" novel, *Children of the New World*. This book, written in the midst of Algeria's revolution against French colonialism, shares much of the context and excitement of Fanon's later writings (especially *The Wretched of the Earth*). The novel is set (and was written) at a time when the outcome of the revolution remained uncertain. In the town where this novel takes place (Blida, where she went to secondary school and where Fanon himself served as head of the psychiatry department at Blida-Joinville hospital) the French remain, on the surface anyway, still very much in control, and for that reason the resistance the novel depicts is largely conspiratorial (taking that term in its more ordinary usage). The novel is constantly marked by a contrast between the tension of the town where life continues to have some semblance of normality (if the humiliations and injustices of colonialism can be called "normal") and the mountains, which are permanently visible from the town and which represent a much purer form of fighting and resistance (and upon which bombs are dropped, on which forests are burned and planes swoop). Furthermore, the majority of the novel's protagonists are women who are often fated (with some exceptions) to wait in the town while their husbands go off to fight in the mountains. The atmosphere of the novel, then, is one of deep anxiety, waiting, and gloom but it is also broken up with moments of real joy and optimism. Yet the kind of hope that Djebar's characters hold out for is never fully realized. Their dreams of a kind of perfect, revolutionary redemption are tantalizingly close but never come to fruition. Here again, the text seems to defeat the expectation of the characters and perhaps even the author. Djebar's prose is too complex, too nuanced to afford the outcomes that the characters hope for. In the frustration of those hopes, in the deferral of revolution and "freedom," we see glimpses of the bonds, identities, and communities that are indeed "already here," already available.

The two central characters of the book, Cherifa and Lila, are sisters-in-law; Cherifa's brother, Ali, is Lila's husband. At the time the novel begins, Ali has already left for the mountains to fight against colonialism. Cherifa's husband, Youssef, remains in town but clandestinely supports the insurgents. Eventually, he too opts to the mountains to fight. In the great contrast between Cherifa's and Lila's attitudes about the war, and about their own lives as wives, women, and Algerians, we see Djebar working with some of the same vocabulary that we saw in Fanon: the question of action, of overcoming the traps of identity and history, of reformulating what is in order to come to some new kind of understanding of self, society, and politics. We also see once again the key role misrecognition plays, as representation and in particular self-representation allow both of these women to navigate (or be navigated in) an impossible situation, to conspire when they were neither necessarily willing nor able to do so before.

Cherifa is portrayed as a very traditional and devoted wife. For much of the book she is utterly passive (although not necessarily in a wholly negative way). She calls herself her husband's "mirror," an idea that fills her with "vague joy."[51] When she finds out that her husband is under suspicion for his clandestine meetings (her neighbor Hakim is the local Arab police inspector), she vows to go to warn him, despite her fears and the many risks such a move involves. In so "deciding," Cherifa

> stretches her willpower to make her mind go blank; to catch the decision by surprise: she wants to act. A strange desire overtakes and worries her, to do something, something daring whose luminosity will astound Youssef . . . "I have to act," she says cautiously, invaded by a vague fear . . . It is a new word [*Mot nouveau*] toward which fate is pushing her ("fate, really?") and suddenly she sees it emerge, rich in promises and results: "Me, act? Me?"[52]

Note here that even in this moment of "self-discovery," Cherifa is experiencing her transformation toward action in semiotic terms; fate is pushing her toward a "new word" (i.e., the word "act"). Thus she experiences her own transformation as coming from an external, representational source (she also calls it a "foreign word" [*Mot étrange*]).[53] As with Benjamin, such a desire "overtakes" her, coming from beyond herself and reshaping who she is in the process. In this way, Cherifa can be seen as being inculcated into a conspiracy with language wherein her own acts become a product of her new relationship with ("self") representation.

In her response to the crisis she faces, Cherifa overcomes a lifetime of conditioning, an entire set of strictures on how a "virtuous woman" behaves. She crosses town alone (something forbidden for a traditional Muslim Algerian woman) enduring the catcalls of men, and the fear of discovery and exposure, to find the store where Youssef works (she has only the vaguest idea where it is). When she finally sees him and warns him, he resolves to flee into the mountains right away. Yet at this point, Cherifa's resolve to act slips away. Later, she tells Lila, "What I wanted to say was, 'Take me along too, since there are other women up there. . . .' But I didn't dare."[54] Asked by Lila if she regrets not going she says:

> I don't know! . . . There are moments when certain things seem so near, so easy, but then a minute later, a second later . . . it's not the same anymore, and those same things become . . . extraordinary and distant?[55]

Here we can see both the transformative power of new ways for Cherifa to understand and represent herself and also the limitations of such approaches. In Cherifa's case, her devotion to her husband gets her to do even the unimaginable; it enables a "conspiracy with language" on her part in which "new" and "strange" words guide her. In a time of near-perfect contingency, Cherifa is able to act in ways that surprise her so that she does indeed become un- (or mis-) recognizable to her self. Yet she does not become some new and perfect postcolonial subject but rather a different iteration (however uncanny) of herself. Part of what she has always been remains; she is still hesitant, uncertain, self-doubting but now she can act.

In Lila's case, the call to action comes much later and in an entirely different fashion. Lila's marriage to Ali is troubled from the beginning; she is not a conventional or traditional wife by any means. Although she loves her husband, she also argues with him and frequently challenges him. Lila's response to Ali leaving for the front is to feel abandoned, to take his politics as a personal affront. Prior to his leaving, she displays little interest in his political activities, preferring to indulge in long philosophical conversations with him. As Djebar writes of Lila, "She couldn't be interested in the future, hers or that of others, settled as she was inside her abounding present."[56] Ali for his part "wag[ed] war against her animal self-centeredness" but ultimately simply leaves her behind.[57]

Lila does not understand her husband until she spends a long night talking to her cousin Bachir (who is fresh from burning down the storehouses of a rich French landowner). When Bachir announces that he will join the resistance, Lila thinks of Ali: "Why hadn't she been close to [Ali], inside his head, when he was talking to himself like this [i.e., as Bachir is doing], as he [Ali] must have been?"[58]

When Lila is arrested for being associated with her cousin (who is himself gunned down as he is leaving her house), she thinks: "from here on in it's actually a question of her being born—of a true awakening."[59] She further considers "what marvelous luck to finally be nondescript on an earth and at a time that are no longer so!" ("quelle merveilleuse chance d'être enfin quelconque sur une terre, à une époque qui ne le sont plus!").[60] The juxtaposition of these two considerations is telling. While the first seems to augur the usual "rebirth" into her true self that is promised by revolution and social change, we see that for Lila, such a change renders her "nondescript" (quelconque has the literal meaning of "whoever" or "anyone"). This is not meant in a negative, pejorative way. Instead it points to the way that Lila is precisely *not* in command, not in charge of her own transformation. Whereas once she was "out of time," lost in her own fantasies of love and power (and hence, in a way, participating in the timelessness that afflicts so many of us under conditions of phantasmagoria), Lila has become "nondescript," that is to say, in conformity with action, with the transformations of her time. It is now time itself that has taken on the burden of being extraordinary, and Lila, not unlike Poe's narrator, holds on (once again in the guise of self-moving) to the events and times themselves, to the constitutive parts of the symbolic order she occupies. Even if she remains trapped in a French jail, Lila has been transformed, taken out of herself not just by love, but also by the events and representations of the revolution that are swirling around her and to which she accommodates herself.[61]

Yet the novel, for all its hopefulness and possibility, engages with the same kinds of worries as Fanon. Djebar too sees that the path of "self-determination" is not so simple, not so sustainable in the long run. For one thing, there is not one single source of oppression to combat, but several. Throughout the novel—and throughout much of Djebar's work—there is a running parallel between Algerians fighting French occupation and women fighting men. When Cherifa defies and divorces her first husband, Djebar writes: "It was a feeling of having faced an enemy at last, if only for an instant, and of having been able to stand up to it, to be."[62] After a long night in which he tortures and then kills a suspected insurgent, Hakim, the police inspector who works for the French, goes home and begins to beat his own wife. The entanglements of gender are complex and not by any means an exact parallel to colonialism, but Djebar is attuned to the erotics of power, to the desire that animates so much of our connection to that which we both succumb to and resist. In *Children of the New World*, both France and masculinity have their allures; as in *The Castle*, such notions serve as the center point around which many lives revolve.[63]

In some ways, the battles waged between genders may offer an even better rendition of the problematics of power for Djebar than does the struggle against colonialism. Colonialism seems like something that can be "lifted" (even though as we see this is easier said than done).[64] Gender and its entanglements, on the other hand, are not going to go away. There is no delivery from something that animates and forms the basis of life for so many of the women in this novel. Although the parallels between gender and colonialism are imperfect, they suggest that the characters' struggle with colonialism may similarly not turn out quite as they hope or intend. What emerges in Djebar's own rendition of struggle is less a war against a clear enemy than a complicated engagement with the elements that constitute the most intimate and basic aspects of her characters' lives.

The Possibility of a Future

Although we can see that, for Djebar, the situation in Algeria frustrates any easy or swift resolution, her characters remain deeply engaged with the question of the future. In *Children of the New World*, Djebar shares Fanon's desire for the future not to be merely an iteration of the present, determined by the precise historical and social context that the revolutionaries sought to extricate Algerians from. Djebar is interested in a different (I would say conspiratorial) temporality, a different sort of future.

For all of the its elusiveness, there are moments in *Children of the New World* when the future (or rather its representation) becomes quite palpable, reminiscent of Arendt's idea that one could "dispose of the future as though it were the present."[65] For example, she writes of Mahmoud, one of the resistance fighters, that

> Although Mahmoud was well past the age of easy romanticism, a glow of happiness came over him—and for him happiness always surfaced like this: on the eve of an undertaking, when circumstances granted a reprieve from the excitement of approaching peril . . . all those all-too-unwavering feelings, for a split second made room for the soul's strange jubilation at perceiving the future as a field, unexpectedly unfolding [de voir devant soi l'avenir comme un champ, d'un coup, déployé].[66]

The idea of the future as a "field, unexpectedly unfolding" speaks to a central premise in Djebar's work (something that can be found in Fanon's as well, but perhaps not always as clearly), namely, the idea that whatever the future is, it cannot be controlled or anticipated; the future becomes revealed unexpectedly and often, as we have already seen, is revealed to be something that was always in our midst. In the original French, even more than in the English translation, we get a sense of the future being "before" us in a sense more physical than temporal ("de voir devant soi l'avenir comme un champ, d'un coup, déployé"). Here, the future is a field that lies before us; it is, once again, already "here."

In Lila's magical night spent talking with her cousin Bachir, we see evidence of this unfurling future that is "before" (*devant*) us as well. At first, in talking with her cousin, Lila is transported away from her worries: "As she was listening to Bachir, she found herself receptive, liberated from the past and, for a while, from the future. The peaceable flow of moments was like a marvelous vacation."[67] The release from the anxiety of temporality is blissful for Lila, but it also provides her with the possibility of a future that she never imagined; letting go of the future she desires (one of safety, order, "normalcy"), Lila is taken out of time as she knows it and thereby presented with the possibility for another life. Djebar writes that whereas for Lila "reality . . . had been a man who loved her . . . for Bachir it was the future [that was real] with all its hesitations [l'avenir avec ses hésitations]."[68] Here again, we see a sense of a future that is neither perfect nor fantastic.

As we have already seen, this "new" sort of future may not be so dramatically different from what already is. When Lila does finally embrace the cause of revolution, when she is in fact living in the "future" that she has denied and ignored all of her life, she realizes:

> No, nothing will be similar to the dizziness that once used to possess her, those magic spells. She's mistaken: she thinks she's relearning the challenge, while everything behind her has abruptly found its course.[69]

We see here more of the necessary practice of misrecognition. In her own mind, Lila may imagine that she has made a choice or determined something about herself and her position in time. In fact, however, the world has changed around her and she has merely stepped into its rhythms. This is the moment of redemption, if there is one to be had, in this novel. The "future" Lila gives herself over to, then, is actually a way to confront what is already present (only not to her).

And what is true for Lila as an individual is also true in some sense for Algeria as a whole. We see in particular in the figure of Youssef a vision of what the revolution could have been, could still be, if it too were allowed to be in alignment with the symbolic order that enables and produces it. In a key passage already discussed in the introduction, at an anti-French demonstration wherein "the green flags of Islam, of the rediscovered dignity of his people, kept advancing," Djebar tells us that

> Youssef, whose only true love was for this shifting reality, this flood tide of wretchedness, would continue his tale. Then his jaws would tighten and he'd add, "Of course, they were simple rags, bits of sheets patched and sewn by the women for their luminous songs." "Filthy rags!" the police yelled, giving their first warning that they'd have to disappear. The flags kept moving forward.[70]

We see here the power of conspiracy even in its ability to redeem a revolution that is impossible and hopeless. The "green flags of Islam" are a sign like any other and easily (and usually) lend themselves to being fetishes of a nation or movement, at best replacing one set of fetishes with another. Yet in this moment, the flags become legible (at least potentially) for what they are, "simple sheets patched and sewn by the women." As with Benjamin's treatment of Jesus, the symbol is exposed and rendered allegorical. In moments such as this, the grand narratives that a flag represents, along with the hope for full redemption that revolution brings, are disrupted, denuded. In the wake of such a disruption, a different kind of community becomes visible; while being identical to the community that "believes" in transcendent revolution, this community now becomes legible as a "shifting reality, this flood of wretchedness." Here, minus its grand organizing "meaning," the texture, the variety, and the multitudinousness of this community become clearer to us. We think of the women and their "luminous songs"; the meaning of their labor, their contribution, takes on a different valence.[71] We think, as with Jesus, of lives lived, tasks accomplished in the service of an overarching truth that has now been (temporarily) removed or displaced. But note that we need "the flag" as the centerpiece to organize and retain this community. Exposing the flag "for what it is" does not end its role as the centerpiece of forming a community, it only allows that community to become legible to itself without being completely overwritten by the mythologies that the flag also brings into being.

Youssef sees this community in the same way he sees the flags of Islam; no longer fetishized, they become simply markers of a continuity and a narrative—the "unfolding field" of the future. Such a future lies literally "before" him. To see the crowds in all of their humanity and plurality we need to see the materiality of the ragged sheets that represent them in their collectivity. Thus is our own "self"-determination (but in this case on a collective rather than individual level) once again a product of our alliance with the sign, our conspiracy with language.

Paradoxically, in addition to Youssef, the police too see the flags for what they are ("filthy rags"). But such an insight does not inculcate them with the conspiracy with language. Even when faced with the materiality of the sign, they remain bound by and in the service of the fetish. In classical fetishist style, they seek to remove the flags as if removing a bunch of sheets would eliminate "what it stands for." We see here more evidence of the dissymmetries that are produced by the conspiracy with language (dissymmetries we first saw with Machiavelli and his use of adianoeta). The same gesture, the exposure of the sign as "merely material," provides access to the communities it is purported to stand for (but usually supplants) even as it keeps the fetishists bound by their delusion. Although revolution is impossible, the police don't know that. The community doesn't know it either, but in their case, their misrecognition can be the basis for a kind of redemption, however unanticipated. In the meantime, in the face of this semiotic struggle, "The flags [keep] moving forward."

Algerian White

In *Algerian White* we see the other end of revolution, the failures and disappointments that follow (which Fanon also seems to have divined, however much he resisted such conclusions). *Algerian White* in some sense is "the future" of *Children of the New World*, but it is a future in the more ordinary sense of the word, the future that lies ahead in our phantasmic sense of time and "progress." In the disappointment that characterizes much of the book we see that *this* understanding of the future offers not redemption but more of the same.

Yet, for all of its sadness, *Algerian White* remains engaged with other possibilities, other futures, as well. Perhaps even more than *Children of the New World*, this book is explicitly and uniquely textual; in this way even its message of disappointment and failure is in some ways redeemed, rendered other than what it is meant to be. *Algerian White* is essentially a remembrance of a number of Algerian writers, playwrights, and intellectuals that Djebar knew personally. Here she conspires not just with "language" per se but with myriad, now dead writers, her friends. In her recollection of such writers and their lives, now rendered as text, Djebar literalizes a sense of a transtemporal community, one that is summoned and even produced in the pages of *Algerian White*. In this way, Djebar offers us a way to understand what a textual conspiracy looks like; she gives a human face to our textual allies, assigning agency (even if it is misrecognized) to the only forces that can possibly redeem us. As with *Children of the New World*, in *Algerian White* Djebar gives us a texture and a specificity to the kinds of identities, communities, and futures that are produced out of conspiracy.

The writers that Djebar describes (including Frantz and Josie Fanon) were assassinated or died of other causes during the struggle for liberation in the late fifties and early sixties or in the revolution's aftermath. Despite the years since their deaths, we see that Algeria has not changed all that much. After the revolution ended and France withdrew, Algeria's revolutionary party established a de facto dictatorship. Dissident voices were throttled and a new round of violence erupted as Islamic radicalism rose to challenge the state and the party. The state's response to the threat of Islamic radicalism reminds Djebar of the very violence that gave birth to Algerian independence in the first place. She points repeatedly to the commonalities between the revolutionary struggle against France and the struggles of Algeria some thirty years later. She tells us that the forests are burning with napalm "again" ("à nouveau"),[72] and the Barberousse prison, a notorious prison used by the French to torture and terrorize Algerian fighters, is also in use (and for similar purposes), once again.

In the face of such an outcome, Djebar both mourns and celebrates the lives of an entire generation of Algerian writers, in the process seeking to discover what Algeria has become, what, in other words, the revolution has "accomplished" and what the future of that revolution could yet be. In seeking a "scrupulously faithful account" of the lives of the writers she contends with, Djebar tells us:

> I have been brought to note that new rituals were in ... coming into being: the writer once dead, his texts not yet reopened [l'écrivain une fois mort, et ses textes pas encore rouverts], it is around his buried body that several different Algerias are being sketched out.[73]

We see here an attempt to sketch out "several different Algerias" that currently exist only (at least in terms of our access to them) in the form of text; these different visions or futures seem to belong only to the dead. But Djebar has a unique relationship to the dead; she actively allows herself to be haunted by the ghosts of these writers in the same way that Benjamin allowed himself to be haunted by Charles Baudelaire, among others. Here again, we see an example of the constellative method at work.

Djebar tells us that these ghosts talk to and argue with her; they shun her when she pries too much into their lives. Although dead, they form an integral part of the fabric of her ordinary lived experience—at least insofar as she expresses her life in texts. Such a view is reminiscent of Benjamin's own appreciation for and identification with the dead: "*even the dead* will not be safe from the enemy if he wins."[74] Directly summoning an image of an alliance with texts, Djebar tells us "they speak to me, those close to me, my allies [mes alliés]."[75] These allies speak to her (and she to them) "in Arabic, in my Arabic, with its flattened out dentals."[76] They also speak in

> a French with neither nerves nor veins, nor even memories, a French both abstract and carnal, warm in its consonances . . . freed from the shroud of the past, the French of the old days now begins to be generated within us, between us, transformed into a language of the dead.[77]

We see here Djebar gaining a sense of her own multiply stranded identity—even her own agency—by communing with her textual allies. In these conversations, the "shroud of the past" ([le] linceul du passé) is lifted, the determinations of ordinary time are displaced, allowing "different" understandings of time and identity to emerge.[78]

As a memorial to actual persons, *Algerian White* is marked by a wistfulness for what Algeria could have been, had these writers been more able to influence the nation while they were still alive.[79] At one point, Djebar expresses a fear that the only possible saviors of Algeria are all dead:

> How then can we get out of this mire—in what language, in what aesthetic form of denunciation and anger—how can we give an account of these changes? The only question which should have taken root in the heat of a living Algerian culture continued to remain a gaping hole, a dead eye—with just two exceptions in the theater: in French the farcical, ironic foresight of Kateb Yacine, and, in a witty

and vigorous dialectical Arabic, the dramatic works of Abdelkader
Alloula, which even now remain so fresh.

Yet both, as I write, are dead. And we miss them.[80]

Here we see a temporal despair, another dead end of time, but it is a despair tempered by the fact that the text gives testament to the way that the
irony of Kateb Yacine and the "vigorous dialectical Arabic" of Abdelkader
Alloula are in fact still with us, present in the very act of commemorating
their loss. In a sense, Djebar herself provides the "Algerian White" a
blankness that (conspiratorially) conceals what it supposedly mourns as
lacking: the presence of the dead, now rendered as textual "allies," the ongoing possibility of resistance, of other voices joined in conspiracy.[81] Djebar's acts of "commemoration" could be read as another version of
Machiavelli's "hiding in plain sight": a book that looks on the surface like
a mournful eulogy (she tells us at one point, "All I do in these pages is
spend time with a few friends")[82] can instead be reread as a conspiracy
with the dead. As with the ghosts she encounters throughout the book,
the declarations of loss and mourning permit the unexpected; just when
we are most assured that Algeria is doomed and the only voices that
could save it are lost (i.e., where the texts are "not yet reopened"), we can
perhaps encounter their voices anew, this time as purely textual and as if
from another (material) world that is not quite as determined or hopeless as our own.

Conspiring with the Dead

In this way, when Djebar marks her textual allies as dead and failed, we can
see she is not giving up on them but depicting their true source of power
and resistance. Such a stance may be suggested by one of the book's
epigraphs, by Kateb Yacine himself: "Hurry up and die, then you will speak
as ancestors."[83] Only as dead writers, as text (in whatever form that takes),
can these writers whom she calls "*my brothers of the pen* [*mes confrères*]"
successfully evade their own temporality; we can read them, as if for the
first time, from a perspective not already determined by what we know to
be true.[84] As we have already seen, by becoming "ancestors" as well as her
contemporaries, these authors scramble the polarities of time that bound
them while alive, allowing Djebar herself to be "freed from the shroud of
the past." The failure of these authors thus becomes reinterpreted as a textual failure, a failure to convey the inevitability of colonialism, a failure to

be bound by a particular time and context (or indeed a particular, and sure, doom).

By putting a human face on her conspiracy with language, Djebar makes such a communion more palatable, more approachable, and, indeed, more legible. Rendering her own friends as textual allies, as allegorical figures, allows Djebar to see that in a sense the future and community that she seeks for Algeria have already existed amid the slaughter and disappointment of the last few decades. This community is rendered invisible by the fetishes that its members inevitably subscribe to, but when abstracted (when rendered "both abstract and carnal"), when rendered into its representational components, such a community reemerges.

The text *Algerian White* thus serves as a site for revealing the community that already exists. At the very end of the book, Djebar writes:

> In the brilliance of this desert, in the safe harbor of writing in quest of a language beyond languages, by trying fiercely to obliterate all the furies of the collective self-devouring in oneself, finding "the word within" [dedans de la parole] again that, alone, remains our fertile homeland.[85]

This may be the closest that she comes to an answer for the question, what is Algeria? Algeria is a "fertile homeland," a site in which representational schemes vie for determination. It is a site, too, where Djebar can "meet" with her textual allies, now misrecognized as human beings (or, alternatively, such a move allows her to put a human face on her textual allies, making them less alien, and alienating, than they would otherwise be). Such misrecognition disguises the nature of her allies as well as the source of resistance that Djebar draws from; it allows her to continue to believe in a communion with texts without giving up on her own sense of agency as well as to hold the site of Algeria as an ongoing possibility or even reality rather than as a successfully determined thing (which would hence no longer need to be represented at all). While the Algeria that emerges, this "fertile homeland," is of necessity more fractured, more compromised, more ordinary and less enticing than the dreams of unity and identity offered by the phantasmagoria, it has the virtue of avoiding the endless deferment that is the hallmark of mythology. Djebar's alliance with texts shows that the future of Algeria is a place she has always lived in (without realizing it); her task in the face of this other sense of time (a time of constellations, of historical—and textual—materialism) is to make its presence clear and known (that is to say, misrecognized) to herself and to her readers.

Conclusion: Recycling Reality

In looking at what Fanon and Djebar have to offer us, we see that in some sense, they offer us only what we already have but do not realize. Such an approach is reminiscent of the Jewish idea that when the Messiah comes she or he will change virtually nothing, the very same notions that we explored with Kafka in chapter 3. The encounter with representational materiality, this alliance with textual allies that we see becoming literal in *Algerian White*, is transformative not in the sense that our reality changes but rather insofar as we change our relationship to that reality, to the way we understand its makeup and our own role (and possibility) in it.[86]

Fanon's and Djebar's (like Arendt's, and for that matter, Benjamin's) anxieties, hesitations, and ambivalences can be read through a conspiratorial lens as guarding against their own desire for easy, and phantasmal, fixes.

The future that Fanon and Djebar are describing—the "fertile homeland" that is Algeria—is just another misrecognition, but it is one that proves fruitful, enjoyable, and already within our reach. We see that both Fanon's and Djebar's work is tempered by their experience of revolution and war and its aftermath; rather than escape that experience they use it as the basic elements to build what comes "next." When they come to understand (as they do, each in a different way) that the future is not "over there" but right here—right in the realm or field of representation itself—we find that we have far more access to it than we thought we ever could. When we politicize the ways we depict and represent the future and our community to ourselves, we are merely reclaiming a power that has always been in our grasp—a power to misrecognize, to fail to read the world as a coherent whole. The signs of our community (like the green flag of Islam) become a "mighty paw," a vital aspect of an ongoing conspiracy.

In addition to this overall view of their contributions to our conspiracy, both of these authors contribute something unique. In keeping with his explicit focus on politics, Fanon, not unlike Machiavelli, offers us strategies to engage with as part of our conspiracy. Specifically, he offers the strategy of violence, of dramatizing our break with the phantasmagoria in a way that renders the kinds of communities and future that are overshadowed by our own fetishism legible and accessible to us. While he may (or may not) mean literal violence, we can see that what is crucial for Fanon is the dramatization conveyed by violence, the announcement to the self and to others that a rejuxtaposition of reality is actually occurring (just as the narrator of Poe's "A Descent into the Maelström" dramatized a break with hope). Hence we do not require violence per se but only what it semiotically signifies. Fanon also shows us how one can engage in mis-recognitions (the idea of revolution, the idea of the "third world") without merely reproducing the fetishism that such ideas purport to fight against. This problem of the traps of history lies at the core of Fanon's work, and, like Machiavelli, he turns to textual solutions as a way out of his dilemma.

For her own part, Djebar offers us a richer sense of the communities that are rendered legible by conspiracy. We see in her work the complex-ity, the interweaving, and the bonds of these communities. We see in stolen moments (like the night Lila spends talking with Bachir) the differ-ent kinds of temporal states, relationships, and potentialities that exist in the interstices of the phantasmagoria. We also see in her work a way to hu-manize this conspiracy, to give it a face or faces, to guide our misrecogni-tion and our own sense of agency and possibility toward a different and "fertile" homeland.

The main question to face at this point is whether such a conspiracy, such communities, such a "future" can ever spill over out of the pages of these books. Can our conspiracy with language produce anything akin to the actual politics that we live and experience every day? Even if Algeria can be shown to be "redeemed," even if it has a future and a community that are in effect "already here," the fact of the matter is that Algeria and Algerians suffer from brutality, from hierarchy, from phantasms and in-justice. And not just Algerians, but people and communities all over the world. For the work of Fanon and Djebar to be more than a solace or a ro-mance of the nobility (and futility) of the Left, it must be able to translate into a politics that affects and alters our daily experience of life amid the phantasmagoria. We must do more than merely point to instances and flashes of redemption; we must in effect learn how to extend our conspir-acy into the unreal and timeless world we (currently) occupy. It is to this question that we will now turn for the book's conclusion.

Conclusion | A Faithless Leap: The Conspiracy That Is Already Here

Having looked at a series of writers, activists, political theorists, and creative artists, we are in a better position to consider the conspiracy described in this book as a whole, to ask what the upshot of this conspiracy is for our own time, for our own sense of what is and is not possible (insofar as even our conceptions of the possible are a reflection of the way we situate ourselves in a particular temporal and historical context). Above all, we must contend with the question of what it means to be in a "conspiracy with language" and what kind of politics and strategies issue from such a conspiracy.

As stated in the introduction, one of the aims of this book has been to take Benjamin seriously as a political theorist (and by extension, the other authors who are in constellation with him). In so doing, we constantly come up against the ways in which, from the perspective of political theory, Benjamin's analysis seems strange, antihuman, and mystical, and therefore problematical from a political perspective. We are returned, in other words, to Adorno's complaint that Benjamin's work seems marked by "magic and positivism."[1] In order to think about the politics of a Benjaminian conspiracy, therefore, we must directly contend with these critiques, as well as with our own conceptions of what politics consists of.

Accordingly, in this conclusion I will reexamine these questions, looking at the nature of textual materialism and textual messiahs and how they affect us, the human subject. I will look at this with an eye toward better understanding the question of "recognizing misrecognition," the idea that we must remain bound to and by the sign even as we seek to escape the effects of the phantasmagoria that the sign has built.

I will then move on to a direct consideration of the "positive" contribution that a Benjaminian conspiracy might make not only to political theory, but also to resistance and the forms of politics it might produce. To make this argument, I will first contrast this conspiracy with the kind of "radical hope" offered by Jonathan Lear in his book of the same name. I will argue that the kind of "hope" Benjaminian conspiracy offers is utterly unlike Lear's depiction of strategy and survival by the Crow Nation in the face of a threat of cultural and physical extermination. Although Lear promises a transformative and ethical response to loss and despair that seems to match the strategies offered by Benjamin himself, I argue that he does not allow us to address the basic problem of fetishization and hence does not overcome the central challenges of the phantasmagoria. By contrast we can better see just how radical, how altering a Benjaminian conspiracy (and hope) might be.

This argument will be followed by a consideration of Benjaminian conspiracy as fomenting a kind of anarchistic politics. In making this argument, I recognize that Benjamin did not always have positive things to say about anarchism. Yet, this is the name I would append to his practice of politics (his own preferred term was "communism"). In looking at such questions, I will ask what "democracy" becomes when it is no longer a fetish; what do we do with democracy as a sign and how do we organize ourselves under this sign when it has been displaced and decentered? My answer is a practice of anarchism (something Jacques Rancière, with some vital qualifications from Jodi Dean, helps us to think about). Anarchism, as I see it, is precisely the name for the antifetishistic, peripheral "side communities" that we have been looking at throughout this book. Anarchy already thrives in the unseen corners of the phantasmagoria, usually unbeknownst to itself. A politics based on misrecognition and antifetishism is an anarchist politics and might (or might not) become the basis for a more powerfully or successfully resistant form of practice. We look at such possibilities with an aim toward retrieving hope (even if it is a hope that is "not for us") for the Left as we find ourselves in our current, seemingly endless, dark times.

Material Alliances

As we have seen throughout this book, the idea of human subjects being in a conspiracy with material allies, with texts, seems to defy our understanding of politics and/or human agency. How can a text be an ally and a coconspirator? Even more puzzling, both Benjamin and Kafka seem to give the text pride of place in this alliance, making us, as it were, a junior partner in our own acts of resistance. This decentering of human agency may strike us as strange, as antipolitical. It may indeed explain why Ben-

jamin is not often considered a "political" theorist at all but usually an aesthetic or literary philosopher.

Yet as we have seen throughout this book, to say that human beings
can and do conspire with language does not remove a human role in this
conspiracy; rather it restores our role insofar as the acts and thoughts and
deeds that we ordinarily consider to be "our own" are in fact the product
of our deep compromise with the phantasmagoria. Insofar as human beings are always in the service of the sign, because we always misrecognize
the world around us, we will always attribute an agency to ourselves. This
agency, however delusional it may be, delineates who "we" are and what
is properly "ours." Such an agency cannot be read out of the human experience, but it can be alienated, made captive to the idolatry of the
phantasmagoria.

We have already seen in the previous chapter how Assia Djebar depicts
our textual alliances in a way that is not as threatening or as alienating as
we might think. She portrays her textual allies as departed friends and colleagues; she humanizes these alliances and in so doing expands her sense
of her own (and our own) agency. Hers is clearly a practice of "recognized
misrecognition," of attributing an agency and a power to a set of events
that otherwise seem wholly material and external to us.

Even so, we may worry that putting a human face on our textual allies
only disguises a de facto surrender of human agency (or at least what feels
to us, in our current phantasmagoric state, as our agency). But here we can
return to Benjamin's earlier understanding of plotting in his *Origin* to see
that this is not the case. Recall that even as early as the *Origin*, Benjamin
was beginning to work out an idea of conspiracy, of overcoming conscious
intention in order to subvert what passed for reality. In a passage that we
considered in the introduction to this book, Benjamin tells us that the
courtiers that were portrayed in the German *Trauerspiel* were treacherous
plotters as regards the person of the sovereign even as they remained loyal
to the signs and symbols of sovereignty:

> Crown, royal purple, scepter are indeed ultimately properties, in
> the sense of the drama of fate, and they are endowed with a fate, to
> which the courtier, as the augur of this fate, is the first to submit.
> His unfaithfulness to man is matched by a loyalty to these things to
> the point of being absorbed in a contemplative devotion to them.
> . . . Clumsily, indeed unjustifiably, loyalty expresses its own way, a
> truth for the sake of which it does, of course, betray the world.

Melancholy betrays the world for the sake of knowledge. But in its tenacious self-absorption it embraces dead objects in its contemplation, in order to redeem them.[2]

With our deeper exploration of Benjamin's conspiracy, we can perhaps make better sense of this passage than the first time we encountered it. Here, once again, we see that the plotters conspire *malgré eux* against the narrative of sovereign power that they subscribe to. They do this (as we have also seen on many occasions in this book) via the very material objects that constitute that power; the idols that form the basis for sovereignty become a "mighty paw" with which to subvert the specter of sovereign authority. We see in this passage an early inkling of a kind of textual alliance that will become more evident in Benjamin's later works. The plotters demonstrate a "loyalty" to objects and signs rather than people. While Benjamin calls this "unfaithful," it is a faithlessness committed against an idol (i.e., the sovereign), in the same way that the intention of allegory "faithlessly leaps forward to the idea of resurrection."[3] If such an action "betray[s] the world," it is only the world of the phantasmagoria. In their faithless treachery and their betrayal, these plotters are serving a "truth" (the truth of the material objects themselves); they plot "for the sake of knowledge," for an understanding of reality that has now turned against the phantasmagoria that it serves (that is, they employ the strategy of the antidote).

While this set of actions depicts the plotters as being somewhat hapless in their defiance of sovereignty, we also see that for Benjamin they participate in something that both affects and involves them very intensely. In his description of the plotters of the *Trauerspiel,* let us recall once again, Benjamin alludes to "a progressive deepening of . . . intention" that is at play in their accidental and even unwanted acts of conspiracy.[4] The larger passage from which this phrase is drawn connects this deepening of intention to a state of mourning that afflicts the characters and playwrights of the *Trauerspiel* alike. This state of mourning reflects the fact that the rescues promised by the phantasmagoria have been either abandoned or simply have become unsustainable, unbelievable as such.[5] In other words, mourning is a state of giving up on hope, the hope for all that the phantasmagoria promises but never delivers; by our own standards, such mourning is the prerequisite for—or even the substance of—any form of conspiracy.

In the abject failure of the German *Trauerspiel* to produce a credible belief in sovereignty, we see cracks in the symbolic armor of the phantas-magoria, an opportunity for other ways of thinking and seeing, possibly even another form of hope. Of this Benjamin writes:

> Mourning is the state of mind in which feeling revives the empty world in the form of a mask, and derives an enigmatic satisfaction in contemplating it. . . . For feelings, however vague they may seem when perceived by the self, respond like a motorial reaction to a concretely structured world. If the laws which govern the *Trauer-spiel* are to be found, partly explicit, partly implicit, at the heart of mourning, the representation of these laws does not concern itself with the emotional condition of the poet or his public, but with a feeling which is released from any empirical subject and is inti-mately bound to the fullness of an object. This is a motorial attitude which has its appointed place in the hierarchy of intentions and is only called a feeling because it does not occupy the highest place. It is determined by an astounding tenacity of intention [die erstaun-liche Beharrlichkeit der Intention], which, among the feelings is matched perhaps only by love—and that not playfully. For whereas in the realm of the emotions it is not unusual for the relation be-tween an intention and its object to alternate between attraction and repulsion, mourning is capable of a special intensification, a progressive deepening of its intention.[6]

In this view human intention and the "intention of the sign" come to align themselves one with the other via the state of mourning, via a necessary kind of hopelessness. The progressive deepening of intention Benjamin refers to is the intention of mourning itself. Mourning is a mood, a re-sponse, and an attitude; it is both a sign and a human response to the fail-ure of mythology in the world. Although the deepening of intention be-longs to "it," we see that mourning elicits and connects with other human emotions and feelings, producing a "motorial reaction" to the world which can, for all its seeming inhumanness, be called a feeling. The plot-ters themselves are brought along, caught up and changed by this mood. We see here an "astounding tenacity of intention" as our misguided, fallen, and satanic human intentionality gropes toward the "Intention" that in some ways has always belonged to it (i.e., the intention that is pre-served/produced by the sign). In this way, we can see that the "progressive deepening" of mourning's intention is also the deepening of our own.

In his lifelong work, Benjamin never lost sight of this basic connection or alliance between human beings and signs. In his later work, he grew only more conspiratorial; his early interest in the baroque plotters developed into a broader set of strategies. In the progression of his work we can see further how a move toward a "progressive deepening" of intention potentially takes us from a sense of loss, a recognition of the failures of the phantasmagoria, toward (or perhaps more accurately backward to) a kind of intention that is "intimately bound with the fullness of an object," a conspiracy with language.

A Historical Materialism

This understanding of how our agency is reconcilable with "the intention of the sign" is reinforced by Benjamin's understanding of historical materialism; it is his response to the problem of history and our position within it. In speaking of historical materialism, in Konvolute N in *The Arcades Project*, Benjamin writes:

> On the elementary doctrine of historical materialism. (1) An object of history is that through which knowledge is constituted as the object's rescue. (2) History decays into images, not into stories. (3) Wherever a dialectical process is realized, we are dealing with a monad. (4) The materialist presentation of history carries along with it an immanent critique of the concept of progress. (5) Historical materialism bases its procedures on long experience, common sense, presence of mind, and dialectics.[7]

This short paragraph contains within it a summary of the entirety of Benjamin's understanding of historical materialism, his ambivalences, and, in a sense, a resolution of sorts. The first four points in this passage tell us, in order, that (1) any given object becomes subject to knowledge, to the satanic practices of human understanding and hence, to representation (which "rescues" the object from being merely inert, dust); (2) what is preserved as a historical object is not a concrete story, a complete narrative unto itself, but just a particle, an image; (3) what we understand as a dialectic, a tension that operates in time and space as we know it, is in fact (also) the workings and unfurlings of the monad; (4) to understand this undermines our belief in progress, in time as an artifact of knowledge.

The fifth sentence is perhaps key for our current purposes. Historical materialism is the means for human beings to come to terms with a "God's eye view" that is denied to us. It allows us to be informed by the object—

even by the monad itself—through the screen of our infinitely compromised forms of knowledge, our misrecognition. Although we contemplate these things that cannot be known by any human sense, historical materialism yet "bases its procedures on long experience, common sense, presence of mind, and dialectic." Here Benjamin is openly stating that the human perspective, for all its flaws, must draw upon its own resources as best it can, the resources of "experience, common sense, presence of mind, and dialectic." Of course, these very same elements are the basis of our intentionality, our compromise with the phantasmagoria. Yet, revealing the strategy of the antidote that he consistently engages with, Benjamin offers that these same faulty organs of discernment can, when set into alliance with signs as objects, potentially redeem us from the idolatry to which we usually subscribe. Rather than try to take on a superhuman, godlike perspective that will only lead us further into the phantasmagoria, we must accept our misrecognition (indeed, we must "recognize" it). We see here that Benjamin will not turn his back on the human perspective. On the contrary, he enshrines it dead center in the conspiracy that he helps to set forward.

Accordingly, many of the paradoxes that we have encountered in this book, those between the sign and the object, between the human subject and the "intention of the sign," and between the author and the text, can be read not as an either/or choice but as just what Benjamin suggests they are, an alliance, a partnership. This partnership does not (and must not) lead to perfect truth or redemption, as we have seen, but it does subvert and resist what would otherwise be a nearly perfect substitute for reality, the phantasmagoria.

This alliance with texts redeems us because, while human beings have long been divorced from God's perspective, the signs by which we perceive the world have not. Although we are banished from a God's eye view, our textual allies are not. If there is no "hope" for us, we can partake in an alliance with that which has never been excluded, never truly broken by the fall and the onrush of hubris and time and history that it produced. This is what allows mourning, the sadness of the *Trauerspiel* (mourning plays), to lead to a "progressive deepening of its intention."

Mourning gestures toward what was lost. Although the original, Adamic act of naming was a direct link between the human and the material, we can no longer have this relationship. While, as we saw in chapter 1, in paradise "ideas are displayed, without intention, in the act of naming,"[8] in our own postlapsarian time, there is no getting away from intention. Yet Benjamin tells us in the very next phrase of that sentence that such ideas "have to be renewed in philosophical contemplation."[9] We cannot name, we cannot truly know, but we can, and must, gesture. This, for Benjamin, is the business of philosophy and, I would add, conspiracy, the basis for his "historical materialism."

Navigating Desire

A final way to think about an alliance with texts comes when we focus directly on the human side of this equation, on the personal experiences and attitudes we can and must have when engaging in conspiracy. If we are meant to give ourselves over to an alliance with the sign, how do we experience such an alliance? Such a move may yet feel like a surrender of autonomy, something fearful and self-denying. Even if we accept that our conscious intention is complicit in ways that we cannot ordinarily fathom, it is still "our" consciousness that we are talking about, something deeply intimate and personal, something that we (for obvious reasons) are reluctant to call into question, much less potentially suspend or resign.

In order to further understand how an alliance with materiality might produce rather than undermine human subjectivity, we can turn once again (albeit with some important reservations, as we will see further) to the work of Joan Copjec. In her analysis of the art of Jasper Johns, Copjec considers something Johns once said to the critic Leo Steinberg. Steinberg notes that many of the materials that Johns uses for his art are commonplace. He notes, for example, that the stencils Johns uses for his paintings are the ordinary store-bought kind rather than some custom-made and presumably more "artistic" version. Copjec describes the conversation as follows:

> [Steinberg asks,] "Do you use these letter types [commercial stencils] because you like them or because that's how the stencils come?"—to which Johns replies "But that's what I like about them, that they come that way." Bull's-eye! This answer hits its mark and Steinberg, recognizing this, uses it to summarize Johns's relation to his objects: "He so wills what occurs that what comes from without becomes indistinguishable from what he chooses."[10]

Copjec offers that, given this alignment with the materiality of representation, "Johns seems to disappear, leaving his objects to stand by themselves."[11] Yet she resists this conclusion, writing:

It is not exactly correct to say with Steinberg that [Johns's works] are "relieved of man's shadow" or that they "insinuate our absence." What they insinuate is the absence of that egoistic self-consciousness which causes us to bow to external circumstances, to the wills and desires—the preferences—of others or to be moved to pity by their pains and sorrows. Johns's work is affectless only in the sense that it is not passively affected by the objects it paints. But this is not to say that there is no subject, no will or passion discernible in the work which, on the contrary, displays a remarkable passion for and satisfaction in the plain object.[12]

Copjec herself is interested in how this understanding illuminates the drive as a Freudian/Lacanian concept, how such a "non-chosen choice" offers human beings freedom and satisfaction in the object that is otherwise generally denied to us. As we have already seen, for Copjec, we can be satisfied by our drive when we give up the "perfect" icon, the pure image, and settle for the plain representational object that is available to us. In terms of the conspiracy we have been describing, this amounts to taking a satisfaction in the idol, not as a substitute for God but as itself, as a material, tangible object (although, she takes pains to point out, these objects "are always more than themselves").[13]

Copjec's point here is that Johns is able to find a "passion for and satisfaction in the plain object" in such a way as to avoid many of the traps of intentionality (or "preferences," to use Copjec's term). The example of Johns's use of stencils illustrates the idea of allowing the materiality of representation to, as it were, "speak for us" without necessarily erasing our own interest or pleasure in the process. In so doing, we see, not the ending of human subjectivity, but its possibility, exactly insofar as a person "so wills what occurs that what comes from without becomes indistinguishable from what [one] chooses." To desire the materiality of the world is only to desire what already is, to take satisfaction in the act of representation as opposed to using representation to grasp at some illusive and unobtainable distant truth (guaranteeing our perpetual frustration in the process).

For all the immense value of such an illustration, such an optimistic view needs to be qualified. As we have already seen (in chapter 4) with Jodi Dean's implicit criticism of Copjec's ideas about the virtues of the drive, there is a danger that even a turn to materiality, to a drive shorn of its goal (but not its aim), can simply reinforce the masochistic pleasures of loss and dissatisfaction that the drive may help us to sidestep. We have seen throughout this book the concern that the idea of "finally" being free from fetishism can be the greatest fetishism of them all. We need, therefore, not only to take refuge in the object but also to "recognize our misrecognition" when we do so. We need to remain cognizant of the power of the sign and its effects on us even as we accept the "mere" object that presents itself to us.

The distinction I would make from Copjec is that her solution is, in my view, insufficiently anti-idolatrous. So long as we believe that we can be free from the pull of the object as goal (by turning to the drive, the aim), we remain in its power.[14] To recognize our misrecognition means that we acknowledge that we are not so free. Insofar as the sign has a power that is independent of us, we must respect its autonomy and heed what it has to teach us; even as we take satisfaction in the object "directly," we remain susceptible to its phantasms.[15]

Poe's metaphor of a maelstrom (at least when read as such via Žižek's gloss) helps us to understand this negotiation with desire more clearly. It will be recalled that the maelstrom reveals that the object of our desire ("the truth") has been removed or at least displaced, revealing a swirling horror or emptiness in its stead. By circumnavigating this horror, without being any less drawn by it (that is to say, without being any less in its orbit), we can learn to take satisfaction in the objects (the "water casks" and "wax plugs") to which we cling, but we must not lose sight of the maelstrom itself.

To say that the water cask that Poe's narrator clings to has become a "destination" in its own right does not mean that it has become equivalent to our original goal, the heart of the maelstrom. We cannot merely substitute the object as an aim in its own right (lest it become a mere reiteration of our original goal). Poe's narrator remains cognizant of the great pull of the maelstrom; he remains in its orbit even as he is saved from annihilation. Thus he does not merely substitute one set of goals for another but clings to the object as an ally, a means of safety and protection in the face of the maelstrom's awful power (a power that the object is itself part and parcel of).

Without such a recognized misrecognition, we are left with the phantasmic wish of escaping representation altogether, a wish that leads back to the center of the maelstrom, to the belief that we are no longer deluded. We have seen many, perhaps all, of the conspirators we have treated in this text at times succumbing to or at least flirting with this belief. Thus Arendt's belief in a politics of pure appearance, Tocqueville's claim that Anglo Americans existed without "fiction," and Fanon's stated belief in an objective "reality" are examples of this temptation. Yet in each case, these authors have been delivered from such beliefs by their own texts, by the resistances that their texts produce.

We see this struggle against the tendency to do away with representation altogether literalized in Poe's other key tale that we analyzed in chapter 4. In the *Narrative of Arthur Gordon Pym,* the white sailors who visit Tsalal are attacked by the black sign marks. Here, the signs are not allies but enemies; their attack reminds us that signs will not always "modestly lie at the feet of the doctrine." Against the sailors' fantasy of a pure image, free of representation (where they could do without the black marks altogether, hence eliciting a fantasy of genocide against the very figures they depend upon), the Tsalalians assert the power and necessity of the sign. They resist being ruled out even as they are simultaneously revolting against the racist and imperialist phantasms that come with the belief that one community can eschew representation at the expense of all others (a belief we see Tocqueville, Fanon, and Djebar all addressing and which for Arendt continues down to the level of the individual). Even the final image of the *Narrative,* the sheet of white that threatens the very soul of representation (and which kills Nu-Nu, the living incarnation of the sign, in the process), is itself marked by representation (the ghostly figure). In his typical subversive yet brilliant style, Poe conspires against, rather than delivers, the promise of final truth to the sailors and to the readers of the *Narrative.* In this final ghostly image, he shows that even when representation is finally defeated, it reasserts itself, delivering us from the phantasm that we could (or should) be free of representation in the first place.

Although the Tsalalians' uprising may indicate that the sign does not always need us, it remains true that we always need the sign; we need those letters, those water casks and wax plugs, to have a sense of our own agency. These objects produce our belief in our own self-steering, however delusional such a belief may be. From the perspective of the allure of the phantasmagoria, which promised real self-mastery and perfect autonomy, such a stance looks passive, accidental, incomplete. Yet if we turn to the phantasmagoria instead, we in fact suffer a nearly perfect and totalizing delusion, losing selfhood once and for all. The "agency" that is afforded to us by our conspiracy with language comes, as we saw with Copjec's analysis of Johns, from choosing what already is, as opposed to grasping at things that manifestly are not. But such a "choice" needs to be informed by all that we cannot know, the choices that we cannot avoid.

And this works, as we have seen, not just for individuals but for entire communities as well; the exposure of the mythologies of power (of both divine and human varieties) allows the circumnavigating "side" communities that we are members of to become more legible to us. Although they are organized and built, as we saw with Kafka, expressly in the (idolatrous) service of the mythologies of power, when those mythologies have been voided or displaced, these communities do not disappear. Not unlike Poe's narrator who survives in the orbit of the maelstrom, these side communities exist and persist even when the center is voided or exposed. We do not need to start new communities from scratch, nor do we need to engage in brand-new and unheralded forms of political life (we do not need to pine for utopias). As Benjamin tells us, in keeping with the Jewish mystical tradition he both conforms with and diverges from, when the messiah comes, it will "only make a slight adjustment in [the world]").[16] In fact the world we need, the "future" we hope for, is already here, the communities we require already exist (as the work of J. K. Gibson-Graham attests).[17] Yet as long as we keep our eye on the illusive perfection that comes with dreams of sovereignty (of the personal, political, and theological varieties), we can never see what we already have; we can find neither satisfaction in our collective and existing practices nor resistance to those phantasms to which we all subscribe.

Is There a Messiah in the Text?

If we are allied with material objects, it remains to understand how we come to view that alliance, how we think about an alien intention that we take on as our own. One way that we have seen authors addressing this idea is through the text as messiah. Throughout this book, we have seen discussions and hints of this textual messianism, some self-voiding power that delivers us from the full maw of phantasm, without, however, removing delusion altogether. Once we (mis)encounter this messiah, we remain, as we have seen, bound by our misrecognitions, but in ways that allow us more leeway to determine ourselves even as we are, in a sense, determined by the texts that afford us this leeway in the first place. Yet to speak of a "textual messiah" once again sounds rather odd—it suggests a kind of mystical attitude toward something that is in fact as banal as black marks on a white page (although Poe shows us how such a banality can be infused with a kind of mysticism).

Yet it remains useful to speak of a textual "messianism"—even without necessarily making recourse to some actual deity—insofar as it helps us to understand how the text delivers us from our own phantasms (to think otherwise would be to suggest that one needs to be religious to engage in textual conspiracy). As we have seen, from the perspective of this conspiracy, the text is not merely a humble servant that we employ to denote our thoughts. Nor is it a cruel trickster who seduces us into a phantasmagoria that we cannot even see. Instead, the text, as we have seen, always stands as a potential ally and redeemer. In the very way that texts and signs can lead to misreading the world in order to produce the phantasmagoria, we can also be misled, as it were, to misread the world in other, more productive and antifetishistic forms.

In considering these texts as potentially containing or performing a messianic function, we have been maintaining a disconnect between authors and their texts. This disconnection is evidence of something particular (although not unique) to the texts we have examined, a quality whereby the authors' own authority is subverted by the text they themselves have written. Here, the text voids its own pose as meaningful or "true" in a way that delivers the author (and the reader) from a particular and fated perspective. To understand this as a messianic delivery may just be a shorthand way of saying that this delivery must be read as happening without the author's "permission" or intention coming into play (if it did, we would be right to suspect this as yet another false prophecy, another form of self-denying idolatry). Its source is external, miraculous (to us). It comes unexpectedly and, as we have seen, without being recognized for what it is.[18]

Given the permanent and ongoing possibility of such textual rescues, the idea of a textual messiah (an idea suggested in Benjamin's work and illuminated by Kafka but legible in other conspiratorial works we have read) ensures that this form of delivery remains out of our reach, beyond the scope of human intentionality. It accomplishes this removal even while the elements that compose the text are just words and pictures. Lorca's plays may demonstrate this power most clearly of all of the authors we have examined. We see his characters turning to representation, to plays and disguises, for their redemption. They are indeed redeemed by their alliances but in ways that simultaneously rescue them from what they were actually seeking. Such a textual intrusion saves us not just from one manifestation of truth, but also from all truths (which are by definition mythological, phantasmagoric).

On the other hand, we could choose to be mystical (although still not necessarily religious). We could say, as Benjamin or Kafka would, that the depiction of a textual messianism gestures toward the anticipation of "divine violence," an act that wipes out idolatry, redeeming us in the process.

In his "Critique of Violence" Benjamin writes: "Just as in all spheres God opposes myth, mythical violence is confronted by the divine."[19] Such divine violence is not ours to dispense, nor ours to know. The God's eye viewpoint—the viewpoint that sees the monad and the idea—is not ours, but by gesturing toward it, we are perhaps pointing toward what is also pointing (or gesturing) toward us.[20]

The simultaneity of messianic deliverance (if that is what it is) and our own acts of conspiracy has been a central, ongoing theme of this book. This is a basic idea that we find in Benjamin, the idea that the coming of the revolution and the coming of the messiah are the very same moment. The simultaneity of these gestures produces a kind of balance. On the one hand, given the nature of the messiah in question, we cannot "wait for God" to save us. As we have seen, God has already come and left. On the other hand we cannot "take matters into our own hands," because to do so would simply be to return us to the phantasmagoria that we remained mired in and desirous of in the first place. Our misrecognition of the messiah is what allows us to understand the self-voiding of the messiah as our own gesture; it is what allows this simultaneity to function, to make our resistance both possible and potent. Through this combination of messianic deliverance and our own conspiracy, we can remain innocent of the way the text determines us, avoiding idolatry even while the idols themselves have been subverted and displaced.

Radical Hope?

In the preceding, we have considered how Benjamin's conspiracy is neither necessarily mystical (although it could be) nor antihuman (at least taken in some senses of that term). It is hence amenable to our understandings of politics even as those understandings are themselves problematic, reflective of our compromised (but not irredeemable) positions. The remainder of this conclusion will be devoted to a consideration of the direct, political upshot of this conspiracy.

As a starting point, to understand how such a conspiracy would work in the world, I would like to contrast the strategies employed in the texts we have read to that suggested by a relatively recent book entitled *Radical Hope*. In that book Jonathan Lear makes an argument about how politics can defy and overcome a sense of what is possible that in many ways seems to echo what I have been claiming we find in Benjamin's work. Yet I will argue that these conceptions are utterly different. In my view, what Lear proposes is neither radical nor hopeful, and by distinguishing his argument from what might truly produce "radical hope" (i.e., a hope that is not for us) I seek to make my own position more clear.

Radical Hope is purportedly a consideration of the situation of the Crow Nation during the late nineteenth century, a time when they seemed to be completely out of options (more accurately, Lear projects onto the screen of Crow history a set of his own beliefs and philosophical insights, ones that probably have very little to do with the Crow per se). Lear tells us that with the decimation of the buffalo herds they relied on, massive losses to their numbers from diseases introduced from Europe, endless war, and pressures from other Native American communities such as the Sioux, Arapaho, and Cheyenne who encroached upon their land, and of course, the encroachment of the Europeans themselves, the Crow faced the end of their culture, of their sense of self, their sense of time, and even of meaning. Lear's book is inspired by the example of Plenty Coups, their chief at that time, who navigated these challenges. In particular he is struck by Plenty Coups's claim that "After [the end of our life as we knew it] nothing happened."[21] Lear interprets this to mean that the very idea of happening itself is produced out of a particular sense of time, reality, and meaning, one that is in this case completely tied up with Crow culture and political life. In this way, not unlike as with Benjamin, we could say that Plenty Coups found himself at a temporal dead end. He knew that he could not imagine a world where Crow identity and subjectivity had ceased to have meaning; a product of his time and his world, he is limited by who he is and how he perceives that world.

Yet for Lear, Plenty Coups successfully negotiates this challenge by sacrificing virtually everything that made the Crow who they were without sacrificing the most basic essence of "Crowness." In doing so, he allows his people to survive and possibly even thrive in the face of their many challenges. Following a series of visions, Plenty Coups sees (or rather Lear sees on behalf of Plenty Coups) that "it is nevertheless possible to commit to a goodness which transcends [self] understanding. He need not claim thereby to have any grasp of what that is. It is a commitment to a goodness that transcends his understanding."[22] This argument is heavily indebted to Kierkegaard (as Lear acknowledges) and has therefore very little to do with Plenty Coups's own perspective. The very idea that God and the universe God created are good allows what Lear, citing Kierkegaard himself, calls a "teleological suspension of the ethical,"[23] that is to say, a suspension of what one knows and believes to be ethical in the face of some greater and transcendent source of ethics (the chief example of course being Abraham's willingness to sacrifice his own son when God commanded that he do so). Connecting this back to Plenty Coups, Lear writes:

> What is so striking about Plenty Coups's situation is that it was a nonmythical, realistic, and plausible account of someone who experienced himself as receiving a divine call to tolerate the collapse of ethical life. This would include even a *collapse of the concepts* with which ethical life had hitherto been understood.[24]

Lear calls such a collapse a "thinning" out of the Crow's concepts, reducing "Crowness" to a kind of essential, and ethical, pith.

Lear distinguishes between radical hope and optimism (as well as fatalism; the last being some kind of stubborn clinging to the past that certainly dooms any individuals who chose that route). Optimism is a kind of wishful thinking where you allow what you wish to be true to determine your actions. For Lear, such thinking is pure delusion. Lear tells us that Plenty Coups's practice of radical hope is responsive to reality as it is, to the anxiety that permeated his time. Hence, his visions, reflecting that anxiety, do not need to be genuinely prophetic to be valid, nor do they serve as mere instances of wishful thinking.

Plenty Coups and Benjamin

Given this articulation of radical hope, it might seem as if Benjamin is advocating something quite similar to what Lear describes. There are several ways in which the argument Lear makes might seem to depict a real-world, historical example of escaping the temporal doom Benjamin engages with. If anything, Lear seems to do one better than Benjamin, apparently offering a story of "success," whereas Benjamin himself looked only at failures. In terms of the respective theologies that we encounter in their texts (keeping in mind that for Lear it does not have to be a theology at all), we can see in Lear's articulation of a transcendent goodness that permits a "thinning" (and thereby a survival) of our concepts, something seemingly similar to the way Benjamin trusts in the "God's eye view" as a corrective to our own participation in the phantasmagoria. Thanks to a "teleological suspension of the ethical" (i.e., of what we think and believe—and know—to be good and true), it seems as if in both cases we can avoid being determined by our limitations because goodness exists independently of human agency (or intentionality). If this insight is true, we can risk, as Plenty Coups and Benjamin both do, a leap of faith into the unknown. Because their respective theologies show them that the world is not perfectly evil, it seems as if there is in fact a possibility for (radical) hope after all.

Yet without denying all of the important and valuable connections established above, and certainly without detracting from Plenty Coups's experiences and choices, I would argue that there are important reasons to distinguish such actions from the conspiracy I am trying to describe in these pages. Clearly, the position of a leftist who finds her- or himself trapped in the early twenty-first century and the position of the Crow are quite different. In our own time, not all of us face the total annihilation that the Crow did. The attack on the Left, while ongoing and fierce, takes multiple forms, and we should be careful to keep such events separate and distinct from the genocide facing Native Americans throughout their history of contact with Europeans. In our own time, the conquest of communities by the phantasmagoria has been generally (although not entirely) completed, and so we are facing a life in the maw rather than on the edge of such a threat. In our own time, too, nothing "happens," as Benjamin tells us, but unlike the Crow, we have no point of reference for understanding how or that this is so. For the Crow, the change from their own life to one determined by alien narratives dramatized the potential end of their existence as an independent people. In our own time, we don't generally have such markers.[25] Indeed, as Benjamin points out, we believe that we exist very much in time, in a world of "happening," of change, progress, and history; these notions are in fact the hallmark of the phantasmagoria in its current guise.

Even leaving these dissimilarities to the side, I would argue that the strategies Lear puts forth in Plenty Coups's name would not serve the Left in its own striving for resistance. To put it plainly, Lear advocates a total collapse in the face of one's adversaries, a way to endure terrible suffering and to survive through a pure act of self-reimagining. I am not writing this to judge either Plenty Coups or the Crow Nation; one can only admire a people who have stared genocide in the face and survived, and I do not doubt that they have maintained many of their cultural concepts albeit in radically altered form. Furthermore, despite the fact that he is interpreted largely through Lear's own perspective, I'm not sure Plenty Coups doesn't have his own, conspiratorial side that Lear is ignoring—or at least not highlighting.[26] Yet when treated as a representative of Lear's proscription for dealing with a sense of being trapped by time and circumstances, this articulation of what Plenty Coups did is a strategy that will lead only to more phantasmagoria and not less.

In seeking to have his people endure, Plenty Coups collaborates with the white soldiers against other Indian people, principally their traditional enemies, the Sioux. If we keep the analogy (however faint) between the condition of the Crow and our current condition of already living in a place where "nothing happens," we can see that to follow this strategy amounts to learning to live with capitalism, with the overpowering force of the phantasmagoria, that is, to do more of what we are already doing, a formula for more, and further leftist defeat.

The central problem is that Plenty Coups's strategy is an accommodation to a terrible storm that his visions tell him his people will not otherwise survive. In the face of that accommodation, we get no meaningful resistance, no challenge to or altering of a sense of time and space that confines and condemns the Crow to a life that is almost completely determined by white power and narratives. Lear makes much of the fact that the Crow are on at least part of their ancestral land today and that they have held onto an idea of "Crowness" despite what they have gone through. But as I see it, as a parallel, this is only offering those of us on the left the option to remain embedded in a system and find a way to make our peace with it. This is the stance we perforce have already taken, and it leads not to life but to political death, to more phantasmagoria. This is a fate Tocqueville foresaw even before the events Lear describes (and which Jodi Dean warns us about in her own work as well).

As I see it, the hope that Benjamin offers is far more radical than what Lear describes (in fact, I don't see any "hope" in what Lear offers at all, radical or otherwise). Indeed, as we saw in chapter 4, one must abandon hope as it is currently constituted, hope for redemption, for meaning and truth before any kind of "radical" hope (a hope that is not for us, which emerges from a different temporal conception) can emerge. As I see it, Lear's account of "radical hope," for all of its pruning away or "thinning" of our concepts, holds onto a piece of our current conceptions (including the conception of hope itself) and thus ensures that whatever emerges in the transformation that such hope allows will not be radically different. One key way to distinguish these authors is to note that Lear's account of Plenty Coups calls for a leap of faith, whereas Benjamin calls for a "faithless leap"—akin to the leap that the narrator in Poe's "A Descent into the Maelström" took off his boat and into the whirlpool.[27] In Benjamin's case (as we see illuminated by our reading of Fanon and Djebar as well), the subject that emerges from his conspiracy is a rearrangement of the materials that compose it, not the preservation of some core element that persists; such a subject has given up on faith, gone into mourning for all that she or he once hoped for (hence "deepening" and altering her or his intention). To hold onto faith is to maintain a "core" of ourselves, preserving the very intentionality that traps us by impossible odds in the first place.

And yet, although the subject is even more radically thinned out in Benjamin's reading than Lear's, the content of our subjectivity is in some ways much thicker than it is for Lear himself. A turn to the materiality of texts, of signs, and of images preserves far more than it leaves behind; what we "become" is virtually identical to what we "were" given that we are merely rejuxtaposing the signs that deliver our narrative to ourselves; as we saw in the previous chapter, the future is already here, we are already "redeemed." Thanks to our ongoing acts of misrecognition (or our recognition of such misrecognition) we retain *more* of a sense of our own agency (however false) than do the Crow, who have had the permanent loss of their own agency demonstrated quite clearly to them.

We thus do not need, as Lear claims, to be open to whatever the future brings, because in rediscovering the material reality of representation, we learn that our world and even time itself (including the future we await) are artifacts of our reading, produced by the juxtapositions of objects that we engage with. The Left does not have to abandon everything that it is in order to resist the phantasmagoria; indeed, as we have seen in earlier chapters, our resistance, our narratives, and the communities that we have already formed are exactly what keep us from being completely determined by the phantasmagoria. What needs to change is the way we understand and read this situation.

Sitting Bull Revisited

For these reasons, I would not include Lear in this textual conspiracy—the radical hope he promises seems to me to be merely a recipe for acquiescence, for more of the same. Perhaps perversely, I would, however, extend this conspiracy to the apparent failure of his book (or at least the book's straw man), Sitting Bull. Sitting Bull was Plenty Coups's contemporary. Unlike Plenty Coups, Sitting Bull went to war against the white soldiers (and lost—although he managed to win a few major victories along the way). Much of Lear's criticism of Sitting Bull comes from the latter's half-

hearted support for the Ghost Dance, a messianic movement among Indian people in the late nineteenth century led by the prophet Wovoka that
held that participating in such a dance would mean the end of white
power. Sitting Bull paid dearly for this support; U.S. agents seeking to stop
the Ghost Dance came to arrest him in 1890, and he was killed in the ensuing struggle. For Lear, Sitting Bull "deployed a messianic vision that
fueled the Ghost Dance in a wishful way."[28] It will be recalled that for Lear,
wishfulness, that is to say, optimism, is not radical hope because it does
not deal with reality. But of course the problem here is that Lear denies
one form of reality (that produced by the Ghost Dance) but accepts another (the reality produced out of white power and authority). What Sitting Bull is doing may be delusional from the perspective of white reality,
but it is an attempt, however failed, to alter that reality (not unlike Fanon's
seeking to alter the "reality" of white/European power in his own time).
Thus Sitting Bull evokes a strategy of misrecognition, of failure to read
white power as a permanent and irresistible fate. His failure, as I see it,
does not suggest the uselessness of his strategy but only suggests the result
of one iteration, one outcome of struggle.

If we could read both Sitting Bull and perhaps even Plenty Coups's responses to the onslaught of white authority in a conspiratorial way, we can
see that "reality" is always an open question and that more options remain
open to them than Lear himself seems to suggest.[29] The fact of the "success" or "failure" of these endeavors in resisting white power is not in and
of itself definitive (in fact the Crow and the Sioux ended up with a relatively similar fate despite their very different strategies). We have seen
from Benjamin how historical failure can in fact remain a source of potential resistance long after that moment has passed into history, a point of
constellation to connect to other acts of resistance.

It is probably the case that no amount of rereading or textual (or other
forms of semiotic) materialism would have saved the Crow or the Sioux in
the short—or even long—run. Overwhelming military and socioeco-
nomic power is what it is. However, once that defeat has occurred, then
the idea of conspiracy becomes useful. Even after failure and loss, or perhaps especially after failure and loss, conspiracy becomes a way to avoid
being perpetually defined by that loss. It is never too late to conspire; as we
saw with Machiavelli, it is even always possible to conspire retroactively.
My argument is that if we truly want a "radical hope" we must follow the
path of Benjamin's conspiracy rather than choose the path of assimilation,
accommodation, and, ultimately, permanent defeat that Lear suggests.

The Politics of Misrecognition: Democracy and Anarchism

For all of this, from a political perspective it seems that at some point, defeat is defeat. If every revolution is doomed to fail, if valiant resisters ranging from Sitting Bull to Fanon wind up losing time after time (or in Fanon's case, perhaps more accurately losing by winning), what is the political valence of a conspiracy that merely strings together these various defeats? What lessons and advantages can we draw from this analysis of conspiracy for our own time and context?

The first thing to consider is that the hopelessness we face on the left is itself an artifact of our ongoing captivity to the phantasmagoria, of the kinds of things we hope for, and not simply a reaction to an impossible situation. As we have seen, the very idea of the possible is produced out of a context that we participate in far more than we generally realize. Hopelessness is not "realistic" so much as a reflection of the reality that produces it. Against such a loss of hope, Benjamin offers mourning, a complex set of emotions that both recognizes the failures of the phantasmagoria and produces subversive alternative ways of seeing and acting (a "motorial" reaction on our part).

By the same token, the political models that we work with also reflect the temporalities that we inhabit and are conditioned by. Thus the very idea that politics has to deliver some final redeeming decision or solution leads us to expect definitive acts such as revolution (taken in its more ordinary sense) in order to pass muster as being properly "political." These expectations for definitive and final acts further lead to the expectation of final and perfect redemption, of the "end of history," or some other form of political cessation. In light of this calculation, other forms of politics, other forms of resistance, are not recognized as being viable, not even as being alternatives. Insofar as they do not fit into our vision of time and history, it is as if they don't or can't "happen" (to cite Plenty Coups).

Of course, the idea that resistance may take new or different forms is not unique to Benjamin. We see such an idea in most Nietzschean-inspired philosophy, in Foucault, in Derrida, and in many others (although I suspect that Benjamin has played a role in passing that idea along to many of those who follow after him, temporally speaking). Nor is the idea of conspiracy solely Benjamin's province. Yet when we think about conspiracy as a form of resistance, one that is open-ended, even endless, rather than definitive, we redefine a history that we have read as a string of defeats and failures as being instead a string of resistant moments. It is Benjamin's key insight, made very near the end of his life, that such moments are already not failures when we think of them in constellation, that is to say, when we read them as being part of an ongoing intertemporal conspiracy.

But I can imagine a skeptical (and not unreasonable) person saying, that is all well and good, but a string of resistant moments is a far cry from the kinds of self-assertions or self-determinations that a left politics promises. In the (vast) spaces between these resistances, we see capitalism busily organizing the world, and ourselves. Even if we feel better about our own past and our role in it, even if we take solace in the fact that the future will continue to have such moments of resistance, what difference does that make in concrete terms, in terms of the world we live in and the conditions that organize that life?

It is here that it is helpful to think further about a "politics of misrecognition," that is to say, a politics of resistance that accepts misrecognition as a basic component of politics, and in that acceptance resists, not merely in isolated moments but in a way that might produce greater spaces in which leftism can thrive and grow. This could also be called a politics of circumnavigation, one based precisely on the kinds of communities that spring up in the wake of grand narratives but which, as we saw with Kafka, are not entirely beholden to or derived from those narratives.

The very idea of a politics of misrecognition or circumnavigation, in its halting and incomplete sense of "What is to be done?" tempers the frequent utopian visions that come out of the Left, visions that can seduce and overcome even the greatest and brightest of resisters with promises of avoiding representation altogether in the name of truth, reality, and purity. Insofar as capitalism has proven itself remarkably good at adapting to the delusions of the moment, whether it is civic republicanism, fascism, liberal democracy, authoritarianism, or various other variations of political mythology, a politics that forswears such ultimate truths, goals, and other mythological achievements better avoids merely reiterating what the phantasmagoria already is. A politics of misrecognition does not come from the perspective of "false consciousness" or the need to reeducate the human race to learn objective truths. It accepts that misrecognition is inevitable and seeks only to combat delusion when it is idolatrous in nature, when it affirms, rather than resists, the central narratives of our time.

Although I earlier stated that we don't have to be mystical in our understanding of how this conspiracy works, using a theological vocabulary, particularly in terms of idolatry, helps make sense of the politics that would be practiced in the absence of such fetishism. The phantasmagoria is an idolatrous use of representation, the production of mythologies about God, about the state, about society, and about the individual. Each of these idols can also be read as a "sign," a representational building block that collectively forms the fabric of our contemporary reality. What would it mean to cease to read these things in an idolatrous fashion, to cease to look for their meaning and truth and instead to read them "merely" as signs (a question we first asked in the previous chapter when considering the green flags of Islam)?

Democracy and Anarchism

To take just one (but clearly vital) example, let us consider a nonidolatrous reading of the term "democracy." This sign has done much to serve (but also to resist) the phantasmagoria. Hardly any nation on earth today forebears calling itself a democracy, so if we just went on terminology alone, we could say that democracy is pretty much triumphant. But what about democracy as a practice? Where (if anywhere) are the "real" democracies to be found?

It is here that we begin to see the phantasmic nature of democracy as a practice. Any "rule of the people" must contend with an enormous store of fantasies: fantasies of sovereignty, of self-determination, of nation, of kinship, and of myriad other forms of political association. In one sense, such fantasies are the necessary fabric of any community, the basis for narrativity. Yet such narratives easily slide into idolatry; in an effort at "self-representation," these visions interfere with or even replace any sense of a community's material existence, the multitudinous life that springs up in the periphery of what it is meant to serve and be.

In light of this idolatrous reading of the sign "democracy," we might be tempted to just give up on the idea. If we can't even summon a vision of the "people" that democracy reflects, how can we think of having something called democracy? Does the problem of representation doom our project from the outset? In his own work, Jacques Rancière offers a different way to understand how to read and think about democracy, one that aligns him at least partially with the conspiracy that we are describing in this book (although, as we will see, with a few important caveats). In *Hatred of Democracy*, Rancière takes great issue with what democracy has become without giving up on "democracy" altogether. He sets out to knock down the sacred cows of liberal democracy one after another. He tells us that the system that we call democracy today is in fact the product of a fantasy invented by Plato—and a hateful fantasy at that. We often forget (but Rancière reminds us) that Plato used the term "democracy" as an insult, meant by its negative example to secure a rule by the best (or at least by those who thought they were the best). For Rancière the concept of democracy in fact disguises an oligarchic monopoly of power. Notions like voting and representation, which are understood as part and parcel of "real" democracies, are in fact artifacts of oligarchic rule. Political representation is originally "the exact contrary of democracy," a form of political organization that ruled via "estates" (in France anyway) that allowed minorities a huge and disproportionate amount of power.[30] Even voting comes in for attack in Rancière's treatment as a false symbol of equality that in its origin is meant to reduce and not expand popular representation. Rancière tells us that voting is "originally the expression of a consent that a superior power requires and which is not really such unless it is unanimous."[31] He prefers the Athenian method of drawing lots.

In what amounts to adding insult to injury, opponents of democracy in all of their guises blame the people themselves (whatever that means) for the ills of a democracy that exists in name alone. They lay blame on the people's consumerism, frivolity, and excess, their corruption and cravenness, even though these qualities are a reflection of the fact that democracy is everywhere and always curtailed and thwarted. Rancière tells us that the hatred of democracy is

> not the simple expression of an aristocratic mood. It serves to ward off an anarchy or an "indistinction" . . . the primary indistinction between governors and governed, one which becomes evident when the obviousness of the natural power of the best or of the highborn is stripped of its prestige—the absence of a special title to govern politically over those assembled other than the absence of title. Democracy is first this paradoxical condition of politics, the point where every legitimation is confronted with its ultimate lack of legitimacy, confronted with the egalitarian contingency that underpins the inegalitarian contingency itself.[32]

Thus democracy is conceived of as a storehouse for the vulnerabilities of oligarchic rule; it becomes a site by which the resistance to such rule can be neutralized, hidden behind the name of democracy. When oligarchs rule, not by title, but by "representation" (as they do in the liberal democracies of the West) the democratic "excess," the anarchic remnant that is excluded from power, is redirected and reacted to as an understanding of the citizen as remorselessly private, selfish, and usually ignorant. As Rancière also tells us, "Popular sovereignty is a way of including democratic excess, of transforming into an *arkhè* the anarchic principle of political singularity—the government of those who are not entitled to govern."[33] Thus "democracy" as a faux populism is conceived and deployed as a way to suppress and replace exactly what it seeks to stand in for. In my own terms, I would say that the sign for democracy is therefore treated, as we have already seen, as an idol, superimposing itself over the people in whose name it is promulgated (a danger Tocqueville obviously anticipates in his own work) even as it helps to organize and produce that people in the first place. But as with all signs, there is another way to read things; Rancière himself suggests an anarchic possibility beneath this false reading and use of the concept of democracy; even if it serves as a response to the "anarchic principle," democracy remains engaged with—and reflective of—that principle. Even though it is read as an idol, democracy can never be so reduced that it doesn't evoke or even produce what it sets out to deny.

Just as with Kafka's depiction of peripheral communities that are produced in the face of false and hubristic narratives (such as the city that grows around the Tower of Babel or indeed the village that rises up around the Castle) so too with democracy we find an entire way of life, an anarchic principle being produced via the name of the very sign that would deny such communities in the first place. So long as the idol remains, these anarchic communities remain at the level of subcurrent and rumor. The occupants of this community—which is in a sense all or most of us—do not recognize themselves as such, so seduced are they by the spectacle of capitalism and the state power that goes with it. But that anarchic "excess" which lies at the radical heart of democracy remains as a potent and already existent full-blown alternative to the power arrangements of the phantasmagoria. It exists, as Ziarek tells us, as "decentered, heterogeneous, built without any governing idea,"[34] amid the full manifestations of sovereign, phantasmic power. The more literary authors we have looked at, ranging from Kafka to Poe to Lorca and Djebar, have depicted those communities and the lives within them in great detail, to give us a sense of their depth and granularity, their resilience and endurance even under conditions of phantasmagoria.

To engage in a nonidolatrous reading of the sign democracy is not to do away with democracy altogether (that is certainly not Rancière's project). Rather, it is to engage with the sign and what it stands for in the face of a radical voiding of its central meanings and purposes. As we saw with Djebar, when the "green flags" of Islam are revealed as ragged sheets—without ceasing to be flags—then and only then can the anarchic communities that have come together in its name appear to themselves in all their complexity, and plurality. The anarchic politics that are disguised under the grand narrative of democracy are also produced, in a sense, out of an anarchic reading of the sign, a move away from the center toward the periphery, a circumnavigating politics. To make our communities more legible to ourselves is to be in a better position to "steer" them (at least from our own, deluded, perspective) when and if periodic voidings of the central idol of "democracy" come to pass (an event that can be triggered by conspiracy itself).

In thinking about such a nonidolatrous form of democracy, we must once again proceed with caution. Here too, Jodi Dean alerts us that even a democracy that has seemingly turned away from mythology can be a trap. Specifically writing against Rancière himself, Dean warns of what she calls the leftist "fantasy of a politics without politics"[35] As I see it, this is another—but in this case explicitly political—version of the fantasy of being non- or "post-" representative that I have described throughout this book, a deliverance from politics akin to Augustine's notion that the ultimate victory over sin is liberation from the temptation to sin, that is to say, from desire altogether.[36]

The key question to ask here is what do we do with our desire, that is to say, with our intentions insofar as these tend to lead us into the trap Dean describes? If we can't be freed from our intentions, what kind of relationship to desire can we safely have (and with what political implications)? Using an explicitly Lacanian (and more particularly Žižekian) lexicon, Dean argues that "democracy" is the *objet petit a* of the Left. It is a desire that is endlessly deferred. It (to cite Žižek directly) "exists only qua anticipated or lost."[37] In saying this, Dean is directly critiquing Rancière, but by implication also Copjec and others.[38] For Dean the satisfactions of the drive, that is to say, the satisfaction of giving up on the goal (or the *objet petit a*), are no satisfaction at all.[39] What Dean calls the "democratic drive," that circulation around the object (akin to the circumnavigation we have been describing), is (as we saw earlier) simply the satisfaction of loss, of having one's status (as a failure, as a political loser) endlessly reconfirmed, reexperienced.[40] In my own terms, this amounts to replacing the fetishes of grand narratives with a fetishism of failure. It may seem like turning away from the *objet petit a,* but it is simply enjoying the futility of the ride around it. This is circumnavigation, too, but one that reconfirms our fetishism. We are left with what Alenka Zupančič calls the "metonomy" of desire, its endlessness, its nonsatisfaction.[41]

In speaking of such a fetishism of futility, Dean tells us that "a reading of politics as rooted only in its own contingency is too close to a state of nature or view from nowhere to be useful for thinking through the challenges of contemporary politics."[42] Such a view returns us to the position we articulated earlier in this conclusion: too much nostalgia for ancient Athenian democracy (such as it was), too much romance of leftist failure, does not make for a politics with content and possibility. It only makes for more failure.

At the heart of Dean's criticism is a most valuable insight: *aporia*, failure, and contingency do not in and of themselves serve as guarantors of anything like democracy or equality or any other values that we may hold. The fact of circumnavigation is not a guarantee that something good, useful, or particularly *leftist* will be happening. An ethos of resistance may be well and good, but if it is just resistance for resistance's sake, is it necessarily more *democratic?* Is the concept of democracy merely a reactive, antithetical practice? In Dean's reading of him, Rancière embodies a "politics without politics," a formal allegiance to an empty category.[43] In his claim that politics is the response to democracy, to the anarchic excess that is always present, we see the risk of assuming that the excess itself is a "pure political," and hence we risk, as we have seen Arendt and others similarly risk, a fetish that we do not recognize as such, a fetish without remedy.

Keeping Dean's critique in mind, I would not so much abandon Rancière's insights (nor Copjec's) so much as show that they may be infused with the same "recognized misrecognition" that we have been looking at throughout this text, to draw them, too, into our conspiracy. To think that resistance qua resistance is a good in and of itself is to risk the mistake that I see Lear making with his analysis of Plenty Coups: it is the risk of assuming that just because the universe is not perfectly evil (Kierkegaard's position) that a leap into the unknown is at the same time a leap toward the good. As we saw in the case of Lear's analysis of the Crow Nation, this is not actually always the case. To assume that this leap will always produce good is to fail to appreciate the fundamental lesson of Benjamin's understanding of the God's eye view. This view is *not ours;* we have no access to it. The idea that we can leap into the void and trust that we will be rescued is another form of idolatry. We leap from one idol to another (possibly worse) one. This is the key difference, then, between a leap of faith and a faithless leap. In the latter case, we must know (and mourn) all that we do not and cannot know in order not to be totalized by our temporal and contextual circumstances.

To make a faithless leap, to recognize our misrecognition, is to avoid the hubristic assumption that the God's eye view is our own. It is to remain cognizant of the fact that we remain semiotic creatures, dependent on the sign even when we rebel against what it appears to represent. We have no outside view, no privileged perch from which to look down on the ruin of representation. We are in representation and we are of representation in all of its imperfection and delusion. For this reason, we can neither give up on the sign altogether nor discover the "true" sign hidden under the mythology (the fetish within the fetish) that Dean accurately sees many left thinkers succumbing to (potentially including Rancière himself).

In our clinging to the sign "democracy" we see that without this sign, we would not have those anarchic excesses, those side communities that represent the "future" that is already here. Yet here, too, we must recognize that existing in a peripheral community is not in and of itself "democratic." As Kafka shows us, in the shadow of grand narratives an infinite number of injustices and hierarchies lurk, just as an infinite number of justices and friendships may also lurk. We see from Dean that it is a mistake to prematurely declare ourselves "democratic"; to assume that we have extricated ourselves from the *objet petit a* is to deny the ongoing structuring power of the sign. What we *can* have in such an instance is a space where democracy may in fact be *possible,* a space where politics is not perfect or good but where it is legible, available. What we actually would do in such a space becomes an open question. Quite possibly we would fail, we would reproduce the phantasmagoria all over again (Benjamin shows us how readily resistance turns into its opposite and visa versa). We are, as Alenka Zupančič shows us, always "on the hook" ethically speaking even as we remain unaware of what ethics consists of, what is required of us.[44] The point may simply be that only in a space cleared of our own complicit intentionality, however partially and imperfectly, is it possible for the anarchism that underlies "democracy" to be legible or practicable. Only then can we begin to speak of ourselves as a "self-determining" political community.

From the perspective of the God's eye view, such a self-determination is ludicrous. It is akin to Poe's narrator "steering himself" around the swirling miasma of the maelstrom. It is akin to the hubris of Ulysses thinking that he fooled the Sirens. Yet from our own perspective, this is what agency and self-determination look like. This is the fruit of our alliance with the signs, the benefit of our recognized misrecognition.

In the face of such "self-determination" the content of our "democratic" acts that follow (again, if we dare use the word) comes not entirely out of the ether, not from our whim or "free" choice, but from the de facto "anarchisms" that have evolved and have already been practiced in the orbit around the grand narratives and referents that already organize our lives. When our own intentions align with the "intention of the sign," the phantasmagoria, at least for a moment, dissolves away—it becomes invisible to us in the same way that the anarchic practices that we practice are rendered invisible when the phantasmagoria overshadows them. Yet the promise of the Left comes not from merely (mis)recognizing those practices (this is why I think even the noble work of J. K. Graham-Gibson is not the whole picture—something I imagine that they would agree with) but from developing and engaging in them in a sustained, "self-steering" fashion. It is only then that something like democracy might be possible as afforded by the sign "democracy."

Based on these points, I would argue that the form of politics that is produced by a Benjaminian conspiracy, by a politics of misrecognition, is an anarchic one. As Benjamin tells us so clearly in "Critique of Violence," the dreams of state power, of sovereignty, the political forms that the phantasmagoria takes, are merely instances of mythology, subject to the annihilation afforded by acts of divine violence (and conspiratorial justice—the two acts may be one and the same). If we want our resistance to be more than mere episodes, if we want in fact to escape the dictates of a temporal calculus that always will reduce the Left to an episodic repetition of failure, we must become more attuned to our misrecognition, to the opportunities that come from resistance and to the anarchic practices that already exist even as we worship at the altar of the phantasmagoria. I would argue that from the position of Benjaminian conspiracy, anarchism is the proper stance to take in the face of our exclusion from the God's eye view; in the face of the endless unfurlings of the monad, in our ambiguity and unknowingness, anarchism is the form of politics that best reflects our position. Anarchy is the one form of politics that resists idolatry; we might say that it is what politics is when it is not overdetermined and overwritten by anything else.

Hope . . . but Not for Us

With this understanding of politics in mind, let us move toward a final conclusion by briefly considering some of the ideas that we have encountered in this book and discussing a few crucial remaining issues. The main question to address is how, in the juxtapositions and constellations that form between the authors we have considered, does one go about actually conspiring? How does one make the transition from text to world? To think a bit more about this, it would behoove us to return to one of the first authors that we considered in depth, Machiavelli, perhaps the greatest theorist of conspiracy the Western world has ever produced. Machiavelli shows us above all how a conspiracy can be spread, how it can (to use a contemporary term) go "viral." In his plays and books, Machiavelli demonstrates and actually deploys a strategy of recasting the deluded, depoliticized, and self-regarding citizens of Florence into active conspirators. As we saw, it becomes possible to extend participation in conspiracy to nearly every citizen because all are in fact already participating in it, whether they realize it or not. The same actions, the same antipolitical, idolatrous readings we devote to the phantasmagoria, are just a razor's edge from becoming the anarchic and conspiratorial forms of resistance that we have been considering in this book. Machiavelli shows how to enable this transformation, to produce an outcome that is "useless for the purposes of fascism."

Such a conspiracy is also constituted and marked above all by a method—Walter Benjamin's anarchic and anti-idolatrous method of reading the world, ourselves, and our relationship to politics. This method, as I see it, is Benjamin's main contribution to political theory (not to mention to literature and other fields); it is the method of conspiracy. It amounts to a sustained and particular practice of anti-idolatry, of strictly obeying (like Kafka) the Second Commandment (or at least Benjamin's version of it). Wherein in the usual (let us call it "Protestant") versions of anti-idolatry or iconoclasm, God is meant to be directly accessed, bypassing the signs and symbols that stand in for the Deity, in a Benjaminian, conspiratorial form of anti-idolatry we do almost the opposite: we deny God altogether and cling to the sign, not, once again, to actually deny God but rather because we recognize our misrecognition; we know that we can never know God directly. Such a move permits us to keep God as an *aporia* and to become (at least relatively) undetermined by the false narratives we otherwise inevitably subscribe to.

In terms of such a conspiracy leading to a larger politics that resists racism, imperialism, colonialism, and capitalism, we have seen the value and power of resistance as a basis for its own counterontology. We see this most clearly in our analysis of Fanon, Djebar, and to some extent Tocqueville as well. A community's narrative, its ongoing self-understanding, is not in and of itself "true," and yet it becomes an artifact of representation, a water cask or a ragged sheet that we require to help us navigate the symbolic order. As a rule, our communities are either themselves geared toward some perfect or ideal destination, a break with representation altogether (as we saw with Tocqueville's analysis of Anglo Americans), or forced into supporting such a goal, by playing the role of the representative other (Native and African Americans in Tocqueville, Tsalalians in Poe, Algerians and Antilleans with Fanon, and postrevolutionary Algerians with Djebar). Resistance to such narratives disrupts these relationships and allows communities access to the signs that resist and distort their own original purposes. Such a decentered, non-goal-oriented circumnavigating community can be a different model for politics, a politics based on misrecognition.

In speaking of a politics of misrecognition or the misrecognition of our various conspirators, I am not trying to signal that I myself, as author of this book, have access to what isn't being recognized by anyone else. To speak of misrecognition seems to bring in an implicit belief in "recognition," a basic reality that is being denied by our delusions. But such a reality is exactly what we do not have access to. To say that the authors we have studied in this book misrecognize reality is not to belittle them but rather to point to the way that their own texts have interfered with and redeem them from their own complicity in the phantasmagoria. I find this admirable even in a figure like Arendt, where such a move seems neither perfectly conscious nor desired on her part. Arendt has the grace to allow her own prose to be troubled by its contradictions; she does not try to render her text coherent to the extent that it delivers nothing but more (disguised) idolatry. Her phantasms, as with the other authors that we have studied, serve a better politics without being any less deluded. As we saw with Machiavelli's use of adianoeta the kinds of "knowledges" that we adopt in this conspiracy are simply an account and expression of our own perspectives. Yet when they are properly shared and promulgated, as we have seen, such knowledges can redeem our communities from that which they pay homage to.

As mentioned in the preface to this book, younger leftists today, having grown up in the ruins of leftist dreams, are less despairing than their elders. They are more comfortable with partial, temporary, and limited forms of resistance. But, as I suggested in the preface too, this stance is in and of itself not a sufficient challenge to global capitalism or the phantasmagoria that issues from it. Nonetheless, their style of leftism is perhaps a better anticipation of the politics that come out of a Benjaminian conspiracy than older styles of left politics (at least since anarchism itself was a widespread aspect of the leftist political spectrum). Insofar as the vast majority of Marxist and other leftist understandings of politics subscribe to a progressive view of time, a sense of lasting and widespread accomplishments, such views are bound to be disappointed, and see no hope at all in the practices a Benjaminian conspiracy both uncovers and produces. But if we stay true to the anarchist implications of our method, we must be suspicious, as always, of any solution that leads to a permanent leftist paradise. The disappointment that we often feel at the notion that anarchism (and, by extension, democracy) is already here, that the world we are seeking is not much different from the world we have, indicates the extent to which we are fixed on a certain definition of politics and even a certain definition of success. What this conspiracy can produce besides what we "already have" is not necessarily a sustained practice in terms of covering large portions of time and space. Instead we can have political practices that are "sustained" in the sense that such anti-idolatrous moments will be deep and rich, vastly connected to a myriad other moments across time, a constellation or web of interactions. That sort of sustenance is perhaps what we might finally be able to "hope for" even though we ourselves have no hope at all.

The final thing to add in terms of hope is that this conspiracy requires a great deal of courage, but courage of a particular and difficult sort. As we have seen, we must give up all hope to get hope, and this is a difficult thing to contemplate. We must learn to imitate the way that allegory "faithlessly leaps forward to the idea of resurrection," to take a "faithless . . . leap" ourselves.[45]

To illustrate what I am referring to, a cinematic example may be useful. A few years ago a movie came out called *Touching the Void*. The film (a semidocumentary) depicted two climbers that went into the Peruvian Andes to scale a dangerous mountain. One of the climbers, Joe Simpson, breaks his leg en route, and his partner, Simon Yates, begins to slowly lower him down the mountain by a rope. But Simpson gets hung over a crevasse, and as he begins to be lowered over it, the angle of his descent gets too steep, threatening to pull Yates in with him. Yates decides to cut the rope rather than join his partner in death. And yet as it turns out Simpson survives his fall into the crevasse. He finds himself at (what he thinks is) the bottom of the crevasse alive but trapped. What he does next defies most conventions of bravery; knowing that with a broken leg, he cannot climb up the sides of the crevasse, he decides to go deeper *down* into the bowels of the thing in the hopes that it will lead him out of his trap (indeed it does; he lives to tell the tale, write the book, and star in his own movie). In essence he has to give up all hope for a rescue, all hope in the ordinary usual sense of that word, in order to be redeemed.

His act is particularly courageous because he does *not* know that a universal God is there to rescue him, to make his actions okay and safe. It remains his responsibility to save himself. The "God's eye view," exactly because it is not our own, cannot guarantee anything for any one of us. All it can do is announce that we are not certainly doomed, that there is hope out there, even if it is not for us. That alone makes it possible to bear the leaps (or plunges) that Simpson takes and that Benjamin's conspiracy requires of us. That insight alone reminds us that the building blocks of the phantasmagoria are potential allies, and antidotes to the very darkness that engulfs us. The rest is literally up to us.

The courage to go further down, down into the belly of the phantasmagoria without succumbing to it, is exactly what Benjamin's conspiracy calls for; it epitomizes the strategy of the antidote. Rather than looking "up" toward some external salvation, it looks down, toward the signs that serve as guides, havens, and a "mighty paw" of resistance.[46] The choice of "going down" seems indeed quite awful until we realize that we are already stuck in the cave. We are, not unlike Socrates' cave dwellers, trapped in a world of delusions. But in this case, rather than go out to see the sun (the ultimate delusion, perhaps), we have to burrow deeper into the recesses of the cave. If we have no choice but to go deeper, let us go together, fighting and resisting every step of the way. We may, indeed must, have no hope, but in that hopelessness we can, just maybe, fight to see another day.

Notes

PREFACE

1. Jodi Dean, "Politics without Politics," *Parallax* 15, no. 3 (2009): 20–36.
2. Walter Benjamin, "Franz Kafka: On the Tenth Anniversary of His Death," in *Illuminations,* ed. Hannah Arendt, trans. Harry Zohn (New York: Schocken, 1968), 116.

INTRODUCTION

1. Walter Benjamin, "Theses on the Philosophy of History," in *Illuminations,* 255.
2. Ibid., 263.
3. Ibid.
4. Assia Djebar, *Children of the New World: A Novel of the Algerian War* (New York: Feminist Press at the City University of New York, 2005), 120.
5. Ibid.
6. This is the usual and quite inaccurate English translation of *Ursprung des deutschen Trauerspiels*—inaccurate because Benjamin actually opposes tragedy to the *Trauerspiels*—the mourning plays. *The Origin of German Tragic Drama,* trans. John Osborne (New York: Verso, 1998), was written in 1924–25, published in 1928.
7. Carl Schmitt, *Political Theology: Four Chapters on the Concept of Sovereignty* (Cambridge: MIT Press, 1985), 5. Giorgio Agamben, "The State of Exception," in *Politics, Metaphysics and Death: Essays on Giorgio Agamben's "Homo Sacer",* ed. Andrew Norris (Durham, NC: Duke University Press, 2005), 284–98. Samuel Weber, *Benjamin's -abilities* (Cambridge: Harvard University Press, 2008), 188.
8. Ibid., 142.
9. Benjamin, *Origin,* 156.
10. Walter Benjamin, *Ursprung des deutschen Trauerspiels* (Frankfurt am Main: Suhrkamp Verlag, 1978), 135.
11. Benjamin, *Origin,* 156–57.
12. Ibid., 139. In fact the intention referred to here is not directly that of the plotters but that of the state of mourning that drives the plotters to do what they do. We will explore this idea in the conclusion. As we will see further, for Benjamin the symbols, signs, and allegories have an "intention" of their own and serve as the source for this deepen-

ing (human) intention as well. Ibid., 133. In this sense, the intention of mourning and the intention of the plotters can be said to converge.

13. Ibid., 158.

14. Walter Benjamin, "The Paris of the Second Empire in Baudelaire," in *The Writer of Modern Life: Essays on Charles Baudelaire* (Cambridge: Belknap Press of Harvard University Press, 2006), 126.

15. This claim has been made in both stronger and weaker versions by thinkers ranging from Theodor Adorno (more of a rebuke than a claim on his part) to Michael Steinberg, who claims that Benjamin offers not theory but "practice." See Walter Benjamin and Theodor Adorno, *The Complete Correspondence 1928–1940* (Cambridge: Harvard University Press, 1999); Michael Steinberg, *Walter Benjamin and the Demands of History* (Ithaca, NY: Cornell University Press, 1996).

16. Walter Benjamin, "Exposé" of 1939, in *The Arcades Project*, trans. Howard Eiland and Kevin McLaughlin (Cambridge: Belknap Press of Harvard University Press, 2002), 22.

17. Borges offers a great quote to understand how influences can work backward and forth in time: "If I am not mistaken, the heterogeneous pieces I have listed resemble Kafka; if I am not mistaken, not all of them resemble each other. This last fact is what is most significant. Kafka's idiosyncrasy is present in each of these writings, to a greater or lesser degree, but if Kafka had not written, we would not perceive it; that is to say, it would not exist. The poem 'Fears and Scruples' by Robert Browning prophesies the work of Kafka, but our reading of Kafka noticeably refines and diverts our reading of the poem. Browning did not read it as we read it now. The word 'precursor' is indispensable to the vocabulary of criticism, but one must try to purify it from any connotation of polemic or rivalry. The fact is that each writer *creates* his precursors. His work modifies our conception of the past, as it will modify the future." Jorge Luis Borges, "Kafka and His Precursors," in *Jorge Luis Borges: Selected Non-Fictions,* ed. Eliot Weinberger, trans. Esther Allen, Suzanne Jill Levine, and Eliot Weinberger (New York: Viking, 1999), 365. Sandra Luft brought this wonderful passage to my attention.

18. Benjamin, *Origin,* 34.

19. Ibid.

20. Ibid.

21. Benjamin, "Franz Kafka," 129.

22. Margaret Cohen, "Benjamin's Phantasmagoria: *The Arcades Project,*" in *The Cambridge Companion to Walter Benjamin,* ed. David S. Ferris (New York: Cambridge University Press, 2004), 207. For more on the history and meaning of the term see Terry Castle, "Phantasmagoria: Spectral Technology and the Metaphorics of Modern Reverie," *Critical Inquiry* 15, no. 1 (1988): 26–61.

23. Thomas Hobbes, *Leviathan,* ed. Richard Tuck (New York: Cambridge University Press, 1996), 446, 466.

24. Ibid.

25. "Of the Kingdome of Darknesse" is the title of the fourth part of *Leviathan.*

26. This is an idea I will return to in chapter 4. As we will see in that chapter, "navigation" of the symbolic order is itself a form of misrecognition since in fact we are merely holding onto signs that do the navigating for us. But we will read this, nonetheless, as self-steering and fortunately so, for without some sense of our own agency or power, the redemptions that come from texts would be worthless for us.

27. Walter Benjamin, "Some Reflections on Kafka," in *Illuminations*, 143–44.

28. Benjamin, *Origin*, 207.

29. Benjamin, "Franz Kafka," 116.

30. The kind of "redemption" offered by Nietzsche can be read in *Thus Spoke Zarathustra* when a group of variously disabled beggars asks Zarathustra to restore them to health. Zarathustra replies that he will not. He says, for example, that "when one takes away the hump from the hunchback one takes away his spirit—thus teach the people." Friedrich Nietzsche, *Thus Spoke Zarathustra,* trans. Walter Kaufmann (New York: Modern Library, 1995), 137.

Here we come to the kind of messianism that underlies Nietzsche's and Benjamin's respective projects. If the savior were to come down to earth and "heal" us, we would be reconfirmed in our self-hatred and self-denial. Such a delivery, from Nietzsche's perspective, is not a redemption but a condemnation. We are only truly "redeemed" when we encounter the messiah—and are left exactly the way she or he finds us, throwing us, finally, back onto our own devices.

31. Benjamin, *Origin*, 165–66 and 229 respectively.

32. See Wendy Brown, *Politics Out of History* (Princeton, NJ: Princeton University Press, 2001); Susan Buck-Morss, *The Dialectics of Seeing: Walter Benjamin and the Arcades Project* (Cambridge.: MIT Press, 1991).

33. For that matter, I would say it is "afoot" in his earlier work as well, only not as fully developed as a strategy.

34. The same could be said for non-Western political theory as well, albeit in very different forms and contexts. In the case of one of the most canonical figures of non-Western political theory, Frantz Fanon, we will deal with this question directly.

35. Jacques Derrida, *Politics of Friendship*, trans. George Collins (New York: Verso, 1997), 27.

36. Benjamin, "Some Reflections on Kafka," 144.

37. James Martel, *Subverting the Leviathan: Reading Thomas Hobbes as a Radical Democrat* (New York: Columbia University Press, 2007).

CHAPTER 1

1. In fact, this "book" is only the second of three proposed parts of a book to be entitled "Charles Baudelaire: A Lyric Poet in the Era of High Capitalism." Presumably, much of part 1, "Baudelaire as Allegorist," can be found in his separate essay "On Some Motifs in Baudelaire," in *Illuminations*. See Benjamin, *Writer of Modern Life*, 1. See also Benjamin, *The Arcades Project.*

2. By the same token, the idea that the phantasmagoria is "merely" representational can also be combated.

3. For more on Benjamin's understanding of dialectics and in particular, the dialectical image, see Buck-Morss, *The Dialectic of Seeing,* as well as her *The Origin of Negative Dialectics: Theodor W. Adorno, Walter Benjamin, and the Frankfurt Institute* (New York: Free Press, 1979). See also Rolf Tiedemann, "Dialectics at a Standstill: Approaches to the *Passagen-Werk* (1982)," in *On Walter Benjamin: Critical Essays and Recollections,* ed. Gary Smith (Cambridge: MIT Press, 1988); Steven Helmling, "Constellation and Critique: Adorno's 'Constellation,' Benjamin's 'Dialectical Image,'" *Postmodern Culture* 14,

no. 1 (2003); Max Pensky, *Melancholy Dialectics: Walter Benjamin and the Play of Mourning* (Amherst: University of Massachusetts Press, 2001); Rainer Nägele, "Thinking Images," in *Benjamin's Ghosts: Interventions in Contemporary Literary and Cultural Theory,* ed. Gerhard Richter (Stanford, CA: Stanford University Press, 2002), 23–40.

4. Benjamin, "Paris of Second Empire," 47.

5. Benjamin, *The Arcades Project* (Konvolute V), 611.

6. Ibid., 607.

7. Ibid., 618–19.

8. Benjamin, "Paris of Second Empire," 129.

9. Benjamin, *The Arcades Project,* 26 ("Exposé" of 1939).

10. In Konvolutes V and X (the latter dealing with Marx specifically), among other places, he is of course merely quoting Marx (usually) without comment (although his choice of quotes is telling in and of itself). But in the Baudelaire "book," Benjamin draws upon many of these same quotes seemingly to elaborate his own views (whether by contrast or agreement remains to be determined).

11. Benjamin, "Paris of Second Empire," 48.

12. Benjamin, *The Arcades Project,* 605 (Konvolute V).

13. Benjamin, "Paris of Second Empire," 48.

14. Ibid., 51.

15. Ibid., 52.

16. Benjamin refers to Blanqui on several occasions as a "professional conspirator." See, for example, his "Exposé" of 1939. This "Exposé" is written in French, and so he uses the term "conspirateur professionnels," referring to Blanqui. The earlier "Exposé" of 1935, which is written in German, uses the term "Berufsverschwörern" but does not refer directly to Blanqui himself. See Walter Benjamin, *Das Passagen-Werk,* vol. 1 (Frankfurt am Main: Suhrkamp, 1991), 54. In "Zentralpark," Benjamin links Blanqui to the term "Berufsverschwörers." Walter Benjamin, "Zentralpark," in *Gesammelte Schriften,* vol. 1.2 (Frankfurt am Main: Suhrkamp, 1991), 687. In English, see also *The Arcades Project,* 21 ("Exposé" of 1939), and "Central Park" in *Writer of Modern Life,* 166 (section 40).

17. Walter Benjamin, "Das Paris des Second Empire bei Baudelaire," in "Charles Baudelaire: Ein Lyriker im Zeitalter des Hochkapitalismus," *Gesammelte Schriften,* vol. 1.2: 513–19. He also uses the French term "conspirateurs de profession." Ibid., 514.

18. Benjamin, "Paris of Second Empire," 52.

19. In the *Origin,* Benjamin writes: "Magical knowledge, which includes alchemy, threatens the adept with isolation and spiritual death. As alchemy and rosicrucianism, and the conjuration-scenes in the *Trauerspiel* prove, this age was no less devoted to magic than the renaissance. Whatever it picks up, its Midas-touch turns it into something endowed with significance. Its element was transformation of every sort; and allegory was its scheme." Benjamin, *Origin,* 229.

20. Although of course, Benjamin's own intentions are paramount here. For an example of the role of rhetoric in Benjamin's writing see Timothy Bahti, "History as Rhetorical Enactment: Walter Benjamin's Theses 'On the Concept of History,'" *Diacritics* 10 (Fall 1979): 2–17.

21. Benjamin, *The Arcades Project,* 605–6 (Konvolute V).

22. Benjamin, "Paris of Second Empire," 52.

23. Ibid.

24. Ibid., 53.

25. Benjamin acknowledges that "the ragpicker cannot, of course, be considered a member of the *bohème*." Ibid., 54. Yet he argues that "everyone who belonged to the *bohème* could recognize a bit of himself in the ragpicker." Ibid.

26. Benjamin and Adorno, *The Complete Correspondence,* 283.

27. Ibid.

28. Ibid.

29. Benjamin, "Paris of Second Empire," 126; emphasis added.

30. Benjamin, "Das Paris des Second Empire bei Baudelaire," 601.

31. Benjamin, "Paris of Second Empire," 124.

32. Ibid., 128.

33. Benjamin, "Das Paris des Second Empire bei Baudelaire," 603.

34. Benjamin, *Origin,* 165–66. This concept of the "intention of the sign" can be seen as having its linguistic expression in the French way of saying "What does it mean?" The term, *Qu'est-ce que ça veut dire?* (literally: what does it want to say?), suggests a source of meaning that comes not from the speaker but from the very terms that are conveying the speaker's "message," offering a countermessage of its own.

35. Ibid. 229. Something of this same sentiment can be seen in Benjamin's "The Task of the Translator," in *Illuminations.* I am indebted to Ruth Sonderegger for this insight, among others.

36. Benjamin is not always consistent on this point. He does sometimes speak of the allegorist as if that figure were in command of the allegory and not the other way around.

37. Benjamin, *Ursprung,* 205.

38. Benjamin, "Paris of Second Empire," 128, and "Das Paris des Second Empire bei Baudelaire," 603. Note here that "Intention" is not used in the German.

39. Benjamin and Adorno, *The Complete Correspondence,* 292.

40. See Buck-Morss, *Origin of Negative Dialectics,* and John McCole, *Walter Benjamin and the Antinomies of Tradition* (Ithaca, NY: Cornell University Press, 1993).

41. In her own work, Beatrice Hanssen shows that Benjamin can be considered to be, if not a "humanist," then at least not as "antihuman" as his interest in nonanimate objects may suggest (indeed, she shows that the two gestures are not contradictory, although she does fault him for avoiding a direct engagement with politics). See Beatrice Hanssen, *Walter Benjamin's Other History: Of Stones, Animals, Human Beings, and Angels* (Berkeley: University of California Press, 2000).

42. Walter Benjamin, "Central Park," trans. Lloyd Spencer, *New German Critique* 34 (1985): 46.

43. Benjamin, *The Arcades Project,* 377 (Konvolute J). Margaret Cohen also speaks of an antidote when she discusses "the antidote Lukács proposed to reification," and its relationship to Benjamin, although she doesn't expand upon that point. Cohen, "Benjamin's Phantasmagoria," 208.

44. See Jacques Derrida's "Plato's Pharmacy," in *Dissemination,* trans. Barbara Johnson (Chicago: University of Chicago Press, 1983).

45. Benjamin, "Paris of Second Empire," 56.

46. Benjamin, *Origin,* 233.

47. Ibid., 37.

48. Ibid., 34, 37.

49. Ibid., 229.

50. Giorgio Agamben, "Walter Benjamin and the Demonic: Happiness and Historical Redemption," in *Potentialities*, ed. Warner Hamacher and David E. Wellbery (Stanford, CA: Stanford University Press, 1999), 138. Samuel Weber also discusses this treatment of the figure of Satan in *Benjamin's -abilities*, 215–18.

51. Agamben, "Walter Benjamin," 139.

52. Benjamin, "Theses," 255.

53. Benjamin, *Origin*, 233.

54. Ibid.

55. Ibid.

56. Ibid., 235.

57. Ibid., 229.

58. Ibid., 230.

59. Benjamin, *The Arcades Project*, 21 ("Exposé" of 1939).

60. Benjamin, "Paris of Second Empire," 57; emphasis added.

61. Benjamin, "Das Paris des Second Empire bei Baudelaire," 526.

62. Peter Fitzpatrick, *Modernism and the Grounds of Law* (New York: Cambridge University Press, 2001), 47.

63. Benjamin, *Origin*, 182.

64. Ibid., 183.

65. Ibid.

66. Ibid.

67. Walter Benjamin, "Critique of Violence," in *Reflections: Essays, Aphorisms, Autobiographical Writings*, ed. Peter Demetz, trans. Edmund Jephcott (New York: Schocken, 1978), 300.

68. In fact, as we will see in the next chapter, it is a bit more complicated than this because we are not in fact "saving ourselves" but only think that we are. We are saved, not by our own actions per se, but by our alliance with signs, with material forms of representation that we cling to (and which once were the source of our idolatry).

69. Benjamin, *Origin*, 233.

70. Ibid., 28–29. Rainer Nägele discusses this reconstruction or regathering in "Thinking Images," 35–37.

71. Benjamin, *Origin*, 34.

72. Ibid., 35.

73. Ibid., 47.

74. Ibid.

75. For more on the connection (and differences) between Leibniz and Benjamin, specifically on the monad, see Peter Fenves, *Arresting Language: From Leibniz to Benjamin* (Stanford, CA: Stanford University Press, 2001).

76. Benjamin, *Origin*, 48.

77. Ibid., 234.

78. Ibid., 232.

79. Ibid., 233.

80. We see another side of Kant, for example, in the work of Lacanians such as Slavoj Žižek, Alenka Zupančič, and Joan Copjec. See Slavoj Žižek, *The Ticklish Subject: The Absent Centre of Political Ontology* (New York: Verso, 2000); Alenka Zupančič, *Ethics*

of the Real: Kant and Lacan (New York: Verso, 2000), Joan Copjec, *Imagine There's No Woman: Ethics and Sublimation* (Cambridge: MIT Press, 2004).

81. Benjamin, "Theses," 255.

82. "The Invention of the Devil" ("Die Erfindung des Teufels"), in Franz Kafka, *Parables and Paradoxes: Bilingual Edition* (New York: Schocken, 1961), 119.

83. Franz Kafka, "Paradise," in *Parables and Paradoxes*, 29.

84. Benjamin, *The Arcades Project* (Konvolute J), 368–69.

85. Benjamin, *Origin*, 232.

86. Benjamin, *The Arcades Project* ("Exposé" of 1939), 22.

87. Ibid., 329 (Konvolute J).

88. Ibid., 370.

89. As occurs, for example, in Benjamin's tale of Dickens seeing the words "Coffee Room" backward through the glass and appearing as "MOOR EEFFOC," giving him "a shock." Ibid., 233.

90. The value of this misreading (i.e., his mistaken belief in novelty) will be analyzed in some detail in the next chapter.

91. The 1939 version was written in French.

92. Benjamin, "Paris of Second Empire," 129.

93. Ibid.

94. Ibid.

95. Ibid.

96. Benjamin, *The Arcades Project* ("Exposé" of 1939), 25. See also Cohen's "Benjamin's Phantasmagoria," 209.

97. Cohen, "Benjamin's Phantasmagoria," 212. In *The Dialectics of Seeing*, Buck-Morss associates Fourier with Benjamin's notion of the wish image. She writes of this, "Wishes and dreams are psychological categories which for Benjamin have no immediate status as philosophical truth. Parting company with the romanticism of Ernst Bloch . . . Benjamin was reluctant to rest revolutionary hope directly on imagination's capacity to anticipate the not-yet existing. Even as wish image, utopian imagination needed to be interpreted through the material objects in which it found expression." *The Dialectics of Seeing*, 114–15.

98. Benjamin, *The Arcades Project* ("Exposé" of 1939), 26, and in original French, *Das Passagen-Werk*, 76.

99. On a very helpful reading of the idea of resigning (particularly in terms of Thoreau), see Thomas L. Dumm, "Resignation," *Critical Inquiry* 25, no. 1 (1998): 56–76.

100. Margaret Cohen speaks of Benjamin's "Marxisms": See Margaret Cohen, *Profane Illumination: Walter Benjamin and the Paris of Surrealist Revolution* (Berkeley: University of California Press, 1993), 17. The book considers Benjamin's relationship to Marx more broadly. See also Christopher Norris's chapter entitled "Image and Parable: Readings of Walter Benjamin" in *The Deconstructive Turn: Essays in the Rhetoric of Philosophy* (London: Methuen, 1983), 107–27. For more on Benjamin's historical materialism see Howard Caygill, "Walter Benjamin's Concept of Cultural History," in Ferris, *Cambridge Companion to Benjamin*, 73–96.

101. Benjamin, *The Arcades Project* (Konvolute J), 303. See also 307.

102. Benjamin, "Theses," 254.

103. And, I would argue, it does redeem us in the Nietzschean sense of the word.

CHAPTER 2

1. Benjamin, "Franz Kafka," 116.

2. Franz Kafka, *The Trial* (in *The Metamorphosis and the Trial*) (Ann Arbor, MI: Borders Classics, 2007), 226, and *Der Prozess* (Frankfurt am Main: Fischer Bücherai, 1958), 165.

3. Kafka's earliest reputation was largely tied up with the religious aura instilled by his friend Max Brod. This reputation is also the one that Benjamin to a great extent draws from, although in his case, Kafka's religiosity and politics are clearly intertwined. For a writer who focuses largely on Kafka's connection to matters Jewish and Zionist, see Iris Bruce, *Kafka and Cultural Zionism: Dates in Palestine* (Madison: University of Wisconsin Press, 2007). For those who read Kafka as a political radical see, most famously, Theodor Adorno, "Notes on Kafka," in *Prisms* (Cambridge: MIT Press, 1983), 243–71, and Gilles Deleuze and Felix Guattari, *Kafka: Toward a Minor Literature,* trans. Dana Plan (Minneapolis: University of Minnesota Press, 1986).

For a good overview of the political readings of Kafka, see Bill Dodd, "The Case for a Political Reading," in *The Cambridge Companion to Kafka,* ed. Julian Preece (New York: Cambridge University Press, 2002), 131–49. In terms of an approach to Kafka's writing as a rhetorical practice, Stanley Corngold tends to see him as a writer whose distrust of figuration is such that his prose self-destructs. See Stanley Corngold, "The Author Survives on the Margin of his Breaks: Kafka's Narrative Perspective," in *The Fate of the Self: German Writers and French Theory* (New York: Columbia University Press, 1986). In terms of the question of Kafka's "Zionism," as Nasser Hussain pointed out to me in conversation, Arendt herself explains that Kafka is neither a Zionist nor an anti-Zionist. For more on this question see Ritchie Robertson, "'Antizionismus, Zionismus'; Kafka's Responses to Jewish Nationalism," in *Paths and Labyrinths: Nine Papers Read at the Franz Kafka Symposium Held at the Institute of Germanic Studies on 20 and 21 October 1983* (London: University of London, Institute of Germanic Studies, 1985), 25–42.

4. For more about failure and the relationship between Benjamin and Kafka see Ewa Plonowska Ziarek, "'The Beauty of Failure': Kafka and Benjamin on the Task of Transmission and Translation," in *The Rhetoric of Failure: Deconstruction of Skepticism, Reinvention of Modernism* (Buffalo: SUNY Press, 1996), 123–55.

5. I discuss this issue futher in a forthcoming book, *Divine Violence: Walter Benjamin and the Eschatology of Sovereignty* (Routledge).

6. When Benjamin writes that "Kafka did not always evade the temptations of mysticism" ("Franz Kafka," 124), it is not at all certain that he is being critical. For more on the relationship between Benjamin and Kafka and the gesture, see Werner Hamacher, "The Gesture in the Name: On Benjamin and Kafka," in *Premises: Essays on Philosophy and Literature from Kant to Celan,* trans. Peter Fenves (Stanford, CA: Stanford University Press, 1996), 294–336.

7. Benjamin, "Franz Kafka," 129. See also Klaus Mladek, "Radical Play: Gesture, Performance, and the Theatrical Logic of the Law in Kafka," *German Review* 78 (2003): 232. And see also Samuel Weber's *Benjamin's -abilities,* 206–7; Tzvetan Todorov, *Theories of the Symbol,* trans. Catherine Porter (Ithaca, NY: Cornell University Press, 1982).

8. For a good exposition of Kafka's own attitude toward writing and his role as author (which the author points out has tremendous political consequences), see David

Constantine, "Kafka's Writing and our Reading," in Preece, *Cambridge Companion to Kafka,* 9–24.

9. Benjamin, "Some Reflections on Kafka," 144–45.

10. The whole question of whether that book is "optimistic" or not is highly fraught; it appears to be, on the surface anyway, a dark and savage dismantling of a Horatio Alger–style epic of a young man's journeys to the West.

11. Benjamin, "Franz Kafka," 124–25.

12. Walter Benjamin, "The Work of Art in the Age of Mechanical Reproduction," in *Illuminations,* 232.

13. Benjamin, "Franz Kafka," 129.

14. Ibid., 122.

15. Benjamin, "Some Reflections on Kafka," 144.

16. Ibid. In her own work, Ewa Plonowska Ziarek makes much of this phrase. For a larger consideration of Benjamin and trasnsmissibility see Samuel Weber's *Benjamin's -abilities.*

17. Benjamin, "Franz Kafka," 124.

18. Ibid., 122. Benjamin goes on to say: "all we can say [about whether there is some central doctrine that Kafka's prose illuminates] is that here and there we have an allusion to it. Kafka might have said that these are relics transmitting the doctrine, although we could regard them just as well as precursors preparing the doctrine."

19. Franz Kafka, "On Parables," in *The Complete Stories,* ed. Nahum N. Glatzer (New York: Schocken, 1971), 457.

20. Ibid.

21. Paul de Man, *Allegories of Reading: Figural Language in Rousseau, Nietzsche, Rilke and Proust* (New York: Yale University Press, 1979), 14.

22. Kafka, *The Trial,* 212. For his well-known reading of this parable, see Jacques Derrida, "Before the Law," in *Acts of Literature,* ed. Derek Attridge (New York: Routledge, 1992), 181–220.

23. Kafka, *The Trial,* 214.

24. Ibid., 215–16.

25. Ibid., 217.

26. Rhetorically speaking, this reading can be said to duplicate the "plot" of the parable itself.

27. Sander Gilman argues that *The Castle* represents an elaboration of "Before the Law." He notes that Kafka told Max Brod that he intended to have *The Castle* end much as "Before the Law" did, whereby K. is finally, while dying, told that "although [his] claims to staying in the village are not valid, nevertheless . . . he would be allowed to live and work there." Sander L. Gilman, *Franz Kafka* (London: Reaktion Books, 2005), 118.

28. There is a fugue-like quality to his arrival, and indeed many critics have noted the dreamlike state of this novel (as is the case in so many of Kafka's writings). See John Zilcosky, "Surveying the Castle: Kafka's Colonial Visions," in *A Companion to the Works of Franz Kafka,* ed. James Rolleston (Rochester, NY: Camden House, 2002), 298–99. Zilcosky notes that although a surveyor, K. sees nothing. He spends the second half of the novel almost entirely in interior spaces and sees only "myopically" at best (300).

29. Franz Kafka, *Das Schloß* (Frankfurt: Fischer Taschenbuch Verlag, 2007), 10.

30. Richard Sheppard tells us others have said that the name suggests decay (*ver-*

wesen) and essence (*Wesen*). Richard Sheppard, *On Kafka's Castle: A Study* (London: Croom Helm, 1973), 198.

31. In English we have the term "clam up" and in German we have the term *Klammheimlich,* meaning sneaky or secretive.

32. Franz Kafka, *The Castle,* trans. Mark Harman (New York: Schocken, 1998), 69.

33. Ibid., 71.

34. Ibid., 175.

35. Ibid., 176.

36. Ibid., 177.

37. Ibid., 36.

38. Jodi Dean has pointed out to me that this is an almost perfect illustration of Lacan's *objet petit a.*

39. Ibid., 197.

40. Mark Harman notes that in his editing of the original version of *The Castle,* Kafka eliminated certain references that made the sleigh/carriage even more overtly a religious symbol, such as the invocation of the word *verboten* (forbidden) and a reference to a golden eagle crowning the carriage. Mark Harman, "Making Everything 'a little uncanny': Kafka's Deletions in the Manuscript of *Das Schloß* and What They Can Tell Us About His Writing Process." In Rolleston, *Companion to Franz Kafka,* 341.

41. Kafka, *The Castle,* 103–4.

42. Ibid., 104–5.

43. Ibid., 105.

44. As Richard Sheppard notes, Max Brod and others promoted (and edited) *The Castle* as having a religious theme. Yet following the novel's publication, scholars such as Wilhelm Emrich, Klaus-Peter Philippi, and Erich Heller argued that the book was a political parable (or at least not a religious one). In Sheppard's opinion, Kafka deliberately (i.e., rhetorically) left the matter ambivalent. Sheppard, *On Kafka's Castle,* 199. In my own view, Brod does misinterpret Kafka, but the book remains a messianic text nonetheless (only not in a way that Brod himself seems to understand).

45. Kafka, *The Castle,* 106.

46. Ibid.

47. Ibid.

48. Benjamin, "Franz Kafka," 134.

49. Simone Weil, *Waiting for God,* trans. Emma Craufurd (New York: Harper, 1992).

50. Benjamin, "Critique of Violence," 300.

51. The only difference being that one comes from "above" and one comes from "below" (although as we will see further that such a directional distinction becomes very murky, difficult to keep distinct).

52. Benjamin, "Theses," 254.

53. "The Silence of the Sirens" ("Das Schweigen der Sirenen"), in Kafka's *Parables and Paradoxes,* 89.

54. In fact in the actual story, Ulysses blocks the ears of the oarsmen and binds himself to the mast. That way he can hear the song of the sirens but not be tempted to his doom. But the way Kafka has it, the story becomes a parable about misrecognition itself. The editor of the book suggests that this is no true misreading on Kafka's part but a "bold . . . rewrit[ing]." Ibid., 190. But of course, the question of what is "deliberate" in misrecognition is itself a bone of contention.

55. Ibid., 89 ("Beweis dessen, dass auch unzulängliche, ja kindische Mittel zur Rettung dienen können"); ibid, 88.

56. Another example of the same dynamic comes in Kafka's treatment of Abraham, in his parable of the same name. Here, Kafka conjures up "another Abraham" ("einen anderen Abraham," "Abraham," 40 [German], 41 [English]), an "ugly old man [with a] dirty youngster that was his child." Ibid., 43. *This* Abraham, Kafka speculates, may have misunderstood or not heard God right in the first place when God demanded his sacrifice: "It is as if, at the end of the year, when the best student was solemnly about to receive a prize, the worst student rose in the expectant stillness and came forward from his dirty desk in the last row because he had made a mistake of hearing, and the whole class burst out laughing. And perhaps he had made no mistake at all, his name really was called, it having been the teacher's intention to make the rewarding of the best student at the same time a punishment for the worst one." Ibid., 45.

57. Ziarek, "The Beauty of Failure," 123.

58. Kafka, "The City Coat of Arms" ("Das Stadtwappen"), in *Parables and Paradoxes*, 37.

59. Ziarek, "The Beauty of Failure," 145.

60. Ibid.

61. Kafka, "City Coat of Arms," 39.

62. Although we have plenty of examples of such cases: the figure of Moses springs immediately to mind.

63. Harman, "Making Everything," 329.

64. Ibid.

65. Ibid.

66. Ibid., 326–27.

67. Kafka, "The Silence of the Sirens," 91.

68. Another example of this other, more conscious form of conspiracy can be found in the ultrashort Kafka story "The Truth about Sancho Panza," in *The Complete Stories*, 430.

69. Kafka, "The Coming of the Messiah" ("Das Kommen des Messias"), in *Parables and Paradoxes*, 81.

CHAPTER 3

1. Niccolò Machiavelli, *The Prince and the Discourses*, trans. Luigi Ricci, revised by E. R. P. Vincent (New York: Modern Library, 1950), 410. Henceforth either *The Prince* or *The Discourses*. All translations from these two books come from this edition, although at times I supply the Italian when I deem it useful. The original Italian comes from Niccolò Machiavelli, *Opere* (*Il Principe* and *Discorsi Sopra la Prima Deca di Tito Livio*), in *La Letteratura Italiana: Storia e Testi*, vol. 29 (Milan: Riccardo Ricciardi Editore, 1963), 320.

2. Machiavelli, *Opere*, 320.

3. Ibid.

4. The argument that Machiavelli's sympathies lie with the people, although not uncontested, is not in and of itself particularly novel. Even if we leave Machiavelli's own contemporaries out of the equation, Rousseau, for one, made this argument: Machiavelli "professed to teach kings; but it was the people he really taught." Quoted in Louis

Althusser, *Machiavelli and Us,* ed. François Matheron, trans. Gregory Elliot (New York: Verso, 1999) 30. Some of the better-known texts that advance this view include J. G. A. Pocock, *The Machiavellian Moment: Florentine Political Thought and the Atlantic Republican Tradition* (Princeton, NJ: Princeton University Press, 2003); and Hanna Pitkin, *Fortune is a Woman: Gender and Politics in the Thought of Niccolò Machiavelli* (Berkeley: University of California Press, 1984). Another tangentially related debate that dominates Machiavelli studies is whether he is part of the humanist tradition or more of an advocate of realpolitik. For the connection to humanism, see Hans Baron, *The Crisis of the Early Italian Renaissance* (Princeton, NJ: Princeton University Press, 1966); and, in a slightly different vein, Quentin Skinner, *The Foundations of Modern Political Thought: The Renaissance* (New York: Cambridge University Press, 1978). Those who distance themselves from this position include Felix Gilbert, "The Humanist Concept of the Prince and *The Prince* of Machiavelli," *Journal of Modern History* 11 (1939): 449–83; J. R. Hale, *Machiavelli and Renaissance Italy* (New York: Collier, 1963); and Mark Hulliung, *Citizen Machiavelli* (Princeton, NJ: Princeton University Press, 1983). More recent scholarship on such issues includes Victoria Kahn, *Machiavellian Rhetoric: From the Counter-Reformation to Milton* (Princeton, NJ: Princeton University Press, 1994); Miguel Vatter, *Between Form and Event: Machiavelli's Theory of Political Freedom* (Boston: Kluwer Academic Publishers, 2000); and Victoria Kahn, "Virtù" and the Example of Agathocles in Machiavelli's *Prince,*" in *Machiavelli and the Discourse of Literature,* ed. Victoria Kahn and Albert Russell Ascoli (Ithaca, NY: Cornell University Press, 1993), 199. Readings of Machiavelli by certain Straussians notwithstanding, many contemporary Machiavelli scholars acknowledge a thinly or perhaps not so thinly disguised republican sentiment on Machiavelli's part (particularly in the *Discourses*). But even this camp is not uniform in its view of what Machiavelli is up to. For example, Victoria Kahn in *Machiavellian Rhetoric* argues that Machiavelli is often misread as a humanist philosopher, and, by extension, as a particular kind of republican theorist.

5. Benjamin, "Work of Art," 218.

6. Benjamin, "Theses," 263.

7. See Antonio Gramsci, *The Modern Prince and Writings,* trans. Louis Marks (New York: International Publishers, 1959).

8. Machiavelli, *The Discourses,* 416.

9. Garrett Mattingly, "Machiavelli's *Prince:* Political Science or Political Satire?" *American Scholar* 27 (1958): 491. The *Art of War* was the only major text of Machiavelli's that was actually published in his lifetime. Niccolò Machiavelli, *The Art of War,* intro. Neal Wood (New York: Da Capo Press, 1965), introduction, xviii.

10. Mattingly, "Machiavelli's Prince," 491. Mattingly points out that this copy has never been seen since, possibly implying that the idea of this copy was a joke on Machiavelli's part.

11. Machiavelli, *The Discourses,* 431.

12. Ibid., 512. And *Discorsi,* 398.

13. Machiavelli, *The Art of War,* 129.

14. *Discorsi,* 398. Perhaps Machiavelli's most famous passage concerning glory comes in *The Prince* when he describes Agathocles, the commoner who rose to power via sheer brutality. He famously writes: "It cannot be called virtue to kill one's fellow citizens, betray one's friends, be without faith, without pity, and without religion; by these methods one may indeed gain power, but not glory." *The Prince,* 32. In her consideration

of this passage, Victoria Kahn contends with various interpretations, specifically comparing Machiavelli's treatment of Agathocles in chapter 8 of *The Prince* and his treatment of Cesare Borgia in the preceding chapter. Borgia, although equally brutal, was the more popular of the two, and Machiavelli seems to consider his actions more favorably than Agathocles himself. Kahn shows quite effectively that Machiavelli does not merely describe but practices the manipulations of public esteem (taken in its broadest sense) on his own readers. To get the reader to accept a more destabilized and contingent notion of *virtù*, the very question of what they find worthy of esteem must itself be explored and exploited. Kahn, "Virtù," 205.

15. Machiavelli, *The Art of War*, 164.

16. Elsewhere in his work, Machiavelli supplies examples of the political effects of glory. We have already seen his discussion of Manlius, whose corrupt ambitions, Machiavelli tells us, were thwarted by the judgment of the people of Rome. Quoting Livy himself, Machiavelli writes of Manlius, "Thus ended the career of this man, who would have been memorable had he not been born in a free community." *Discourses*, 439. And he goes on to write: "The means of attaining glory are different in a republic that is corrupt from what they are in a republic that still preserves its institutions pure." Ibid. But even in a corrupt (or at least semicorrupt) republic, glory can still have a positive effect insofar as "all states necessarily come to [corruption], unless (as we have shown above) they are frequently reinvigorated by good examples, and brought back by good laws to their first principles." Ibid., 440.

17. Machiavelli, *The Prince*, 4.

18. Machiavelli furnishes many instances of such dissymmetries not only of epistemology but also of effectiveness. He describes, for example, how at various times Rome produced a Fabius when it needed to protract a war and then a Scipio when it needed to end it. *The Discourses*, 442. Here, the very plurality of people is an advantage, for it supplies the right person for the right time in every case.

19. Niccolò Machiavelli, *Mandragola*, in *The Chief Works and Others*, vol. 2, trans. Allan Gilbert (Durham, NC: Duke University Press, 1989), 777–78.

20. This is more or less the way that Hanna Pitkin interprets the play. Pitkin, *Fortune is a Woman*, 30.

21. Machiavelli, *Mandragola*, 820–21. And in *Opere*, 1033.

22. Ibid.

23. Machiavelli, *The Discourses*, 403.

24. Such a conspiracy might be literally true insofar as a few years after the play was finished (in 1522), a conspiracy featuring Machiavelli's friends Luigi Alamanni (to whom he had dedicated his *Life of Castruccio Castracani*) and Zanobi Buondelmonte (to whom he had also dedicated the *Life of Castruccio Castracani* as well as the *Discourses*) was foiled by the Medicis. Many in Machiavelli's intellectual circle at Orti Oricellari, the estates of the family of the now deceased Cosimo Ruccelai, were implicated and arrested and/or exiled. Machiavelli got let off the hook, despite great suspicion of being involved. Ross King, *Machiavelli: Philosopher of Power* (New York: HarperCollins, 2007), 202–3. Mark Hulliung also connects Machiavelli's writings in the *Discourses* with this foiled conspiracy in *Citizen Machiavelli*, 95.

25. Machiavelli, *The Discourses*, 403–4. And *Discorsi*, 315.

26. Machiavelli, *Clizia*, in *Chief Works and Others*, 861.

27. Ibid. And *Clizia* in *The Comedies of Machiavelli: Bilingual Edition*, ed. David

Sices and James B. Atkinson (Hanover, NH: University Press of New England, 1985), 386. "Risappia," a term used in another form by Sofronia herself (right after the passage cited above), is a conjugation of the verb *risapere*, which means to make known (from *sapere*, to know).

28. Ronald Martinez points out that the name "Sofronia" is etymologically related to the Greek virtue of *sophrosyne*, i.e., self-restraint. Ronald L. Martinez, "Benefit of Absence: Machiavellian Valediction in *Clizia*," in Kahn and Ascoli, *Machiavelli and the Discourse of Literature*, 132.

29. In his analysis of *Clizia*, Martinez makes this claim although he does not do so in terms of conspiratorial politics. For Martinez, the character of Nicomaco represents, not some princelike figure, but rather Machiavelli himself, the name Nicomaco being, once again, a shortening of Niccolò Machiavelli—an argument that might be extended to "Nicia" in *Mandragola* as well, although Hanna Pitkin disputes that. Pitkin, *Fortune is a Woman*, 30.

30. See King, *Machiavelli*, 202–3.

31. This is an argument that links, I believe, Machiavelli and Arendt despite the fact that the latter tends to have a fairly low opinion of him.

32. Benjamin, "Some Motifs in Baudelaire," 182.

33. He also seems to have more noble or at least political motivations as well, attesting to his link with Machiavelli himself. He tells Callimaco early on that he can trust him because "even if there weren't as much profit in the business as I think and hope, you and I have a natural affinity, and I want you to carry out your wish almost as much as you do yourself." *Mandragola*, 784.

CHAPTER 4

1. See, for example, Alexis de Tocqueville, *Travail sur L'Algérie*, in *Oeuvres Complètes* (Paris: Gallimard, Pléiade, 1991).

2. Even when he is not connected to Benjamin, Tocqueville has been read, especially recently, as being more radical than he appears—at least potentially. The most famous recent work making this point is Sheldon Wolin's *Tocqueville Between Two Worlds: The Making of a Political and Theoretical Life* (Princeton, NJ: Princeton University Press, 2001); see also Mark Reinhardt, *The Art of Being Free: Taking Liberties with Tocqueville, Marx and Arendt* (Ithaca, NY: Cornell University Press, 1997); Morton Schoolman, "Aesthetic Individuality as a Democratic Achievement," in *Reason and Horror: Critical Theory, Democracy and Aesthetic Individuality* (New York: Routledge, 2001), 248–99; and Roger Boesche, *The Strange Liberalism of Alexis de Tocqueville* (Ithaca, NY: Cornell University Press, 1987). See also Claude Lefort's essay on Tocqueville in *Writing: The Political Test* (Durham, NC: Duke University Press, 2000).

3. Thomas Jefferson, *Notes on the State of Virginia* (Chapel Hill, NC: University of North Carolina Press, 1982).

4. Alexis de Tocqueville, *Democracy in America* (New York: Bantam, 2000), 1:16.

5. Ibid., 2:535. Original version: Alexis de Tocqueville, *De la démocratie en Amérique* (Paris: Gallimard, 1986), 2:42.

6. Tocqueville, *Democracy in America*, 2:535. And *De la démocratie en Amérique*, 2:42.

7. Tocqueville, *Democracy in America,* 2:535.

8. Ibid.

9. Ibid., 536.

10. Ibid, 1:100. In original, *De la démocratie en Amérique,* 1:154.

11. Tocqueville, *Democracy in America,* 1:99.

12. Ibid., 98.

13. Ibid.

14. Ibid., 107.

15. Ibid., 99.

16. Benjamin, "Work of Art," 242.

17. *Democracy in America,* 1:60.

18. Although some scholars see a radical discontinuity between the two volumes, James T. Schliefer argues that they "remain two segments of the same work." James T. Schliefer, "Tocqueville's Democracy in America Reconsidered," in *The Cambridge Companion to Tocqueville,* ed. Cheryl B. Welch (New York: Cambridge University Press, 2006), 121–38.

19. Tocqueville, *Democracy in America,* 1:61.

20. Ibid.

21. Ibid., 63. In original: *De la démocratie en Amérique,* 1:109.

22. Ibid., 2:844.

23. Ibid., 845.

24. Ibid., 870.

25. Ibid.

26. For Tocqueville, the critical difference between this form of pseudodemocratic power and other forms of political organization is that in this case, "the state" is in a sense hardly distinguishable form the people it serves (Tocqueville says that in America the people "are alternately made the playthings of their ruler, and his masters—more than kings, and less than men"). Ibid., 872.

27. Tocqueville, *De la démocratie en Amérique,* 1:51.

28. See also Alexis de Tocqueville, *Writings on Empire and Slavery,* ed. and trans. Jennifer Pitts (Baltimore: Johns Hopkins University Press, 2003). See Jefferson's *Notes on the State of Virginia,* 137–43. The question of whether Tocqueville himself is a racist remains ongoing in contemporary scholarship. See for example George M. Fredrickson, *The Black Image in the White Mind: The Debate on Afro-American Character and Destiny, 1817–1914* (Middletown, CT: Wesleyan University Press, 1987), which argues that Tocqueville is indeed racist when it comes to African Americans. For a different view see Andrew Hacker, *Two Nations: Black and White, Separate, Hostile and Unequal* (New York: Ballantine, 1995). See also Margaret Kohn, "The Other America: Tocqueville and Beaumont on Race and Slavery," *Polity* 35, no. 2 (2002): 169–93; Joel Olson, *The Abolition of White Democracy* (Minneapolis: University of Minnesota Press, 2004).

29. Tocqueville, *Democracy in America,* 1: 384–85.

30. Ibid., 386.

31. Ibid., 386–87.

32. Ibid., 387.

33. Ibid., 413.

34. Ibid., 403, note s.

35. Ibid., 399–400, note q.

36. Ibid., 403, note s. Such language is reminiscent of Henry David Thoreau's own musings about the French and the Irish in America. Henry David Thoreau, *Walden and Civil Disobedience* (New York: Norton, 1966), 99–101 and 139 respectively.

37. Tocqueville, *Democracy in America*, 1:388.

38. Ibid., 389.

39. Ibid., 2:622.

40. Ibid., 8.

41. Tocqueville, *De la démocratie en Amérique*, 1:43.

42. One could even read Tocqueville's call for a new materialism in America along Benjaminian lines: "The reproach I address to the principle of equality, is not that it leads men away in the pursuit of forbidden enjoyments, but that it absorbs them wholly in quest of those which are allowed. By these means, a kind of virtuous materialism may ultimately be established in the world, which would not corrupt, but enervate, the soul, and noiselessly unbend its springs of action." *Democracy in America*, 2:658. Of course, Tocqueville goes on at great length to denounce materialism (but as it is currently practiced and conceived).

43. For a discussion of Baudelaire's French translation of the *Narrative* see Mary Ann Caws, "Insertion in an Oval Frame: Poe Circumscribed by Baudelaire, Part II," in *French Review* 56 (1983): 891. See also Edgar Poe, *Les Aventures d'Arthur Gordon Pym,* trans. Charles Baudelaire (Paris: Gallimard, 1977).

44. R. E. Foust, "Aesthetician of Simultaneity: E.A. Poe and Modern Literary Theory," *South Atlantic Review* 1981: 17–25. See also Benjamin, "Some Motifs in Baudelaire," 181–83.

45. Charles Baudelaire, "Edgar Poe: Sa vie et ses oeuvres," in *Histoires Extraordinaires par Edgar Poe* (Paris: Michel Lévy Frères, 1869), 4. For more on Baudelaire's translation of Poe see Léon Lemonnier, *Les Traducteurs d'Edgar Poe en France de 1845 à 1875: Charles Baudelaire* (Paris: Presses Universitaires de France, 1928).

46. Baudelaire, "Edgar Poe," 7–8. This quote and the prior one are my own translations.

47. Poe's reputation as being subversive and complicated dates from the beginning of his career. Among the relatively recent works that take part in this tradition, perhaps the most well known is John Muller and William J. Richardson, eds., *The Purloined Poe: Lacan, Derrida and Psychoanalytic Reading* (Baltimore: Johns Hopkins University Press, 1988). This book contains both Lacan's own "Seminar on the Purloined Letter" and Derrida's "The Purveyor of Truth" (in abbreviated form). See also Stanley Cavell's "Being Odd, Getting Even (Descartes, Emerson, Poe)," in *In Quest of the Ordinary: Lines of Skepticism and Romanticism* (Chicago: University of Chicago Press, 1988), 105–49; Joan Dayan, *Fables of Mind: An Inquiry into Poe's Fiction* (New York: Oxford University Press, 1987); Kenneth Dauber, *The Idea of Authorship in America: Democratic Poetics from Franklin to Melville* (Madison: University of Wisconsin Press, 1990); Evan Carton, *The Rhetoric of American Romance: Dialectic and Identity in Emerson, Dickinson, Poe, and Hawthorne* (Baltimore: Johns Hopkins University Press, 1985).

48. The idea that with Poe, bodies turn into corpses belongs to Stephanie Sommerfeld.

49. Geoffrey Sanborn argues that the *Narrative* also performs a devolution of subjectivity as the character undoes his own stated desire for normalcy. See Geoffrey San-

born, "A Confused Beginning: The Narrative of Arthur Gordon Pym, of Nantucket," in *The Cambridge Companion to Edgar Allan Poe,* ed. Kevin J. Hayes (New York: Cambridge University Press, 2002), 163–77. For a general overview of scholarship on Poe's *Narrative,* see Ronald C. Harvey, *The Critical History of Edgar Allan Poe's "The Narrative of Arthur Gordon Pym: A Dialogue with Unreason"* (New York: Routledge, 1998). See also John T. Irwin, "The Quincuncial Network in Poe's Pym," in *Poe's Pym: Critical Explorations,* ed. Richard Kopley (Durham, NC: Duke University Press, 1992), 175–87. For an engagement with Poe's analysis of slavery in that book, see John Carlos Rowe's "Poe, Antebellum Slavery and Modern Criticism" in the same volume, 117–40; John T. Irwin, *American Hieroglyphics: The Symbol of the Egyptian Hieroglyphics in the American Renaissance* (New Haven: Yale University Press, 1980).

50. Edgar Allan Poe, *The Narrative of Arthur Gordon Pym of Nantucket* (New York: Penguin, 1999), 1.

51. Ibid., 37.

52. Ibid., 38.

53. Ibid., 39.

54. Ibid.

55. Ibid.

56. Benjamin, *Origin,* 207.

57. Ibid., 207–8.

58. Ibid.

59. Heidegger makes essentially the same point in *What is Called Thinking?* (New York: Harper Perennial, 1976).

60. Poe, *Narrative,* 56.

61. This is a version of Hegel's "night of the world," where the symbols take on a life of their own and swirl around. Žižek references this image in *The Ticklish Subject,* 29–30.

62. Poe, *Narrative,* 216–17.

63. Ibid., 217.

64. Ibid., 4. Such a statement points to the book's own origin as an actual hoax, a fiction posing as true. That Poe conceived of and executed such a hoax reinforces the way that he connects the "real" world to the symbolic—a connection that we saw in Tocqueville as well (in Poe's case, such a connection takes on a darker and more subversive form than with Tocqueville). Here the exposure of the hoax threatens to expose the larger "hoax" of how we read and respond to our so-called reality.

65. Ibid., 220.

66. Ibid., 221.

67. Slavoj Žižek, *The Plague of Fantasies* (New York: Verso, 1997), 239.

68. Edgar Allan Poe, "A Descent into the Maelström," in *Complete Tales and Poems of Edgar Allan Poe* (New York: Vintage, 1975), 138.

69. Ibid., 139.

70. Ibid.

71. Žižek, *The Plague of Fantasies,* 239.

72. Žižek ends his analysis of "A Descent into the Maelström" (and *The Plague of Fantasies* itself) by writing: "Is not Lacan's entire theoretical edifice torn between these two options: between the ethics of desire/Law, of maintaining the gap, and the lethal/suicidal immersion in the Thing?" Ibid.

73. See Copjec, *Imagine There's No Woman.*

74. Dean, "Politics without Politics." The focus of Dean's article is on Jacques Rancière, but the same point could be applied to Copjec, among others.

75. Here again, I am grateful to Jodi Dean for her helpful clarity in the signification of the real.

76. Brown, *Politics Out of History,* 4.

77. Poe, "A Descent into the Maelström," 136.

78. Ibid., 135. The same sentiment is expressed by Pym in the *Narrative* when, while scaling some high cliffs and feeling terrified, he finds that his "whole soul was pervaded with a *longing to fall.*" *Narrative,* 206.

79. Poe, "A Descent into the Maelström." 139.

CHAPTER 5

1. For an investigation of Lorca's death, and the cultural meaning imputed to it, see Melissa Dinverno, "Raising the Dead: García Lorca, Trauma and the Cultural Mediation of Mourning," *Arizona Journal of Hispanic Cultural Studies* 9 (2005): 1–24. See also Ian Gibson, *Federico García Lorca: A Life* (New York: Pantheon, 1997).

2. For an overview of Lorca's politics see Nigel Dennis's entry "Politics" in *A Companion to Federico García Lorca,* ed. Federico Bonaddio (Rochester, NY: Tamesis, 2007), 170–89.

3. Speaking of his own time, Benjamin famously writes, "This is the situation of politics which Fascism is rendering aesthetic. Communism responds by politicizing art." Benjamin, "Work of Art," 242.

4. Hannah Arendt, *Willing,* in *The Life of the Mind* (New York: Harcourt Brace Jovanovich, 1978), 67.

5. Hannah Arendt, "Truth and Politics," in *Between Past and Future: Eight Exercises in Political Thought* (New York: Penguin, 1968), 241.

6. As Lisa Disch points out, Iris Young speaks of a "metaphysics of presence" (borrowing a phrase from Derrida), a term that seems to well describe this view. She writes about this in "How Could Arendt Glorify the American Revolution and Revile the French? Placing *On Revolution* in the Historiography of the French and American Revolution," 2. This is a paper she presented at the University of Pennsylvania in January 2008 (among other places). Cited with permission from the author.

7. Arendt, *Willing,* 195.

8. Ibid., 29. Many scholars, such as Elisabeth Young-Bruehl, do not see Arendt as opposing willing at all. It may be, however, that we are simply focusing on different aspects of what is, for Arendt, a very complex and ambivalent phenomenon. See Elisabeth Young-Bruehl, *Hannah Arendt: For Love of the World* (New Haven: Yale University Press, 1982), 444–45.

9. Hannah Arendt, "What is Freedom?" in *Between Past and Future,* 159.

10. Arendt, *Willing,* 63.

11. To some extent, Arendt's suspicion of the will may reflect her personal experience of Nazism; the projection of phantasms, claims of truth and order, and general indifference to human suffering and plurality that the Nazis embodied suggest the extreme form of a critique that she had of the will and its political effects more generally.

For an account of the way Arendt understands Nazism, particularly as a moment of an imagination that is at once too active in projecting its phantasms and too passive in terms of imagining its effect on others, see George Kateb, "The Adequacy of the Canon," *Political Theory* 30 (2002): 482–505, especially 488 and 501–5.

12. Arendt, *Willing*, 64.

13. Ibid.

14. Ibid.

15. Ibid.

16. Benjamin, "Critique of Violence," 300.

17. Arendt, *Willing*, 67; emphasis added.

18. Ibid., 70.

19. Hannah Arendt, *The Human Condition* (Chicago: University of Chicago Press, 1958), 179.

20. Ibid., 239.

21. Ibid., 199.

22. Ibid., 243.

23. Hannah Arendt, *On Revolution* (New York: Penguin, 1965), 273.

24. In an earlier essay, I have described Arendt's connection between sovereignty and the will. James Martel, "'*Amo: Volo ut sis*': Love, Willing and Arendt's Reluctant Embrace of Sovereignty," *Philosophy and Social Criticism* 34, no. 3 (2008): 287–313.

25. Arendt, "What is Freedom?" 163.

26. Disch, "How Could Arendt Glorify," 2–3.

27. Ibid., 4.

28. Arendt, *On Revolution*, 237.

29. Ibid.

30. Ibid.

31. Ibid.

32. Disch, "How Could Arendt Glorify," 17.

33. Ibid.

34. See Bonnie Honig, "Declarations of Independence: Arendt and Derrida on the Problem of Founding a Republic," *American Political Science Review* 85, no. 1 (1991): 97–113.

35. Agnes Heller, "Hannah Arendt on Tradition and New Beginnings," in *Hannah Arendt in Jerusalem*, ed. Steven E. Aschheim (Berkeley: University of California Press, 2001), 20.

36. We see this sentiment very clearly in Arendt's work. In *On Revolution*, in a passage Heller herself cites, Arendt writes: "If foundation was the aim and the end of revolution, then the revolutionary spirit was not merely the spirit of beginning something new but of starting something permanent and enduring; a lasting institution, embodying this spirit and encouraging it to new achievements, would be self-defeating. From which it unfortunately seems to follow that nothing threatens the very achievements of revolution more dangerously and more acutely than the spirit which has brought them about. Should freedom in its most exalted sense as freedom to act be the price to be paid for foundation?" *On Revolution*, 232.

37. Heller, "Hannah Arendt on Tradition," 25.

38. It is perhaps for this reason that, for all of her lauding of the spontaneous and free Greeks, we see (as Jacques Taminiaux and Roy Tsao have suggested) a preference for

278 | Notes to Pages 168–77

the tradition-bound Romans. See Jacques Taminiaux, "Athens and Greece," in *The Cambridge Companion to Hannah Arendt*, ed. Dana Villa (New York: Cambridge University Press, 2000), 165–77; Roy T. Tsao, "Arendt Against Athens: Rereading the Human Condition," *Political Theory* 30, no. 1 (2002): 97–123.

39. Arendt reads *The Castle* as involving "situations and perplexities distinctive of Jewish life." Hannah Arendt, "The Jew as Pariah: A Hidden Tradition," in *The Jewish Writings* (New York: Schocken, 2007), 290.

40. Ibid., 292.

41. Ibid., 293.

42. Ibid.

43. Ibid., 294.

44. Ibid.

45. Ibid., 294–95.

46. Ibid., 295.

47. Ibid.

48. Ibid., 297.

49. Ibid.

50. Ibid., 292.

51. Federico García Lorca, *The Shoemaker's Wonderful Wife*, in *Plays: Two* (London: Methuen, 1990), 3. For more on this play, see Andrew A. Anderson, *Garcia Lorca: La Zapatera Prodigiosa* (Rochester, NY: Tamesis, 1991).

52. Lorca, *The Shoemaker's Wonderful Wife*, 4. In Spanish it says "*El Autor mira un poco cohibido al público y se retira de espaldas lleno de ironía*"—literally, he retreats backward filled with irony (or in an ironic way). Federico García Lorca, *La zapatera prodigiosa*, in *Obras Completas II, Teatro* (Valencia: Galaxia Gutenberg / Círculo de Lectores, 1997), 197.

53. Lorca, *The Shoemaker's Wonderful Wife*, 3.

54. Ibid. In this exchange, as Sarah Wright informs us, "the Author's character rebels against her creator." Sarah Wright, *The Trickster-Function in The Theatre of García Lorca* (Rochester, NY: Tamesis, 2000), 24. In speaking of Lorca's concept of "comedias irrepresentables," Wright further writes, "At first sight, it would appear that authorial intent seems to provide a justification for this choice, but paradoxically . . . the role of the author is evacuated of authority, and. . . . the theatrical space is opened out into a dialogue of signs and signifiers. The author function is thus replaced by the trickster-function" (15).

55. Lorca, *The Shoemaker's Wonderful Wife*, 30.

56. Ibid.

57. Ibid., 31.

58. Ibid., 34.

59. Ibid.

60. This can be read as another version of "raising a mighty paw" against the idea of truth itself by use of (mis)representations of both the deliberate and unknowing variety (functionally speaking, there may not be much of a difference between these two kinds of misrepresentation for Lorca).

61. Lorca, *The Shoemaker's Wonderful Wife*, 34.

62. Ibid., 36.

63. Ibid., 40. In original: *La zapatera prodigiosa*, 237.

64. Lorca, *The Shoemaker's Wonderful Wife,* 41.

65. Recall that for Benjamin the messiah "would only make a slight adjustment in [the world]." Benjamin, "Franz Kafka," 134.

66. As with Žižek's reading of Poe's narrator, they aren't steering but they think they are.

67. There is a temptation with Arendt's notion of "who" a person is to also think of it as being somehow authentic, but this is once again to fall into the very delusions of being non- or postrepresentative that Arendt herself engages with but fortunately pulls away from (or is pulled away by the text).

68. Actually it is not so much that Marcolfa talks him into it as he enchants him into it. Their dialogue has a surrealistic quality (one that is repeated occasionally in the rest of the play) and in it Don Perlimplín replies "*as in a dream*" (in Spanish: *Distraído,* or distracted). *The Love of Don Perlimplín,* in *Plays: Two,* 44. In Spanish, *Amor de Don Perlimplín con Belisa en su jardín,* in *Obras Completas: Teatro,* 242. For analyses specifically of *The Love of Don Perlimplín,* see Pamela Bacarisse, "Perlimplín's Tragedy," in *Lorca, Poet and Playwright,* ed. Robert Havard (Cardiff: University of Wales Press, 1992), 71–92. For an analysis of that play based on sexuality, see Paul Binding, *Federico García Lorca: The Gay Imagination* (London: GMP Publishers, 1985).

69. Lorca, *Love of Don Perlimplín,* 49.

70. Ibid., 51. In Spanish: "Me casé . . . ¡por lo que fuera!, pero no te quería. Yo no había podido imaginarme tu cuerpo hasta que lo vi por el ojo de la cerradura cuanda te vestían de novia. Y entonces fue cuando sentí el amor, ¡entonces!, como un hondo corte de lanceta en mi garganta [like a deep cut of a lancet in my throat]." *Amor de Don Perlimplín,* 249. In this glimpse through a keyhole, we are reminded of the way K. glimpses Klamm in *The Castle.*

71. Lorca, *Love of Don Perlimplín,* 54.

72. Ibid.

73. Ibid.

74. In this he goes against the advice of Marcolfa, who, regretting his earlier machinations, tells him, "You love [Belisa] too much." Ibid., 56.

75. Ibid., 57.

76. Ibid.

77. Ibid., 58.

78. Ibid., 60.

79. Ibid., 62. In original: *Amor de Don Perlimplín,* 261.

80. Lorca, *Love of Don Perlimplín,* 63.

81. Ibid.

82. Ibid., 63–64. In original: *Amor de Don Perlimplín,* 263.

83. Lorca, *Love of Don Perlimplín,* 64.

84. Ibid.

85. Ibid. In original: *Amor de Don Perlimplín,* 263–64.

86. *Amor de Don Perlimplín,* 252.

87. In the end, Lorca may be more successful at such an endeavor in the sense that he offers us a more coherent vision of how such strategies might be employed. Yet, at the same time, he does not share Arendt's burden of having to produce a political theory out of his work—he can merely gesture in a particular direction.

88. Brown, *Politics Out of History,* 4.

89. For two very helpful works on the question of materialism, agency, and human action see (specifically on Arendt) Roger Berkowitz, "Solitude and the Activity of Thinking," in *Thinking in Dark Times: Hannah Arendt on Ethics and Politics*, ed. Roger Berkowitz, Jeff Katz, and Thomas Keenan (New York: Fordham University Press, 2010). See also (on Hobbes but with broader applications as well) Samantha Frost's *Lessons from a Materialist Thinker: Hobbesian Reflections on Ethics and Politics* (Stanford: Stanford University Press, 2008).

CHAPTER 6

1. Assia Djebar, *Algerian White* (New York: Seven Stories Press, 2003), 221.
2. Clarisse Zimra, afterword to Assia Djebar, *Women of Algiers in Their Apartment*, trans. Marjolijn de Jager (Charlottesville: University Press of Virginia, 1992), 190. And Clarisse Zimra, afterword to Assia Djebar, *Children of the New World*, 206. See also David Macey, *Frantz Fanon: A Biography* (New York: Picador, 2002), 387.
3. Homi Bhabha, "Foreword," in Frantz Fanon, *The Wretched of the Earth*, trans. Constance Farrington (New York: Grove Press, 2004), xxviii–xxix. Nasser Hussain pointed this out to me.
4. Fanon, *Wretched of the Earth*, 2.
5. Ibid., 18–19.
6. Ibid., 37.
7. Ibid., 140.
8. Ibid., 142.
9. Ibid., 20–21.
10. Ibid., 184–85 n. 23. In the original French, *Les damnés de la terre* (Paris: La Découverte Poche, 2002), 243.
11. Fanon, *Wretched of the Earth*, 184–85 n. 23.
12. Ibid.
13. Frantz Fanon, *Black Skin, White Masks*, trans. Charles Lam Markmann (New York: Grove Press, 1967), 116.
14. Frantz Fanon, *Peau noire, masques blancs* (Paris: Éditions du Seuil, 1952), 88.
15. David Macey, "Fanon, Phenomenology, Race," *Radical Philosophy* 9 (May–June 1999): 1.
16. Lewis R. Gordon, *Fanon and the Crisis of European Man: An Essay on Philosophy and the Human Sciences* (New York: Routledge, 1995), 35. See also Ato Sekyi-Otu, *Fanon's Dialectic of Experience* (Cambridge: Harvard University Press, 1996).
17. Fanon, *Wretched of the Earth*, 93.
18. Frantz Fanon, *A Dying Colonialism*, trans. Haakon Chevalier (New York: Grove Press, 1965), 47.
19. Fanon, *Black Skin, White Masks*, 14. And *Peau noire*, 11.
20. Fanon, *Wretched of the Earth*, 131, and *Les damnés de la terre*, 180. David Macey writes that Fanon's adoption of an Algerian "We" should not surprise us since he did not believe that his earlier Martinican identity was "real" (it was produced in regard to the white "gaze" and had no substance of its own). Through struggle and the building of new postcolonial nations, Fanon held in the creation of new and indeed "real" identities;

hence it becomes possible for him to shed one identity and adapt another. *Frantz Fanon: A Biography,* 374–75.

21. Fanon, *Wretched of the Earth,* 134.

22. Ibid., 135.

23. Fanon, *Black Skin, White Masks,* 102–3.

24. Assia Djebar perhaps best articulates Fanon's shifting yet consistent identity when she calls him "Algerian-Martinican." *Algerian White,* 107.

25. Fanon, *Black Skin, White Masks,* 26. Although he doesn't here seem to mean closer in a racial sense, it still suggests that the color of one's skin is not in and of itself determinant.

26. Ibid.

27. For more on Fanon's understanding of the relationship between the psyche and colonialism, see Hussein Abdilahi Bulhan, *Frantz Fanon and the Psychology of Oppression* (New York: Plenum Press, 1985).

28. Fanon, *Black Skin, White Masks,* 12.

29. In his analysis of Jean Vaneuse, a black character in a book written by René Maran, Fanon writes that "Jean Vaneuse is a neurotic, and his color is only an attempt to explain his psychic structure. If this objective difference had not existed, he would have manufactured it out of nothing" (*Black Skin, White Masks,* 78–79).

30. Ibid., 161.

31. Ibid.

32. Ibid., 162.

33. Ibid., 109. *Peau Noire,* 88. David Macey discusses this in *Frantz Fanon: A Biography,* 166.

34. Fanon, *Black Skin, White Masks,* 109.

35. The same thing can be said of culture, another key element of "reality" for Fanon. Distinguishing between culture and "custom" (the latter being the kind of false sense of authenticity that Fanon espied, for example, in the negritude movement), Fanon seems to imply that culture can in fact actually *be* authentic (*Wretched of the Earth,* 160). Yet, as Fanon shows, as in the example of psychology, reality and "truth" only come from the struggle against colonialism: "Truth is what hastens the dislocation of the colonial regime, what fosters the emergence of the nation. Truth is what protects the 'natives' and undoes the foreigners. In the colonial context there is no truthful behavior. And good is quite simply what hurts *them* most" (*Wretched of the Earth,* 14).

Thus struggle itself produces, in effect, an ontology of permanent resistance. For that reason it does not end in perfect and transcendent victory. Fanon thus foments a conspiracy instead of a rebellion; in this way he preserves exactly what he is struggling against, but struggle itself, as we have already begun to see, scrambles the existing building blocks of reality to produce other, possible alternatives, new versions of reality and new "futures" as well.

36. Hannah Arendt, "On Violence," in *Crises of the Republic* (New York: Harcourt Brace Jovanovich,1972), 116 n. 19. See also Nigel C. Gibson's chapter "Violent Concerns" in *Fanon: The Postcolonial Imagination* (Cambridge: Polity Press, 2003).

37. Fanon, *Wretched of the Earth,* 51.

38. Arendt, "On Violence," 163.

39. Ibid., 122.

40. Ibid., 151.

41. Ibid., 123.

42. Hannah Arendt, "Thoughts on Politics and Revolution," in *Crises of the Republic*, 210–11.

43. Macey, *Frantz Fanon: A Biography*, 469–70. See also Alice Chekri, *Frantz Fanon: A Portrait* (Ithaca, NY: Cornell University Press, 2006), 180–81.

44. For an excellent overview of the question of Arendt on race and the way it affects her political theory, see Jimmy Casas Klausen, "Hannah Arendt's Antiprimitivism," *Political Theory* 38, no. 3 (2010): 394–423. See also Anne Norton, "Heart of Darkness: Africa and African Americans in the Writings of Hannah Arendt," in *Feminist Interpretations of Hannah Arendt*, ed. Bonnie Honig (University Park: Pennsylvania State University Press, 1995), 247–61. See also Richard H. King and Dan Stone, eds., *Hannah Arendt and the Uses of History: Imperialism, Nation, Race, and Genocide* (New York: Berghahn Books, 2007).

45. In response to Arendt's critique that the idea of third world solidarity is suspect because it is a reworking and a reapplication of a previous and "failed" (Marxist) ideology: it seems to me no failure at all but a perfect instance of transtemporal conspiracy working precisely the way Benjamin claims it can. Two moments, completely separated by time, by context, become, as it were, coterminous, mutually implicating and mutually inspiring one another.

46. Interestingly, Djebar's own name comes from a kind of misrecognition. While her original last name (the surname of her father) is Imalayen, which she calls "*gloriously Berber*" (in an interview with Clarisse Zimra in the afterword to Assia Djebar, *Women of Algiers in Their Apartment*, 185), Djebar chose as her nom de plume *djebbar*. one of the ninety-nine ritual modes of address to Allah, meaning "Allah the intransigeant." Inadvertently however she wrote down *djébar* (the accent dropped away subsequently), meaning "healer." Ibid., 160.

47. This term "chopped up" comes from the way that Proust describes Baudelaire's notion of time as cited by Benjamin, "Some Motifs in Baudelaire," 181.

48. Macey *Frantz Fanon: A Biography*, 387.

49. Djebar, *Algerian White*, 104.

50. Ibid., 107.

51. Djebar, *Children of the New World*, 25.

52. Ibid., 84. And Assia Djebar, *Les enfants du nouveau monde* (Paris: René Julliard, 1962), 137.

53. Djebar, *Children of the New World*, 84; *Les enfants du nouveau monde*, 137.

54. Djebar, *Children of the New World*, 145.

55. Ibid.

56. Ibid., 107.

57. Ibid.

58. Ibid., 186.

59. Ibid., 198.

60. Ibid. *Les enfants du nouveau monde*, 310.

61. Of course this is not the fate of all the characters in this novel. The traitorous Touma, a young woman who informs on the resisters and flirts dangerously with Europeans, ends up being killed by her own brother. Hakim, the police inspector whose sub-

jection to colonialism becomes increasingly legible to him as the contradictions between his "European" training and the reality of what he has to do becomes explicit, slowly rolls toward madness.

62. Djebar, *Children of the New World*, 14.

63. For a discussion of the feminist gender implications of Djebar's work see Clarisse Zimra's afterword to *Women of Algiers in Their Apartment*, especially 201–2. See also Djebar's own "postface" to that book entitled "Forbidden Gaze, Severed Sound," where she discusses Baudelaire, 133–51. See also Clarisse Zimra's "Writing Woman: The Novels of Assia Djebar," in *SubStance* 21, no. 3 (1992): 68–84; Priscilla Ringrose, *Assia Djebar in Dialogue with Feminisms* (New York: Rodopi, 2006); Laurence Huughe, "Ecrire comme un voile: The Problematics of the Gaze in the Work of Assia Djebar," *World Literature Today* 70 (1996): 867–76.

64. When contemplating the (successful) end of the war, one of Cherifa's neighbors says, "The end . . . That will be a marvelous awakening, a deliverance." Djebar, *Children of the New World*, 8.

65. Arendt, *The Human Condition*, 245.

66. Djebar, *Children of the New World*, 164–65; *Les enfants du nouveau monde*, 260.

67. Djebar, *Children of The New World*, 184.

68. Ibid., 185; *Les enfants du nouveau monde*, 290.

69. Djebar, *Children of the New World*, 197–98.

70. Ibid., 120. The coda "would continue his tale" does not appear in the French original. *Les enfants du nouveau monde*, 192.

71. I am indebted to Bonnie Honig for this observation.

72. Djebar, *Algerian White*, 47; *Le blanc de l'Algérie* (Paris: Éditions Albin Michel, 1995), 51. For more on *Algerian White* see Clarisse Zimra, "Introduction to Assia Djebar's *The White of Algeria*," *Yale French Studies* 87 (1995): 149–70.

73. Djebar, *Algerian White*, 14; *Le blanc de l'Algérie*, 12. She goes on to write: "A nation seeking its own ceremonial, in different forms, but from cemetery to cemetery, because, first of all, the writer has been offered as propitiatory victim: strange and despairing discovery!" *Algerian White*, 14.

74. Benjamin, "Theses," 255.

75. Djebar, *Algerian White*, 18; *Le blanc de l'Algérie*, 18.

76. Djebar, *Algerian White*, 17.

77. Ibid. 18.

78. Djebar, *Le blanc de l'Algérie*, 18.

79. At one point, when contemplating the death and loss of Albert Camus (a complicated and controversial figure for Djebar) and his own prescriptions for a multiracial, federal Algeria, she wonders why Algeria could not have experienced "a solution like the one Mandela found in South Africa." *Algerian White*, 109. Even in saying this, she concedes that such talk by Camus and the hope it inspired "later on . . . would seem to belong to another epoch" (109).

80. Ibid., 128.

81. Writing of *Algerian White*, Jane Hiddleston reminds us that the "white of the title evokes the emptiness of a blank page" (it is also the color of mourning in the Muslim world). Jane Hiddleston, *Assia Djebar: Out of Algeria* (Liverpool: Liverpool University Press, 2006), 122.

82. Djebar, *Algerian White*, 218.
83. Ibid., 11. In French: "Hâtez-vous de mourir; après vous parlerez en ancêtres ..." *Le blanc de l'Algérie*, 9.
84. Djebar, *Algerian White*, 114; *Le blanc de l'Algérie*, 122.
85. Djebar, *Algerian White*, 230; *Le blanc de l'Algérie*, 245.
86. In *Imagine There's No Woman*, Joan Copjec examines the paintings of Kara Walker in ways that also suggest the power of rejuxtaposition as a way to resist the legacy, in this case, of slavery. As Copjec says of Walker's work: "History flows through these figures but it does not contain them." *Imagine There's No Woman*, 107.

CONCLUSION

1. Benjamin and Adorno, *The Complete Correspondence*, 283.
2. Benjamin, *Origin*, 156–57.
3. Ibid., 233.
4. Ibid., 139.
5. Samuel Weber asks, "What does the German baroque mourning play mourn?" His answer is "the death of tragedy." *Benjamin's -abilities*, 156.
6. Benjamin, *Origin*, 139; *Ursprung*, 120.
7. Benjamin, *The Arcades Project* (Konvolute N), 476.
8. Benjamin, *Origin*, 37.
9. Ibid.
10. Copjec, *Imagine There's No Woman*, 39.
11. Ibid.
12. Ibid., 40.
13. Ibid.
14. To be fair, Copjec acknowledges the endlessness of our relationship to the object. She writes that the drive "does not finish so easily with its object but keeps turning around it," yet such a turning seems, in her view, to remain free of the phantasms that come with the object as goal. Ibid., 38.
15. It may be that Copjec herself allows for the ongoing effect of the goal as with her already cited comment that the objects are "always more than themselves."
16. Benjamin, "Franz Kafka," 134.
17. See, for example, J. K. Gibson-Graham, *A Post-Capitalist Politics* (Minneapolis: University of Minnesota Press, 2006) and *The End of Capitalism (as We Knew It): A Feminist Critique of Political Economy* (Minneapolis: University of Minnesota Press, 2006).
18. In a way, we could say that even to call this delivery "messianic" is just another form of misrecognition, another false attribution. And of course it is, but that is not to say that it is not *also* messianic.
19. Benjamin, Critique of Violence," 297.
20. Here, I borrow an image from Heidegger. See Martin Heidegger, *What is Called Thinking?*
21. Jonathan Lear, *Radical Hope: Ethics in the Face of Cultural Devastation* (Cambridge: Harvard University Press, 2006), 2.
22. Ibid., 95.
23. Ibid., 92.

24. Ibid.

25. This is not to suggest that the Crow are somehow lucky that their loss is legible to them (for in fact, as Lear ably points out, it is not; the very markers of legibility are themselves erased along with the culture that produced them). But it is to point out that our current crisis is more a crisis of perception than of tangible destruction. We have *already* been destroyed, but the problem is we don't have the concepts by which to make this fact evident to ourselves.

26. We learn (via Lear) that he did not tell Linderman, his original translator, everything, for in addition to his vision of the Chickadee, an animal sign that foretold the fate (and survival strategies) of the Crow, Plenty Coups retained one other icon from Crow tradition, that of the war eagle (Lear, *Radical Hope,* 91), possibly suggesting both a more traditionalist and more aggressive side to Plenty Coups himself.

27. Although recognizing that the "actor" taking the faithless leap in Benjamin's account is not a person but allegory itself, we have seen how human beings can learn from and imitate the sign and its intentions.

28. Lear, *Radical Hope,* 150.

29. At this point, the fact that we are hearing from Plenty Coups always through a white interlocutor, whether Linderman or Lear, becomes an issue. We can't be sure what Plenty Coups thought about anything (and to his credit, Lear does not try to impose a reading on him, he just discusses what it would mean if Plenty Coups's words were read in a particular way).

30. Jacques Rancière, *Hatred of Democracy* (New York: Verso, 2006), 53.

31. Ibid.

32. Ibid., 94. Rancière discusses how Tocqueville has been implicated in this debate; his fears of a genuine tyranny have become reconstituted as a critique of consumer society. Ibid., 20.

33. Ibid., 76.

34. Ziarek, "The Beauty of Failure," 145.

35. Dean, "Politics without Politics," 24.

36. St. Augustine, *The City of God* (New York: Penguin Classics, 2003).

37. Dean, "Politics without Politics," 26.

38. Dean adds Derrida's notion of "democracy to come" to the mix as well.

39. Although Dean tells us: "Drive circulates around an object, generating satisfaction through this very circulation." Dean, "Politics without Politics," 26.

40. Ibid.

41. Alenka Zupančič, "Ethics and Tragedy in Lacan," in *The Cambridge Companion to Lacan,* ed. Jean-Michel Rabaté (New York: Cambridge University Press, 2003), 184.

42. Dean, "Politics without Politics," 31.

43. Dean writes: "Rancière's emphasis is on the disagreement between those who claim the equality of speaking beings and those who deny it. Such disagreement is not essential to equality but can be made to appear through other counter-factual claims. We can imagine the inscription of liberty as a claim to freedom in conditions of unfreedom; or the converse: a claim of unfreedom in conditions of freedom. One says an unfettered market in commodities is freedom. The other responds: I disagree. We can imagine the inscription of ownership in the commons, a claim to privacy property in conditions of common goods. One says: this is mine. The other responds: I disagree. And we can imagine claims of belonging in conditions of fear and exclusion. The one

says: I am one of you. The other says: I disagree. Each of these instances of liberty, ownership, and belonging stages a conflict with a given partition of the perceptible and attempts to make an alternative partition appear. But none is the same as the egalitarian inscription and none is strictly speaking democratic. There are non-democratic stagings of disagreement. And because there are non-democratic stagings, politics is not necessarily democratic." Ibid., 34.

44. As Zupančič tells us, the situation of the subject vis-à-vis ethics is "*I couldn't have done anything else, but still, I am guilty.*" Zupančič, *Ethics of the Real*, 27.

45. Benjamin, *Origin*, 233.

46. Thoreau offers us a similar sentiment about going "down" instead of up when he writes: "Time is but the stream I go a-fishing in. I drink at it; but while I drink I see the sandy bottom and detect how shallow it is . . . I would drink deeper; fish in the sky, whose bottom is pebbly with stars. . . . My instinct tells me that my head is an organ for burrowing, as some creatures use their snout and fore paws, and with it I would mine and burrow my way through these hills" (perhaps the same hills that are the site of vengeance at the end of "A Descent into the Maelström"). Thoreau, *Walden*, 66.

Bibliography

Abdilahi Bulhan, Hussein. *Frantz Fanon and the Psychology of Oppression.* New York: Plenum Press, 1985.

Adorno, Theodor. "Notes on Kafka." In *Prisms.* Cambridge: MIT Press, 1983.

Agamben, Giorgio. "The State of Exception." In *Politics, Metaphysics and Death: Essays on Giorgio Agamben's Homo Sacer,* ed. Andrew Norris. Durham, NC: Duke University Press, 2005.

Agamben, Giorgio. "Walter Benjamin and the Demonic: Happiness and Historical Redemption." In *Potentialities,* ed. Warner Hamacher and David E. Wellbery. Stanford, CA: Stanford University Press, 1999.

Althusser, Louis. *Machiavelli and Us.* Ed. François Matheron. Trans. Gregory Elliot. New York: Verso, 1999.

Anderson, Andrew A. *Garcia Lorca: La Zapatera Prodigiosa.* Rochester, NY: Tamesis, 1991.

Arendt, Hannah. *Between Past and Future: Eight Exercises in Political Thought.* New York: Penguin, 1968.

Arendt, Hannah. *Crises of the Republic.* New York: Harcourt Brace Jovanovich, 1972.

Arendt, Hannah. *The Human Condition.* Chicago: University of Chicago Press, 1958.

Arendt, Hannah. *The Jewish Writings.* New York: Schocken, 2007.

Arendt, Hannah. *On Revolution.* New York: Penguin, 1965.

Arendt, Hannah. *Willing.* In *The Life of the Mind.* New York: Harcourt Brace Jovanovich, 1978.

Augustine. *The City of God.* New York: Penguin Classics, 2003.

Bahti, Timothy. "History as Rhetorical Enactment: Walter Benjamin's Theses 'On the Concept of History.'" *Diacritics* 10 (Fall 1979): 2–17.

Baron, Hans. *The Crisis of the Early Italian Renaissance.* Princeton, NJ: Princeton University Press, 1966.

Baudelaire, Charles. "Edgar Poe: Sa vie et ses oeuvres." In *Histoires Extraordinaires par Edgar Poe.* Paris: Michel Lévy Frères, 1869.

Benjamin, Walter. *The Arcades Project.* Cambridge: Belknap Press of Harvard University Press, 2002.

Benjamin, Walter. "Central Park." Trans. Lloyd Spencer. *New German Critique* 34 (1985): 32–58.

Benjamin, Walter. *Gesammelte Schriften.* Frankfurt am Main: Suhrkamp, 1991.

Benjamin, Walter. *Illuminations: Essays and Reflections.* Ed. Hannah Arendt. Trans. Harry Zohn. New York: Schocken, 1968.

Benjamin, Walter. *The Origin of German Tragic Drama.* Trans. John Osborne. New York: Verso 1998.

Benjamin, Walter. "The Paris of the Second Empire in Baudelaire." In *The Writer of Modern Life: Essays on Charles Baudelaire.* Cambridge: Belknap Press of Harvard University Press, 2006.

Benjamin, Walter. *Das Passagen-Werk.* Vol. 1. Frankfurt am Main: Suhrkamp, 1991.

Benjamin, Walter. *Reflections: Essays, Aphorisms, Autobiographical Writings.* Ed. Peter Demetz. Trans. Edmund Jephcott. New York: Schocken, 1978.

Benjamin, Walter. *Ursprung des deutschen Trauerspiels.* Frankfurt am Main: Suhrkamp, 1978.

Benjamin, Walter, and Theodor Adorno. *The Complete Correspondence 1928–1940.* Cambridge: Harvard University Press, 1999.

Berkowitz, Roger. "Solitude and the Activity of Thinking." In *Thinking in Dark Times,* ed. Roger Berkowitz, Jeff Katz, and Thomas Keenan. New York: Fordham University Press, 2010.

Binding, Paul. *Federico García Lorca: The Gay Imagination.* London: GMP Publishers, 1985.

Borges, Jorge Luis. "Kafka and His Precursors." In *Selected Non-Fictions,* ed. Eliot Weinberger, trans. Esther Allen, Suzanne Jill Levine, and Eliot Weinberger. New York: Viking, 1999.

Brown, Wendy. *Politics Out of History.* Princeton, NJ: Princeton University Press, 2001.

Bruce, Iris. *Kafka and Cultural Zionism: Dates in Palestine.* Madison: University of Wisconsin Press, 2007.

Buck-Morss, Susan. *The Dialectics of Seeing: Walter Benjamin and the Arcades Project.* Cambridge: MIT Press, 1991.

Buck-Morss, Susan. *The Origin of Negative Dialectics: Theodor W. Adorno, Walter Benjamin, and the Frankfurt Institute.* New York: Free Press, 1979.

Boesche, Roger. *The Strange Liberalism of Alexis de Tocqueville.* Ithaca, NY: Cornell University Press, 1987.

Carton, Evan. *The Rhetoric of American Romance: Dialectic and Identity in Emerson, Dickinson, Poe, and Hawthorne.* Baltimore: Johns Hopkins University Press, 1985.

Castle, Terry. "Phantasmagoria: Spectral Technology and the Metaphorics of Modern Reverie." *Critical Inquiry* 15, no. 1 (1988): 26–61.

Cavell, Stanley. "Being Odd, Getting Even." In *In Quest of the Ordinary: Lines of Skepticism and Romanticism.* Chicago: University of Chicago Press, 1988.

Caws, Mary Ann. "Insertion in an Oval Frame: Poe Circumscribed by Baudelaire, Part II." *French Review* 56 (1983): 885–95.

Caygill, Howard. "Walter Benjamin's Concept of Cultural History." In *The Cambridge Companion to Walter Benjamin,* ed. David S. Ferris. New York: Cambridge University Press, 2004.

Chekri, Alice. *Frantz Fanon: A Portrait.* Ithaca, NY: Cornell University Press, 2006.

Cohen, Margaret. "Benjamin's Phantasmagoria: *The Arcades Project.*" In *The Cambridge Companion to Walter Benjamin,* ed. David S. Ferris. New York: Cambridge University Press, 2004.

Cohen, Margaret. *Profane Illumination: Walter Benjamin and the Paris of Surrealist Revolution.* Berkeley: University of California Press, 1993.

Constantine, David. "Kafka's Writing and Our Reading." In *The Cambridge Companion to Kafka,* ed. Julian Preece. New York: Cambridge University Press, 2002.

Copjec, Joan. *Imagine There's No Woman: Ethics and Sublimation.* Cambridge: MIT Press, 2004.

Corngold, Stanley. "The Author Survives on the Margin of His Breaks: Kafka's Narrative Perspective." In *The Fate of the Self: German Writers and French Theory.* New York: Columbia University Press, 1986.

Dauber, Kenneth. *The Idea of Authorship in America: Democratic Poetics from Franklin to Melville.* Madison: University of Wisconsin Press, 1990.

Dayan, Joan. *Fables of Mind: An Inquiry into Poe's Fiction.* New York: Oxford University Press, 1987.

Dean, Jodi. "Politics without Politics." *Parallax* 15, no. 3 (2009): 20–36.

Deleuze, Gilles, and Felix Guattari. *Kafka: Toward a Minor Literature.* Trans. Dana Plan. Minneapolis: University of Minnesota Press, 1986.

de Man, Paul. *Allegories of Reading: Figural Language in Rousseau, Nietzsche, Rilke and Proust.* New York: Yale University Press, 1979.

Dennis, Nigel. "Politics." In *A Companion to Federico García Lorca.* Ed. Federico Bonaddio. Rochester, NY: Tamesis, 2007.

Derrida, Jacques. "Before the Law." In *Acts of Literature,* ed. Derek Attridge. New York: Routledge, 1992.

Derrida, Jacques. *Dissemination.* Trans. Barbara Johnson. Chicago: University of Chicago Press, 1983.

Derrida, Jacques. *Politics of Friendship.* Trans. George Collins. New York: Verso, 1997.

Dinverno, Melissa. "Raising the Dead: García Lorca, Trauma and the Cultural Mediation of Mourning." *Arizona Journal of Hispanic Cultural Studies* 9 (2005): 1–24.

Disch, Lisa. "How Could Arendt Glorify the American Revolution and Revile the French? Placing *On Revolution* in the Historiography of the French and American Revolution." Paper presented at the University of Pennsylvania, January 2008. Cited with permission of author.

Djebar, Assia. *Algerian White.* New York: Seven Stories Press, 2003.

Djebar, Assia. *Le blanc de l'Algérie.* Paris: Éditions Albin Michel, 1995.

Djebar, Assia. *Children of the New World: A Novel of the Algerian War.* New York: Feminist Press at the City University of New York, 2005.

Djebar, Assia. *Les enfants du nouveau monde.* Paris: René Julliard, 1962.

Djebar, Assia. "Forbidden Gaze, Severed Sound." In *Women of Algiers in Their Apartment,* trans. Marjolijn de Jager. Charlottesville: University of Virginia Press, 1992.

Dodd, Bill. "The Case for a Political Reading." In *The Cambridge Companion to Kafka,* ed. Julian Preece. New York: Cambridge University Press, 2002.

Dumm, Thomas L. "Resignation." *Critical Inquiry* 25, no. 1 (1998): 56–76.

Fenves, Peter. *Arresting Language: From Leibniz to Benjamin.* Stanford, CA: Stanford University Press, 2001.

Fitzpatrick, Peter. *Modernism and the Grounds of Law.* New York: Cambridge University Press, 2001.

Frost, Samantha. *Lessons from a Materialist Thinker: Hobbesian Reflections on Ethics and Politics.* Stanford, CA: Stanford University Press, 2008.

Gibson, Ian. *Federico García Lorca: A Life.* New York: Pantheon, 1997.

Gibson, Nigel C. *Fanon: The Postcolonial Imagination.* Cambridge: Polity Press, 2003.

Gilbert, Felix. "The Humanist Concept of the Prince and *The Prince* of Machiavelli." *Journal of Modern History* 11 (1939): 449–83.

Gordon, Lewis R. *Fanon and the Crisis of European Man: An Essay on Philosophy and the Human Sciences.* New York: Routledge, 1995.

Fanon, Frantz. *Black Skin, White Masks.* Trans. Charles Lam Markmann. New York: Grove Press, 1967.

Fanon, Frantz. *Les damnés de la terre.* Paris: La Découverte Poche, 2002.

Fanon, Frantz. *A Dying Colonialism.* Trans. Haakon Chevalier. New York: Grove Press, 1965.

Fanon, Frantz. *Peau noire, masques blancs.* Paris: Éditions du Seuil, 1952.

Fanon, Frantz. *The Wretched of the Earth.* Trans. Constance Farrington. New York: Grove Press, 2004.

Foust, R. E. "Aesthetician of Simultaneity: E. A. Poe and Modern Literary Theory." *South Atlantic Review* 1981: 17–25.

Fredrickson, George M. *The Black Image in the White Mind: The Debate on Afro-American Character and Destiny, 1817–1914.* Middletown, CT: Wesleyan University Press, 1987.

Gibson-Graham, J. K. *The End of Capitalism (as We Knew It): A Feminist Critique of Political Economy.* Minneapolis: University of Minnesota Press, 2006.

Gibson-Graham, J. K. *A Post-Capitalist Politics.* Minneapolis: University of Minnesota Press, 2006.

Gilman, Sander L. *Franz Kafka.* London: Reaktion Books, 2005.

Gramsci, Antonio. *The Modern Prince and Other Writings.* Trans. Louis Marks. New York: International Publishers, 1959.

Hacker, Andrew. *Two Nations: Black and White, Separate, Hostile and Unequal.* New York: Ballantine, 1995.

Hale, J. R. *Machiavelli and Renaissance Italy.* New York: Collier, 1963.

Hamacher, Werner. "The Gesture in the Name: On Benjamin and Kafka." In *Premises: Essays on Philosophy and Literature from Kant to Celan.* Trans. Peter Fenves. Stanford, CA: Stanford University Press, 1996.

Hanssen, Beatrice. *Walter Benjamin's Other History: Of Stones, Animals, Human Beings, and Angels.* Berkeley: University of California Press, 2000.

Harman, Mark. "Making Everything 'a little uncanny': Kafka's Deletions in the Manuscript of *Das Schloß* and What They Can Tell Us about His Writing Process." In *A Companion to the Works of Franz Kafka,* ed. James Rolleston. Rochester, NY: Camden House, 2002.

Harvey, Ronald C. *The Critical History of Edgar Allan Poe's "The Narrative of Arthur Gordon Pym."* New York: Routledge, 1998.

Heidegger, Martin. *What is Called Thinking?* New York: Harper Perennial, 1976.

Heller, Agnes. "Hannah Arendt on Tradition and New Beginnings." In *Hannah Arendt in Jerusalem,* ed. Steven E. Aschheim. Berkeley: University of California Press, 2001.

Helmling, Steven. "Constellation and Critique: Adorno's 'Constellation,' Benjamin's 'Dialectical Image.'" *Postmodern Culture* 14, no. 1 (2003).

Hiddleston, Jane. *Assia Djebar: Out of Algeria*. Liverpool: Liverpool University Press, 2006.

Hobbes, Thomas. *Leviathan*. Ed. Richard Tuck. New York: Cambridge University Press, 1996.

Honig, Bonnie. "Declarations of Independence: Arendt and Derrida on the Problem of Founding a Republic." *American Political Science Review* 85, no. 1 (1991): 97–113.

Hulliung, Mark. *Citizen Machiavelli*. Princeton, NJ: Princeton University Press, 1983.

Huughe, Laurence. "Ecrire comme un voile: The Problematics of the Gaze in the Work of Assia Djebar." *World Literature Today* 70 (1996): 867–76.

Irwin, John T. *American Hieroglyphics: The Symbol of the Egyptian Hieroglyphics in the American Renaissance*. New Haven: Yale University Press, 1980.

Irwin, John T. "The Quincuncial Network in Poe's Pym." In *Poe's Pym: Critical Explorations*, ed. Richard Kopley. Durham, NC: Duke University Press, 1992.

Jefferson, Thomas. *Notes on the State of Virginia*. Chapel Hill: University of North Carolina Press, 1982.

Kafka, Franz. *The Castle*. Trans. Mark Harman. New York: Schocken, 1998.

Kafka, Franz. *The Complete Stories*. Ed. Nahum N. Glatzer. New York: Schocken, 1971.

Kafka, Franz. *Parables and Paradoxes: Bilingual Edition*. New York: Schocken, 1961.

Kafka, Franz. *Der Prozess*. Frankfurt am Main: Fischer Bücherai, 1958.

Kafka, Franz. *Das Schloß*. Frankfurt am Main: Fischer Taschenbuch, 2007.

Kafka, Franz. *The Trial*. In *The Metamorphosis and the Trial*. Ann Arbor, MI: Borders Classics, 2007.

Kahn, Victoria. *Machiavellian Rhetoric: From the Counter-Reformation to Milton*. Princeton, NJ: Princeton University Press, 1994.

Kahn, Victoria. "Virtù and the Example of Agathocles in Machiavelli's *Prince*." In *Machiavelli and the Discourse of Literature*, ed. Victoria Kahn and Albert Russell Ascoli. Ithaca, NY: Cornell University Press, 1993.

Kateb, George. "The Adequacy of the Canon." *Political Theory* 30 (2002): 482–505.

King, Richard H., and Dan Stone, eds. *Hannah Arendt and the Uses of History: Imperialism, Nation, Race, and Genocide*. New York: Berghahn, 2007.

King, Ross. *Machiavelli: Philosopher of Power*. New York: HarperCollins, 2007.

Klausen, Jimmy Casas. "Hannah Arendt's Antiprimitivism." *Political Theory* 38, no. 3 (2010): 394–423.

Kohn, Margaret. "The Other America: Tocqueville and Beaumont on Race and Slavery." *Polity* 35, no. 2 (2002): 169–93.

Lear, Jonathan. *Radical Hope: Ethics in the Face of Cultural Devastation*. Cambridge: Harvard University Press, 2006.

Lefort, Claude. *Writing: The Political Test*. Durham, NC: Duke University Press, 2000.

Lemonnier, Léon. *Les Traducteurs d'Edgar Poe en France de 1845 à 1875: Charles Baudelaire*. Paris: Presses Universitaires de France, 1928.

Lorca, Federico García. *Obras Completas II, Teatro*. Valencia: Galaxia Gutenberg / Círculo de Lectores, 1997.

Lorca, Federico García. *Plays: Two*. London: Methuen, 1990.

Macey, David. "Fanon, Phenomenology, Race." *Radical Philosophy* 9 (May–June 1999).

Macey, David. *Frantz Fanon: A Biography*. New York: Picador, 2002.

Machiavelli, Niccolò. *The Art of War*. Intro. Neal Wood. New York: Da Capo Press, 1965.

Machiavelli, Niccolò. *The Chief Works and Others.* Vol. 2. Trans. Allan Gilbert. Durham, NC: Duke University Press, 1989.

Machiavelli, Niccolò. *The Comedies of Machiavelli: Bilingual Edition.* Ed. David Sices and James B. Atkinson. Hanover, NH: University Press of New England, 1985.

Machiavelli, Niccolò. *The Prince and the Discourses.* New York: Modern Library, 1950.

Machiavelli, Niccolò. *Opere.* In *La Letteratura Italiana: Storia e Testi.* Vol. 29. Milan: Riccardo Ricciardi Editore, 1963.

Martel, James. "'*Amo: Volo ut sis*': Love, Willing and Arendt's Reluctant Embrace of Sovereignty." *Philosophy and Social Criticism* 34, no. 3 (2008): 287–313.

Martel, James. *Subverting the Leviathan: Reading Thomas Hobbes as a Radical Democrat.* New York: Columbia University Press, 2007.

Martinez, Ronald L. "Benefit of Absence: Machiavellian Valediction in *Clizia.*" In *Machiavelli and the Discourse of Literature,* ed. Victoria Kahn and Albert Russell Ascoli. Ithaca, NY: Cornell University Press, 1993.

Mattingly, Garrett. "Machiavelli's *Prince:* Political Science or Political Satire?" *American Scholar* 27 (1958): 482–91.

McCole, John. *Walter Benjamin and the Antinomies of Tradition.* Ithaca, NY: Cornell University Press, 1993.

Mladek, Klaus. "Radical Play: Gesture, Performance, and the Theatrical Logic of the Law in Kafka." *German Review* 78 (June 2003): 223–49.

Muller, John P., and William J. Richardson, eds. *The Purloined Poe: Lacan, Derrida and Psychoanalytic Reading.* Baltimore: Johns Hopkins University Press, 1988.

Nägele, Rainer. "Thinking Images." In *Benjamin's Ghosts: Interventions in Contemporary Literary and Cultural Theory,* ed. Gerhard Richter. Stanford, CA: Stanford University Press, 2002.

Nietzsche, Friedrich. *Thus Spoke Zarathustra.* Trans. Walter Kaufmann. New York: Modern Library, 1995.

Norris, Christopher. *The Deconstructive Turn: Essays in the Rhetoric of Philosophy.* London: Methuen, 1983.

Norton, Anne. "Heart of Darkness: Africa and African Americans in the Writings of Hannah Arendt." In *Feminist Interpretations of Hannah Arendt,* ed. Bonnie Honig. University Park: Pennsylvania State University Press, 1995.

Olson, Joel. *The Abolition of White Democracy.* Minneapolis: University of Minnesota Press, 2004.

Pensky, Max. *Melancholy Dialectics: Walter Benjamin and the Play of Mourning.* Amherst: University of Massachusetts Press, 2001.

Pitkin, Hanna. *Fortune is a Woman: Gender and Politics in the Thought of Niccolò Machiavelli.* Berkeley: University of California Press, 1984.

Pocock, J. G. A. *The Machiavellian Moment: Florentine Political Thought and the Atlantic Republican Tradition.* Princeton, NJ: Princeton University Press, 2003.

Poe, Edgar Allan. *Complete Tales and Poems.* New York: Vintage, 1975.

Poe, Edgar Allan. *Les Aventures d'Arthur Gordon Pym.* Trans. Charles Baudelaire. Paris: Gallimard, 1977.

Poe, Edgar Allan. *The Narrative of Arthur Gordon Pym of Nantucket.* New York: Penguin, 1999.

Rancière, Jacques. *Hatred of Democracy.* New York: Verso, 2006.

Reinhardt, Mark. *The Art of Being Free: Taking Liberties with Tocqueville, Marx and Arendt.* Ithaca, NY: Cornell University Press, 1997.

Ringrose, Priscilla. *Assia Djebar in Dialogue with Feminisms.* New York: Rodopi, 2006.

Robertson, Ritchie. "'Antizionismus, Zionismus'; Kafka's Responses to Jewish Nationalism." In *Paths and Labyrinths: Nine Papers Read at the Franz Kafka Symposium Held at the Institute of Germanic Studies on 20 and 21 October 1983.* London: University of London, Institute of Germanic Studies, 1985.

Rowe, John Carlos. "Poe, Antebellum Slavery and Modern Criticism." In *Poe's Pym: Critical Explorations,* ed. Richard Kopley. Durham, NC: Duke University Press, 1992.

Sanborn, Geoffrey. "A Confused Beginning: The Narrative of Arthur Gordon Pym, of Nantucket." In *The Cambridge Companion to Edgar Allan Poe,* ed. Kevin J. Hayes. New York: Cambridge University Press, 2002.

Schliefer, James T. "Tocqueville's Democracy in America Reconsidered." In *The Cambridge Companion to Tocqueville,* ed. Cheryl B. Welch. New York.: Cambridge University Press, 2006.

Schmitt, Carl. *Political Theology: Four Chapters on the Concept of Sovereignty.* Cambridge: MIT Press, 1985.

Schoolman, Morton. "Aesthetic Individuality as a Democratic Achievement." In *Reason and Horror: Critical Theory, Democracy and Aesthetic Individuality.* New York: Routledge, 2001.

Sekyi-Otu, Ato. *Fanon's Dialectic of Experience.* Cambridge: Harvard University Press, 1996.

Sheppard, Richard. *On Kafka's Castle: A Study.* London: Croom Helm, 1973.

Skinner, Quentin. *The Foundations of Modern Political Thought: The Renaissance.* New York: Cambridge University Press, 1978.

Steinberg, Michael P. *Walter Benjamin and the Demands of History.* Ithaca, NY: Cornell University Press, 1996.

Taminiaux, Jacques. "Athens and Greece." In *The Cambridge Companion to Hannah Arendt,* ed. Dana Villa. New York: Cambridge University Press, 2000.

Thoreau, Henry David. *Walden and Civil Disobedience.* New York: Norton, 1966.

Tiedemann, Rolf. "Dialectics at a Standstill: Approaches to the Passagen-Werk (1982)." In *On Walter Benjamin: Critical Essays and Recollections,* ed. Gary Smith. Cambridge: MIT Press, 1988.

Tocqueville, Alexis de. *De la démocratie en Amérique.* 2 vols. Paris: Gallimard, 1986.

Tocqueville, Alexis de. *Democracy in America.* 2 vols. New York: Bantam, 2000.

Tocqueville, Alexis de. *Travail sur L'Algérie.* In *Oeuvres Complètes.* Paris: Gallimard, Pléiade, 1993.

Tocqueville, Alexis de. *Writings on Empire and Slavery.* Ed. and trans. Jennifer Pitts. Baltimore: Johns Hopkins University Press, 2001.

Todorov, Tzvetan. *Theories of the Symbol.* Ithaca, NY: Cornell University Press, 1982.

Tsao, Roy T. "Arendt Against Athens: Rereading the Human Condition." *Political Theory* 30, no. 1 (2002): 97–123.

Vatter, Migue. *Between Form and Event: Machiavelli's Theory of Political Freedom.* Boston: Kluwer Academic Publishers, 2000.

Weber, Samuel. *Benjamin's -abilities.* Cambridge: Harvard University Press, 2008.

Weil, Simone. *Waiting for God.* Trans. Emma Craufurd. New York: Harper, 1992.

Wolin, Sheldon. *Tocqueville Between Two Worlds: The Making of a Political and Theoretical Life*. Princeton, NJ: Princeton University Press, 2001.

Wright, Sarah. *The Trickster-Function in The Theatre of García Lorca*. Rochester, NY: Tamesis, 2000.

Young-Bruehl, Elisabeth. *Hannah Arendt: For Love of the World*. New Haven: Yale University Press, 1982.

Ziarek, Ewa Plonowska. *The Rhetoric of Failure: Deconstruction of Skepticism, Reinvention of Modernism*. Buffalo: SUNY Press, 1996.

Zilcosky, John. "Surveying the Castle: Kafka's Colonial Visions." In *A Companion to the Works of Franz Kafka*, ed. James Rolleston. Rochester, NY: Camden House, 2002.

Zimra, Clarisse. Afterword. In Assia Djebar, *Women of Algiers in Their Apartment*, trans. Marjolijn de Jager. Charlottesville: University of Virginia Press, 1992.

Zimra, Clarisse. "Introduction to Assia Djebar's *The White of Algeria*." *Yale French Studies* 87 (1995): 149–70.

Zimra, Clarisse. "Writing Woman: The Novels of Assia Djebar." In *SubStance* 21, no. 3 (1992): 68–84.

Žižek, Slavoj. *The Plague of Fantasies*. New York: Verso, 1997.

Žižek, Slavoj. *The Ticklish Subject: The Absent Centre of Political Ontology*. New York: Verso, 2000.

Zupančič, Alenka. "Ethics and Tragedy in Lacan." In *The Cambridge Companion to Lacan*, ed. Jean-Michel Rabaté. New York: Cambridge University Press, 2003.

Zupančič, Alenka. *Ethics of the Real: Kant and Lacan*. New York: Verso, 2000.

Index

Printed and bound by CPI Group (UK) Ltd, Croydon, CR0 4YY

09/06/2025

14685670-0005